𝕿𝖍𝖊 𝕾𝖚𝖓𝖉𝖆𝖞 𝕿𝖊𝖑𝖊𝖌𝖗𝖆𝖕𝖍

Guide to Commuterland
Finding a home within reach of London

The Sunday Telegraph
Guide to Commuterland

Finding a home within reach of London

Caroline McGhie

AURUM PRESS

This revised and extended edition first published in 2004 by
Aurum Press Ltd, 25 Bedford Avenue, London WC1B 3AT.

A catalogue record for this book is available from the
British Library.

1SBN 1 84513 035 9

6	5	4	3	2	1
2009	2008	2007	2006	2005	2004

Edited by Jane Hutchings
Line Drawings by Vincent Design
Rail travel information by Barry Doe
Book designed by Roger Hammond @ Blue Gum

Printed and bound by Creative Print and Design (Wales),
Ebbw Vale

CONTENTS

(✓) only the London Bridge trains

((✓✓)) good for city but not for Mercer

7   **Introduction**
10 **Acknowledgements**
11 **Notes on Rail Travel Information**

STATION-BY-STATION GUIDE

(✓) 14 Liverpool Street > **Norwich**
(✓) 34 Liverpool Street > **Southend**
✓ 40 Fenchurch Street > **Shoeburyness**
✓ 46 Fenchurch Street > **Pitsea** (via Tilbury)
(✓) 50 Liverpool Street > **Cambridge**
64 Kings Cross > **Newark Northgate and King's Lynn**
(✓) 90 Moorgate > **Stevenage**
96 Kings Cross Thameslink/St Pancras > **Bedford and Leicester**
112 Euston > **Rugby** (via Northampton)
130 Marylebone > **Aylesbury** (via Chorleywood)
136 Marylebone> **Leamington Spa**
148 Paddington > **Reading and Bristol**
172 Paddington > **Oxford and Evesham**
180 Paddington > **Castle Cary**
192 Waterloo > **Reading**
208 Waterloo > **Salisbury and Southampton**
234 Waterloo > **Portsmouth**
250 Victoria/London Bridge > **Arundel and Brighton**
276 Victoria/Waterloo > **Horsham**
282 Victoria/London Bridge> **East Grinstead and Uckfield**
292 Charing Cross/Cannon Street > **Hastings**
304 Charing Cross/Cannon Street > **Canterbury** (via Tonbridge and Ashford)
312 Victoria > **Ashford International** (via Maidstone)
320 Charing Cross/Victoria > **Herne Bay and Canterbury** (via Rochester)

337 **Index of stations, towns and villages**

120 min

90 min

60 min

30 min

London

King's Lynn
Leamington Spa
Leicester
Norwich
Cambridge
Evesham
Diss
Northampton
Ipswich
Aylesbury
Peterborough
Oxford
Colchester
Bristol
St Albans
Chelmsford
Frome
Southminster
Bath Spa
Southend
Swindon
Basildon
Andover
Canterbury
Guildford
Salisbury
Ashford
Chandler's Ford
Winchester
Lewes
Horsham
Brighton
Rye
Southampton
Hastings
Glynde

6

INTRODUCTION

It might seem cynical to present the English countryside as one huge emporium from which we can pick a lifestyle, calculate a journey, choose a school for our children and buy a house. But the truth is that in the 21st century we are rich in choice and there are many different lives we could lead, in many different places. The force for change is usually a house move – the biggest financial decision any of us ever makes.

What gathering of friends, especially in London, is complete without its stock-in-trade conversation about the quality of life? The questions are always the same. What point is there in slaving round-the-clock at the office if our precious leisure hours have to be spent in urban parks and shopping malls? What point is there in sitting daily in traffic jams if the local schools are inadequate, the air quality too poor and the garden too small for the lifestyle we feel we deserve? How can we inject more pleasure into our lives and reduce the stress?

Repeated property booms have created the economic lever to make it happen. If we decide that the good things in life – the things that really matter – are walks from the back door, views over the hills, awareness of the changing seasons and shopkeepers who know your name, then selling up and moving out of town is often the answer. For years the price of a Victorian semi in London has paid for the pretty country cottage, the old vicarage, even the pony paddock. Now prices are much higher all over the country. In 2003 the Nationwide and the Halifax recorded average price-increases nationally of around 15 per cent. While rises have fallen back in London and the South East, there have been high increases in the North (the North East has gone up by 30 per cent, the North West by 22 per cent) as the boom has rippled outwards. To put it bluntly, you can't get as much for your money any more.

The magic carpet of Commuterland appeals to many. People who have reached pivotal points in their lives are especially prone to restlessness. Older couples whose children have left home inevitably feel tempted. Perhaps a flat in town and a cottage in the country might be the answer? Younger couples with new babies wonder if they want children who are hip and streetwise, or ruddy-cheeked and nature-loving. First-time buyers leave the decision to buy until later these days (often not until their early thirties), and want to look out of London to find areas where they can afford to buy.

New technology has dramatically loosened the chains of the workplace since the first *Guide to Commuterland* appeared in 1992. With mobile phones and laptops we can work on the train, prepare for meetings, sort domestic hiccups. Increasing numbers of people can now work from home, or part-time commute by travelling to the office only two or three days a week. This has allowed them to look further afield and find new areas to enjoy. People who once thought of living in Cambridgeshire will now look at Lincolnshire.

Wherever your chosen place, don't make an ill-considered, badly researched plunge. The reality is that a manageable commute coupled with a genuinely enhanced lifestyle is possible only after careful consideration of a wide range of factors. You may never find exactly what you want, but you need to be happy with the compromise.

For full-time commuters the first consideration is the length and convenience of the rail journey. Decide which London terminus you want to arrive at. If you work in the City, for instance, then London Bridge and Liverpool Street win hands down over Paddington or Victoria. The conventional wisdom is that the journeys which sandwich the main commute (home to station, London terminus to place of work) are best kept down to 15 minutes each. The maximum sensible number of changes en route is two. Each extra change increases the likelihood of missed connections or other unplanned delays. Most people find that 90 minutes is the maximum tolerable limit for a journey – a time-band which has an inevitable influence on property prices.

It is no good consulting a map to estimate your likely journey time, the rail networks make a nonsense of geography. You will find throughout this book that stopping services from stations closer to London take longer than faster trains from places further out. Frequency of service is just as important. If you miss your train, how long will you have to wait for the next? This is especially important if you need to work flexible hours and you don't want to turn into an office clock-watcher.

The purpose of this book is to do as much as possible of the initial homework for you. It follows the railway lines out of London in all directions and describes villages within reach of each station. It tries to encapsulate the character of each town and village, the landscape that surrounds them, the quality of schools and communications, journey times to London, the range of available property and what it costs. The detail is not comprehensive, but it should be enough to give you a clear idea of where to look – and where to avoid.

What to watch for

• Be quite certain about whether you want to live in the country, or whether you would be happier living in a town with the country a short drive away. If you want people close by, shops within walking distance, roads that are well lit at night, then the deep countryside is not for you. Look at the towns.

• What are your primary needs? Proximity to a good school, supermarket, fashion and foodie shops? Isolation, great walks, big views, village life?

• If village life is what you want, find out how the village of your choice works socially. Are you prepared to put time into keeping the cogs of the village turning? Will you shop locally and support the local post office and farmers' market?

• Make sure you have allowed for inflation, increasing petrol prices, interest rate rises and house market fluctuations in your house-price-plus-season-ticket calculation (and mounting school fees if they are part of the package).

• Remember that villages with cohesive centres and period houses will have the highest prices. You can be quite sure that wherever a modern developer has been too heavy-handed the prices will be lower. Areas hit hardest in the slump were those that lacked architectural distinction.

• Beware taking on too much land unless you really have the time to garden it or can afford to hire a gardener.

Caroline McGhie
North Norfolk
May 2004

ACKNOWLEDGEMENTS

This book is the result of team effort. It has been put together by dedicated researchers – Christine Webb, Heather Devany, Catherine Coley, Jane Hutchings, Jenny Knight, Rosalind Russell, Ginetta Vedrickas – who have talked to estate agents, parish clerks, town and county councils up and down the country in order to update the original text. Crucial information about season tickets, journey times and frequency of trains has been prepared by the public transport travel consultant, Barry Doe, who sifted all the timetables and fares' manuals of all the rail companies crossed by the guide. His knowledge is encyclopaedic.

Emily Clark turned to the School League Tables to pick out the highest-performing schools in each locality, both state and private. There are many more good schools in all the areas, but we were only able to mention those with the best results.

Useful sources of further information include local government websites, the *Shire County Guides* (Shire Publications Ltd), and *The Villages of Britain* series (Countryside Books), which are marvellous repositories of oral history prepared by the Women's Institute.

Supreme efforts have been made to achieve factual accuracy in a world where perceptions of people and places vary, and where the pace of physical change in our towns and villages is now extremely rapid. We are grateful to all those people who have shared their local knowledge with us to make this book such a useful source of information.

I would like to thank the editor of *The Sunday Telegraph*, Dominic Lawson, for continuing to have faith in the idea and Jane Hutchings for being such a calm editor.

NOTES ON RAIL TRAVEL INFORMATION

For more detailed information consult National Rail Enquiries.

Journey time
This is the time taken by the fastest train to London in a normal off-peak hour. Any significant differences between peak and off-peak services are indicated.

Peak trains
Except where indicated, this represents the number of through trains per hour arriving at the London terminus between 0730 and 0930. (A margin has been allowed to take account of trains arriving within a few minutes either side of these times.) Note that there may well be a greater overall frequency offered by changing en route. Some detail on this is given where the difference is significant.

Off-peak trains
Except where indicated, this is the total number of through trains to the London terminus in a normal off-peak hour. Where there is no off-peak through service, but one exists locally, details are given about alternative services by changing. Note that even where an off-peak service exists there may well be a greater overall frequency offered by changing, as for the peak hour.

Season tickets
The price quoted is for the Standard Class Annual. The cost of a weekly season is obtained by dividing the annual rate by 40. A monthly season is the weekly rate x3.84. These are the only rates available, which means that, for example, a season for six months is charged at six times the monthly rate with no further discount. However, it is possible to buy any season ticket for any length of time above a month, in odd days, at pro rata the monthly rate. First Class season tickets, where available, are 1.5 times the standard rate except for a small group of seasons which are 1.6 times the standard rate. The small group includes stations between

Ipswich and Norwich, stations between Wellingborough and Leicester, and to Peterborough, Grantham and Newark Northgate.

Out-of-town commuters can pay a supplement to incorporate a Travelcard with their annual season ticket. This offers unlimited travel on trains, Underground and buses in Greater London. The annual supplement is around £380 to £450 (£450 to £650 First Class), which is good value as the normal cost is £1532 Standard Class.

At most stations, an annual season ticket (with or without Travelcard) automatically becomes a "Gold Card", entitling the holder to a third off off-peak rail fares for any journey in London and the South East. Prices are correct as at early May 2004. Few, if any, changes are likely until January 2005.

Season tickets are valid to any appropriate London terminus. For example, tickets from Brighton cover not only the services shown to Victoria or London Bridge, but also to Cannon Street, Blackfriars, Waterloo and Charing Cross by changing at London Bridge. Similarly, tickets from stations on the Bristol/Paddington line are also valid to Waterloo via Staines. Seasons issued for stations between Bedford and St Albans to Kings Cross Thameslink and from stations south of the Thames to London Bridge can now be obtained to allow travel across London on Thameslink services without extra charge – but not, of course, on the Underground, for which a Travelcard remains necessary.

Note that some stations now have dual prices for seasons. This means that one season is available on all services, and another may be for just one operator. Note that season tickets are often available at slightly higher prices from stations on different nearby lines. For example the annual from Uckfield quoted here is £1740 and from Haywards Heath it is £2800, but a version is available for £2880, which allows use from either station to London.

Charing Cross/Waterloo (East)

All trains to Charing Cross stop at Waterloo (East) and most trains also serve London Bridge. In the peak hours on these lines there are also additional trains into Cannon Street.

Rail maps

The maps are schematic diagrams only and are not drawn to scale.

Norwich

Bury St Edmunds
Thurston
Diss
Elmswell
Stowmarket
Saxmundham
Needham Market
Wickham Market
Melton
Woodbridge
Westerfield
Ipswich
Sudbury
Manningtree
Harwich Town
Bures
Mistley
Dovercourt
Chappel & Wakes Colne
Harwich International
Wrabness
Colchester
Walton on the Naze
Marks Tey
Hythe
Thorpe-le-Soken
Frinton
Braintree
Colchester Town
Wivenhoe
Weeley
Kirby Cross
Cressing
Alresford
Great Bentley
White Notley
Kelvedon
Clacton
Witham
Hatfield Peverel
Chelmsford
Ingatestone
Shenfield

Liverpool Street

Liverpool Street
> **Norwich**

Journey: 21 min
Season: £2060
Peak: 10 per hr
Off-peak: 8 per hr

SHENFIELD is a mutated village, but nonetheless the greengrocer and butcher know you by name. There are three parts to it: the village itself, with bread-and-butter Victorian and Thirties' streets; Hutton Mount, where avenues of huge double-garaged detached houses priced at £750,000 to £1m peep out from between the trees; and Hutton proper, which is strictly Sixties, congested but more affordable. It is on London's doorstep, just outside the M25, with the result that the station car park has been extended and is considered expensive.

Journey: 30 min
Season: £2260
Peak: 3 per hr
Off-peak: 1 per hr

INGATESTONE This is a village with small-town pretensions and well over 3000 inhabitants, many of them East Enders who have moved up and out. Its best features are a collection of 19th-century almshouses and the High Street, which is on a reassuringly human scale. A three-bedroom semi-detached will cost £265,000 to £300,000; a five-bedroom house in a smart address such as Chantry Drive, £700,000. One of its greatest attractions is the Anglo-European School, to which parents send their children from all over Essex. Many of the passengers drive south to avoid the parking problems at Chelmsford, though they lose with one hand what they gain with the other because it is more difficult to get a seat at Ingatestone.

Journey: 31 min
Season: £2520
Peak: 8 per hr
Off-peak: 8 per hr

CHELMSFORD has just billowed with new developments. Broomfield and Links Drive are the right side of the railway tracks, Boarded Barns the wrong side. A lot of investment has been made in shopping. There are several out-of-town superstores, including Tesco and Sainsburys, two malls – High Chelmer and The Meadows – while the Thursday antiques and secondhand market continues to draw the bargain-hunters. Essex Country Cricket Club is in the centre. The brilliant grammar schools are a magnet to those disillusioned with London state schools. A family house in a leafy street will cost £350,000 to £450,000. The town is due to sprout a further 14,000 homes in the next few years as it has been zoned for growth. The surrounding countryside, despite its savaging from developers, still contains some wonderful surprises. The station lays claim to being the busiest in the country, funnelling 15,000 people each morning into London. Extra trains start here, rather than further up the line, in an attempt to provide more seats.

Close in on the east flank of the town is **Sandon** with a pretty village green. Two-bedroom cottages just off the green cost around £200,000, while a five-bedroom Georgian house would fetch £850,000. Modern four-bedroom houses are £350,000 to £450,000. The village is very much a dormitory, protected by the A12 bypass – though the roar of the traffic is still audible in some of the houses. The excellent comprehensive school has a large sixth form and draws children from further afield, including Maldon and South Woodham Ferrers.

A little further out is **Danbury**, larger than most people's concept of the archetypal village and on the busy A414. It has its own shops and pubs, some of them 16th-century, and the Common, woods and lakes are big attractions. A period house with four bedrooms would cost £600,000 at least. "It's a commuter village, but not posh. It's not a don't-touch-me place. Everyone and his grandmother goes there on Sundays for a walk," was how one local pundit described it. Others, however, consider it very smart. The heather and bracken of Danbury and Lingwood Commons (National Trust) provide one of the few known breeding grounds for the Rosy Marbled Moth. Blake's Wood also offers 100 acres of hornbeam and chestnut coppice carpeted with bluebells in the spring. **Little Baddow**, scarcely separated from Danbury, has more airs and graces. It has a post office, and a lovely cricket pitch in the woods and huge six-bedroom houses on The Ridge that sell for £600,000 to £1m or more.

Another classic commuter village is **Stock**, with its cluttered narrow streets, pond and village green, though it suffers from the traffic on the B1007. It has recently lost its butcher and greengrocer, but has its own wine store, post office, general store, newsagent, a florist and hairdresser, and a wealth of societies from flower arranging to drama and the British Legion. There are some staunch churchgoers and the local church is worth visiting in order to admire its intricately constructed timber belfry. The village also has a brick tower windmill with two sails attached, which is tucked down the aptly named Mill Lane. It is one of several surviving mills which are quite a feature in the Essex countryside. A Tudor house with a quarter of an acre on the main road would cost £650,000; a three-bedroom Thirties' semi around £350,000.

To the west of Chelmsford is a clutch of picturesque villages. **Writtle** is close in enough to be a suburb, with 16th- and 17th-century houses costing up to £620,000. Its green and duck pond are the envy

'Danbury is a commuter village, but not posh. It's not a don't-touch-me place. Everyone and his grandmother goes there on Sundays for a walk'

House style in East Anglia

This is a region where stonelessness has led to resourcefulness. Without stone with which to build, early residents turned to timber and plaster, and later brought in the first Flemish bricks as ballast in returning wool boats. Hand-made bricks can still be bought at Bulmer in Suffolk.

It was to timber, though, that the early builders on the Essex marshes turned, around the horizontal mudflats and sea wall walks of the Blackwater estuary. Here you find modest white weatherboarded cottages like land-locked boats or beach-huts that have strayed on to solid ground. The cleft oak boards are laid with the seasoned bark-edge to the outside of the building in order to give the walls maximum protection from the elements.

Once the lovely pastoral landscape of Suffolk unfolds, it reveals some of the best medieval houses in the country, built on the early profits of the wool trade at a time when this was one of the richest and most densely populated regions of the country. Streets full of drunken timbered houses, their first-floor jetties projecting over the road, built long before the chimney or the water closet had even been thought of, are the survivors of a veritable building boom. They are now fiercely guarded by the Suffolk Preservation Society, the headquarters of which is among the silvery-timbered buildings of Lavenham.

Suffolk also offers a wonderful architectural palette of colours with distinctive buffs, creams, yellows and pinks. Old manor houses with many gables often have plastered and colour-washed wattle-and-daub walls. Others have distinctive pargeting where the plaster is raised into patterns of foliage or figures to make the walls resemble skilfully iced cakes.

of the county. Hylands Park is a Grade II star, restored Neo-Classical wonder with its grounds open to the public. It provides the setting for the annual Chelmsford Spectacular, when people take their own deckchairs to hear popular music and watch the synchronised firework displays.

Nearby is a collection of hamlets, linked to Chelmsford by an intermittent bus service, where four-to-five-bedroom houses cost anything from £365,000 to £850,000. **Mashbury** is without a pub or shop or jumble sales, but remarkable for its togetherness. **Good Easter** has one of the oldest barns in the county and a village green with a pump on it, where a two-bedroom period semi with half an acre will cost £360,000. **High Easter** is the prettiest, with a café and a restaurant. A two-bedroom listed thatched cottage here is £315,000. **Chignall Smealy** and **Chignall St James** have some timbered houses and a pub called the Three Elms. **Pleshey,** on the other hand, is particularly sought after because of its thatched cottages, church and motte-and-bailey castle. A four-bedroom listed farmhouse could cost £850,000.

Journey: 43 min
Season: £2700
Peak: 3 per hr
Off-peak: 1 per hr

HATFIELD PEVEREL This is commuterland in the lee of the A12. Good-neighbourliness shows itself in the form of Neighbourhood Watch and a wine club set up by bibulous incomers. A cottage on the green in **Hatfield Peverel** would start at £230,000 for two bedrooms, though a small two-bedroom house elsewhere in the village could cost £145,000. New-home lovers should watch for a new Countryside Properties development of houses known as Beaulieu Park, between Hatfield Peverel and Chelmsford, an interesting mix of mock

Victorian and New England weatherboarded houses. A three-bedroom period farmhouse with five acres and stables at Great Leighs, a good six-mile drive from the station, might cost around £500,000.

Journey: 43 min
Season: £2820
Peak: 7 per hr
Off-peak: 4 per hr

WITHAM The smart set don't live in Witham itself, which has become a town that people shop in (no large department store) or pass through on their way to the station. The detective-story writer Dorothy L Sayers was not so proud, however. She lived and wrote in Newland Street and a plaque is there to prove it. The town still serves as the social hub for the surrounding villages, which feed commuters on to the fast main line train services to Liverpool Street. Car parking spaces are plentiful.

The conservationist lobby is strong, with old stalwarts belonging to the Witham and Countryside Society; culture vultures join the Witham Operatic Society. The entire 18th- and 19th-century High Street has been designated a conservation area. Other than Bramston Sports Centre, there is little to entertain the young. The nearest cinema is miles away in Colchester or Chelmsford. In the Seventies the town was identified as a London overspill, which is why it now contains an array of modern estates. A two-bedroom listed cottage might be bought for £145,000. Bovis is selling five-bedroom two-bathroom houses for £325,000.

All the surrounding villages are significantly more expensive. Scarcely separated from Witham itself is **Chipping Hill**, with the Woolpack Inn, a triangular green and a manor house. The view from here was described by Horace Walpole in 1749 as "sweet meadows falling down a hill and rising again on the other side of the prettiest winding stream you ever saw". **Wickham Bishops**, set on a hill a couple of miles out, looks down its nose at the others. A five-bedroom mock-Georgian house with a generous garden will command £395,000 here. **Great Braxted** is slightly cheaper, as is **Great Totham**, which is further from the station. The yachting fraternity flock to **Tollesbury**, 12 miles away, where there is a large modern marina on a creek of the Blackwater.

> Branch line to **Braintree** via **White Notley** and **Cressing**

Through trains:
2 per hr (peak)
1 per hr (off-peak)
Journey time (from Braintree): 63 min
Season ticket from Braintree: £2940

The through train service to Liverpool Street on this line was introduced in 1990 as a result of vigorous lobbying by the Witham and Braintree Rail Users Association. People still take the shuttle into Witham and wait five minutes for a fast connection. The early departure of the last through train used to strand passengers in London, but there are now later trains to Braintree, which solves the problem.

Few commuters use **White Notley**. The station is kept open because there is a level crossing here, manned by human hand until very recently, but now automatic. **Cressing** is another walk-to-the-station village. The station is no more than a country halt with a platform and shelter. The village has 1700 inhabitants and two pubs. It has lost its butcher and newsagent, but the post office now sells almost everything. It also has its own primary school, though the nearest secondary schools are in Braintree. A three-bedroom bungalow could be bought for at least £210,000. Old Cressing, part of which is a conservation area, is scissored from new Cressing by the main road. As one parish councillor put it, "Nobody would ever describe it as quaint, or even picturesque, but it is a good working village." **Braintree** is the birthplace of the Crittall window and about as pretty – but it has improved hugely in the last decade. There are entire estates built on the outskirts, which are full of former Londoners, happy to swap the East End for a slower pace of life, better schools and no traffic jams. It also now has the new Freeport shopping village and Great Notley Village, a new development of 2000 homes with some smart detailing. A further 7700 new homes are planned. Property prices in Braintree vary from £130,000 for a three-bedroom semi to £415,000 for a four-bedroom detached house, and £325,000 for a thatched cottage with three bedrooms in a third of an acre.

Traditional Essex weatherboarded house

> Continuation of main line

Journey: 44 min
Season: £2880
Peak: 4 per hr
Off-peak: 1 per hr

KELVEDON is sought after for its strong village heartbeat. St Peter's church and the Kelvedon Players organise endless activities, including children's groups and an annual pantomime. Once people have settled here they rarely move out. A three-bedroom period cottage with a long rear garden will cost £232,000. An 18th-century house with eight bedrooms, indoor swimming pool, tennis courts, and six-and-a-half acres would sell for £1.6m. **Feering**, less than two miles away, is almost umbilically linked. It has a new community centre and village school, an art club, and choir, a WI, bowls, badminton, Scouts and Guides. The villages share a cricket club. On May Day the pubs stay open all day while the village green throbs with dancers. Newcomers quickly become assimilated. A Victorian detached house with five bedrooms and two bathrooms would cost £495,000.

Journey: 46 min
Season: £2940
Peak: 4 per hr
Off-peak: 1 per hr

MARKS TEY All the Teys, **Marks Tey**, **Little Tey** and **Great Tey**, are within a 10-minute drive of this or Colchester station. Parking here is easy. Marks Tey has large Seventies' estates where you can buy a two-bedroom flat for £105,000, or a four-bedroom detached for £225,000 to £250,000. Little Tey next door is also a grazing ground for first- and second-time buyers. Great Tey is a little more remote, with its own village shop, post office and village hall. **Coggeshall**, a couple of miles from this and Kelvedon station, is much more seductive, wonderfully medieval, with lace-making traditions and a much-loved inn called The Woolpack. It has a regular Thursday market, which sells everything from buttons and WI jam to fruit and veg. Another feather in its cap is Paycocke's House (National Trust), one of the most famous Tudor houses in the country. A period four-bedroom terraced house might cost £330,000 to £385,000.

> Branch line to Sudbury via Chappel & Wakes Colne and Bures

No through trains.
Trains to Marks Tey: 1 per hr
Journey time (from Sudbury): 72 min
Season ticket from Sudbury: £2952

Villagers living down this branch line would be just as likely to drive to Colchester and catch one of the more frequent trains from there. **Chappel** and **Wakes Colne** are two villages sewn together by a vast and spectacular Victorian viaduct. The River Stour, crossed by a small bridge, marks the line which slices **Bures** up between Essex and Suffolk. It therefore has two of everything, from parish clerks downwards. The cricket club and green are picturesque. There is conspicuous wealth here, and some weekend cottages. The odd pop musician sweeps through in his Rolls Royce. A little two-bedroom Victorian cottage costs £135,000; a detached three-bedroom house on a modern development will fetch £190,000 or more, while a five-bedroom house in half an acre might reach £395,000.

Sudbury's irresistible charms compensate for the inconvenience of the journey for the brave few who commute from here. The jumble of historic cottages, churches and grander gabled houses, Gainsborough's birthplace among them, sit in the arm of the River Stour, cushioned by water meadows. The market square is filled with stalls on Thursdays and Saturdays. The Sudbury Dramatic Society raised money to establish The Quay Theatre and it is home to the First Call theatre for teenagers. Down towards the water meadows there are the tennis club, rowing club and cricket club. The Kingfisher Leisure Pool provides a dash of Disneyland with flume rides, a wave machine and giant bouncing rubber balls.

> **'The jumble of historic cottages, churches and grander gabled houses sit in the arm of the River Stour'**

A few commuters choose to live in the town and walk to the station, or even drive to Marks Tey or Colchester. You might get a little one-bedroom flat for around £80,000 to £110,000, or a three-bedroom house standing in its own garden for £239,000. Five-bedroom Georgian houses in large gardens on the outskirts can be bought for £445,000. Great Cornard was originally a London overspill zone and somewhat stigmatised as such, but people have bought their council houses and the area has lifted. Around 1200 new homes are now to be studded into the fabric around the town.

Most people opt for the villages. **Long Melford**, three-and-a-half miles out, is one of the most admired in the county with an achingly lovely long main street (hence the name of the village) which eventually erupts on to the green and a cathedral-sized church. No wonder it was used as the backdrop to the television series *Lovejoy*. The Hall is National Trust. The Green is one of *the* addresses. A four-bedroom house with beams, peg-tile roof and an inglenook

Thatched cricket pavilion, Bures

'Lavenham is a film-set village with 300 listed buildings'

fireplace would cost £550,000, though you can get a three-bedroom Grade II listed cottage for £160,000. The village has its own school, post office, grocery stores, butcher and baker. It crawls with antique dealers and American tourists in the summer.

Lavenham, four miles from Sudbury, is another film-set medieval village, with restaurants, dried flower and teddy bear shops, 300 listed buildings and the home of the Suffolk Preservation Society. A three-bedroom period terrace would cost £210,000. "A place caught in time" is how one resident describes it – but unfortunately it is beyond the 10-mile belt round Colchester and therefore a stretch for regular commuters to reach at the end of a long day. **Cavendish** on the River Stour is another with a village green, antiques shops and restaurants, but think hard about the journey before you look at it. A converted barn with two bedrooms will cost £395,000.

> Continuation of main line

Journey: 49 min
Season: £3100
Peak: 8 per hr
Off-peak: 6 per hr

COLCHESTER People have time for Colchester, which is the oldest town in Britain, with a show-stopping Norman castle built on the foundations of a Roman Temple. The medieval alleyways in the old quarter harbour specialist shops such as a teddy bear shop, while the two pedestrianised shopping centres serve up all the usual chain stores. In the next six years it is due to grow by 17,000 homes as brownfield sites have been assembled for builders to develop. For now, however, three-bedroom terraced houses in town cost £200,000 to £300,000. A five-bedroom period semi with a generous garden in one of the best areas such as Lexden will cost £275,000 to £750,000. There are any number of societies, including archaeological, jazz, folk and choral. It has two theatres – the Mercury repertory company and the new Headgate Theatre for amateurs. In addition, there is St Mary's Arts Centre and a six-screen cinema. Colchester Leisure World is an impressive new multi-sports stadium. Annual events include summer concerts in the park and the rather bizarre Oyster Feast in October, at which assorted media figures are invited to gorge themselves.

The Colchester bag is brimming with goodies. The Colnes (see Chappel & Wakes Colne) are handsome, but not glamorous, and all have a gas supply – no dreaded oil tank lurking in the garden. **Earls Colne**, two miles away, is the biggest and is self-contained, with a supermarket, restaurants, banks and individual shops in the period High Street. A Victorian family house will cost £350,000, a three-bedroom, part-tiled, part-thatched cottage will fetch £375,000. **White Colne** is merely a ribbon settlement along the main A604 to Earls Colne. It has no shop, but properties along the main road come considerably cheaper – possibly 10 per cent less than those on quieter roads. **Colne Engaine** is the most desirable of this group. It has a classic village green framed with period houses, a village shop, a pub, a church and a primary school. You need £140,000 for a two-bedroom cottage, but more than £200,000 to start looking for a family house here.

    Eight Ash Green is also highly prized. The A1124 cuts through the centre, skirting the green and the little houses that circle it. It has a village store, a primary school, a church and a petrol station, as well as a gas supply. There is a mix of houses, from ex-local authority selling from £175,000, to small peg-tiled timbered cottages at £130,000 to £180,000; or you might get a four-bedroom house in half an acre for just under £360,000. **Fordham**, on the River Colne, is rather more dislocated. It does a kind of vanishing act half way along the main street, then gives you a second helping as you turn the bend. Children travel up to 20 miles to Colchester Royal Grammar School (boys) or The County High (girls) if they can get a place.

    The Horkesleys are not greatly loved, though you could pick up a cottage in **Little Horkesley** for £250,000. **Stoke-by-Nayland**, however, eight miles from Colchester, is where the poetry begins and drunken timber-frame houses splashed with Suffolk pink-wash colour the landscape. It is set high on a ridge over the Stour, with a church that commands a giddy view of Constable country in all directions. **Boxford**, a couple of miles further out, is as pretty and quieter.

> Branch line to **Clacton** or **Walton on the Naze** via **Colchester Town, Hythe, Wivenhoe, Alresford, Great Bentley, Weeley, Thorpe-le-Soken, Kirby Cross** and **Frinton**

For train information see page 24

WIVENHOE is subject to commuter clotting. It is a little quayside town which grows lumps of commuter cars each day, left here by those who want to avoid the stressful drive into Colchester (which can take 45 minutes). Parking spaces are so precious that the public car park, which is meant for shoppers only, is locked between 5.30am and 8.45am. Local councillors have even considered buying houses to knock them down, simply to create more parking spaces.

    The village is gradually metamorphosing from a working port where the oyster catch was all important, to a boating village with craft shops that attracts local artists and writers. The pubs bulge with students at certain times of year and parties of foreign students at others, brought in by Essex University, based in the tower blocks in

Through trains
from Clacton: 3
per hr (peak)/1 per
hr (off-peak)
Journey: 80 min
(from Clacton)
Season: £3500
(from Clacton)
This service is
from Clacton,
Thorpe-le-Soken
and Wivenhoe only.
Other stations:
change at
Colchester, except
for 2 peak hr
trains from Walton
on the Naze.

'Weed your
front garden in
Kirby-le-Soken
and you could
spend all day
talking to
passers-by'

Wivenhoe Park. It is distinct from Colchester five miles away, cushioned by green fields which are fiercely defended from development. Old shipyards are being turned into new houses and prices vary from £160,000 for a two-bedroom flat to £350,000 for a five-bedroom town house. The ferry to Rowhedge (once rowed by an elderly man who smoked a pipe) now operates only on summer weekends. Detached period houses on the quay cost over £500,000. Smaller three-bedroom Victorian terraced houses can be had for less. It has an infant and a primary school, and local societies including the Gilbert and Sullivan Society, the Wivenhoe Players and the Pantomime Group. There is also an annual regatta. The new Colne Barrier controls the tidal flow to the south of the town in order to protect homes from flooding during surges.

Great Bentley is chiefly notable for the extraordinary size of its village green. At 45 acres it swallows the cricket green, two football pitches and the annual gymkhana – and the houses on it are the ones to aim for. Something with three bedrooms off the green might cost £145,000. There is a baker and pharmacy, a Tesco, a primary school and allotments for residents only.

Clacton may one day find itself a conservation area. It epitomises the pre-war seaside resort, where those with fond memories of holidays in bed-and-breakfasts and days on the pier might choose to buy their final bungalow and take up a round of golf on Sundays. The average three-bedroom semi costs £125,000; a two-up-two-down £110,000. It is described by some as being full of "East Enders-made-good driving their Range Rovers".

My dear, if you live in **Frinton**, you have arrived. That is to say that you have certainly distanced yourself from that frightful candyfloss and razzmatazz in Clacton. The old railway level-crossing gates are the heavenly portals to Frinton. Outside is where the modern estates are to be found, and it isn't Frinton proper, for Frinton is *very* proper. There was a huge fight to stop the arrival of a pub (nicknamed locally The Stick and Zimmer), a fish-and-chip shop and even the first ice-cream shop is set back from the beach in a discreet position in Connaught Avenue. It also has its commuters who use the direct trains to Liverpool Street. Solicitors, doctors, dentists and accountants are attracted to the cavernous houses, servants' quarters and tennis courts included, worth over £500,000, that sit in swathes of gardens in The Avenues. Rare ingredients are easy to find. Connaught Avenue, with its designer clothes shops, jewellers and delicatessens, is known as the Bond Street of Essex. The list of local clubs and societies covers three foolscap pages, but it is bridge evenings that make the world go round, coupled with the

Frinton Summer Theatre, the annual tennis tournament and the 18-hole links.

You get sand as fine, but house prices considerably cheaper in **Walton on the Naze**. A three-bedroom semi on the outskirts could take £195,000 off you. There are regulation, seaside resort chip shops, safe bathing, fresh lobster to be bought in the summetime and a pier, but the main attractions are the sheltered inlets behind The Naze where the yacht club is located. The saltings and mudflats, designated as a Site of Special Scientific Interest, are a staging post for flocks of migrating birds and there are monthly guided walks.

Kirby-le-Soken, two miles away, is sought after because of its proximity to Frinton. It was originally threaded on to a single long main street, in the Essex tradition, but has since sprung bungaloid growths around it. One village shop has closed, leaving a post office stores and two pubs. Everybody knows everybody in this village. Cottage windows are papered with posters flagging local events, and gardens are regularly thrown open to the public for good causes. Weed your front garden here and you could spend all day talking to passers-by.

> Continuation of main line

| Journey: 50 min |
| Season: £3460 |
| Peak: 5 per hr |
| Off-peak: 3 per hr |

MANNINGTREE This station is often preferred to Colchester because it is marginally easier to park the car (though nothing is free) and easier to get a seat. **Manningtree** town itself has a charming frontage on to the Stour, known as the Walls, where homeowners have houses worth from £300,000 up to £1m. "Legoland" executive houses have leeched on to it. Visitors to the port are struck by the swans and sailing barges. The social life is mixed – old skippers and commuters drink together in the pubs – and the Manningtree Society and Stour Music Society add a cultural note.

East Bergholt is one of the set-piece villages in this area, sprawly, but prime commuter territory, where houses go for up to 25 per cent more than similar ones nearby. Constable wrote of it in 1776: "I even love every stile and stump and every lane in the village." He painted it enough times, and the cottage he used as a studio is still here – as is Willy Lott's cottage, which he made famous by painting. It doesn't seethe with tourists quite as much as other local sightseeing spots. A late-Georgian house with three bedrooms might sell for £250,000. A modern four- or five-bedroom detached house that would sell for £400,000 in Ipswich would fetch at least £100,000 more here. Houses at **Flatford Mill**, the hamlet nearby, are similarly fought over. The mill, which was owned by Constable's father and painted by the man himself, attracts so many visitors that there are now one-way lanes.

'Flatford Mill, which was owned by Constable's father, attracts so many visitors that there are now one-way lanes'

Dedham is positively stockbroker now. In spite of the paralysing tourist influx in the summer, it is a place that people still dream of moving to. Sir Alfred Munnings's home, Castle House, where his paintings are on display, lies just to the south. Those who live in the High Street are martyrs to the tourists who make parking and shopping impossible. Even a little two-bedroom thatched cottage here will cost £285,000 and most properties cost around 25 per cent more than those in other villages. One resident of 17 years remembers how quiet it used to be. "It looks beautiful at eight o'clock at night when nobody is here." Her husband used to park in a field to catch the train at Manningtree. Now he will delay his journey by three hours to get on a train that assures him a seat.

> Branch line to Harwich Town, via Mistley, Wrabness, Harwich International and Dovercourt

Peak: 1 through train per hr plus 2 per hr changing at Manningtree

Off-peak: 1 per hr changing at Manningtree

Journey: 83 min (from Harwich Town)

Season: £3500 (from Harwich Town)

While Manningtree benefits from the stops made by fast trains coming through from Harwich and Norwich, the small stations out along the tidal estuary towards Harwich do not. Properties are scattered and isolated along this out-of-the-way bit of coastline, and the journey, which usually involves a change at Manningtree, is slow but spectacular.

> Continuation of main line

Journey: 66 min

Season: £3920

Peak: 5 per hr

Off-peak: 4 per hr

IPSWICH itself is described as a town of convenience, good for shopping. There is a theatre and a live rock venue. Two-bedroom terraced houses to the east, near the well-respected Northgate comprehensive, can be bought for around £175,000; three-bedroom Victorian terraced houses for £245,000 and detached houses for £350,000 to £500,000. A huge £350m development has transformed the waterfront into a hip venue where penthouses have been selling at £600,000. The prices rise when you get close to a park, especially Christchurch Park where the private schools are located. Here a substantial family house will cost £650,000. An old rectory in a

Schools in Suffolk

One of the honeypots is Ipswich, which has two star private schools, Ipswich School for both sexes and Ipswich High for girls. Another is Bury St Edmunds (now more accessible by train), which has Culford independent school and two comprehensives, King Edward VI and St Benedict's Catholic co-educational school.

Woodbridge (also more accessible) has a pair of independent schools – Framlingham College and Woodbridge School – as well as the comprehensives Thomas Mills High and Farlingaye High. For girls, another school with good results is St Felix at Southwold overlooking the Blyth estuary.

dishevelled state in a nearby village might be expected to cost £500,000. Restored, with 20 acres of meadowland and a range of outbuildings, the price will rise to £900,000. The Shotley Peninsula, in the tongue of land just below Ipswich, is where the naturalists and yachting types gather. It has the River Orwell to one side, the Stour to the other and oozing mudflats between that attract wildfowl and waders. **Stutton** is the popular village here, on the Alton Reservoir which is the sailing centre. **Shotley Gate**, out on the tip, provides a vantage point from which to watch the ships ploughing in and out of Harwich.

To the west of Ipswich is Hadleigh, a classic period market town untouched by the deadening hand of the vast supermarket – though Tesco is queuing for admittance. Eight miles out, it is a model collection of medieval and Georgian houses, and provides everything that a small town should, from wine bars and interior designers to banks and solicitors. A small two-bedroom Tudor cottage here would cost £125,000 to £150,000; a large Georgian town house £390,000.

'The price of houses in Kersey depends on how desperate people are to buy their fantasy'

Just two miles beyond it is **Kersey**, where the price of the houses depends on how desperate people are to buy their fantasy. The hillside, running steeply down to a watersplash and up again, is stacked with remarkable lichen-cloaked half-timbered houses, built 500 years ago on the profits of the cloth industry. A three-bedroom thatched cottage sitting in a third of an acre would sell for around £375,000.

To the east is **Woodbridge**, one of the most sought-after towns in this part of Suffolk. It has its own station and has a new direct service into Liverpool Street – members of the commuter club here pay for their tickets monthly by direct debit. High ranking, high salaried types buy up the 16th-century houses round this old port on the Deben estuary. It is serious boating and foody country. You can buy a three-bedroom terrace close to the ancient weatherboarded tide-mill and old quayside buildings in the town itself from £250,000 with on-road parking. Or you could spend over £1m on a period house with six bedrooms and exposed beams. It also has the highly respected co-educational Woodbridge School and a prep. Prices have been rising fast here.

> Branch line to Saxmundham via Westerfield, Woodbridge, Melton and Wickham Market

Few through trains: 1 per hr (peak) plus 1 changing at Ipswich; 1 every 2 hrs (off-peak) changing at Ipswich

Journey: 114 min (from Saxmundham)

Season: £4488

Much of this remarkable coast has been too far for daily commuters because there were so few direct services. Starting in December 2004, it will have more through trains than the rather quaint current arrangement of one train out at breakfast and one tea-time train home. Beyond Saxmundham the line continues to Lowestoft.

Those who can't afford **Woodbridge** (see page 27) might consider **Little** and **Great Bealings** where a two-bedroom cottage can be bought for £200,000 or **Grundisburgh** (pronounced Grundsbra), which is cheaper and popular with families because it has a good primary school, or **Ufford**, which is very pretty and unspoilt. **Wickham Market** is also an unpretentious little town with a market square fringed with white-fronted Georgian houses. An end-of-terrace two-bedroom cottage recently sold for £140,000. The station is a mile out of town.

Or you could journey on to **Saxmundham** and head for **Aldeburgh**, described by E M Forster as "a bleak little place, not beautiful". Most people find it enchanting (fresh fish can be bought off the boats on the beach every morning) and many like to retire or take second homes here, intending to commute during the summer months only. Prices vary from £300,000 for a three-bedroom cottage in the town centre to £380,000 for a four-bedroom semi with a garden and garage. The internationally renowned music festival is held down the road at **Snape**. In the Edwardian seaside model village of **Thorpeness** there are the holiday villas that sell for £180,000 for two bedrooms to £600,000 for five bedrooms.

Beyond the Sizewell power station, which is not everyone's idea of a scenic embellishment, you come to the villages of **Westleton** and **Middleton**. These are hugely popular with escapees from the City who want to don Barbours, wellies and tweed hats and visit those wonderful vanishing cliffs at Dunwich (National Trust) or the Royal Society for the Protection of Birds reserve at Minsmere. Westleton has a village green and duck pond to go with its Suffolk thatch, colour wash and wattle-and-daub cottages. You could get a three-bedroom end-of-terrace for £220,000, but it would need a lot of renovation.

Suffolk half-timbered and thatched cottage

Yoxford is worth thinking about, too. Peasenhall is also pretty, and Framlingham provides the nearest classic country town, with a market square and old castle at its heart, and a good independent school, Framlingham College. Though it is rather too far for commuters.

> Continuation of main line

Journey: 94 min
Season: £4000
Peak: 1 through train plus 1 per hr changing at Ipswich
Off-peak: 1 every 2 hrs changing at Ipswich

NEEDHAM MARKET has plenty of old houses, some with Georgian facades, and a wondrous 15th-century chapel with a roof that sent the architectural historian Pevsner into orbit. He described it as "a whole church with nave, aisles and clerestory seemingly in the air". Buyers are drawn to the villages to the west that bask in the reflected glow of nearby Lavenham. A shock to the system is likely to arrive in the form of a £25m indoor ski centre called Snoasis attracting 200,000 visitors each month, with extra housing and a hotel. Nearby **Hitcham** has the crucial ingredients of shop and a densely-packed parish calendar. **Bildeston** has all the black-and-cream wickerwork architecture of a village built on the profits of the medieval clothing industry. It also has restaurants and a doctor's surgery. To the east of Needham Market the houses have much humbler origins.

Journey: 82 min
Season: £4040
Peak: 3 per hr
Off-peak: 1 per hr

STOWMARKET has a strategic position just on the lip of the Suffolk prairie. Beyond the A45 all the last dimples in the countryside have been ironed flat, and the trees and hedges unpicked from a landscape which blazes yellow with rape in the summer. Little two-up-two-downs cost £110,000; modern three-bedroom detached houses £160,000. **Haughley**, however, is pretty enough to have been colonised by commuters to Bury or Ipswich. It combines new developments on the outskirts with an intimate old village street and a green with a 60-ton parish coal-house on it, built in 1861. It also has shops, restaurants, and a strong interest in organic farming (this is where the Soil Association experiments with pesticide-free crops). **Wetherden** has not been developed quite so much, and its preoccupations are firmly agricultural and horsey – point-to-points are well attended. Newmarket is not that far away. A three-bedroom cottagey semi in either village could be expected to cost £260,000.

> Branch line to **Bury St Edmunds** via **Elmswell** and **Thurston**

Few through trains

Journey time from
Bury St Edmunds:
107 min

Season ticket from
Bury St Edmunds:
£4456 (also valid
Kings Cross via
Cambridge)

Peak: 1 through
train per hr from
Bury St Edmunds
plus 2 per hr
changing at
Ipswich or
Cambridge

Off-peak: 2 per hr
changing at
Ipswich or
Cambridge

This area is not nearly as popular with London commuters as that served by the fast electric trains to Diss. Both **Elmswell** and **Thurston** have grown by a third in recent years, swallowing new houses like packets of sweets. The rail operator's skip-stop policy means that most trains roar straight through to Bury – the occasional one will stop in the mornings and evenings depending on passenger demand.

Bury St Edmunds could be forgiven for regarding itself as the capital of East Anglia. As atmospheric as Norwich, Cambridge or King's Lynn, it sits right at the heart of the region on the conjunction of the A14, A143 and A134. On the rail network it stands on the watershed, suspended 28 miles from Cambridge and Ipswich. People travel west via Cambridge, east via Ipswich. A new breakfast train direct to London each day and home again in the evening makes things easier. Georgian and medieval houses crowd the centre, and in summer the tourists flock in to see the abbey ruins. The street market opens on Wednesdays and Saturdays. British Sugar has made it the base for one of its major production plants. West Suffolk Hospital is also here, and so is the Greene King brewery. Victorian terraced houses stand in appropriately named streets – Queens Road, Kings Road, Albert Crescent and so on. Two-bedroom versions start at around £140,000. Something more lavish at an address such as Home Farm Lane will cost over £250,000.

Three miles to the north is **Culford**, best known for its mixed day and boarding public school. Four-bedroom modern estate houses sell at £265,000. To the north-west you rapidly enter the Fens, and most people tend to prefer the more undulating landscape to the south. **Fornham St Martin** on the northern edge, has recently been relieved by a bypass. Four-bedroom houses skirting the Fornham Park golf course sell at over £280,000. Fornham All Saints is an older village altogether, centred around the church and village green – it also has the Swallow Suffolk Golf and Country Club with a spa and beauty centre. Four-bedroom houses here might fetch £280,000.

To the south is **Horringer** (once known as Horningsheath) with a set-piece church and green beside the entrance to Ickworth House (National Trust). The green is framed by neat cottages in plastered timber, flintwork and white brick that sell in an instant. Or there is **Cockfield**, an extraordinary cluster of hamlets, each with its own green, where a five-bedroom period house with three reception rooms might sell for £500,000. A mile away is Great Green, where you have village cricket on summer Sunday afternoons and four-bedroom period houses selling at £350,000 or more.

> Continuation of main line

Journey: 95 min
Season: £4560
Peak: 3 per hr
Off-peak: 1 per hr

DISS is extremely popular with commuters, because the trains whistle through to London. During the property boom of the late Eighties the town expanded, a few computer companies moved in and prices went up. It currently has a population of around 7,500, and still has a weekly Friday market, though it no longer includes livestock. It has an indoor swimming pool, squash and tennis courts, and an 18-hole golf course, but no cinema. In the town itself (which has mains gas) the most desirable streets include Mount Street, Denmark Street and Friends Road, where older Georgian houses mix with Fifties' properties. A period semi with three bedrooms might sell for £225,000; a four-bedroom detached with large garden £280,000, and a good barn conversion with three to four bedrooms £360,000.

Dickleburgh, three miles to the north, has its own village stores, post office, doctor's surgery and primary school, and it has been bypassed. Or you could look west to **Redgrave**, which has a village green and pub. Much closer to Diss is **Palgrave**, whose residents include a preponderance of artists and a cartoonist, who live in the plastered and thatched cottages and regularly show their work. There is a green and a primary school. Locals complain that the school is cramped Victorian, but it cannot expand because it is built on common land. The only pub closed several years ago and the bar in the village hall is open only occasionally. Houses on the new David Wilson Homes development sell at over £320,000 for four to five bedrooms.

Georgian
farmhouse,
south Norfolk

Schools in Norfolk

In Norfolk the widest choice is in Norwich. Schools here include the two strong independents, Norwich School for boys and Norwich High for girls, as well as the Roman Catholic comprehensive Notre Dame High School.

A particularly interesting school in Norfolk is Wymondham College, probably Europe's largest mixed state boarding school. Here, tuition is free and the cost of boarding lower than at any comparable private school. It is not to be confused with Wymondham High comprehensive, which also does very well. Gresham's, at Holt near the north Norfolk coast, is the dominant co-educational independent school in the area for day pupils and boarders.

South-west is **Mellis**, a tiny scattered village with the most extraordinarily large 237-acre green, the most talked-about feature locally. The Suffolk Wildlife Trust likes to delay the hay-cutting until high summer in order to allow the wild flowers to reseed. The green is bisected by the main railway line which can be noisy, depending which way the wind is blowing. There is a pub, but no post office or shop. Children attend the primary school here, then go to secondary school in Eye, which also has a sixth-form college.

For a very lively village life it would be better to look east to **Hoxne** (rhymes with oxen) which is set around the village green with an outstanding half-timbered priory with herringbone brickwork. It has its modern ribbon development, too. The village has one pub, a shop and a petrol pump, and there is a primary school. Morris dancers visit in summer and the Harvest Breakfast on the green in the autumn is a must. This comes a fortnight after the rousing Harvest Festival and Harvest Lunch. A small terraced house here with two bedrooms could be had for around £150,000. Something bigger with three bedrooms would start at £180,000.

Eye, four miles south, is a typical Suffolk town on the River Dove, with two banks, a florist, butcher and baker, an old castle and a new business park on the old airfield. Though it is no longer a borough, it still has its mayor and deputy mayor. It attracts lots of London commuters and buzzes with societies. These include the Gardening Club, Eye Theatre and Eye Bach Choir. It has a primary school and a small hospital that caters mainly for the elderly. Gardening is competitive – residents open their gardens to the public. Church fund-raising activities are frequent and impressive. A four-bedroom thatched cottage with a separate annexe at **Yaxley**, two miles away, would hit the market with a price tag of around £360,000. New four-bedroom houses cost £290,000.

Journey: 100 min
Season: £4800
Peak: 3 per hr
Off-peak: 2 per hr

NORWICH Few people commute this far, although the more frequent service to London makes the journey easier. The attractions of Norwich are strong, especially with the Broads and the Norfolk beaches just a car drive away. The hospital and the University of East Anglia swell the ranks of the middle-class professionals. The city retains a strong sense of history with the old castle, huge tented market and vibrant shopping centre at its heart, where street buskers, students and wealthy shoppers mix. There have been big changes recently with a new Riverside Complex of properties, cinema and shops and a new hospital on the outskirts. To be near enough to the station you need to look to the south-west, in an area known as The Golden Triangle, where you could pay up to £350,000 for a double-fronted Victorian villa, though there are plenty of cheaper Victorian terraced houses to be had, too. On a modern estate you could buy a detached four-bedroom house for £200,000.

'The attractions of Norwich are strong, especially with the Broads and the Norfolk beaches just a car drive away'

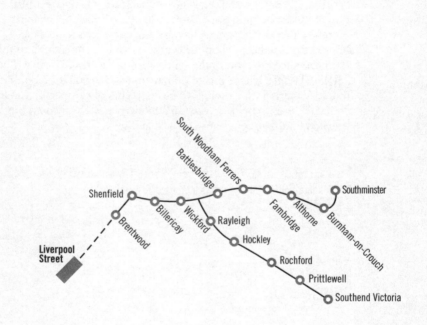

Liverpool Street
> **Southend**

Journey: 35 min
Season: £1880
Peak: 7 per hr
Off-peak: 6 per hr

BRENTWOOD People are fond of Brentwood because of its traditional high street with independent shops and its convenient position. It is right on Junction 28 of the M25, yet within walking distance of fields, woods and the lakes of Thorndon Park. It exudes a sense of wealth, even among the young. Ford and British Telecom have a strong presence as employers; Ford once owned a lot of property which has now been sold off. Modern estates have been grafted on to gracious Victorian terraces and Thirties' cul-de-sacs. In The Homesteads, for instance, mansion-sized houses are packed as tight as country cottages to create a feeling of village intimacy. A four-bedroom property here would cost £550,000 to £600,000. Brentwood's adult population empties into London every weekday, though many opt to catch the train at Shenfield.

Journey: 21 min
Season: £2060
Peak: 10 per hr
Off-peak: 8 per hr

SHENFIELD
See **Liverpool Street to Norwich** line (page 15)

Journey: 28 min
Season: £2260
Peak: 8 per hr
Off-peak: 4 per hr

BILLERICAY is bustling, respectable and genteel. House prices are not as high as at Shenfield, but are similar to those in Brentwood and Chelmsford. The town is close enough to the open countryside to attract a steady drift of people from London's East End. A private golf course has been built on the Chelmsford side. Car park spaces in the station car park are scarce as hen's teeth during peak times and a mobile clamping unit picks off illegal parkers. There is a year-long wait for season ticket parking, and there are between 3000 and 4000 season ticket holders to compete with.

Journey: 34 min
Season: £2460
Peak: 8 per hr
Off-peak: 3 per hr

WICKFORD People who live in Wickford consider themselves superior to those who live in Basildon, but inferior to those from Rayleigh. Commuters pour in from the Dengie peninsula to catch the fast trains here, rather than take the slower service on the Southminster branch line. Some of the trains stop at Stratford, where people can switch painlessly to the London Underground or Docklands Light Railway. The town is a tumour of Sixties' estates built on to the village of Shotgate, with green belt on three sides. You could spend £190,000 on a new three-bedroom semi, or well over £185,000 on a house with four bedrooms. Housing estates are popular. On the Wick housing development a whole new settlement has emerged with houses selling at £160,000 for two bedrooms to £180,000 for two to three bedrooms.

> Branch line to Southminster via Battlesbridge, South Woodham Ferrers, Fambridge, Althorne and Burnham-on-Crouch

Through trains: 2 per hr (peak)/1 per hr (off-peak)

Journey (from Southminster): 83 min (64 min peak)

Season from Southminster: £2800

SOUTH WOODHAM FERRERS is almost other-worldly, epitomising all that the *Essex Design Guide* had to say about the use of traditional materials and regional styles. Building began in 1976, which makes it one of the more recent attempts to create a planned New Town instead of a rash of new developments. Banks are made to look like barns. Everything has steep pitched roofs and eaves. The William de Ferrers school doubles as a public library and the hall for the amateur dramatics society, but a new community centre, Champion Manor Hall, is soon to be opened. Planning regulations are tough. You aren't allowed to park a caravan outside your house at the front. The Round Table and other similar organisations are strong in a place where people were once all newcomers together, forging links for the first time. The town has grown up, and the place once entirely inhabited by thirty-somethings who were all relatively well-off and wrinkle-free, has much more of a mix of ages and income brackets. One-bedroom houses start at £105,000, four-bedroom detached houses at £225,000 to £325,000. The Marsh Farm Country Park offers 350 acres of reclaimed marshland in which to walk the dog. The shopping development offers retail therapy.

At **North Fambridge** you enter yachting country. There is a post office and a general store and an outer fringe of small new estates. A typical large four-bedroom detached house will cost £450,000 to £500,000. **Althorne** is a tiny hamlet, one-and-a-half miles from its station on the river. It is mostly modern, with a post office-cum-shop and a pub, the Ferryboat Inn. A semi here costs £200,000 upwards, a bungalow £250,000 and a detached house £240,000 to £350,000. It is **Burnham-on-Crouch**, however, which is the real yachting capital of the Dengie peninsula, known as the pearl or the

Cowes of the east coast. There are four yacht clubs. Burnham Week attracts hundred of yachts and thousands of visitors every year. The town has a mix of Victorian, Georgian and classic Essex weatherboarded cottages, and a huge modern complex of flats built on the quay, popular with weekenders who want long lonely walks. Overlooking the river you could expect to spend £315,000 for three bedrooms; a studio will go for £70,000. An older two-bedroom cottage could be had for £130,000.

Southminster suddenly seems remote at the end of the line, and house prices dip accordingly. It is a close farming community on the very edge of the marshes that stretch timelessly off into the North Sea. A three-bedroom semi here would cost £180,000. A grander house on the outskirts with a paddock would be upwards of £360,000. Southminster has its own primary school, cricket and football teams and choral society. **Tillingham**, to the north, is the archetypal Essex village with weatherboarded cottages, a green, a church and a pub. A two-bedroom cottage in a terrace starts at £130,000; a Grade II listed house in ample gardens would cost £345,000. Still within reach of Southminster station is **Bradwell-on-Sea**. It has a good collection of cottages, and Bradwell Lodge, a Georgian house near the Blackwater, with internal decorations by Robert Adam. Its church, St-Peter's-on-the-Wall, is one of the earliest in England, built in 654, though only the nave remains. You can walk 12 miles along the sea wall without meeting a soul. Close by is a marina and bird reserve. The area is stigmatised by the presence of the nuclear power station, but it is being de-commissioned.

'Burnham-on-Crouch is known as the pearl or the Cowes of the east coast'

Riverside apartments, Burnham-on-Crouch

> Continuation of main line

Journey: 41 min
Season: £2480
Peak: 6 per hr
Off-peak: 3 per hr

RAYLEIGH mushroomed in the Thirties, and considers itself upmarket of Basildon and Wickford. The large windmill at one end of the High Street adds a gracious note to the place. A modern three-bedroom semi costs £215,000. The nearby village of **Hullbridge** once had the dubious honour of being dubbed by *The Sun* as the sexiest place in England. The reasons given were no more exciting than its high per capita birthrate and a local councillor's claim that the place is so boring that people have nothing better to do than stay at home and make babies. The village should be valued more for the fact that it sits on the Crouch Estuary. You can walk along the sea wall to Battlesbridge, where you can enjoy one of the slivers of Essex landscape which have remained unsullied by modern pressures. It is less expensive than other areas.

Journey: 45 min
Season: £2480
Peak: 6 per hr
Off-peak: 3 per hr

HOCKLEY The Southend area was developed in the 1890s, and the further you come inland from the tip, the more modern it becomes. Hockley and **Hawkwell**, roughly six miles inland, have mostly Sixties' and Seventies' houses. Hockley Woods is the place for Sunday walks along the bridleways, with drinks at The Bull afterwards. Lakeside and Bluewater provide the all-singing all-dancing shopping experiences in this part of the world.

Journey: 49 min
Season: £2500
Peak: 6 per hr
Off-peak: 3 per hr

ROCHFORD is a plain town with a square surrounded by banks and specialist shops, including gift shops, a tea and coffee shop, and a watch repairer. The market is held here every Tuesday. Hall Road is the smart address. The houses here have huge gardens running down to the golf course, and you'll need over £1m to buy. The town tends to feel overshadowed by Southend. It has a reservoir popular with anglers on Sundays. The choice of shops has improved with the opening of the Lakeside shopping centre off the M25 at Thurrock. **Ashingdon**, three miles away, has higher property prices. A modern one-bedroom flat can be had for £90,000, while four-bedroom houses can cost over £260,000. It has a pub, a few shops, and it sits in a patch of rural Essex that is attempting to keep urbanisation at bay. Builders are, however, trying to fill the gaps with new houses.

'I'll tell you how bad Prittlewell used to be,' says one commuter. 'I sent a bottle of wine to the station manager just because my train was on time. Then 77 consecutive journeys were 10 minutes late'

Journey: 53 min	
Season: £2500	
Peak: 6 per hr	
Off-peak: 3 per hr	

PRITTLEWELL is a restrained northern suburb of Southend where two- to three-bedroom semis cost around £160,000. People who travel this line have seen the service improve dramatically. "I'll tell you how bad it used to be," says one commuter. "I sent a bottle of wine to the station manager just because my train was on time. Then 77 consecutive journeys were 10 minutes late."

Journey: 55 min	
Season: £2500	
Peak: 6 per hr	
Off-peak: 3 per hr	

SOUTHEND VICTORIA
See Southend on the **Fenchurch Street to Shoeburyness** line (page 43). Most people prefer to use that line because the journey is quicker.

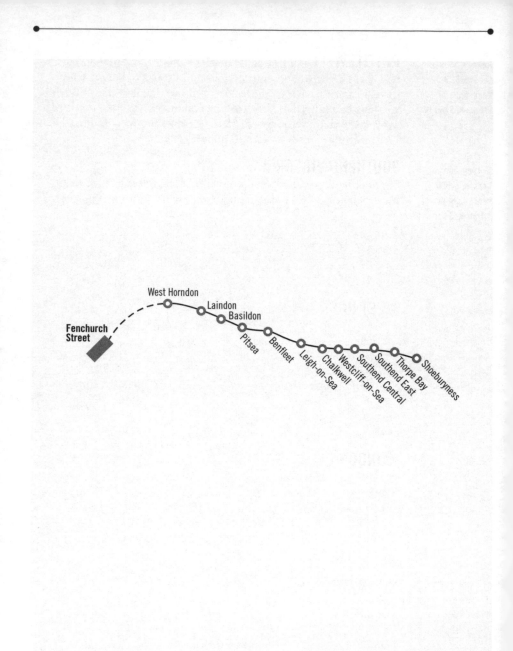

Fenchurch Street

West Horndon

Laindon

Basildon

Pitsea

Benfleet

Leigh-on-Sea

Chalkwell

Westcliff-on-Sea

Southend Central

Southend East

Thorpe Bay

Shoeburyness

Fenchurch Street
> **Shoeburyness**

Note that at all stations out of Fenchurch Street you can buy a season ticket at a discount of around 15 per cent on the prices quoted, which allows travel to Fenchurch Street arriving before 0715 or after 0915 Monday to Friday. There is no time restriction on the homeward journey or in either direction at weekends.

Journey: 29 min
Season: £1400
Peak: 4 per hr
Off-peak: 2 per hr

WEST HORNDON Classic between-the-wars and post-war suburbia has sprouted at West Horndon because of the sheer convenience of the rail service, though it somehow remains rural and most of the Thirties' bungalows have 150ft gardens, many of them backing on to fields. The station attracts commuters along the A128 from Brentwood, who find it easier to drive south and catch the train here rather than tangle with the traffic in Brentwood or Basildon. A three-bedroom bungalow sells for around £290,000; a detached five-bedroom house for around £345,000.

Journey: 34 min
Season: £1820
Peak: 8 per hr
Off-peak: 2 per hr

LAINDON station has the advantage of an extra platform. A number of services start from here, and its commuters are guaranteed a seat. The less expensive area, known locally as Alcatraz, is subject to urban renewal and a three-bedroom terraced house here costs around £117,000. The better area is Langdon Hills, within a few minutes' walk of the station, where modern detached houses sell for about £190,000 to £230,000.

Journey: 33 min
Season: £1820
Peak: 5 per hr
Off-peak: 4 per hr

BASILDON has virtually swallowed up **Laindon** and **Pitsea**. As one of a clutch of new towns planned after World War II to absorb people and industry from London, it exists as a kind of joke to people who once thought we could be weaned away from commuting. The planners decided people could live and work in the same place – industrial development was zoned to the north of the town – and for this reason it was built without a station. They finally had to bow to pressure and build one in the Seventies. The town's phenomenal rate of growth has not been without its problems. Older residents have felt increasingly uneasy about walking alone at night, and sometimes the town has to be heavily policed. Against that, the centre has been given a multi-million-pound makeover, together with a millennium glass bell tower opened by the Queen, and there may be yet more inward investment. You could buy a four-bedroom executive house with garage for £240,000 to £380,000.

Journey: 41 min
Season: £2000
Peak: 4 per hr
Off-peak: 4 per hr

PITSEA is rather more friendly than Basildon proper, with a defined centre and an open-air market in the sea of ex-council housing. Estate agents say it is one of the few affordable areas left. A three-bedroom terraced house can be found for £130,000, an ex-council one-bedroom flat for £80,000. Pitsea Mount offers some of the best private housing very close to the station, with four-bedroom detached houses costing £280,000.

Journey: 40 min
Season: £2180
Peak: 8 per hr
Off-peak: 4 per hr

BENFLEET The Southend Rail Travellers' Association says this is one of the busiest stations on the entire line, serving a huge catchment area swollen with Sixties' development. Benfleet itself is little more than ribbon development along the A130, and it is hard to find anything you could define as a centre. Little weatherboarded cottages could cost anything between £190,000 and £250,000, detached executive houses with four or five bedrooms £320,000 to £380,000.

'Leigh blends a certain eccentricity (of the take-the-tricycle-rather-than-the-bus kind) with airs and graces'

The station also attracts commuters from **Canvey Island**, which is really the scrag end of Essex. So much of it lies below sea level that houses tend to offer views of the sea wall or of oil refineries. You can get a little one-bedroom bungalow for £140,000, or a three-bedroom semi for around £170,000. Traffic in and out of the island strangles the only two roads linking it to the mainland. Peter de Savary once had plans to build 4300 houses, accompanied by a new station just south of Benfleet, but these were shelved and now Wilson Connolly has built a large development instead.

Journey: 45 min
Season: £2180
Peak: 8 per hr
Off-peak: 4 per hr

LEIGH-ON-SEA Leigh blends a certain eccentricity (of the take-the-tricycle-rather-than-the bus kind) with airs and graces, and is more sought-after than its neighbours. The old town in particular is worth just going to see, since it retains its historical integrity as a working fishing village. You can watch the boats landing their catches, and the cockle sheds are well stocked. The two- or three-bedroom terraced cottages rarely come on the market and are quickly snapped up, for £210,000 or more, when they do.

Birdwatchers are treated to endless sightings of migratory birds that stop off at Two Tree Island, a stretch of saltmarsh that was once a refuse dump. Hadleigh Country Park offers 100 acres of grazed downland with birds, butterflies and urbanised wildlife. Many of the larger houses have been filleted into flats. Something with one bedroom might sell at £115,000, two bedrooms at £130,000. Unconverted Twenties' and

Thirties' houses up on the cliffs go for £250,000 to £400,000. There is pressure on properties within walking distance of The Broadway and the station because car parking is impossible.

Journey: 48 min
Season: £2180
Peak: 8 per hr
Off-peak: 4 per hr

CHALKWELL The Chalkwell Hall estate is extremely popular, being south of the London Road, close to the Fenchurch Street line and the bracing breezes from the sea front. Large detached Edwardian houses with four bedrooms cost over £500,000.

Journey: 50 min
Season: £2280
Peak: 8 per hr
Off-peak: 4 per hr

WESTCLIFF-ON-SEA Westcliff is a dignified old Victorian lady of a town which is failing to fend off the encroaching seaside tat. Sadly, her densely layered streets of 19th-century houses, many of them now converted into flats, tend to be jammed with cars that can't find anywhere to park. She has a more cosmopolitan air these days, thanks to her appeal to asylum seekers. Average prices of flats range from around £85,000 for one bedroom to £120,000 for two or £400,000 for something with a good view on the Esplanade. The Cliff Gardens run all the way along the cliffs to Southend.

Journey: 52 min
Season: £2280
Peak: 8 per hr
Off-peak: 4 per hr

SOUTHEND CENTRAL Southend has spent the last few decades adjusting to the death of the Great British Holiday, while simultaneously adapting itself as a London dormitory. A huge injection of European regeneration money has helped, as has the arrival of the £53-million campus for South East Essex College. It remains popular with day-trippers and bank holiday weekenders, and hasn't lost the kiss-me-quick feel of the Fifties. Strolling along the Prom is still a popular Sunday morning pastime. Its efforts in the late 18th and 19th centuries to rival the elegance of other seaside resorts such as Brighton have endowed it with some fine buildings, including the Royal Terrace. The one-and-a-quarter mile pier, which miraculously survived a fire in 1976, was then severed by a boat 10 years later, and is now cherished and restored and joined by the theme park Adventure Island, where thrills are supplied by The Vortex and The Scorpion.

'Westcliff is a dignified old Victorian lady of a town which is failing to fend off the encroaching seaside tat'

The Royal Bank of Scotland and the administrators of VAT are both large local employers. The shopping centre is pedestrianised, though it is but a flea on the backside of the huge Lakeside development nearby at Thurrock. Southend has its own airport with flights to the Channel Islands and plans for a new terminal to open in 2006 offering flights to Europe and the Mediterranean. The sailing fraternity is strong. There are five yacht clubs either side of Southend, along the stretch between **Thorpe Bay** and **Leigh Old Town**. Average house prices run from £140,000 for a two-bedroom house, £170,000 for a three-bedroom semi and well over £190,000 for one in a better area.

Journey: 55 min
Season: £2280
Peak: 8 per hr
Off-peak: 4 per hr

SOUTHEND EAST This is the area known as **Southchurch**. A great web of residential streets extends from Southend Central to Thorpe Bay, stitched together by a long main road of shops and offices. A three-bedroom semi on one of the nicest roads – Southchurch Boulevard or Arlington Road, for example – will cost over £250,000. In less popular streets the price drops to around £200,000. Two- or three-bedroom terraced houses sell for around £180,000 to £190,000.

Journey: 58 min
Season: £2380
Peak: 8 per hr
Off-peak: 4 per hr

THORPE BAY is the most expensive part of Southend, and even those who live on the fringe-of-the-fringe say they live here. Detached houses with four to five bedrooms, built in the early-20th century, sell for £450,000 to £550,000. Those on the seafront might go for anything up to £1 million. The private golf club and Conservative politics feature large on the social circuit, which is fuelled with new money and is anxious to dissociate itself from anything too down-market. There is a wine bar but no pub. The place excites envy in its neighbours, as described by one local cricketer with typical Essex bluntness. "When you played against Thorpe Bay, you bowled at the batsman, not the wicket."

'Even those who live on the fringe-of-the-fringe say they live in Thorpe Bay'

Seafront property, Southend

Schools in Essex

The choice of high-performing grammars, ex-grammars and comprehensives in Essex makes it attractive to ambitious parents with young families who cannot afford or do not wish to use the private sector. Be warned, however, that some of the best schools have five times too many applicants for the number of places. Entrance requirements are stiff.

Many of the schools appear in clusters. Southend, for instance, has Southend Boys' High and Southend Girls' High, both traditional grammar schools, as well as two good state schools, Westcliff High for boys and Westcliff High for girls. Brentwood independent schools include Brentwood and Peniel Academy (non-selective).

The good comprehensives include St Martin's and the Ursuline ex-grammar comprehensive girls' convent. There is also Shenfield High (mixed) at Shenfield. Not far away is the Anglo-European at Ingatestone, a comprehensive which promotes the International Baccalaureate.

Chelmsford has the County High School for Girls and the boys' equivalent, King Edward VI Grammar School, which has choral links with the cathedral. New Hall is the nearby girls' day and boarding school.

Colchester has the Grammar County High School for Girls, and the Colchester Royal Grammar for boys – a descendant of the ancient town school established in 1206. Choices here also include St Benedict's Roman Catholic and Philip Morant co-educational schools.

Other places with strong schools are Hornchurch, which has The Campion boys' Catholic comprehensive; Loughton, which has the Davenant Foundation co-educational school; Saffron Walden with its County High; Hockley which has Greensward College comprehensive; and Woodford Green, which has the girls' grammar Woodford County High.

Journey: 62 min
Season: £2380
Peak: 8 per hr
Off-peak: 4 per hr

SHOEBURYNESS With its sprawling council estates and industrial zones, Shoeburyness has little to offer other than cheapness. A three-bedroom house can be had for around £150,000. It also has a beach which is good for windsurfing, sailing and jet-skiing. There are a few flats right on the beach that sell for around £150,000. The Grade II listed Horseshoe Barracks, not far from the station, is being turned into smart homes and the converted officers' mess sold for £950,000. To the north it becomes a little more sedate and a good house can be bought in the £350,000 range.

Barling, nearby, offers a profound contrast with one foot still firmly planted in the past. Among the 300-year old cottages, it is also possible to buy a detached Twenties' bungalow for £350,000. A period house with a paddock in this area would cost at least £750,000 to £950,000. Alternatively, there is **Great Wakering**, with its church, pubs and shops. A two-bedroom, Grade II listed, mid-terraced house here would cost £150,000; a three-bedroom house with a long rear garden over £190,000.

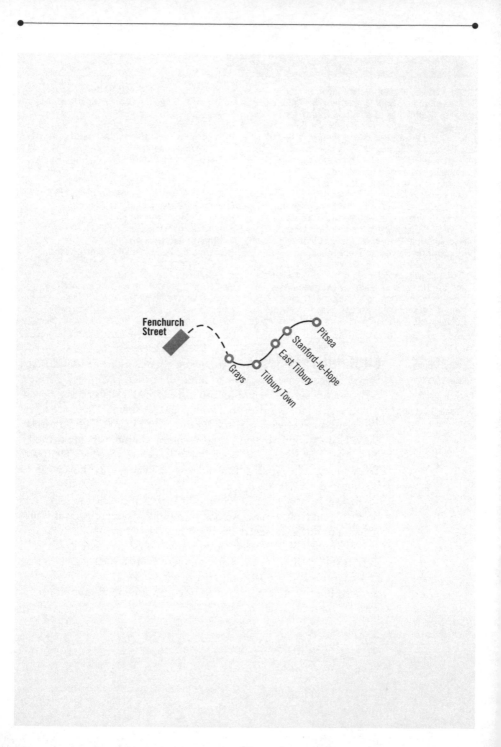

Fenchurch
Street

Grays

Tilbury Town

East Tilbury

Stanford-le-Hope

Pitsea

Fenchurch Street
> **Pitsea** (via Tilbury)

Note that at all stations out of Fenchurch Street you can buy a season ticket at a discount of around 15 per cent on the prices quoted, which allows travel to Fenchurch Street arriving before 0715 of after 0915 Monday to Friday. There is no time restriction on the homeward journey or in either direction at weekends. This is a line where most full-fare season tickets have actually fallen in price in recent years.

Journey: 38 min	
Season: £1400	
Peak: 6 per hr	
Off-peak: 4 per hr	

GRAYS was built in two surges – one in the late-19th century and one in the Thirties – and is now one of the busiest commercial centres in this part of Essex. Cheaper homes in the £120,000 range are being snapped up and price rises at the lower end have been remarkable. The most comfortable area to live is **North Grays**, where the roads are filled with large Thirties' houses. The four-bedroom detached variety would cost between £300,000 and £400,000. **North Stifford** is another popular part, with the remnants of the old village still intact (blink and you miss it). A 15th-century cottage with two bedrooms would sell for around £250,000. The vast Lakeside shopping centre at Thurrock, three miles away, offering one of the largest concentrations of shopping in Europe, a Mississippi steamer restaurant and seven-screen cinema, has had a huge impact. It has also spawned the new Bannatynes Leisure Centre. Grays itself is a good shopping centre with small outlets of the big chains.

Nearby is Chafford Hundred, where a whole new town of 5500 houses is nearly complete on the old chalk pits beside the M25 and the Dartford Tunnel. It has a rich mix of one-bedroom flats for £145,000, two bedrooms at £170,000, up to four-bedroom houses selling for around £330,000, with maisonettes, semis and terraced housing between. It also has its own new main line rail station (on a link between Grays and Upminster); schools are already in place and more housing is to come.

‘At Chafford Hundred, a whole new town of 5500 houses is nearly complete on the old chalk pits beside the M25’

Journey: 40 min	
Season: £1400	
Peak: 5 per hr	
Off-peak: 2 per hr	

TILBURY TOWN

Tilbury itself bears all the warts and eyesores that the 20th century could have thrown at it. When the ships coming up the Thames got so big that they couldn't squeeze up to London any more, Tilbury developed a docks complex so huge that it can be seen for miles around. Housing is very council-orientated and cheap. Many former council tenants have bought their properties and an ex-council house with three bedrooms costs around £120,000. The Tilbury loop line has been furnished with brand new carriages at a cost of £300 million. **Tilbury Riverside** burgeoned on the back of the boat-trains to Europe in the 1850s, but it long ago lost its station and now the only ferry that ploughs in and out is for Gravesend.

Journey: 47 min	
Season: £1820	
Peak: 5 per hr	
Off-peak: 2 per hr	

EAST TILBURY

There are strangely rural, forgotten-about pockets in this town. Around quiet corners you come suddenly upon dirt tracks that open up long walks beside the Thames. The Bata shoe company was started here by Czechoslovakians who built their own distinctive Thirties' flat-roofed houses, schools and cinema, now much admired and designated a conservation area. The factory has closed, but is preserved, and many of the houses have been sold on the open market. The old Bata office block has been converted into flats. A second-hand three-bedroom terraced house here costs about £130,000; you can buy a four-bedroom detached house for about £300,000 to £350,000. The Lakeside shopping centre at Thurrock has sucked much of the retail energy from these nearby areas. Modernisation came late to this line, but the old timber platform in the station has been replaced, and the manually operated level crossing gates now work automatically.

Commuters used to call it the Misery Line, but a great deal of money has been spent on track and signalling improvements. Meanwhile, overcrowding has eased since passenger numbers have dropped from 165,000 per week to 125,000 as more people work from home for one or two days a week or opt to travel by car.

'Tilbury bears all the warts and eyesores that the 20th century could have thrown at it'

'Commuters used to call it the Misery Line, but a great deal of money has been spent on track and signalling improvements, and overcrowding has eased'

Journey: 51 min
Season: £1820
Peak: 5 per hr
Off-peak: 2 per hr

STANFORD-LE-HOPE There are a few late 19th-century streets near the station, but otherwise most of **Stanford le Hope** is an eruption of low-cost Sixties' housing that gathered around **Corringham** and **Coryton** as far as the big oil refineries on the edge of the Thames. Plans are afoot to turn Coryton into a major port and the area is expected to swallow a large amount of new Thames Gateway housing in the next decade. Three-bedroom semis are priced at about £160,000 to £200,000, standard four-bedroom detached houses at £275,000, with the most expensive in the range selling for about £300,000 to £350,000. From here people might prefer to travel by rail up to **Pitsea** and change to the main line into Fenchurch Street, rather than take the slow and indirect route through **Tilbury**.

Journey: 41 min
Season: £2000
Peak: 4 per hr
Off-peak: 4 per hr

PITSEA See **Fenchurch Street to Shoeburyness** line (page 42).

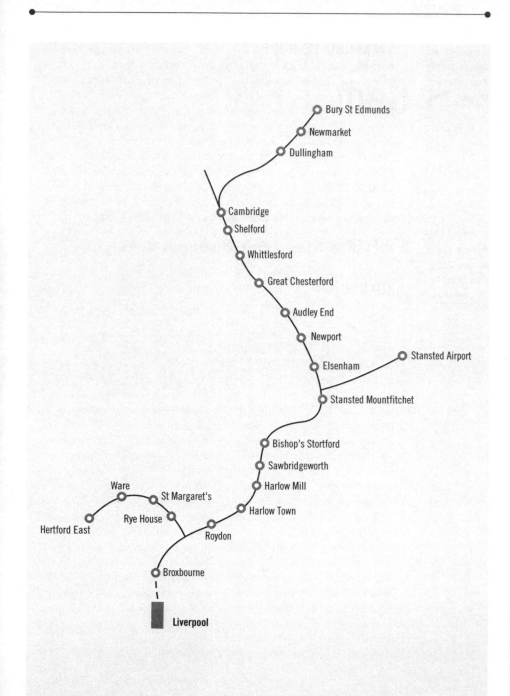

Bury St Edmunds
Newmarket
Dullingham
Cambridge
Shelford
Whittlesford
Great Chesterford
Audley End
Newport
Stansted Airport
Elsenham
Stansted Mountfitchet
Bishop's Stortford
Sawbridgeworth
Harlow Mill
Ware
St Margaret's
Harlow Town
Hertford East
Rye House
Roydon
Broxbourne
Liverpool

Liverpool Street
> Cambridge

For stations as far as Shelford, a lunchtime season ticket allowing travel to Liverpool Street between noon and 2.30pm from the home station on weekdays, is available at an 18 per cent discount on prices quoted. There is no restriction on the homeward journey or in either direction at weekends.

Journey: 27 min
Season: £1712
Peak: 8 per hr
Off-peak: 5 per hr

BROXBOURNE The railway came to Broxbourne in 1840. Victorian houses immediately started going up around the station and it has been commuter country ever since. To the south of it is a soothing pocket of countryside where the New River lazes across the meadows. Other relics of the rural past, including Broxbourne Woods, have been retained by conversion into parkland. The Lea Valley Regional Park runs for 23 miles from Bromley-by-Bow through Broxbourne to Ware, making Broxbourne a handy resort for boating and holiday chalets – the leisure pool competes for people's affections with the Grundy Park Leisure Centre. Detached houses on the more residential western side of the town can sell for £450,000 upwards. Smaller three-bedroom houses to the east fetch up to £290,000. Large amounts of new housing are planned at Canada Fields. There is a vast out-of-town Brookfield Retail Park at Cheshunt to the south. Cheshunt also has a golf course.

Broxbourne doesn't stop before **Hoddesdon** begins, though the atmosphere becomes rather more industrial. Hoddesdon is tightly bound by the green belt and it has a proper town centre with 17th-century buildings set around the old clock tower – an area busy with stalls on market day. The two good state schools attract large numbers of families. Houses on the west and south sides are more desirable, being removed from the more industrial east. In the mix of Victorian, Thirties' and Sixties' houses you could buy a three-bedroom semi for up to £200,000. Larger houses, such as those in the privacy of College Road, sell for £500,000 to £600,000.

Fork to Hertford East via Rye House, St Margaret's and Ware

Journey: 48 min
(34 min peak)

Season: £1728

Peak: 2 per hr

Off-peak: 2 per hr

RYE HOUSE sits on the northern edge of Hoddesdon, on the finger of the Lea Valley Regional Park where the remains of the old Rye House gatehouse still stand. There was once a thriving nursery garden industry here. In the Thirties, says the local council, the Lea Valley had "the world's largest accumulation of glasshouses". Between 1968 and 1971 much of the old nursery land was surrendered to housing, thus creating what is now known as the Hundred Acre Estate, attached to the north side of Hoddesdon. Here you can buy a basic terraced house for £190,000; a three-bedroom semi for £210,000. The 1999 version is Rye House Village, 140 houses built beside the station, where a two-bedroom flat can cost £125,500 and a three-bedroom detached house £250,000. Elsewhere in Rye House, property tends to be fairly cheap. The relative modesty of the houses here is ironic when you remember that there was once a plan to make Rye House into a kind of genteel pleasure garden. The plans were buried when Sir Giles Gilbert Scott's huge power station arrived. Today a combined cycle gas turbine power station does the job. Entertainments at Rye House Stadium include go-kart, speedway and greyhound racing.

Journey: 51 min
(37 min peak)

Season: £1892

Peak: 2 per hr

Off-peak: 2 per hr

ST MARGARET'S The village here is **Stanstead St Margaret's**, divided from **Stanstead Abbots** by the River Lea, though sharing a vicar. A bypass has reduced the amount of through-traffic from 19,000 vehicles a day to 9000. It is a fast-growing village with new houses going up all the time. There is one remaining pub, The Jolly Fisherman. A former pub, The House Up A Tree, had a tree house to which people used to take their pints in the summer. The old malt industry lingers like a ghost. Disused cowls and chutes litter the skyline, and the occasional whiff of it wafts over the terraced cottages and modern estates in Stanstead Abbots. There are some small shops and a post office on this side of the river, with playing fields and sports club just outside at St Margaretsbury. Stanstead Abbots has a primary school attached to the church. Most of the older children attend secondary schools in Hertford or North Hoddesdon. The Stansteads have a marina with narrowboats and cruisers for hire. Property prices are slightly higher than those in Hoddesdon.

Journey: 54 min
(40 min peak)
Season: £2020
Peak: 2 per hr
Off-peak: 2 per hr

WARE People say that this is where the chimneypots stop and the countryside begins. Ware is a good old market town which hasn't been spoilt, and beyond it lies what the estate agents like to call the golden box – a group of handsome villages in a landscape which, despite its proximity to London, preserves a feeling of real remoteness. The town has a strong sense of history. The main local employer is SmithKlineGlaxo, whose factory is set in parkland by the river. In developing new sites it has dug up Roman artefacts and discovered the remains of bodies from the time of the Black Death, shipped out along the River Lea for burial outside London. What Hertfordshire sent in return was water – channelled to London's East End by way of the New River, a canal built in the early 17th century. Much of the town's wealth was created by the malt industry, and many of the old maltings have been converted into flats, mini-Docklands style. You can buy a one-bedroom flat on the water's edge for £145,000; a three-bedroom apartment with parking for £200,000. It is a charming place to live. The narrowboats still come past and there are some pretty walks along the riverbank. These allow you to view the extraordinarily delicate old gazebos behind the houses in the High Street, where the gardens run down to the river.

The town centre also contains quite a few mews houses, developed from the old stables and courtyards behind the High Street. Four-bedroom town houses with paved courtyards at the back cost £350,000. There are some smart modern houses closer to the golf course on the south side of the town, where something with four bedrooms and a double garage would fetch up to £500,000. There are specialist shops, including Victoria Beckham's sister's clothes shop, and little restaurants. The town has lots of clubs and societies, which show themselves off once a year during Ware Festival in July. There are indoor and outdoor heated swimming pools, cricket on the Old Hertfordians ground, Hertford Rugby Club at Hoe Lane, and Ware Football Club.

18th-century
riverfront
gazebos, Ware

The villages are in a quite different price zone. Footballers, pop stars and television personalities lurk down these country lanes, and you could easily pay up to £850,000 for an ex-farmhouse with acreage.

Great Amwell is both the most expensive and the prettiest, with the New River draped in willows. Here it widens to a pool with two islands. These hold monuments to the New River's creator, the engineer Sir Hugh Myddleton. Two miles away are the imposing buildings of Haileybury College. A period house with five bedrooms and two acres in Great Amwell could easily cost £1m, though at the other end of the scale you might find a little two-up-two-down in need of modernisation for £175,000. The village has an annual flower show and every so often it opens its gardens to the public.

To the east is **Hunsdon**. Its timbered and weatherboarded cottages, village school and friendly atmosphere all contribute to its great appeal. Saturday coffee mornings are a regular event in the village hall, and there are societies for toddlers, tennis players and the elderly. Small Victorian cottages cost around £150,000. Three-bedroom cottages can be expected to cost at least £200,000, and farmhouse-sized properties between £500,000 and £600,000. New houses have been built in small handfuls for those at managing director level, priced at £450,000 to £500,000 for five bedrooms.

In the precious northern belt are villages such as **Standon** and **Puckeridge** in the Rib Valley. Standon is favourite, with its wide curving High Street, timber-framed houses and village school. St Edmund's Roman Catholic College is a few miles to the west. Property prices are slightly higher than those in Hunsdon. Puckeridge has a twisting High Street and more the feel of a small town about it, with Sixties' and Seventies' developments tacked on. More new development has followed as a result of the expansion of Stansted Airport. An older two-bedroom terraced house here would cost £135,000; a new four-bedroom house £250,000. The Thurlow Hunt rides out from Brent Pelham nearby.

Braughing is a film-set village built at the confluence of the River Quin with the Rib. The approach to it is by way of a ford known as The Splash that occasionally floods. It has an aviation society, local history society, and active bell-ringing group. There is drama and tennis, too. D White is a superb local butcher selling special Braughing sausages made to a secret recipe. The colour-washed cottages have often been used as backdrops to television feature films, and some have superb pargeting. The smallest cottage here would cost around £165,000, with prices rising to about £750,000 for the larger period houses.

Journey: 58 min
(44 min peak)
Season: £2060
(also valid from
Hertford North)
Peak: 2 per hr
Off-peak: 2 per hr

HERTFORD EAST See **Moorgate to Stevenage** line (page 92).

> Continuation of main line

Journey: 43 min
Season: £1784
Peak: 2 per hr
Off-peak: 1 per hr

ROYDON is a commuter haven, being handsome enough to have a conservation booklet written about it, but not chocolate boxy. Some of the houses are genuinely Georgian; others have false Georgian fronts. The village revolves around the church, the green and the High Street, which has many listed buildings. The school still thrives and, though the butcher has gone, there is a bakery, chemist, part-time doctor's surgery, an Italian restaurant and hairdresser. Historical relics include village stocks and lock-up. Roydon has a flower festival every other year, the tennis court is well-used, the Roydon Players can be relied upon for local drama and there are three conservation societies ready to see off the Government's plans for thousands of new homes. There are some five-bedroom houses with large gardens that sell for £350,000, but they can top £1m; a period house with 13 acres and a swimming pool will cost £950,000 at the very least.

Journey: 33 min
Season: £2132
Peak: 6 per hr
Off-peak: 4 per hr

HARLOW TOWN It has to be said that many people hate Harlow in spite of its parks and Henry Moore sculptures (most of which are now so valuable that they have had to be put away in museums). The New Town was created in 1947, to the masterplan of Sir Frederick Gibberd, as a series of four large residential zones in a rural setting, each with its own infrastructure. The population jumped from 4000 to over 80,000, mostly as a result of London overspill. A two-bedroom terraced house at Church Langley will cost over £140,000 and a five-bedroom detached £320,000. Harlow has a good shopping centre at Broad Walk, its own nightclub, bingo hall and the Playhouse Theatre. There is a sports centre, and Harlow Pool has a trimnasium, solarium and dance studio. The newest canine night spot is the Greyhound Stadium. Two large industrial estates lurk on the edge of the town.

Journey: 50 min
Season: £2172
Peak: 2 per hr
Off-peak: 1 per hr

HARLOW MILL This is the station for some of Harlow's smarter parts – Mark Hall North, for instance, where a three-bedroom house costs £160,000. **Harlow Old Town** is very popular because of the older period properties it contains, together with good little shops, including two bakeries. A house here is likely to cost 10–20 per cent more than its nearest equivalent in the New Town. There are many pretty villages to the east. At **Fyfield** or **Moreton**, for example, you could buy a Victorian terraced cottage for £160,000, or a discreet country house with six bedrooms and 11 acres for £1.3m. People who live in this area are not famous for their liking of Harlow and are more likely to nip south and use the Central Line from Epping.

SAWBRIDGEWORTH is a low-rise town set in the fields and woods between Harlow and Bishop's Stortford and, though at this point you are in Hertfordshire, this is where you begin to see the distinct local building styles of Essex: steep tiled gables and dormers, overhanging upper storeys, timber and weatherboarding. The town has two primary schools and enough shops for day-to-day needs, including bakeries and butchers. There are all the usual societies, plus a lacemakers' group. In a strange reversal of trends, the old cinema has been turned into a Catholic Church. Horse-riding is popular with local children.

Flats by the river overlooking the marina are favoured by commuters who also benefit from being little more than five miles from Stansted Airport. Famous nearby residents include Posh and Becks. Two-bedrooms cost £200,000, three-bedrooms £250,000. Older three-bedroom semis can be bought for £240,000.

Journey: 38 min
Season: £2336
Peak: 2 per hr
Off-peak: 3 per hr

BISHOP'S STORTFORD is a wealthy little market town surrounded by pretty villages. Aircraft coming in and out of Stansted Airport fly around it to avoid causing any distress to those who live here. It has a good shopping centre, with a Sainsbury's, a Tesco and a discreet department store. A market is still held on most Thursdays on the twisting main street. The town buzzes with activities, including both operatic and amateur dramatic societies. The H20 disco and a couple of wine bars cater for ravers.

The older, more attractive buildings are in North Street, Windhill and the Old High Street. It is possible to buy a two-bedroom house in Bishop's Stortford for as little as £170,000, but a three-bedroom semi would take you to £250,000 and you should expect to pay £300,000 for a four-bedroom detached. The better side of town is the north-west corner. The private boys' school Stortford College is here, and the houses are large and secluded. Prices range between £400,000 and £750,000. There is an equestrian centre at Hallingbury Hall, Little Hallingbury. A substantial country house with nine bedrooms and 10 acres on the edge of town might cost £1.5m.

To the west, on the Hertfordshire-Essex borders, are the Hadhams. **Much Hadham** is probably the smartest village in the area. Its fashionable status derives from the fact that the Bishop of London once took up residence here, and subsequent bishops kept the palace going for centuries. It has a charming mix of Elizabethan cottages, 18th-century town houses and Victorian almshouses, and the blacksmith's forge has become part of a crafts museum. The sizes and prices of the houses span a very wide range. The 18th-century four-bedroom town houses with walled gardens can be bought for £500,000. A five-bedroom barn conversion at **Little Hadham** would cost £595,000. Further north are the Pelhams. **Stocking Pelham** is a

Journey: 38 min
Season: £2496
Peak: 7 per hr
Off-peak: 6 per hr

particularly pretty village where a good country house with three acres could easily reach £985,000.

To the south-east is **Hatfield Broad Oak**, built on the edge of Hatfield Forest – more than 1000 acres of National Trust woodland donated by the Puckeridge and Essex hunts. It is a handsome old village full of Georgian buildings. There is some post-war development south and east of the High Street. Hatfield Broad Oak has a post-office-cum-general store and a butcher which also sells fish. Time does not stand still, however: the former craft shop now sells computers. The influx of commuters and working wives who are out of the village during the day, and so shop elsewhere, is making life difficult for the shopkeepers. Barrington Hall, a grand country house set in parkland, is now the office of a perfume company. You do get the occasional stray aircraft overhead, but for the most part they disturb other villages such as Great Hallingbury.

Journey: 49 min
Season: £2520
Peak: 4 per hr
Off-peak: 2 per hr

STANSTED MOUNTFITCHET The expansion of Stansted Airport cannot but have a huge effect on the area surrounding it. The airport is growing steadily towards its predicted passenger total of 15 million a year. A Government White Paper has given the go-ahead for another runway so there is concern about the increase in air traffic and noise. There is, however, a fast service from the airport on a spur line from here with trains dashing into London four times an hour in less than 45 minutes. A four-bedroom converted barn in the area will cost £500,000. One of the nicest villages within striking distance of the railway station is **Manuden**, a tiny one-and-a-half street village on the River Stort with some pretty jettied timber-framed houses. A four-bedroom detached bungalow might cost around £380,000; a three-bedroom, thatched 16th-century cottage would be likely to fetch around £365,000.

> Branch line to Stansted Airport

Journey: 43 min
Season: £2580
Peak: 4 per hr
Off-peak: 4 per hr

As parking is plentiful beside architect Norman Foster's spectacular **Stansted Airport** terminal, and the trains into London are swift, commuters are increasingly tempted to use this station now. This and the M11 brings the land of windmills within easy reach.

> Continuation of main line

Journey: 54 min
Season: £2572
Peak: 2 per hr
Off-peak: 1 per hr

ELSENHAM offers a good view of the air traffic in and out of Stansted, but strangely it is little affected by the noise. Its two most prominent features are a village pump in a domed octagonal well-house and Elsenham Hall, a late-Georgian red-brick mansion next to the church. The village has seen a lot of new development in the last two decades, and the range of property types and prices is large, from £100,000 for a three-bedroom flat to over £300,000 for a modern estate house and £500,000 for a four-bedroom period house on the outskirts. Shops include a post office, newsagent, supermarket and chippie, and there is a hairdresser, garage and pub. Bishop's Stortford is nearby for major shopping. It is a very horsey kind of a village, with plenty of activities: WI, gardening club, allotment association, cricket, football and keep-fit clubs. The eponymous jam factory is not as huge as you would expect.

Ugley just to the north does not deserve its name. Incidentally, the Women's Institute here refers to itself as the Women's Institute of Ugley, rather than the Ugley Women's Institute. And **Quendon**, too, is very pretty. The big house, Quendon Park, is surrounded by a wooded deer-park and has a good William and Mary south front. A five-bedroom Georgian farmhouse with outbuildings recently sold for £1.5m.

To the north-east on the young River Chelmer is **Thaxted**, an impressive old town with a guildhall that broods over the open market place and an old windmill at the end of Fishmarket Street which has been restored as a museum. The church, with 181ft spire and medieval roofs, is one of the finest in Essex. Thaxted's problem is that it lies beneath the flight path to Stansted Airport, though people are so attached to the town that they don't seem to mind. Many of them move house within the village, and some Londoners have second homes here. A two-bedroom terraced house will cost around £150,000; a three-bedroom detached house £240,000.

Journey: 59 min
Season: £2688
Peak: 2 per hr
Off-peak: 1 per hr

NEWPORT has always been more expensive than the neighbouring town of Saffron Walden, to which it long ago lost its market. It has a fine main street of gracious houses, all within easy reach of the station and the M11. A two-bedroom Grade II listed cottage would be snapped up overnight for £175,000. An added attraction is Newport Grammar School for boys, an ex-grammar but still highly respected.

Essex begins to get pricey here, with a collection of very pretty villages. South-west of the station are **Clavering**, with its cluster of cottages around the church, and **Rickling Green**. The latter has a

'Rickling Green has a picture-book green with a cricket pitch overlooked by a pub called The Cricketers'

picture-book green with a cricket pitch appropriately overlooked by a pub called The Cricketers (owned by the parents of the television chef, Jamie Oliver). Two-room thatched cottages sell for £150,000 to £200,000, large country houses with land for £1m to £2m.

Only a mile from the station to the west is **Wicken Bonhunt**, very small and exclusive, where an ordinary five-bedroom house will cost around £650,000. Another mile brings you to **Arkesden**, by a little stream known as Wicken Water. Thatched cottages spread themselves around a green, and there is a good 16th-century hall and 13th- to 14th-century church. A three-bedroom thatched cottage would be likely to fetch over £275,000.

On the east side is **Widdington**, also very small and expensive, a hilltop village with cottages around the green and larger houses hidden in the lanes. A four-bedroom detached house would cost around £400,000; a small lath-and-plaster cottage around £200,000. **Debden** is another thatched village on the way to nowhere, but it does have two pubs and a heroic community shop which has been going for 20 years. A four-bedroom cottage with very little land in the centre of the village will cost £300,000.

Journey: 56 min
Season: £2744
Peak: 4 per hr
Off-peak: 2 per hr

AUDLEY END There is little more at Audley End than the station itself. The town it serves is **Saffron Walden**, known cruelly as Suffrin Boredom to some. It has a handsome market place with narrow medieval rows running off it, small specialist shops, a Waitrose and a branch of the Eaden Lilley department store. It is a stronghold of conservationists who want to protect the charming streets of timber-framed houses. The huge common, once used for grazing cattle and medieval tournaments, now serves as a fairground and recreation area. Its most puzzling feature is a rare turf maze – archaeologists still don't understand its purpose. Friends co-educational private school is a draw for many of the families who come to live here. There are quite a few inexpensive modern estates. A one-bedroom flat will cost around £100,000; a four-bedroom detached Georgian-style house up to £500,000. The town can be rather touristy in summer.

The villages nearby are beyond the reach of most local young couples. At **Wendons Ambo**, one of the (very few) four-bedroom modern houses would be likely to fetch around £325,000. The more substantial five-bedroom, three-reception room houses built in the Sixties would sell for £400,000. The lane to the church has some particularly appealing cottages. **Littlebury** nearby is also expensive, with a good collection of lath-and-plaster cottages beside the miniature River Cam, near the site of an Iron Age camp. A 150-year-old two-up-two-down will cost £150,000; a converted barn would be likely to fetch well over £500,000. On the east side of Audley End is **Wimbish**, which is little more than a smattering of houses through the lanes. The presence of an army barracks pulls the prices down. **Hempstead**, Dick Turpin's birthplace, is very popular, though the road to it is winding and slow. **Finchingfield** is much photographed because of the beautiful juxtaposition of church, pond and cottages, not to mention its windmill and Elizabethan big house. A four-bedroom period house with a garden could be bought for around £400,000.

Journey: 64 min
Season: £2824
Peak: 2 per hr
Off-peak: 1 per hr

GREAT CHESTERFORD Little and Great Chesterford are both

extremely prestigious, having a very popular primary school and being close enough to attract people working in Cambridge. The River Cam splashes through both, and in Great Chesterford it is overlooked by a large watermill converted into flats. The village has a family grocer, a post-office-cum-shop, and some very stylish early houses, one of which has some spectacular pargeting. A four-bedroom period terraced house will cost £300,000. **Hadstock**, to the east, is a pretty village with thatched cottages around a green, but it is less expensive. A four-bedroom period cottage on the green will sell for £300,000.

Journey: 63 min
Season: £2888
Peak: 4 per hr
Off-peak: 2 per hr

WHITTLESFORD, ideally situated close to Cambridge and the

M11, is quite a sizeable village and prices can be higher than neighbouring Duxford. Most people know **Duxford** for its airfield (well to the west), which houses part of the collection of the Imperial War Museum. In addition to the permanent display of historic aircraft there are flying displays and pleasure flights in the summer. There are some nice old pubs and some thatched cottages, though these have been rather swamped by the new estates and bungalows. A two-bedroom detached bungalow will cost around £150,000; a three-bedroom detached house £200,000.

Sawston has an image-problem caused by the large council estates by which it is surrounded. What draws many people to it, however, is the presence of a Cambridge Village College (see Comberton, page 62). Small one-bedroom houses cost around £130,000; three-bedroom semis £110,000; new three- and four-bedroom houses £250,000.

Journey: 76 min
Season: £2960
Peak: 2 per hr
Off-peak: 1 per hr

SHELFORD Great Shelford and Little Shelford, with Stapleford into

which they merge at the base of the Gog Magog Hills, all ooze prosperity. This is where the Cambridge wealthy – businessmen and London commuters and academics – choose to make their homes. The houses are large and secluded, with parks and other green open spaces to enhance the feeling of spaciousness. There are plenty of shops, including a boutique. Period houses in Great Shelford's Mingle Lane and Gog Magog Way, which leads to the Gog Magog Golf Club, are thought to have particular appeal. A seven-bedroom house in 10 acres would cost almost £3m. You don't *have* to be rich to live here, however. There is a development close to the station which has two-bedroom starter homes at £130,000. Sawston Village College, one of the much-admired Cambridge Village Colleges (see Comberton, page 62) is the local secondary school.

To Liverpool Street
Journey: 70 min
Season: £3100
(also valid into
Kings Cross)
Peak: 4 per hr
Off-peak: 2 per hr

To Kings Cross
Journey: 48 min
(56 min peak)
Season: £3100
Peak: 2 per hr
Off-peak: 3 per hr

'The Cambridge Phenomenon predictably delivered an upward thrust to local house prices'

CAMBRIDGE The line beyond here goes to King's Lynn. For villages close to stations on the **Kings Cross to King's Lynn** line via Cambridge and Ely, see pages 72–79.

The property market in Cambridge has a mind of its own, being heavily influenced by the constant comings and goings of university academics and the staff of the high-tech industries that have thrived in the university's shadow. During the Eighties the explosion of scientific, medical and agricultural companies based on university research became known as the Cambridge Phenomenon, and predictably it delivered an upward thrust to local house prices. The boom continues as people pour into the area to work. So tight is the green-belt girth of this beautiful, but quite small city, that an entirely new settlement called **Cambourne** is being completed to the west. Prairie fields have been turned into 3000 houses, with a 50 acre business park, two primary schools and a heavy environmental spin (ponds and trees and walks are high on the agenda). Small three-bedroom houses sell for £218,000, larger versions for £280,000.

To the north of Cambridge lie the Science Park and the stark flat landscape of the Fens. It is the south, therefore, that most people prefer. The station is here, and so are the better schools, including The Perse co-educational private school. The area closest to the station, around Tennyson Road, is popular with professional couples. Two-bedroom Victorian terraced houses in this area cost £250,000. On the other side of the tracks they cost £190,000. Larger four-bedroom Victorian houses in the station area cost around £350,000. The Kite, so-called because of its diamond-shape, is another favoured address, close to the shopping centre. A two-bedroom Victorian house here would cost around £240,000. Alternatively, to the west, there is Newnham, an old-established residential area where a typical bay-fronted three-bedroom Victorian house would cost £330,000. Recently, the highest prices reached in Cambridge have shot through the £2m barrier.

The most expensive, exclusive and attractive village in the area has to be **Grantchester**, two miles to the south. The poet Rupert Brooke lived here as a student at the Old Vicarage, now occupied by Jeffrey Archer. Brooke's best-remembered lines, "Stands the Church clock at ten to three?/And is there honey still for tea?", are a reference to his time in Grantchester. The village's many attractions include walks along the Cam, the old tea-rooms which students punt to, and pretty cottages that sell for enormous sums. You could possibly get a small two-bedroom Victorian terraced house for £250,000; but a favoured five-bedroom house with a large garden is likely to fetch £750,000 and upwards.

To the west of Cambridge is **Comberton**. This is a good village for families since it contains one of the highly-regarded Cambridge Village Colleges. A handful of these were built to embody the ideas of Henry Morris, chief education officer at Cambridge from 1922 to 1954. He believed that secondary schools could be run like small colleges, serving several villages while at the same time fulfilling their cultural needs and providing adult education. Property and prices in the villages (excluding Grantchester) tend to be more family-friendly than in Cambridge itself.

'Madingley has stunning views to the spires and towers of Cambridge'

Due west of Cambridge is **Madingley**, which is worth looking at because of the stunning views to the spires and towers of Cambridge, seen against the backdrop of the Gog Magog hills. Much of the village is owned by the university, and the hall is now a hostel for graduates. Prices are probably up to 10 per cent lower than Grantchester's.

The countryside in the north looks markedly less friendly, but lower prices are increasingly attracting those who want big roomy houses. **Histon**, previously the base of the Chivers jam-making enterprise, is almost a small town now, with shops, sub-branches of banks, building societies and garages. Its main attraction is its proximity to Impington, which has a Village College designed in the early Thirties by Walter Gropius and Max Fry. It is also close to **Girton**, home not only of Girton College, but of Girton Golf Club, too. A two-bedroom house here will cost £150,000.

In the east, on the edge of Fens, which can sometimes look like the edge of the world, are **Swaffham Bulbeck** and **Swaffham Prior**. They are eight miles from Cambridge, but worth considering if you want to escape the academic atmosphere which affects some of the other villages. Both are remarkably unspoiled and have some charming period cottages. At Swaffham Prior (where the poet Edwin Muir once lived) you could buy a three-bedroom cottage in need of

Schools in Cambridgeshire

Educational excellence in Cambridgeshire is centred on Cambridge itself. High-flying state schools include the Village College comprehensives such as Bottisham, Swavesey, Cottenham, Sawston, Comberton, Impington, Linton and Melbourn, from which children can go on to sixth-form centres. In the private sector there is The Leys for both sexes, Sanctum Wood (mixed), The Perse independent school for boys (girls in the sixth), Perse Girls' and St Mary's Roman Catholic day and boarding school for girls. Those who live at St Ives or St Neots often look to Kimbolton in Huntingdon, a co-educational independent day school (with some boarding), which was once a grammar.

modernisation with half an acre for £190,000; a five-bedroom Victorian house with an acre for £350,000 to £450,000.

The A14 is an important dividing line in the east. Anything to the south of it, where the countryside starts to ripple again, will command a higher price. **Fulbourn** serves as a Cambridge suburb, with new developments encroaching on the older houses and thatched cottages. There is a range of shops, a primary school and a mill which is occasionally opened to the public. Nearby is Fulbourn Fen, an educational nature reserve. The old Victorian asylum has been turned into health service offices. A three-bedroom semi on a new estate will cost £165,000; a four-bedroom detached house with two bathrooms around £270,000; a four-bedroom period house over £400,000

> Branch line to Bury St Edmunds via Dullingham and Newmarket

No through trains

Trains to Cambridge: less than 1 per hr

Journey: 85 min (from Newmarket)

Season from Newmarket: £3120

DULLINGHAM is quite remote and therefore suited to two-car families. It has become popular because of its proximity to Cambridge. It is very pretty, with thatch-and-clunch cottages, an old farm and stables and a village green. A little two-bedroom house with half an acre of garden will cost £395,000. **Newmarket** is the place to live if you are a fancier of horseflesh – it is home to 4200 horses and there are more swimming pools here for horses than for humans. The town lives and breathes racing. The chalk downland is peppered with stud farms, shelter belts and exercise areas, with the National Stud at Newmarket Heath. Strings of horses can be seen each day trailing through the town to the horsewalks on to the gallops. There are two racecourses – the Rowley Mile and the July. A large house with stabling and acreage could cost more than £1m. **Kennett** is also rather remote – a very quiet Fenside village that feels a little stranded between Cambridge and Suffolk. It has no shops, but there is a primary school. At secondary age, children must take the bus to Soham Village College eight miles away. The single street has some period houses, flint and half-timbering. At the end of it is the grave of a gypsy boy who was hanged for stealing sheep. He died at least 200 years ago, but the grave always has flowers on it – rumour has it that the flowers laid on Derby Day foretell the colours of the winner. A family-sized house here could be bought for £300,000 to £350,000. For **Bury St Edmunds**, see **Liverpool Street to Norwich** line, page 30.

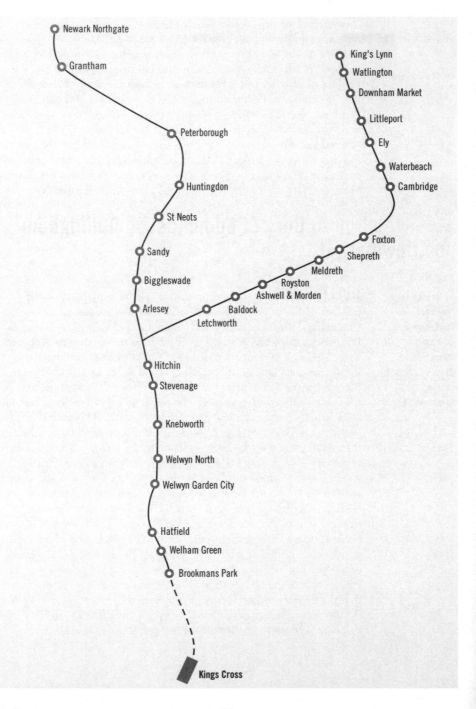

Newark Northgate

Grantham

Peterborough

Huntingdon

St Neots

Sandy

Biggleswade

Arlesey

Letchworth

Baldock

Ashwell & Morden

Royston

Meldreth

Shepreth

Foxton

King's Lynn

Watlington

Downham Market

Littleport

Ely

Waterbeach

Cambridge

Hitchin

Stevenage

Knebworth

Welwyn North

Welwyn Garden City

Hatfield

Welham Green

Brookmans Park

Kings Cross

Kings Cross
> **Newark Northgate and King's Lynn**

To Moorgate
Journey: 37 min
Season: £1560
Peak: 4 per hr
Off-peak: 3 per hr

BROOKMANS PARK This is the world of personalised number plates and golf courses, the playground to **Potters Bar**. Large expensive houses, some of them sealed behind tall hedges, have been built between lakes and woodlands in the grounds of two long-demolished country houses, called Brookmans and Gobions. The railway arrived in 1926, and suburbia gradually ate up the surrounding fields. A four-bedroom house in more exclusive **Brookmans Park** can be bought for £500,000, though prices run into millions with ease. Moffats Farm is thought once to have been the home of Dr Thomas Muffett, author of the nursery rhyme *Little Miss Muffet*.

To Moorgate
Journey: 39 min
Season: £1720
Peak: 4 per hr
Off-peak: 3 per hr

WELHAM GREEN is a step down from Brookmans Park. The village offers a mix of private developments and council estates built around a centre with a green, shops, pubs, restaurants and a garage. A three-bedroom detached house could be bought for £350,000 – possibly 30 per cent cheaper than an equivalent house in Brookmans Park. There is a commemorative stone to the Italian balloonist Vincenzo Lunardi, who made the first balloon ascent outside France in 1784. He landed here to let his cat out of the basket because it was feeling sick.

To Kings Cross
Journey: 24 min
Season: £1920
Peak: 3 per hr
Off-peak: 2 per hr

To Moorgate
Journey: 43 min
Season: £1920
Peak: 4 per hr
Off-peak: 3 per hr

HATFIELD was built in four stages. There was the Old Town, then the New Town and the arrival of the railway – when it became known as 'California' because it was 'out west and bit rough'. Then came the post-war stage of the New Town, and now the old British Aerospace site has sprouted a major shopping mall, multiplex cinema and drive-through McDonald's. The University of Hertfordshire's new De Havilland campus has the Hertfordshire Sports Village, built to Sport England standards, which is open to local residents. Hatfield may be dreary, but it has a brilliant strategic position – being close to the A1, the M25, and only a wingbeat from Kings Cross by train – and it offers lower house prices than surrounding areas. Its greatest public attraction is Hatfield House, built by Robert

Cecil. Among its many distinctions is the fact that it was one of the first houses to be lit by "Edison-Swan electric incandescent light bulbs", patented in 1879.

Most people prefer the red-brick houses of Old Hatfield to the Thirties'-style, bypass variegated houses and shopping parades of the 1948 New Town. A cottage with two bedrooms in Old Hatfield would be likely to cost around £220,000, though a flat of similar size would be slightly cheaper at £160,000. A three- or four-bedroom detached house will cost from £260,000 upwards, but won't have a large garden. Two of the best areas are The Ryde, which has detached houses and bungalows, and Ellenbrook, where there is a mix of Thirties' semis and detached houses. The lowest price for something with three bedrooms here would be £280,000. In New Hatfield the starting price for a four-bedroom detached house is around £260,000, rising to around £300,000.

WELWYN GARDEN CITY

To Kings Cross
Journey: 27 min
Season: £2060
Peak: 5 per hr
Off-peak: 2 per hr

To Moorgate
Journey: 47 min
Season: £2060
Peak: 4 per hr
Off-peak: 3 per hr

Ebenezer Howard, with his chief architect Louis de Soissons, designed Welwyn Garden City as a sustainable town with its own employment zones, but the lure of the commute was not resisted for long. Early residents in the Twenties had to wade through the builders' mud in their wellington boots to get to the station, and changed into their city shoes on the train. The fusion of garden and city still remains very attractive, and the original cottagey houses behind perfectly-clipped hedges are very much sought after. Many have been kept on a ball-and-chain by 99-year or 999-year council leases (inherited from the Welwyn Garden Company), but freeholds are now available. The utilitarian planning means that there is very little sense of one street being more up-market than any other. The wide main shopping boulevards now look strangely dated, and local shops and businesses tend to feel they have lost out to the bustle and variety of St Albans and Stevenage. There is, however, a John Lewis department store, and the Howard Centre close to the station has added greatly to the shopping scene. Sports enthusiasts are catered for by the impressive Gosling Sports Park and two 18-hole golf courses.

The best side of the town is the west, where a three-bedroom semi with a garage in a quiet tree-lined road could cost £280,000 to £320,000. It is possible, however, to buy a two-bedroom terraced house for around £220,000. The town is still evolving: large new private estates have gone up to the east at the Panshanger aerodrome. A three-bedroom semi on a new private estate will cost around £300,000.

There is some very pretty, rolling wooded countryside around Welwyn Garden City, and those who prefer an older village could look at **Wheathampstead** to the west. As you approach the charming

'Exectutive home',
Wheathampstead

High Street from the direction of St Albans you pass a small quay on the River Lea, where people stop to chat or sit and fish. On one side of the road is a 400-year-old pub, The Bull. On the other is a converted watermill which now contains a butcher, art gallery and patisserie. The village has three primary schools, from which children move on to secondary schools in Harpenden and St Albans. There is a library, four churches of different denominations, and lots of clubs and societies, including wine-making and archery clubs, cricket and tennis. You could pay over £210,000 for a Victorian cottage; £580,000 for one of the new five-bedroom houses. Nearby is Brocket Hall, where Lady Caroline Lamb once emerged naked from a soup tureen and where more recently Lord Brocket ran a glitzy hotel and conference centre. He sold it on a 60-year lease 1996 when he was imprisoned for insurance fraud and it is still used for conferences.

Old Welwyn, just to the north of Welwyn Garden City, is so much more refined and mature than its neighbour. It has a mix of houses from one-bedroom cottages with small courtyard gardens, priced at around £280,000, to larger three-bedroom cottages fronting the road at £400,000. On the edge, away from the shops in the main street, is the executive development Danesbury Park where a four-bedroom house will cost £600,000.

Journey: 30 min
Season: £2160
Peak: 4 per hr
Off-peak: 2 per hr

WELWYN NORTH The village best served by this station is **Digswell**, which consists of large detached houses with secluded gardens sewn into the lanes behind high hedges – some of them dominated by the huge viaduct built to carry the Great Northern Railway over the valley. It has the advantage of being close to a main-line station yet only two miles from Welwyn Garden City. Houses tend to be sold very discreetly, and are not cheap. You would need to spend £550,000 for a four-bedroom bungalow. A small, but pretty lake is maintained by the Digswell Lake Society.

Tewin is another wooded dormitory. The sale of the village by the Cowper estate in 1919 led to its rapid expansion, with large new estates leeching on. The Upper Green is still used for tennis, cricket and football matches. A three-bedroom modernised cottage on the green would cost £300,000; larger four- and five-bedroom detached houses in big gardens fetch around £750,000. The tomb of Lady Anne Grimston in the parish church fascinates visitors and locals alike. Before her death in 1713 she had scoffed that the after-life was as likely as a tree growing through her grave. The tomb is now a macabre tangle of root and branch.

The **Ayots** to the west, like Digswell, are very exclusive: **Ayot St Peter** perches on a hilltop, while **Ayot St Lawrence** straddles narrow lanes enclosed between hedgebanks. The latter also has a popular old pub, the Brocket Arms, and George Bernard Shaw's house, the late-Victorian Shaw's Corner, where he lived until his death in 1950. The house, which has Shaw's writing hut at the bottom of the garden, is in the hands of the National Trust. The village's most prominent landmark is the extraordinary Neo-Classical parish church, seen like an 18th-century folly across a meadow. House prices are higher than those in Tewin. Little cottages are thin on the ground as most of the houses are large and expensive, starting at £800,000 and running up into the millions.

Journey: 34 min
Season: £2340
Peak: 4 per hr
Off-peak: 2 per hr

KNEBWORTH

As is the case with most towns and villages in this area, there is an old and a new Knebworth. Old Knebworth grew up around the big house and parkland. The newer part was built around the railway station, which arrived at the turn of the 20th century. Lutyens tried his hand with some cottages in Deards End Lane and Park Lane, and he also produced a golf club-house and the remarkable church of St Martin. Knebworth retains a village atmosphere and has a library and village school as well as a Co-op store. It is hugely popular with commuters, many of whom never escape from the sound of the trains. Because the railway line runs right through the middle, many of the older, quainter cottages back straight on to it. A two-bedroom cottage in this position would cost £220,000 to £240,000. In Deards End Lane, a Lutyens house will cost upwards of £1m. There are plenty of local activities and clubs, including cricket, amateur dramatics and old-time dancing, and there is an annual summer fête. This is in addition to the country shows, concerts and car rallies held at Knebworth House.

Commuters at Knebworth nurture a huge grapevine, planted when the station opened, with its roots in the platform. At one time the station master harvested up to 55lb of grapes from it and made five or six gallons of wine.

Many people prefer the atmosphere of the smaller, more rural villages such as **Datchworth** to the east, where the community spirit remains strong and anyone who falls ill, or who can't fetch the children from school, soon finds their needs catered for. Pony paddocks and riding stables abound. It has a post office and two general stores, a village museum in the old blacksmith's forge, and a sports pavilion with a rugby field behind it. There is a mix of property, from three-bedroom cottages needing a bit of work which sell at around £240,000 to the kind of place that comes with an acre of ground, tennis court and price-tag of around £750,000. The village is spread between a web of greens. The harsher realities of life in the past are recalled at Datchworth Green in the centre, where the children's swings and summer tennis and cricket matches are overlooked by the old whipping post.

STEVENAGE

STEVENAGE offers something like safety-net housing for people who can't afford Hertfordshire's plusher towns and villages. Huge new estates are now zoned west of the A1 and in the north-east of town. It isn't attractive, but the prices are low by comparison and the train service is excellent. The station is served not only by the Cambridge and Peterborough commuter services, but also by the InterCity 125s on the East Coast line into Kings Cross, and Moorgate trains on the Cuffley loop (see page 91). The New Town developments, colour-coded on old maps, have streets fancifully named after famous explorers, cathedrals, inventors, cricketers and so on, but in reality they offer little more than the uniformity of the three-bedroom mid- and end-terraced. Most are designed according to what is called the Radburn principle, which means that motorists and pedestrians are kept well apart.

The beauty of the large modern shopping centre is that it is genuinely traffic-free. The various neighbourhoods, including the industrial area, are joined to each other, and to the centre, by a cycleway, a cleverly designed miniature road network which at peak periods takes up to 1,100 people per hour on their way to and from school or work. The shopping centre offers excellent choice, with all the major chain stores as well as a large range of retail warehouses such as B&Q and Homebase and the Forum shopping centre. But more large-scale town centre re-development is in the pipeline and the area is zoned for growth by the Government. At Poplars there is a giant Sainsbury superstore and starter homes can be bought for £140,000. The covered market under the town centre multi-storey car park is open three days a week, and the stalls for the outdoor market go up on Wednesdays and Saturdays.

Stevenage is very strong on computers and technology, both in the businesses it attracts to its huge

To Kings Cross
Journey: 25 min
Season: £2560
Peak: 6 per hr
Off-peak: 4 per hr

To Moorgate
Journey: 60 min
Season: £2560
Peak: 2 per hr
Off-peak: 1 per hr

Distinctive late-Victorian cottage, Old Stevenage

industrial parks – including GlaxoSmithKline – and in its educational facilities. North Herts College opened in 2003 with spanking new science laboratories and the Gordon Craig Theatre. Leisure facilities are lavish, too, with a huge leisure centre-cum-theatre and exhibition hall. There are three 18-hole golf courses: a municipal course in Stevenage itself, and one each at Knebworth and Graveley. The place for Sunday walks is Fairlands Valley Park, where there is a sailing and fishing lake, a boating lake and a bandstand for open-air concerts.

The Old Town, "Hilton" in EM Forster's *Howards End*, is greatly cherished, and property prices are proportionately higher. A two-bedroom cottage would cost around £165,000; a three-bedroom cottage more than £210,000. On Stevenage's margins are some sedate, tree-lined roads that attract the middle-class professionals: Rectory Lane and Granby Road, for example, where a detached house with four or five bedrooms and a large garden may cost upwards of £350,000.

There is also a leap in house prices between the New Town and the villages that surround it. Sought-after **Benington** in the east, for example, has a picture-postcard village green and timbered cottages – though it also has its share of new developments and local authority housing. An older house with four bedrooms here would take you into the £450,000 range.

Walkern is much busier, with a main street that takes quite a lot of traffic. New estates have sprung up around the old dovecote and pond, and by the chequer-brick Manor Farm. A two-bedroom period cottage will cost around £220,000.

Aston is also popular and much closer to Stevenage, though it is a little hemmed in by Stevenage and has had its own struggle to restrict development – the field in the village centre (with cricket pitch and pavilion) has been fiercely defended. Most of the new housing is kept to small developments in cul-de-sacs. A large four-bedroom detached would cost £500,000.

House style in Hertfordshire

In Hertfordshire you find an essentially modest county, now marbled with stockbroker enclaves and new towns. The prettiest cottages tend to be small and unassuming. Geologically, the county sits on the rim of a saucer of chalk filled with clay and knuckles of flint. Without stone, early builders used timber from the forests.

Every town has a handful of timber-framed buildings, though in the case of Hitchin these were hidden behind brick facades when brick superseded timber as the fashionable material to use.

There are charming cottages built of clunch, a type of chalk stone, some of the best of which can be seen at Ashwell. The county has also borrowed from its neighbours, adopting weatherboarding from Essex and yellowy brick from Cambridgeshire.

Journey: 31 min
Season: £2612
Peak: 6 per hr
Off-peak: 4 per hr

HITCHIN has managed to retain its character better than some of the surrounding towns. Parts of the centre still remain in a medieval time-warp, such as the Market Place, and the lanes leading off it to the cathedral-size St Mary's Church and the River Hiz. Tilehouse Street, now relieved of much of its through traffic, remains as medieval England must have known it; and Bancroft was once admired as one of the best urban streets in England. It is a classic small market town, once famous for straw-plaiting, surrounded by popular commuter villages. The shopping centre is good enough with a large traditional market (three times a week), bars and restaurants. Prices have been rising fast here in the last three years. In the town itself a five-bedroom town house in Tilehouse Street has recently sold for £550,000, though it has only a small garden and no off-street parking. Larger three-bedroom semis on the south side of the town can be bought for around £190,000. The Avenue, Wymondley Road and Benslow Lane are quiet leafy roads only 15 minutes' walk from the station, and contain some rather grand houses. Large Victorian and Edwardian houses in The Avenue tend to sell for up to £800,000.

'Pirton has a compact round shape which affects the social dynamics and makes it a more convivial place to live'

The villages of **Gosmore** and **Charlton** to the south are very close to Hitchin and therefore desirable. Gosmore has a green and some very pretty old houses. You could spend anything from £225,000 for a tiny two-bedroom cottage to over £250,000 for a three-bedroom period house. **Pirton** also scores because it isn't linear like many of the other villages in the area, but has a good, compact round shape which somehow affects the social dynamics and makes it a more convivial place to live. It is a bit cheaper than Gosmore. A Victorian three-bedroom semi will cost around £240,000.

Great Wymondley and **Little Wymondley** also loom in the Hitchin firmament, the irony being that Little Wymondley is by far the larger of the two. Great Wymondley is little more than an untidy crossroads with a few cottages, a pub and the humps of a medieval castle. A bypass has relieved Little Wymondley of traffic, causing house prices to rise. A two-bedroom period cottage will now cost £215,000.

St Ippollits (sometimes just called Ippollits, and spelled in a variety of different ways) is a rather pretty hilltop village with smartly painted timbered houses and a dominating church which gives the village its name. Unfortunately it is threatened by vast new housing estates. New four-bedroom executive homes cost £350,000. Commuters from St Ippollits and the Wymondleys also have the option of travelling from Stevenage, where car-parking is easier.

> Fork to Cambridge and King's Lynn

Journey: 35 min
Season: £2780
Peak: 3 per hr
Off-peak: 2 per hr

LETCHWORTH You need to make sure your face fits in Letchworth. This was the first Garden City, and the dream is still intact, as wholesome as a Hovis advertisement. To those who come from elsewhere to live – and to the groups of Japanese architects who come to gawp at it in summer – it can seem strange indeed. Ebenezer Howard's social experiment attracts a distinct type of middle-class teetotaller, full of good intentions and disposed to vegetarianism. It was a pretty dry town and until recently it had only one pub. Once upon a time there was just the Skittles Inn, which sold only lemonade and ginger beer, but this has been turned into The Settlement community centre. Pleasant evenings are spent in patchwork groups, making friendly quilts or in other activities whose fruits are apt to appear at craft fairs. The beauty of all this is that it is quite safe to roam the streets at night. The town has belatedly acquired a three-screen cinema complex, a new supermarket, sports and leisure centre.

The sought-after properties are the original Garden City houses, which have a rural calm about them. The cottages in Nevells Road, Icknield Way and Wilbury Road are worth just going to look at. An original garden city house with four bedrooms would cost around £400,000 (Sollershott West and East, and The Broadway have good examples), while a two-bedroom Edwardian terraced cottage could be bought for £140,000.

'Outsiders think the people in Letchworth are crazy. It is very tight-knit socially, artistic and rather like a commune'

"Outsiders think the people in Letchworth are crazy. It is very tight-knit socially, artistic and rather like a commune," said one resident who is now devoted to the town and wouldn't live anywhere else. It can afford to be particularly proud of its schools. Not only does it have two well-known public schools, St Francis' College for Girls and St Christopher's (progressive, vegetarian, boarding for boys and girls), but it also has two well-respected comprehensives, Highfield and Fernhill.

The town is still growing, and properties on the newish estates tend to be cheaper than in the Garden City proper. A three-bedroom detached house on the Lordship Farm estate, for instance, will cost £230,000. An old asylum building in parkland is now being developed to produce 900 new homes with garden-city credentials at Fairfield Park.

Of the villages close by, **Norton** has a haphazard charm, a good pub and a common that offers 63 acres of woodland and deer. It also has the local leisure centre. **Willian** is little more than a hamlet, made endearing by its duck pond and some very old houses, but property in both these villages rarely comes on the market.

Journey: 38 min
Season: £2780
Peak: 3 per hr
Off-peak: 2 per hr

BALDOCK is a classic small market town, with an old coaching history and a much admired wide main street. People enjoy living here, and like to protect the place from further development. After years of wrangling a bypass is finally being built to siphon traffic out of the centre. The main asset for shoppers is a vast and impressive Tesco superstore in a converted Neo-Classical hosiery factory which once enjoyed a brief life as a film studio. The traditional High Street has to compete with the shopping centres in Stevenage and Cambridge, but the ancient custom of the Wednesday market has kept it alive. The town musters a butcher and a baker, plus plenty of solicitors and estate agents, antiques shops and restaurants.

Almost anywhere in Baldock is nice to live. There are streets of timber-framed and colour-washed, Georgian and Victorian houses and some modest modern estates. Even the council estates are arranged in well-kept, tree-lined avenues. A two-bedroom mid-terraced Victorian cottage will cost around £150,000; a Georgian house with four bedrooms from £350,000. Baldock is just within range of people who work in Cambridge (20 miles), and this is reflected in the property prices. It is also attractive for its secondary school. Knight's Templar Comprehensive has a high reputation for academic achievement and is the preferred choice of many parents who could afford to have their children educated privately.

Journey: 56 min
(38 min peak)
Season: £2860
Peak: 3 per hr
Off-peak: 1 per hr

ASHWELL & MORDEN The station is too far outside the village to walk, so parking spaces are keenly contested. Waiting to be picked up is no great hardship, though, since there is a country pub right opposite the station. Ashwell is a commuter dormitory, which manages to retain an active village social life. There is a playgroup, a day nursery, a stage school and a dance school, and every year the Ashwell Show grows less like a village flower show and more like a county horse show. It really is the chic village to live on this prairie. The attraction lies in its sense of complete self-containment and in the preservation of its architecture. Timber-framed cottages, some cob, are followed by dignified Georgian town houses. It has a pretty church in clunch and flint, and a primary school that is not only highly thought of educationally, but is also a social engine to the village. It has a bakery, three pubs, an award-winning butcher, a pharmacy, a doctor's surgery, a dentist, a weaver and a potter. There is also the Ashwell Village Museum, housed in an ancient timber-frame cottage and run by volunteers. People expect their houses to sell at a premium in Ashwell, so you have to be ready for this when you go house-hunting. A two-up-two-down here might cost £170,000 – 10 per cent more than it would fetch a few miles away in Royston. A four-bedroom cottage will cost £500,000. **Kelshall** sits in the foothills of the Chilterns, open to views right across the prairies of

Bedfordshire and Cambridgeshire. It is an extremely well-kept and close-knit village. A four-bedroom detached house will fetch around £400,000. **Therfield** is another proud old Chilterns village whose agricultural heritage goes back a very long way, as the long barrows on Therfield Heath testify. A two-bedroom ex-local authority home will cost £250,000; a four-bedroom house around £400,000.

Journey: 46 min
Season: £2980
Peak: 3 per hr
Off-peak: 2 per hr

ROYSTON recovered successfully from the recession in the early Nineties and new shops opened up. It sits on the borders of Hertfordshire and Cambridgeshire, so people have the choice of two education systems. It offers cheap housing and convenience. In addition to the railway line it also has easy access to the A10, M25, A1 and M11. Traditionally, the south side of town is thought to be better than the north, where some of the housing estates have been built at a very high density, close to the huge Tesco. Property prices start at £140,000 for a two-bedroom Victorian cottage and £175,000 for a three-bedroom semi. The modern houses tend to be cheaper than the older Victorian/Edwardian ones which offer more room. The heath, which has a golf course, is the place to walk and ride.

The surrounding countryside offers a wide choice of villages. **Barley**, to the south-east, is a no-frills village with a strong local community, pretty walks and an all-purpose village shop. There is a good local riding school, doctor's surgery with dispensary, two pubs and a primary school. Its greatest assets are an early Tudor restored town house, used for local activities, weddings and harvest suppers, and a small village cage or lock-up, which remains as a curiosity. A two-bedroom cottage will cost £215,000 or more. Barley's position on the chalk toes of the Chilterns accounts for the villagers' historic nickname – "the little men from the hills".

Three-bedroom period cottage, near Royston

Barkway is rather more elegant, with a wonderful array of timber-framed and Georgian brick houses. One of these with four bedrooms and parking on the main street will cost over £450,000. A two-bedroom cottage will cost over £250,000, but these are few and far between. Barkway still has a good village school where the numbers are increasing.

Bassingbourn, to the north, also has an impressive main street lined with period houses. The nearby army barracks does not affect house prices. A five-bedroom detached house with four reception rooms will cost over £500,000.

Journey: 68 min
Season: £2980
Peak: 2 per hr
Off-peak: 1 per hr

MELDRETH This was once serious fruit-growing country, but Meldreth now has only one commercial orchard left with a farm shop attached. It has a recreation ground, and beneath a spreading chestnut tree are the old village stocks and a whipping post. It is an enormously welcoming village, though it is rather scattered. The primary school is well regarded, as is the nearby Melbourn College for 11- to 16-year-olds. Leisure opportunities include tennis, croquet and football. Village people may also use the riding stables attached to the Meldreth Manor School, which is run by Scope. The village contains a mix of old thatched cottages and new developments, though much of the newer housing seems very uniform. Semis sell for around £170,000; four-bedroom detached houses for £370,000.

Melbourn is across the fields. Its attractions include six restaurants and pubs and a very strong community spirit. Property prices are similar to those in Meldreth.

Journey: 71 min
Season: £2980
Peak: 2 per hr
Off-peak: 1 per hr

SHEPRETH The feature of Shepreth village centre is a stream with two old mills on its banks. There are some pretty thatched cottages and several modern closes built in the late Sixties and Seventies. The village has a shop-cum-post-office, a Montessori school and two trout farms. The houses tend to be larger than those in Meldreth. The properties backing on to open fields in Frog End are probably the best for views though furthest from the shops. Two-bedroom cottages start at around £170,000, while four-bedroom detached houses cost around £350,000 upwards. Annual village events include a horticultural show, harvest festival and the Shepreth festival of arts and crafts. Several artists live in the area. It is a horsey area – and you sometimes even spot the odd pony and trap trotting by.

Journey: 73 min
Season: £2980
Peak: 2 per hr
Off-peak: 1 per hr

FOXTON is attractive and quiet, with a pretty, but tiny green and some good timber-framed houses in the long main street. The village has two churches, a shop-cum-post-office, a pub, a new pavilion and primary school and village hall. There are all the usual societies for women, toddlers and the elderly, plus the formidable Foxton Gardeners Association which organises a regular September show. The village is best known to outsiders for being the subject of a highly-praised historical book, *The Common Stream*, by local author Rowland Parker, published in 1975. Foxton tends to be rather sought-after because of the railway station and its proximity to Cambridge. Prices are similar to those in Shepreth.

Nearby **Barrington** has a huge set-piece green with thatched cottages on one side and a fine church on the other. The Cambridge factor is a significant influence on prices. A four- to five-bedroom house on the green cannot be bought for less than £400,000. There are some modern developments discreetly tucked away in cul-de-sacs, where four-bedroom detached houses sell for around £325,000 to £400,000. An acre or two of land, however, could put the price up. Clunch, the chalk-stone used so extensively in local building, was quarried nearby.

Journey: 48 min
(56 min peak)
Season: £3100
(also valid to
Liverpool Street)
Peak: 2 per hr
Off-peak: 3 per hr

CAMBRIDGE See **Liverpool Street to Cambridge** line (page 61).

Most London services from the following stations go to Kings Cross. At peak times there is a limited direct service to Liverpool Street, otherwise passengers for Liverpool Street must change at Cambridge.

Journey: 58 min
(66 min peak)
Season: £3100
Peak: 2 per hr
(plus 1 per hr to
Liverpool St)
Off-peak: 1 per hr

WATERBEACH The trains leaving Waterbeach in the morning are full of children on their way to school in Cambridge or Ely. The village does have its own primary school which doubles as a community centre. Here you can take evening classes, or join the Waterbeach Players or the brass band. Waterbeach has an army barracks, a post office, Chinese takeaway, three grocery shops, fish-and-chip shop, butchers and bakers, and several pubs. There is a Tesco three miles away at **Milton**. The Waterbeach Feast, a procession of floats and stalls, is held every June, when the local women traditionally have always made frumenty – boiled wheat in a thick sweet milk-and-sugar sauce with raisins. The best properties are the Cambridge brick houses in the conservation area around the village green. A two-bedroom version will cost from £170,000. A three-bedroom semi in Waterbeach is likely to cost around £180,000. New housing is going up fast.

Cottenham, also on the edge of the Fens close to Waterbeach station, has a Village College (see Comberton, page 62) and some useful shops in its favour, but it has expanded rather brutally. Its population doubled in only 20 years. A three-bedroom Victorian terraced house will cost £190,000 to £220,000, better value than in nearby Histon, while a four-bedroom modern detached house will cost £250,000 to £300,000.

Journey: 67 min
(75 min peak)

Season: £3160

Peak: 2 per hr
(plus 1 per hr to
Liverpool St)

Off-peak: 1 per hr

ELY had remained aloof, cut off from Cambridge by the Fens for so long that recent property booms arrived as something of a shock. Now, however, it has become an immensely popular alternative to the hothouse of Cambridge and new housing using old styles is springing up around the edges with price tags of £290,000 for four bedrooms. A house with a view of Ely's remarkable 11th-century cathedral is usually thought more desirable than a home in one of the villages. It is a very small, compact city with a tiny High Street, though it does have both a Tesco and a Waitrose. Georgian houses sit quite happily alongside Thirties' semis, and there are no distinct up-market areas. A renovated Grade II listed town house with four bedrooms can be expected to cost £350,000. There are dramatic and choral societies for those inspired by the theatrical Fen landscapes. King's School is situated close to the cathedral.

Some people are also attracted to the area by thoughts of the *Good Life* – the cottage with a productive vegetable garden, a few ducks and a goat. Villages to the south, such as **Witchford, Sutton, Haddenham** and **Stretham**, are the most sought-after. You should expect to pay around £120,000 for a two-bedroom semi; between £205,000 and £250,000 for a four-bedroom detached.

Journey: 75 min
(84 min peak)

Season: £3280

Peak: 2 per hr
(plus I per hr to
Liverpool St)

Off-peak: 1 per hr

LITTLEPORT is a thriving little town on this huge horizontal landscape, with some beautiful old houses as well as plenty of new estates. There are three thatched properties in the town centre (adding a touch of cosiness) and since the Harleys of Harley Davison originally came from here, a 7ft-tall motorbike is soon to be erected as artwork. A huge development of 750 houses is about to start. A four-bedroom timber-framed house on a small plot will cost around £285,000. Littleport has a leisure and sports centre and Littleport Village College provides evening classes. The town has plenty of day-to-day shops, including a wonderful bakery, a butcher and fishmonger, quaint hardware store and a clothes shop. "The best thing about living here is that there are such beautiful sunsets, flooding across acres and acres of open sky," says one local resident.

'The best thing about living in Littleport is that there are such beautiful sunsets, flooding across acres and acres of open sky'

Journey: 84 min
(93 min peak)
Season: £3540
Peak: 2 per hr
(plus 1 per hr to
Liverpool St)
Off-peak: 1 per hr

DOWNHAM MARKET is popular with people who are taking early retirement – over 40 per cent of the population is aged over 60 – but families are being courted with hundreds of new four-bedroom houses. It is a pleasant Norfolk town with plenty of shops, good high school, a floodlit football ground, a swimming pool, and two small industrial estates on the outskirts. It used to be an inland port, but today the river, contained in its high banks, is somewhere to walk beside rather than a busy thoroughfare for imports and exports. This is the kind of place where you can leave your car unlocked all day, and where you don't have to queue in the supermarket. A two-bedroom, turn-of-the-20th-century terraced house will cost around £95,000; a three-bedroom semi with a garage £125,000.

Journey: 90 min
(99 min peak)
Season: £3600
Peak: 2 per hr
(plus 1 per hr to
Liverpool St)
Off-peak: 1 per hr

WATLINGTON The village has fought yet more development, but a decision has been taken to build additional new homes and Watlington will grow by 25 per cent in the next two years. It has a couple of shops, a primary school, a doctor's surgery and a village 'office' with IT, internet and photocopying facilities. It is slightly cheaper than Downham Market – a two-bedroom terraced house would cost around £90,000. A small farmhouse out on the Fens could be bought for £250,000.

Journey: 97 min
(106 min peak)
Season: £3760
Peak: 2 per hr
(plus 1 per hr to
Liverpool St)
Off-peak: 1 per hr

KING'S LYNN The old port of King's Lynn has a definite appeal for birdwatchers, who can be seen in their anoraks and wellington boots scanning the sky with their binoculars. The marshes and mudflats of the Wash are a great attraction for waterfowl and waders. The riverside is a favourite spot for watching the boats come in. Architecturally, King's Lynn lost much of its dignity in the 20th century and its sense of prosperity at the same time. The conservationists now have a firm grip on what is left – a historic legacy which includes the merchants' houses of Nelson Street, Queen Street and King Street, most of which are now used as offices

200 year-old
brick-and-flint
farmhouse,
Downham Market

and occasionally as locations in television costume dramas. The Corn Exchange Theatre attracts big musical and theatrical names, and in the summer it plays host to the King's Lynn Festival, usually attended by one of the Royals (Sandringham is only eight miles away). It has the biggest shopping centre for miles around. Among the older properties you could pick up a three-bedroom semi for £135,000. Even a good period three-bedroom town house will probably not exceed £200,000.

> Continuaton of main line from Hitchin

Journey: 36 min
Season: £2760
Peak: 2 per hr
Off-peak: 1 per hr

ARLESEY You are on to the Bedfordshire plains here, where the low, sprawling, yellow-brick villages can seem monotonous and unimaginative after the variety of Hertfordshire. Arlesey itself might be short on charm, but lays claim to being the longest linear village in the country with a High Street of Victorian brick houses, many of which have been extended at the back to provide bathrooms and kitchens. A three-bedroom detached house will cost around £230,000. The Agricultural Show and the Wives' Pram Race, once key points in the calendar, have now been dropped. Its immediate neighbour, **Stotfold**, is another large village dominated by the local yellow brick, and has the same mix of Victorian and modern housing at similar prices. Stotfold has the additional advantage of having a secondary school, being close to the A1M, and offering the choice of whisking down the motorway to catch the better train service from Stevenage. Letchworth and Baldock are also nearby.

    Shillington is also a large, though rather more rural, village of yellow brick with the occasional timber-framed house and an intimate gathering of 17th-century houses around the hilltop church of All Saints, an impressive local landmark. Closer to Arlesey is **Henlow**, where prices are slightly increased by the proximity of RAF Henlow. This is the village where sports and showbiz personalities come to revitalise at Champneys Henlow Grange Health Farm. Henlow has a few shops and pubs and good sports facilities. County cricket is played at The Pyghtles. Other villages worth looking at in this catchment are **Meppershall**, **Lower Stondon** and **Clifton**.

Journey: 39 min
Season: £2820
Peak: 2 per hr
Off-peak: 2 per hr

BIGGLESWADE has a population of around 17,000 and is very much a dormitory for Cambridge and Bedford as well as for London. It is a town of yellow brick houses and market-gardening set on the River Ivel, which was once just navigable from the sea. Greene King had a brewery here, which may explain why there are so many pubs. There is a busy market on Saturdays. Shops recently enjoyed a £7m town centre makeover, yet people still tend to go to Cambridge for major purchases. Proximity to the A1 (where there is a Sainsbury's) means that Stevenage is also easily accessible. One of the more highly regarded streets is London Road, where large four-bedroom houses can be bought for £250,000 upwards. It is a busy road, however, and seems to have less appeal for incomers than it does for people moving locally.

'In picturesque Old Warden the cottages are thatched with gingerbread trimmings and chimneypots'

Those in search of the rural idyll will have to go west to **Ickwell Green**, where the village green has a cricket club with a maypole on it and is fringed with colour-washed, brick and tiled cottages. Houses for sale here are as rare as hen's teeth and agents are wary about quoting prices because they are all so individual. **Old Warden** is even more picturesque, having been preserved in aspic by the Shuttleworth Estate. The cottages are thatched, with gingerbread trimmings and chimneypots, and very few of them ever reach the open market. But its very presence is a magnet to the area, attracting people to the neighbouring villages. The Shuttleworth Collection of historic aircraft is a major draw to visitors, especially on flying days. **Northill**, the third village in the cluster, is not quite so rarefied. The occasional modern house has crept in beside the older cottages around the pub and the duck pond. A two-bedroom thatched semi will cost around £240,000. There are stables in the area and it is fairly horsey.

Potton, to the north-east, is the size of a small town, with a population of more than 5000. Its market square is much admired, though the only way to live in it would be to buy a flat over one of the shops. The likely price for a two-bedroom cottage is £135,000. Otherwise property in the town tends to be cheaper than Biggleswade and Sandy (see below). It is the headquarters of the eponymous Potton company, makers of neo-Tudor self-build home kits.

Journey: 45 min
Season: £2848
Peak: 2 per hr
Off-peak: 2 per hr

SANDY is plain as can be, an old Bedfordshire village that acquired a station and then sponged up overspilling Londoners into its large council estates and yellow-brick streets. It is perhaps a shade cheaper than Biggleswade. The Royal Society for the Protection of Birds has its headquarters outside the town at Sandy Lodge, and there are some pleasant woodland walks. Two of the more expensive places to live are the large Victorian houses along Bedford Road, which can be a little noisy because of proximity to the A1, and the modern houses on the river-front at Mill Lane. The average price of a two-bedroom house in Sandy is £130,000. Two huge new housing estates, Ivel Park and Fallow Field, offer five-bedroom homes which cost £350,000.

Beeston, on the southern edge of Sandy, is divided by the A1, and quite a few properties are blighted by it. Nevertheless, the conservation area with the green, old thatched cottages and blacksmith's forge offers pleasant relief from some of the other, drearier villages in the area. **Tempsford**, to the north, is also spliced by the A1. Its war-time aerodrome was used by the Special Operations Executive to drop secret agents into occupied France, and it was from here that the American bandleader Glen Miller took off for his final flight in 1944.

Journey: 50 min
(34 min peak)
Season: £3060
Peak: 2 per hr
Off-peak: 2 per hr

ST NEOTS is considerably prettier than many of the towns in the area, and larger, too, with a population of 28,500 or more. The market square with its fine Georgian buildings is alive with gastro-pubs and cafés, and al fresco eating in the summer. The farmer's market appears on the second Saturday of each month, complete with live entertainment. Cricket and rugby are played on the huge, 160-acre common. There are three golf courses and an operatic society, the St Neots Players, which stages productions at the Priory Centre. There is also an annexe of Huntingdon Regional College.

The River Great Ouse contributes both colour and charm. There is a rowing club and two marinas. People come to St Neots to mess about in boats and to fish, or to walk the Ouse Valley Way. Unsurprisingly, some of the nicest places to live are close to the river. **Eaton Ford**, for example, was once a riverside village in its own right, but has now been absorbed by the town. The period architecture, combined with the presence of St Neots Golf Club and the river meadows, have pushed up the price of a four-bedroom detached house to around £260,000.

Semi-detached thatched cottage, Bedfordshire

Also popular is Old St Neots, in the area around the market square and shops, with walks in the woods of Priory Park. A two-bedroom house with a garden will cost about £135,000. Slightly cheaper is **Eaton Socon**, another former village drawn into the St Neots fold, where houses tend to be arranged in terraces. A four-bedroom detached house could cost around £250,000. It has the advantage of being on the A1, convenient for commuting to Stevenage or Hatfield. Less popular is **Eynesbury**, where the council estates have mushroomed through the period houses. Prices are low and homes on new private estates are now appearing at £225,000 to £400,000 for four bedrooms. New housing is planned to the east of the railway – 1000 of the 200,000 homes which the Government says we need.

People looking for a village home tend to head eastwards, where the countryside starts to undulate a little, though property prices also begin to rise as you get closer to Cambridge. **Great Gransden**, **Little Gransden** and **Waresley** have pretty Elizabethan thatched cottages and are particularly popular with professional couples. A three-bedroom semi in one of these villages would fetch around £220,000. **Eltisley** is slightly cheaper. It has an extraordinarily large village green and a lovely thatched cricket pavilion which is used for meetings as well as cricket matches. There is a pub and a popular primary school that also serves the surrounding villages. There are some small new housing estates favoured by young families, and bungalows for the elderly. A three-bedroom detached house would cost more than the equivalent in St Neots, but less than in the Gransdens.

To the north-west is Grafham Water, a huge man-made reservoir that draws people from miles around for walking, water skiing, windsurfing and other watersports. **Perry** was a village that had little to say for itself before Grafham Water was made, but prices are now similar to those in Eaton Ford. One possible drawback of living near open water is that midges can be a problem in the summer.

Journey: 57 min
(45 min peak)
Season: £3264
Peak: 3 per hr
Off-peak: 2 per hr

HUNTINGDON
Most people will probably prefer the neighbouring villages to Huntingdon itself, though the old county town is not unattractive. Oliver Cromwell lived here, and the former school which both he and Samuel Pepys attended has been turned into a Cromwell Museum. The previous house-price boom brought quite a few Londoners in search of cheaper housing, so there is a well-established body of commuters. Builders have been keeping pace with demand and the town centre is due to be revamped. The truth is that people tend to spend their lives trying to move out of this area rather than in. The cheapest housing is

found among the ex-council houses. Better addresses include Hartford and Sapley, where the period properties add a touch of class to the newer developments and bungalows. A modern house with four bedrooms in either area will cost around £190,000.

Across the remarkable 14th-century bridge in **Godmanchester**, the tone is raised by some pretty, pastel-coloured 16th-, 17th- and 18th-century houses, and by pleasant walks along the Great Ouse to Portholme Great Meadow, which is ablaze with wild flowers in spring. Much of Godmanchester is a designated conservation area, and there are some particularly fine houses in Post Street, Earning Street and the Causeway, where some of the gardens run down to the river. A modern five-bedroom house here is likely to fetch between £300,000 and £400,000, while a five-bedroom period house with a garden on the river will push the price towards the £800,000 mark. Not far to the west is **Brampton**, where Pepys lived for a time and where the Brampton racecourse can be found. It still retains its village green, though there have been a lot of new developments. The RAF station here is nothing to worry about – its function is purely administrative. The proximity of Grafham Water makes it a popular village for watersports enthusiasts.

St Ives, five miles to the east, also has more charm than Huntingdon, with a pot-pourri of building styles along the quay and a smattering of pubs and restaurants. The centre is a conservation area, and the threadwork of alleyways between Market Hill and the riverside is particularly intriguing. It grew up on the site of a large Easter Fair, and is the St Ives of the nursery rhyme.

Close to St Ives, nudging the Fens, are some of the most desirable villages in the area. **Hemingford Abbots**, formerly part of the Ramsey Abbey estate, seduces everyone with its thatched cottages and lovely walks. It is full of successful local businessmen and young couples attracted like moths to the Cambridge lamplight – all waxed jackets, Land Rovers and labradors. "You know if someone comes from Hemingford Abbots because they talk down to you," says one local resident. "There is a lot of pride in the village. If there is an art exhibition in the area, it will always be held in Hemingford Abbots." There are two-up-two-down Victorian terraced houses selling for £175,000. The wealthier aim for the small urban palaces in Common Lane. Some of these have river frontages and might sell for around £1m. The walks are idyllic, along footpaths that cross the meadows to Houghton Mill. This is an early Ouse watermill, in a beautiful setting which attracts visitors in search of tea in the summer. Those with less money to spend might look next door in **Hemingford Grey**, which is the poor relation living off the Hemingford name. There are many more family-sized houses here. A four-bedroom modern house would cost around £300,000.

'You know if someone comes from Hemingford Abbots because they talk down to you'

Houghton and **Wyton**, pronounced "Hooton" and "Witton", are also cheaper because they are that much further from the A1. The High Street which links them is punctured by the green and has a supermarket with a deli. The housing market offers a mix of old and new. A four-bedroom modern estate house will cost around £300,000; a five-bedroom period house up to £650,000. To the north is **Woodhurst**, a perfect example of a ring village. Some of the four-bedroom houses on new developments will cost £400,000.

Due north of Huntingdon are **Little** and **Great Stukeley** (where the former Prime Minister John Major lives), which offer a reasonable mix of old and new houses, council estates and chalet bungalows. A modern house with four bedrooms and a plot of land in Great Stukeley is likely to cost around £275,000. A four-bedroom period family house can be bought for £325,000.

Journey: 50 min with dual season, 65 min peak, 71 min off-peak with WAGN season

Season: £4712 (all), £3528 (WAGN only)

Peak: 4 per hr using both options

Off peak: 3 per hr (fast), 2 per hr (WAGN)

PETERBOROUGH

The tower of the Norman cathedral, which contains the tomb of Catherine of Aragon, is just about the only thing of beauty in Peterborough. It is visible from almost anywhere in the city and is illuminated at night. What the city lacks in aesthetics, it might be said to gain in purpose-built leisure facilities – cathedrals of contemporary life. The Queensgate shopping centre's malls and squares, in marble, glass and steel, are air-conditioned, American-style. There is a 13-screen cinema, an ice-rink, a rowing and canoeing centre, an indoor cricket stadium and three golf courses. The city is ringed with fast roads and bypasses, making life easy for drivers and pedestrians, too. The Key Theatre, opened in 1973, keeps the culture vultures happy with everything from opera and ballet to Christmas panto. And the Lady Lodge Arts Centre, in an old farmhouse at Orton Goldhay, puts a crafty-vegetarian spin on photography, music and the theatre.

Those interested in new housing should trawl the streets of the new £500m satellite town to the south called **Hampton**, with homes for over 13,000 people and a separate shopping centre. Four-bedroom houses here cost £185,000 to £260,000. Otherwise househunting becomes a question of working your way around the various Ortons. **Orton Goldhay** has shoals of ex-council terraced properties. At **Orton Malborne** there are more private houses in the mix, but prices remain similar. A three-bedroom semi will cost around £130,000; a three-bedroom detached £165,000. Prices rise sharply in the sumptuous, newly-built estates of **Orton Wistow**, where a family-sized modern house can start at £250,000. Similar properties can also be found in **Werrington** and **Gunthorpe**, both of which retain a core of older housing. Much of central Peterborough is to be avoided, especially the repetitive drabness of the older terraces. **Westown** is a preferred area, where three-bedroom semis with gardens sell at around

£140,000. For real one-upmanship, there are the houses in Thorpe Park Road, Thorpe Road and Westwood Road, where Thirties' homes in voluminous gardens sell at anything over £300,000 to the city's doctors, dentists and solicitors. The less wealthy middle-classes find themselves in **Longthorpe** and **Netherton**, where there is a range of older houses. A three-bedroom thatched cottage could cost £280,000.

To the east of Peterborough is stark Fenland. Most people find it too glum, and head determinedly for the undulating landscape and stone villages to the west. For those who are undeterred, **Whittlesey** in the east is set right in the Fens. Just to the south of it is King's Dyke, designed to introduce a sharp kink into the network of navigable waterways and so limit the size of vessels passing between the Rivers Nene and Ouse. The village has a brickworks, but is still dwarfed by the huge flatness that surrounds it. A two-bedroom detached bungalow might cost £135,000; an older, three-bedroom, bay-fronted semi £130,000. **Thorney**, slightly further north, was kept intact as an estate village throughout the 19th century and so has a greater sense of history. The rather mock-Jacobean water tower adds a flourish to the skyline. An older three-bedroom semi here will cost £130,000.

The villages to the south of Peterborough are also somewhat lacking in visual appeal. **Yaxley**, being so close to the A1, offers the convenience of an easy commute to the towns both north and south. Technically it is a village, though it has all the amenities and proliferating housing estates of a small town. Nearby RAF Alconbury is ear-marked for new development and much has already happened at Ferndale on the edge. The old part of Yaxley is the most sought after, particularly the thatched cottages that skirt the village green and old village pump. Run-of-the-mill three-bedroom semis fetch around £130,000; two-bedroom period cottages £115,000. The countryside around is not for those who want conventional beauty. "There are no hedgerows, no trees and no hills. But it grows on you," said one resident who had been converted. Large tracts between Yaxley and Fletton, including an old brick pit, are being swallowed by the new Hampton township. The villages west of the A1(M) such as **Folksworth**, **Haddon** and **Stilton**, hear the growl of the motorway.

North and west of Peterborough are the best areas to look. **Market Deeping** and its satellites **Deeping St James** and **Deeping Gate** ("Deeping" refers to the deep meadows on the banks of the River Welland), are a major attraction. Market Deeping is an attractive town with wide streets, some old stone houses and pubs, and with good old-fashioned butchers and bakers mixed in between the antiques shops. It has its own library and health centre, and an industrial zone including fireplace manufacturers and double-glazing specialists. There are two primary schools in addition to a good comprehensive

'The tower of the Norman cathedral is just about the only thing of beauty in Peterborough' and leisure centre at Deeping St James. The eight-mile drive to Peterborough station is only a matter of minutes along the A15. An older stone house with three bedrooms will cost £170,000 upwards depending on how much land comes with it. A three-bedroom semi will fetch considerably more than its counterpart in Peterborough. A four-bedroom detached house with a garage on a modern estate would cost around £180,000.

The stone villages in the Deepings corridor are all desirable and have been protected from over-development. They include **Maxey**, **Barnack**, **Ufford** and **Helpston**, the last being where the poet John Clare lived in the 19th century, and where he wrote his poems about the agricultural changes he saw going on around him. He is buried in the churchyard, and there is a memorial to him at the crossroads. A large cottage with four bedrooms might cost £250,000 in any of these villages, or slightly more if it is thatched.

Due west of Peterborough you find a similar kind of charm in villages such as **Wansford**. The village combines with Stibbington, which has a post-office-and-shop serving a population of about 450 between the two communities. A beautiful stone packhorse bridge links the two halves across the River Nene. Every year, the Fitzwilliam Hunt meets outside the Haycock Hotel, an old coaching inn, on New Year's Day.

Close by is **Elton**, which is very much regarded as an aspirational village and carries a premium. It has some good 17th-century houses, with Elton Hall just to the south and a lock on the Nene just to the west. A three-bedroom stone cottage in Elton might cost £300,000. All these villages benefit from being close to Stamford, a pretty medieval town and a good antidote to Peterborough.

'The poet John Clare is buried in the churchyard at Helpston, and there is a memorial to him at the crossroads'

'All these villages benefit from being close to Stamford, a pretty medieval town and a good antidote to Peterborough'

Journey: 69 min
Season: £5392
Peak: 3 per hr
Off-peak: 2 per hr

GRANTHAM A solid band of commuters arrived in Grantham on the crest of the 1988 housing boom as high prices rippled out from London. In those days around 80 per cent of the people looking for houses came from outside the area. During the slump around 90 per cent of the buyers were local. Now we have the "virtual commuter" who needs only to make occasional visits to London. And we have former commuters who have set up local companies here so that they can work nearer to home.

‘Everyone knows that Margaret Thatcher was born here, but not many people remember that Sir Isaac Newton was born here, too’

What everyone knows about Grantham is that Lady Thatcher was born here, in North Parade. Not quite so many people remember that Sir Isaac Newton was born here, too. Thatcher was educated at Kesteven and Grantham Girls' School, which is still doing for girls

Early 20th-century farmhouse, Grantham area

'The limestone
hills around
Grantham
contain some
pretty stone
villages...
Barrowby
stands high
enough to
afford good
views across
the Vale of
Belvoir'

what Kings does for boys. The town also has an associated college of Nottingham Trent University offering courses in building, business studies, engineering and general studies. Leisure is high on the agenda, in the form of the Meres Leisure Centre and athletics and football stadium. There are golf courses at Belton Park, Belton Woods and Stoke Rochford, and good fishing on the River Witham.

Grantham still has a smattering of ancient houses in Castlegate and Church Street, plus the celebrated Angel and Royal Hotel. But much of it now consists of new development. The local authority is anxious to attract more inward investment. At the lower end of the market, two-bedroom period town houses start at £70,000. Four-bedroom detached houses cost between £160,000 and £320,000. The best roads to live in are probably those leading out towards the villages of Manthorpe and Belton. Large detached houses set well back from the road can be bought for £350,000.

The limestone hills around Grantham contain some pretty stone villages, particularly in the west. **Barrowby**, for instance, stands high enough to afford good views across the Vale of Belvoir. A four-bedroom family-sized stone house here might cost £350,000. **Denton** is another handsome stone village, which used to be part of the Welby estate. Denton Reservoir nearby is popular with anglers, and has some pretty pathways along its banks. There is some Sixties' housing in the mix, and a small council estate. You could expect to pay £350,000 for a three-bedroom period house with a garage; £110,000 for a semi.

Closer to Grantham is **Harlaxton**, which is sufficiently attractive to have been designated a conservation area and hasn't been abused by unimaginative modern development. It owes much of its style to the Gregory family, who built the eye-catching manor house in the early 19th century, plus some of the Regency-style houses in the village. A pretty country cottage with three bedrooms might cost £315,000.

Perhaps two of the most exclusive villages are **Manthorpe** and **Belton** to the north, sandwiched by Belton Hall and its magnificent park, now in the hands of the National Trust. Little ever comes up for sale in Belton, but if you were lucky you could expect to pay £450,000 for something with four bedrooms.

Journey: 78 min
Season: £5836
Peak: 2 per hr
Off-peak: 1 per hr

NEWARK NORTHGATE This proud town, once a Royalist stronghold in the Civil War, does its best to ignore the great snake of the River Trent which slithers past, encased inside high banks to prevent it from flooding. The lovely cobblestone market place is a major feature, though the 14th-century draper's shop, which is supposed to be one of the oldest domestic buildings in the Midlands, is now occupied by a building society. The annual diary in Newark is full of antiques fairs – at least six are held each year, including the largest antiques fair in Western Europe. There has been a substantial amount of new housebuilding, including 1000 new homes at Farndon where small two-bedroom houses sell at £104,000 and one-bedroom apartments at £95,000. A new riverside development is planned with 200 apartments overlooking the marina.

'The annual diary in Newark is full of antiques fairs – at least six are held each year'

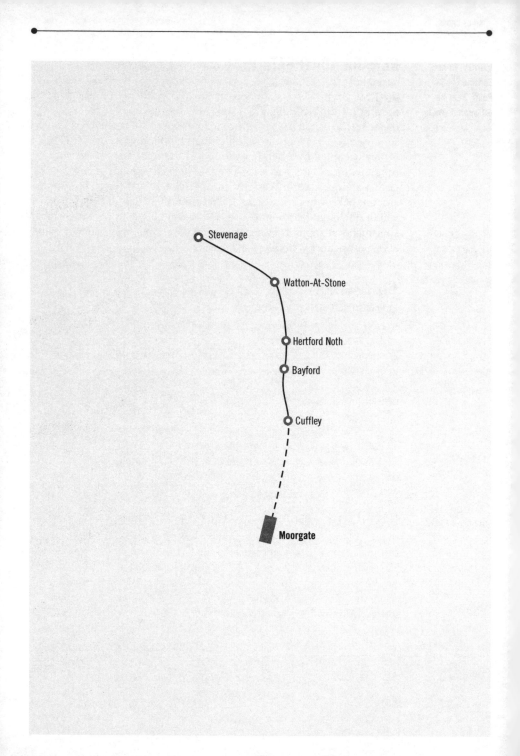

Stevenage

Watton-At-Stone

Hertford Noth

Bayford

Cuffley

Moorgate

Moorgate
> Stevenage

Journey: 38 min
Season: £1280
Peak: 6 per hr
Off-peak: 3 per hr

CUFFLEY is prime commuter country, much of it built in stockbroker Tudor style on what was once a wooded hillside. Though the character of the houses is intensely suburban, the village is still surrounded by proper farmland. Some of the large bungalows in their ample gardens have had new houses squeezed in beside them. Others, most oddly, have been converted into houses by having extra storeys added on top. There is no council housing to speak of. Two-bedroom flats can be bought for around £190,000; three-bedroom semis around £320,000. In the Ridgeway, mansions backing on to woodland can cost well over £1m.

The village has quite a high proportion of commuters, elderly residents, and young families who are moving in. A vociferous group of conservationists opposed the building of a golf course on nearby farmland. The village has enough shops to provide practically two of everything. It also has its own primary school. Older children go to Potters Bar. Leisure activities include the Cuffley Players and an operatic society, plus football club and bowls. There is a tennis club with a two-year waiting list, but public courts are available.

Journey: 43 min
Season: £1780
Peak: 2 per hr
Off-peak: 3 per hr

BAYFORD is significantly more rural than Cuffley. It is set quietly in the heart of the Broxbourne woods, which are full of footpaths and bridleways, and is not so overburdened with modern development. The older Georgian houses have a pleasing presence as a result. The village is rather spread out. It has both a pond and an open space which it treats as a green. There is a cricket field with a new cricket pavilion built with Lottery money. There is a pub, the Bakers Arms, but no post office or shop, and most people stock up from Waitrose

'Bayford is set quietly in the heart of the Broxbourne woods, which are full of footpaths and bridleways' or Tesco in Hertford. The village has its own mixed infants and junior school, but older children go out of the village. Every two years villagers open their gardens to the public, with the admission charges going towards local amenities.

Together with its neighbours – **Brickendon**, **Little Berkhamsted**, **Epping Green** and **Bayfordbury** – Bayford exudes wealth and charm, and there is little point harbouring any ambition to live here unless you're looking in the £300,000 to £700,000 bracket. A two-bedroom mews house recently sold for £300,000. Brickendon is little more than a tiny hamlet set around a green, half a mile's walk from Bayford. Little Berkhamsted is delightfully wooded and has some lovely weatherboarded cottages opposite the church. Bayfordbury is perhaps not so exclusive since it has the B158 running through it.

Journey: 47 min
Season: £2060
(also valid from
Hertford East)
Peak: 6 per hr
Off-peak: 3 per hr

HERTFORD NORTH
Hertford is a surprisingly small, old-fashioned county town, protected by a quilt of green belt at the junction of the Rivers Beane, Lea and Mimram. It is possible to take a boat south to the sea from here by negotiating a series of locks. Much of the town centre is a conservation area, charmingly provincial considering its proximity to London. Family firms still thrive alongside all the antiques shops, and there is a Saturday street market. The cattle market has fallen prey to property developers and been turned into flats. There is a county court, county hospital and all the other public buildings you would expect of an administrative

Period country house in Hertfordshire

centre, the 1939 County Hall on its hilltop being the most ostentatious of the group.

The Round Table has a strong presence and organises the annual fun day. Other prominent social groups include the Company of Players, based at the Little Theatre, and the Dramatic and Operatic Society, which organises the annual theatre week. There are also choral and art societies, and a symphony orchestra. There is a sporting fraternity too: cricket club, canoe club, Hertford Football Club, the Old Hertfordians Rugby Club, and fishing in streams made famous by Izaak Walton in *The Compleat Angler*.

Hertford is generally more expensive than other nearby towns, partly because of its status as county town. Commuters have a good choice of routes into London. The Moorgate/Kings Cross trains from Hertford North provide easy changes to the London Underground at Finsbury Park or Highbury & Islington. Or, if you prefer, there are trains to Liverpool Street from Hertford East (page 54), which connect with the Underground at Seven Sisters and Tottenham Hale. People scuttle through the short cuts converging on Hertford North station in the morning in such large numbers that there is a prescribed route known locally as the Commuter Trail. Not many of them live in the area immediately behind the station, which is dominated by council estates, but there are plenty of good streets within walking distance.

'People are often so fixated on Bengeo that they will consider living nowhere else'

At the cheaper end of the market, modern town houses can be bought for around £300,000. For middle-range, three- and four-bedroom houses with generous gardens you should look in the Fordwich area. Here you will find semis at around £500,000; detached houses around £750,000. For more extravagant housing see High Molewood and Great Molewood, where large detached houses and chalet bungalows are spread along unmade private roads surrounded by woodland. Five bedrooms, two bathrooms and four reception rooms in Thirties' architectural style might cost around £600,000. The smartest suburb to the north is **Bengeo**. People moving to Hertford are often so completely fixated on Bengeo that they will consider living nowhere else, so to a certain extent house prices here are recession-proof. It has a parade of shops and a good preparatory school. A six-bedroom house in an acre or two of garden will cost well over £1m.

However great the appeal of Bengeo for commuters, it is the south side of town which locals consider to be the more desirable.

'Outside Hertford, Hertingfordbury is probably one of the most exclusive villages in the area'

The large Victorian and Edwardian houses of Queen's Road and Highfield Road, enlivened by the occasional architectural curio, sell at over £500,000 for four bedrooms.

In the centre of Hertford, upwardly mobile young couples are attracted to the riverside, where terraced cottages were originally built for mill or malt workers. In the last decade Folly Island has been mercilessly gentrified, regardless of the shortage of parking places, and tiny two-bedroom houses with small gardens now cost around £200,000. The second bedroom tends only to be cot-sized, so those with growing families have to think of moving on.

Outside Hertford, **Hertingfordbury** is probably one of the most exclusive villages in the area. The thriller-writer Frederick Forsyth has a house here. The village has no more than 20-odd houses with a cricket pitch and two pubs, a church and a bridge over the Mimram. Its quaintness sends prices for tiny cottages over £300,000.

Journey: 53 min
Season: £2204
Peak: 2 per hr
Off-peak: 1 per hr

WATTON-AT-STONE is daubing its pretty face with new

development. The main street is where the older properties are – yellow- and red-brick houses, jettied timber and plaster. But most of the rest of the village is new, and building has been more or less constant throughout the last decade. A five-bedroom period house in the main street might cost around £550,000; a four-bedroom modern detached around £450,000. One of the more recent development plans has been to convert an old salmon-smoking factory into flats.

'One of the pubs has the old pudding stone outside from which the village derived its name'

The village combines the best of both worlds by being intensely rural (and horsey), and yet close enough to London for theatre and other trips. There is cricket, football and the most unusual asset of tennis on floodlit courts, in addition to three pubs – one of which has the old pudding stone outside from which the village derives its name – a flower club and other village societies.

The village has the Heath Mount private infant and junior schools, as well a nursery and primary. This is one of the places to benefit from Lottery funding for a new village hall. The spring which gave the village the other half of its name ("wat", meaning watery) and which gave it brief prominence as a popular spa, dried up long ago. But a hedgerow near the station is supposed to be one of the most ancient in Hertfordshire.

To Moorgate

Journey:	60 min
Season:	£2560
Peak:	2 per hr
Off-peak:	1 per hr

To Kings Cross

Journey:	25 min
Season:	£2560
Peak:	6 per hr
Off-peak:	4 per hr

STEVENAGE See **Kings Cross to Newark Northgate** line (page 69).

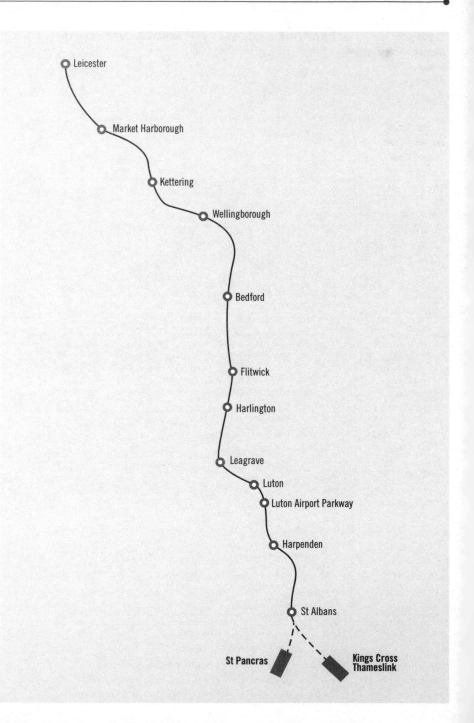

Leicester

Market Harborough

Kettering

Wellingborough

Bedford

Flitwick

Harlington

Leagrave

Luton

Luton Airport Parkway

Harpenden

St Albans

St Pancras

Kings Cross Thameslink

Kings Cross Thameslink/St Pancras
> Bedford and Leicester

From stations to Bedford, Thameslink trains connect to Kings Cross Thameslink rather than St Pancras. They then continue to Farringdon, City Thameslink, Blackfriars, and London Bridge. Season ticket prices quoted are valid to all these London stations including London Bridge (but not on the underground). Beyond Bedford all services are to St Pancras.

Journey: 19 min	
Season: £2120	
Peak: 8 per hr	
Off-peak: 4 per hr	

ST ALBANS Forget the villages around St Albans. The attractions of the town itself, with its medieval centre focused around the cathedral, are such that it has become one of the smartest places to live north of London. Georgian and Edwardian town houses snuggle against quaint old cottages and 15th-century coaching inns. In the cramped, but charming streets in the town centre conservation area you could buy a two-up-two-down cottage for around £250,000.

St Albans has excellent communications. It lies roughly equidistant from the M1 and A1, and only a few miles from the M25. The train journey into London is so fast that, in terms of time, it's hardly further from the City than Clapham. In the last two decades some of the country's biggest accountancy firms have moved here, including PwC, Deloitte Touche, KPMG and others.

The shopping centre feels reassuringly traditional with a bi-weekly street market in St Peter's Street. There are old-fashioned independent shops, antiques shops and at Christopher Place there are smart shops and restaurants, including Carluccio's. The town has three theatres: the Albans Arena, the Maltings and the Abbey Theatre, where the formidable local dramatics society, The Company of Ten, performs. There are also frequent concerts and recitals in the Cathedral.

Schools are another of St Albans's particular attractions. The local state schools all have good reputations, and there are private schools for those who want them (see box, page 98).

The really stylish 15th-, 16th- and 17th-century houses are on Fishpool Street, the old London-Holyhead Road, where a Grade II listed two-bedroom cottage will sell for £300,000 to £400,000. A two-up-two-down cottage in the heart of town will sell for around

97

£250,000. The main residential area is Marshalswick. Three-bedroom semis here cost £300,000 to £320,000. Large detached houses in Marshal's Drive, with tennis courts, come with price-tags in the region of £800,000. Marshalswick has its own small shops, library and free car park. Further out of St Albans you will find roads of semi-detached houses where a three-bedroom Fifties' home will cost around £260,000.

For more modern, executive-style houses, the eastern corridor towards Hatfield, around the Hatfield Road, is the place to look. Three-bedroom semis sell for around £380,000 upwards; four- to five-bedroom detached houses will break £500,000.

Villages in the St Albans catchment include **Chiswell Green** – home of the Royal National Rose Society – **London Colney** and **Shenley**. These are all fairly popular with commuters, and appear reasonably pleasant at first glance. Locals tend to look down their noses at them, however, because of the volume of ex-council housing.

Journey: 26 min
Season: £2380
Peak: 7 per hr
Off-peak: 4 per hr

HARPENDEN is, if such a thing is possible, even smarter than St Albans. It has two cricket clubs, a leisure centre and an indoor swimming pool. People have to travel to St Albans or London for professional theatre, though the local amateur dramatics and operatic societies regularly entertain at the civic hall. It has a Sainsbury's, and plenty of boutiques, gift and speciality shops in the centre of the village. The green runs right through the centre, providing a perfect spot to sit and watch the world go by in

Schools in Hertfordshire

Hertfordshire is well served with good schools. But be aware that many which call themselves comprehensives actually run a selective entry system.

Watford's schools are within reach of people living near Chorleywood. Watford Boy's Grammar and its girls' counterpart are comprehensives with strong academic records. Both are heavily over-subscribed.

Harpenden also has three strong schools: St George's co-educational comprehensive, which takes some boarders, Roundwood Park co-ed, school and The King's School, a non-selective co-ed.

Bishop's Stortford has a good private school in Bishop's Stortford College and three good comprehensives – Bishop's Stortford High, The Hertfordshire and Essex High, and St Mary's

Catholic School. Rich pickings can be had in St Albans, not only with the high-performing St Albans Girls' comprehensive, but also a matching pair of independent schools – St Albans School for boys (with girls in the sixth form) and St Albans High for girls. Two more schools worth mentioning include the private St Columba's College for boys and Loreto College Roman Catholic Girls' comprehensive.

Other good comprehensives can be found in Potters Bar, Hemel Hempstead, Hitchin, Sawbridgeworth and Welwyn Garden City. Strong private schools include Berkhamsted Collegiate in Berkhamsted, Haberdashers' Aske's for boys and for girls in Borehamwood; Haileybury in Hertford and St Francis College in Letchworth.

16th-century
town house,
St Albans

summer. Schools for
all age ranges – both private and state-
run – have a particularly high reputation.

Some of the most desirable properties are those close to the two
golf courses or to the East and West Commons, though The Avenues
have almost overtaken them now with the added attraction of a 10-
minute walk to the station. A four- or five-bedroom detached house
here now tops £1m. East Common has its own golf course; West
Common is more residential. In the area of the Commons you could
pay £275,000 for a two-bedroom terraced house; up to £1m for a
large family house. Properties span various architectural periods from
Tudor right through to the present day, and many of them have large
gardens with the occasional tennis court and swimming pool. Those
with shallower pockets could find a three-bedroom home away from
the Commons at around £300,000.

There are some extremely pretty villages within reach, any of
which might have been lifted straight from the pages of *Country Life*
or *Horse and Hound*. **Redbourn**, five miles away, is a large village with
a population of more than 5000, centred around a classic common
and picture-book High Street. Small shops and a post office provide
for day-to-day needs, and there is an infant and junior school.
However, it lies too close to the M1 for its own good – the roar of
the cars can be heard. A four-bedroom cottage with half an acre will
cost £430,000, while a five-bedroom house in two acres will cost
£750,000. Hunt through the jumble of older cottages in the High

Street to find something smaller and cheaper. For **Wheathampstead** see **Kings Cross to Newark Northgate** line (page 66).

Kimpton to the north-east also has an attractive High Street with small shops and has good walks nearby in Gustard Wood. Commuters rub shoulders with long-established locals. Prices are slightly lower than in nearby Wheathampstead. There are plenty of terraced cottages, but a modern four-bedroom house will cost £520,000. There is a village infant and junior school.

Flamstead, due west, is popular for its conservation-area charm and active village social life. A thick blanket of green belt gives it a very rural atmosphere, and in the Flamstead Society it has an influential local history group. The village now holds an annual charity Scarecrow Festival in August which creates an outlet for creative and artistic talent. Many of the older-established residents are allotment holders, and the garden show is an important annual event. For the amusement of the young there is a football ground and tennis courts. There is a general store with a post office. The village has its own playgroup and junior school, and there are two old pubs which attract customers from miles around. The cottages are a picturesque mix of brick and flint. A two-bedroom example will cost around £240,000-plus; a larger 17th-century three-bedroom house £300,000-plus.

Journey: 32 min
Season: £2540
Peak: 6 per hr
Off-peak: 4 per hr

LUTON AIRPORT PARKWAY Generous and easy parking

arrangements make Luton Airport an attractive alternative to catching the train from Luton proper – anything to avoid stressful early morning traffic jams. For Luton main entry see below.

Journey: 24 min
(34 min
Thameslink)
Season: £2580
Peak: 7 per hr
Off-peak: 5 per hr

LUTON spreads its mess of modern housing estates, industrial

complexes and shopping streets with little grace. It does still have some industrial pride, however, with major local employers including Whitbread and London Luton Airport, and blue chip companies such as Astra Zeneca are now making an entrance. Shopping is unfussy and run-of-the mill, and includes the refurbished Arndale Centre. There is an 11-screen cinema, five sports and recreation centres, two swimming pools and the new Luton University. Luton Town Football Club plays at Kenilworth Road.

There are a few enclaves for those who prefer period homes. Along and just off the Old Bedford Road, about half a mile from the centre, are some period villas which have lavishly restored and now sport multi-bathrooms where there were non originally. A four-bedroom home here will cost between £350,000 and £500,000, depending on how much has been spent on it. Throughout the town there are plenty of detached Thirties' houses selling at over £225,000 for three bedrooms; up to £300,000 for four bedrooms or more.

Kensworth, to the south-west, is a popular commuter village. Cottages line the main road, with a recreation ground and village hall to provide the community focal points. You might get a tiny two-bedroom cottage for as little as £250,000, but the sky's the limit for the large farmhouses in the area. The village has two general stores, a newsagent, a flower shop and its own infant and junior school. There is also some retirement housing.

To the east and south-east of Luton, just over the border into Hertfordshire, are the small villages of **Breachwood Green**, **Bendish** and **Peter's Green**. Bendish is probably the most stylish, being very tiny with old period cottages. A small two-up two-down cottage will set you back by £200,000 here. Prices at Peter's Green are similar, though the place is so small that you could blink and miss it. Prices drop by about 15 per cent here – a spacious converted alehouse could be bought for £545,000. The village lies directly under the flight path to Luton Airport, and the ex-council properties put choosy buyers off.

Timber-framed cottages, Dunstable

LEAGRAVE is hardly distinct from Luton. It has its own small

Journey: 38 min
Season: £2580
Peak: 4 per hr
Off-peak: 4 per hr

precinct of shopping streets, but otherwise can be considered part of the town. In the centre of Leagrave, two- and three-bedroom pre-war terraced houses sell for between £120,000 and £150,000. On the outskirts you find the occasional new development where two-bed terraced houses start at around £135,000.

Dunstable, two miles west at the threshold of the Dunstable Downs, is far more captivating. The old town centre is dotted with timber-framed buildings, old coaching inns (Dunstable was an important coaching stop on Watling Street), and some attractive Victorian terraces. It is has a bi-weekly outdoor market, and lots of small designer-shops, good for birthday presents, though for mundane household purchases most people go into Luton. State schools include middle schools and an upper school which also provides adult evening classes. All have good reputations. Dunstable has its own leisure centre, swimming pools, theatre and a nightclub. The Downs, too, provide plenty of leisure opportunities and the landscape for a golf club and Whipsnade Wild Animal Park. They are also a favourite haunt for hang-gliders and kite-fliers. Victorian terraced homes with two or three bedrooms fetch around £130,000 to £150,000. A two- or three-bedroom semi on a modern estate would cost around £190,000; a three- or four-bedroom detached house from £250,000 upwards.

Also in the Luton catchment area is **Houghton Regis**, a former village of about two miles square, not quite swallowed up by encroaching development. Modern estates and Thirties' semis make up the bulk of the property stock, with prices hovering at £120,000 to £140,000 for three bedrooms. At its heart it has some small quality shops around Bedford Square.

Journey: 44 min
Season: £2660
Peak: 5 per hr
Off-peak: 4 per hr

HARLINGTON, on the very tip of the Chiltern Hills, has an

attractive core of timber-framed houses and thatched cottages grouped around the church. They are in a conservation area, and anything with two bedrooms will cost at least £160,000. On the outskirts are two estates built around 30 years ago. Three-bedroom semis are priced at around £170,000 to £220,000; four-bedroom detached houses at £235,000 upwards. A five-bedroom detached house in one and a half acres, with stables, is £695,000. A few local shops and a post office serve a population of around 2300, but the place is hammered by commuter traffic. There is a good infants' school, an upper school and a sixth-form college. The nearest middle school is at Toddington (see below), a few miles to the south-west. There is quite a strong sporting tradition in the village.

Toddington, which lies just off the M1, is much larger, with a population of about 5000 and a range of shops and schools. There are a few elegant houses around the green and some intriguing old pubs. Toddington Manor was the home of Henrietta Wentworth, mistress of the Duke of Monmouth, the illegitimate son of Charles II. The town has grown paunchy with new development. Property prices are slightly lower than Harlington's, with three-bedroom semis from around £200,000 upwards.

Prettier villages in the Harlington area include **Tingrith** and **Milton Bryan**. Both these are hamlets of no more than 40 picture-postcard cottages each, plus the occasional Georgian farmhouse. There are no shops or schools, and both appeal to the better-heeled commuter. Cottages cost around £235,000; family-sized period houses with stables and a paddock can cost £695,000.

Journey: 48 min
Season: £2660
Peak: 6 per hr
Off-peak: 4 per hr

FLITWICK Little is left of old Flitwick, which was just a cluster of timber-framed houses and brick cottages. New development has entirely changed its character. Much of the new building has been for the benefit of commuters, whose trains come thundering straight through the centre of the town. Apart from the railway, the most noticeable central landmark now is a huge branch of Tesco. Flitwick has three lower schools and one middle school, though upper-school children have to travel to Ampthill (see below). For those with surplus energy there is a sports centre with a dance studio, swimming pool and squash courts.

Prices in the modern estates range from £155,000 to £190,000 for a three-bedroom semi; over £240,000 for a four-bedroom detached house. A three-bedroom Victorian house in the centre could be bought for £220,000 to £250,000. Commuters from as far afield as Daventry flood in to street park here and save on the price of a season ticket.

Ampthill, a small Georgian market town with a population of around 7000, makes Flitwick look like an ugly sister. Its picturesque centre is set around a market square, dotted with antiques shops and other small specialist shops. It also has a supermarket, schools for children of all ages, and a handsome park of around 160 acres. It is believed that Catherine of Aragon once lived here and received visits from Henry VIII. A three-bedroom peg-tiled estate cottage might be picked up at £250,000; a four-bedroom detached period house over £400,000; or a rare Georgian gem with a bit of land £700,000.

Steppingley, a tiny village a mile to the west of Flitwick, has little more than 40 Duke of Bedford peg-tiled estate cottages, a cricket

Duke of Bedford
cottages,
Steppingley

club, pub and a good restaurant. The atmosphere is upmarket and horsey. Prices for three-bedroom cottages are in the region of £250,000. A four-bedroom detached period house will fetch over £400,000. Out of the village along one of the lanes you could expect to pay over £700,000 for a Georgian farmhouse with a bit of land.

**Journey: 39 min
(45 min
Thameslink)
Season: £2880
Peak: 7 per hr
Off-peak: 4 per hr**

BEDFORD
Though still a market town, Bedford has to a certain extent allowed its individuality to become submerged by its own commercial success. Modern office blocks have appeared in the historic centre. Multi-national companies located here include Unilever. The Harpur Centre, a modern shopping mall, is complemented by quality small shops along the High Street, plus big-name stores, supermarkets and a bi-weekly market. The Bunyan Centre is the place for most sports and there are three swimming pools, including the Oasis "beach pool". The Civic Theatre provides a forum for amateur dramatics, but is upstaged as a venue by the Corn Exchange. The Aspects leisure centre has restaurants, a bowling alley and multi-screen cinema. The town is also a centre of learning having Bedford College, De Montfort University and nearby Cranfield University.

Along the embankment by the River Great Ouse, where people stroll and sit in summer to watch the waterfowl, are some large, tree-shaded Victorian houses – probably the nicest properties in the town. One of these with five to seven bedrooms would cost over £550,000. There are also some purpose-built flats in the same area. The smallest one-bedroom apartment starts at £150,000. A three-bedroom Victorian terraced house nearby would cost £170,000; a three- to four-bedroom semi up to £200,000. For the rest of the town the general rule is that the houses are more modern the further out you go, but prices do not vary much. You can expect to pay around £170,000 for a three-bedroom semi; £180,000 for a three-bedroom detached house.

Most of the sought-after villages in the flat countryside around Bedford are to the north. **Oakley,** just over four miles to the north-west, has in its High Street some old brick farmworkers' cottages that once belonged to the Duke of Bedford's estate. You would pay from around £170,000 for one of these with two bedrooms and a long garden. There is also a good deal of modern development where you

Schools in Bedfordshire

Bedford's strongest suit is its independent sector, which includes Bedford High and Dame Alice Harpur for girls, Bedford for boys and Bedford Modern for boys and girls, all of which have pupils bussed in from the surrounding large catchment area.

'The local water mill is restored and actually mills flour'

would pay about £155,000 for a three-bedroom semi; from £230,000 for a four-bedroom detached. Youngish families mix with the small number of commuters. Village social life revolves around the village hall, cricket and football teams, the gardening club and the two pubs. There is a village store, a post office, primary and middle schools.

Bromham, on the Ouse three miles north-west of Bedford, is a large village with a population of 5000. Many of the local families have lived here for generations. The limestone cottages in the village centre are surrounded by modern housing and building is still going on. There is a supermarket, post office, two general stores, a petrol station, hairdresser, fish-and-chip shop, health centre, two pubs and a lower school. Bromham House, an old manor house, now has its grounds filled with new housing, the local watermill is restored and actually mills flour. The town holds an annual apple day. A nice three-bedroom semi could be bought for £172,00, a detached four- to five-bedroom house in Bromham House grounds for £500,000.

Biddenham, due west of Bedford, is the favourite village for London commuters. It is so close to the town (the station is but a brisk 15-minute walk), yet it feels deliciously remote and is set around a classic village green. All this makes it one of the most expensive villages in the area. Properties range from 17th-century thatched cottages to imposing Thirties' houses, plus a few modern developments built with managing directors in mind. Prices range from £150,000 for a two-bedroom cottage to £600,000 for a substantial family house. A development of 300 houses has been built with a shop, a cricket field, tennis courts and a community centre as part of the package. Four-bedroom houses here cost £250,000. There is a cricket club and tennis club. The village hall is packed at parish council meetings, and everyone gets involved in local events, including an annual summer show. Conservation issues are policed by the Biddenham Society. A Grade I listed Queen Anne house with estate cottages and 36 acres of parkland was recently marketed at £2.75m.

'Biddenham village hall is packed at parish council meetings, and everyone gets involved in local events, including an annual summer show'

> Beyond Bedford, all services are to St Pancras.

Journey: 55 min
Season: £3864
Peak: 3 per hr
Off-peak: 2 per hr

WELLINGBOROUGH is so plain it defies description yet the improved train service is bringing in new life-blood in the form of commuters. It has a good range of major chain stores, several supermarkets including a Sainsbury's and a modern shopping mall, the Swansgate Centre. Schooling is good, with three state secondary schools and one private school, Wellingborough School for boys. A night out in Wellingborough used to mean going to a pub, but the town now also has a theatre, The Castle, an arts complex and a leisure centre.

The town has a mix of Victorian terraced houses, smart newish developments and some not-so-nice council estates. Developments around the railway station are popular as starter homes. A two-bedroom quad (a quarter of a house split into four) will cost £80,000; a three-bedroom semi £125,000; a four-bedroom detached just over £160,000. There are some pleasant older properties in Northampton Road, where you could expect to pay over £180,000 for a three-bedroom Thirties' house. For Victoriana, look in Hatton Park where houses cost £200,000 upwards. A four-bedroom modern detached house on one of the better developments – the Gleneagles Estate, for instance – would cost between £210,000 and £250,000.

Rushden, a few miles to the east, is about one-third the size of Wellingborough and rather less attractive, with some charmless early Seventies' architecture and the extra dollop of houses planned which might simply add to the anywhere-land feel. The consolation for house-buyers are some reasonably-priced Victorian terraced houses, ranging from around £100,000 to £120,000 for two or three bedrooms. A four-bedroom detached modern house will cost over £180,000. Shopping is adequate: there is a Safeway on the edge of town and a Budgens within. The main source of local pride is the sports centre and the splash-leisure pool. There is no cinema since the old picture house was converted into a theatre for amateur dramatics and bingo. Rushden was the birthplace of the novelist H E Bates, who used Rushden Hall – one of the few historic buildings surviving in the town – as the model for Evensfield in *Love For Lydia*.

A favourite state school is Ferrers School in **Higham Ferrers**, four-and-a-half miles to the east of Wellingborough. The village has now become a town, hardly separated from Rushden, with an attractive High Street lined with period stone properties and new developments fanning out on

Red-brick and stone cottage, Wellingborough

either side. A four-bedroom stone house here will cost over £350,000. A rare, rambling, five-bedroom terraced house on the market square will cost over £500,000. Some of the villages close to it are worth looking at, too. **Wymington** has a good mix of stone and thatch, with a spread of old farmhouses down the lanes, and **Podington** has a quality of timelessness that is very attractive. You could find a period three-bedroom stone house for around £360,000.

Wollaston, about seven minutes' drive due south of Wellingborough, is centred around a cluster of old cottages, with modern developments, an industrial estate and council housing on the outskirts. The makers of Doc Martens have their headquarters here. It has small shops, a post office and its own primary and secondary schools. The conservation watchdogs of the Wollaston Society have enjoyed some triumphs, including the arrival of a bypass to take the strain of the A509. Property prices start at £140,000 for a three-bedroom semi; £210,000 for a four-bedroom detached; and £370,000 for a 17th-century stone cottage. A four-bedroom, double-garaged detached house overlooking the fields might cost £320,000.

For real village atmosphere, however, you should head south to **Grendon**, about five miles from Wellingborough. This pretty village consists of 18th-century cottages gathered around the church, with some Victorian terraces and a few individual modern properties. Villagers get by with one pub and a good primary school. There is a limited bus service. The population of more than 500 includes young families, commuters and some elderly residents in bungalows. Village life centres around the Church Social Committee, Village Hall Committee, WI and cricket team. There is an annual church fête and periodic fund-raising ventures which attract considerable support. Expect to pay at least £195,000 for a period cottage; upwards of £140,000 for a two-bed Victorian terraced house.

East of Wellingborough is **Raunds**, a small town not to everyone's taste, with a 14th-century manor house and Victorian buildings surrounded by modern estates. Its tightly-knit community of about 8000 is served by two supermarkets, a post office and smaller shops. Little terraced houses can be bought for £90,000; three-bedroom Victorian semis for £120,000; and modern three-bedroom detached houses for £150,000 upwards.

Also on this side of Wellingborough are **Great** and **Little Addington**. Both are cottagey with some modern development on the wings, mainly four-bedroom detached houses. The two villages share a vicar, a playing field, a youth club and WI, though there is still a certain amount of friendly rivalry which brings people out in summer and winter for inter-village sporting contests. Another highlight of the social calendar is the annual horticultural society show. There is a Church of England primary school and a playgroup for tots, of which

> 'Grendon is a very pretty village consisting of 18th-century cottages gathered around the church'

'Green wellies, Land Rovers and waxed jackets are common currency in the Addingtons'

there are a fair number. New housebuilding is seriously restricted here, so prices can only go up. You would have to pay around £225,000 for a three-bedroom stone cottage, possibly thatched; around £250,000 for a modern four-bedroom detached. A five-bedroom stone country house with an acre of land could cost up to £600,000. The area is so seriously horsey that estate agents say that anything with a pony paddock is bound to sell. Green wellies, Land Rovers and waxed jackets are common currency here.

Journey: 62 min
Season: £4284
Peak: 4 per hr
Off-peak: 2 per hr

KETTERING is a no-nonsense East Midlands market town, well-supplied with leisure opportunities and good shopping. All the big-name stores are here, including Tesco, Sainsbury's and Marks and Spencer, and the modern Newland Shopping Centre is useful if not inspiring. Kettering Leisure Village encompasses a sports arena, conference facilities and a lakeside bar, as well as offering tennis, squash, a gym and fishing. Not far from here is the 180-acre Wicksteed Park with its fairground theme park. Those addicted to more sedentary pleasures will be pleased to hear that there is a 10-screen cinema.

The town has a few old Georgian terraces in the centre, larger Victorian houses forming a ring around them, and modern estates on the outskirts. You might pick up a two-bedroom Victorian terraced house for £90,000, or a three-bedroom Victorian house with original features and a good garden for around £130,000.

The countryside here at last begins to pick itself up off the Bedfordshire plains. It is a mellow, slightly rolling, farmland landscape, which draws people from Kettering out into frankly villagey little market towns that surround it. Look at **Rothwell** and **Desborough** to the north, and **Burton Latimer** to the south. All are similar, with Victorian market places, small shops and their own primary and secondary schools. Property prices are similar to those in Kettering. Rothwell is particularly pretty and has a gem of an Elizabethan market hall. The centre is a designated conservation area. It also has the benefit of a state secondary school, Montsaye, with a very good academic record. A two-up-two-down terraced house will cost £85,000; a three-bedroom terraced £100,000; a three-bedroom semi £125,000 to £135,000; a four-bedroom detached £195,000.

One of the more notable smaller villages is **Geddington**, four miles north of Kettering, with a population of around 1400. A medieval bridge crosses the River Ise here, with a forested hillside providing an attractive green backdrop. It has three pubs, a village hall, a post office and a primary school. Its heart is a cluster of old cottages, though new housing has forced itself in and there are some Victorian terraces, too. For a two-bedroom terraced house or a small cottage you would have to pay upwards of £180,000. Closer to Kettering on this side is the tiny village of **Weekley**. There are possibly no more than 150 people living here altogether, many of them from old farming families, some of them elderly (the former vicarage is now a residential home). Among the thatched cottages there is a pretty thatched post office, also home to Jessica's Tea Shop, which is much photographed. There is no school or pub, but the tea shop, village hall and church provide venues for coffee mornings, sports club meetings and choirs. Weekley is a quiet, compact, well-heeled and tight-knit village where a cottage – should you be lucky enough to find one for sale – would cost around £210,000.

Journey: 76 min
Season: £4976
Peak: 3 per hr
Off-peak: 2 per hr

'People grow very fond of Market Harborough, home of the first liberty bodice'

MARKET HARBOROUGH

People grow very fond of Market Harborough, home of the first Liberty Bodice, with its distinctive half-timbered Old Grammar School on stilts in the centre, now used for public functions. The population is a manageable 19,000. Georgian-built offices and shops are still in place in the town centre, and the office blocks of large local employers such as Golden Wonder crisps manage not to be too intrusive. Other companies in the town include Harper Tungsten Batteries and the Harboro Rubber Company, and there is a large industrial park on the outskirts. The new St Mary's Place shopping centre in the old cattle market has a Sainsbury's and an indoor market. There is a leisure centre and swimming pool, a 100-seat theatre large enough for local productions, but no cinema.

Some of the nicest properties are the large Victorian villas along the Northampton Road, where three-bedroomed houses start at £230,000. There are also some rather gracious tree-lined avenues in which mature Thirties' semis and detached houses are likely to cost £200,000 to £350,000. Victoria Avenue, actually a cul-de-sac, and Lubenham Hill, are both popular.

North of Market Harborough you enter the wide-open, rolling countryside of the Welland Valley, where villages of thatch and stone are connected by unhurried roads. This is Quorn territory and serious hunting country. Life in The Langtons – **Church Langton**, **Tur**

Schools in Leicestershire and Rutland

Leicester itself has The Beauchamp College, a co-educational comprehensive with a reputation both for being liberal and achieving good results.

There are three independent schools in the city: Leicester Grammar for boys, the High School for girls and Irwin College non-selective mixed school. The Leicester Islamic Academy and Soar Valley College comprehensive also do well in the school league tables.

Other dominant public schools in the area include Uppingham, the boys' and girls' boarding school – and Oakham, which takes boarding and day boys and girls.

Langton, **West Langton**, **East Langton** and **Thorpe Langton** – revolves
around horses and farming. Church Langton is the largest of this
idyllic clutch of villages and West Langton the smallest, though they
are all really little more than hamlets, clusters of stone and thatched
cottages. All except West Langton and Tur Langton have a pub.
Church Langton has the only primary school. Prices vary according
to how much land comes with the house and how good the views are,
but you could reckon on paying over £250,000 for a three-bedroom
stone cottage; up to £500,000 for four bedrooms and an acre of land
on a hilltop.

Another gem is **Foxton**. It lies about two-and-a-half miles north-
west of Market Harborough on the Grand Union Canal. Its famous
series of locks – 10 altogether in two flights rising through 75ft – and
an inclined-plane boat-lift (which is being restored) are a great
attraction to tourists in the summer. The village itself is pretty, too,
with old stone and thatched cottages and only a few ex-council
houses. Swingbridge Street is possibly the nicest. The population is a
friendly mix of young families, commuters and farmers. There is a
village hall, infant and junior schools and three pubs. A three-
bedroom detached cottage will cost £200,000, rising to around
£500,000 if it has an acre or two of land. Ex-council houses fetch
around £160,000 to £200,000. It is worth noting that in the villages to
the north of Market Harborough you might still find old manor
houses which make very compact, manageable homes. For six or
seven bedrooms, a few acres of land and stabling, you would pay
around £1m.

Close to Foxton is **Gumley**, a tiny one-street village on a hill. There
is a pub, but no shop or school. Many of the villagers own horses and
have farming interests. Property rarely comes on the market and
price depends on the quality of the view. You might find a two-
bedroom Victorian brick cottage for £170,000, or a modern four-
bedroom house for £325,000.

Journey: 71 min
Season: £5792
Peak: 4 per hr
Off-peak: 4 per hr

LEICESTER This gutsy, modern Midlands city is not likely to woo
the heart of too many London commuters though it is very
conveniently placed close to the M69, M6 and M1. Its prosperity was
built on hosiery, then on the mass production of boots and shoes,
and more recently on engineering and computing. The city has
cleverly married public and private spending to good effect, and
private developers have turned former warehouses and factories into
fashionable lofts and flats. For example, in the Pick Building, where
army uniforms were made, a one-bedroom apartment can be bought
for around £145,000, two bedrooms for just under £200,000. There is
a large student population from both Leicester and De Montfort
universities, and the fact that 32 per cent of the population is non-

white means that the city is culturally fabulously varied. This is the land of steam, antiques and agricultural fairs, but also the land of many cultures, where the Caribbean Festival in August attracts 60,000 people and the Hindu celebrations of Diwali and Navratri eclipse those of anywhere else in Europe. The Leicester covered market is renowned for its cheeses and pies.

The Golden Mile on Belgrave Road attracts shoppers from all over the world in search of silks, sarees, jewellery and spices. Leisure here means sport. For participants, the city has bowling rinks, BMX and skate facilities, tennis courts, cricket and football pitches, swimming pools and leisure centres. For spectators, there are Leicester City FC, Leicestershire County Cricket Club and the indomitable Tigers – Leicester Rugby Football Club.

Highfields, the red light district that has been cleaned up, is generally avoided. So are some of the ugly council estates, though these offer cheap housing – three-bedroom semis at £120,000. Just to the south of the city is the comparative comfort of **Stoneygate**, where there are large Victorian and Edwardian villas, some of which have been converted into flats. A three-bedroom Victorian house here will cost £275,000; a five-bedroom detached £400,000. Prices are similar in **Oadby**, which also has its share of older streets and a gentle mix of new housing.

There are some very pretty villages nearby in the Charnwood Forest and along the Wreake Valley, though perhaps some of the most unspoilt stone villages lie slightly out of reach towards Oakham. To the east is classic hunting country, where the Fernie Hunt borders with the Quorn. **Hoby** in the Wreake valley is particularly charming. In this and any of the villages close by, a four-bedroom detached period house might cost £400,000 to £500,000, while the smaller two-bedroom variety will cost £150,000 to £200,000. In the Charnwood Forest you come close to the old coal-mining area of Coalville and granite quarrying area of Mountsorrel, but the forest itself is completely unspoilt and fiercely protected. Prices of small cottages in **Quorn** are similar to those in the Wreake Valley, but large period properties with six to eight bedrooms and one and a half acres of land can be priced at £750,000 to £850,000.

'The Golden Mile on Belgrave Road attracts shoppers from all over the world in search of silks, sarees, jewellery and spices'

'To the east is classic hunting country, where the Fernie hunt borders with the Quorn'

111

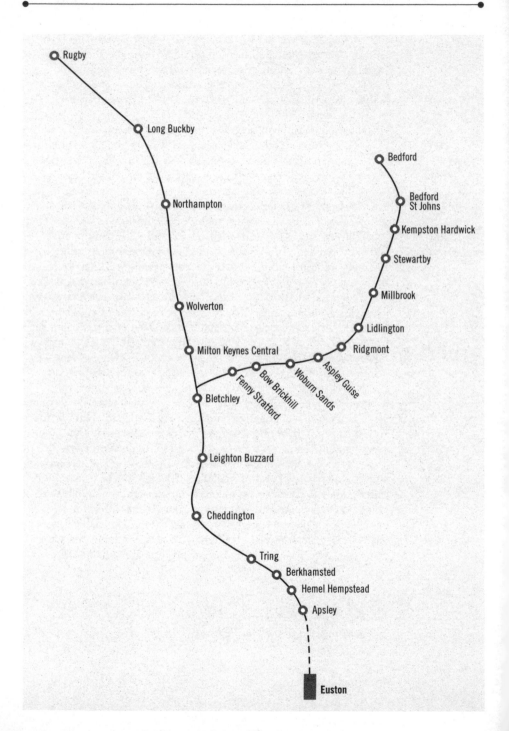

Rugby

Long Buckby

Northampton

Bedford

Bedford St Johns

Kempston Hardwick

Stewartby

Millbrook

Wolverton

Lidlington

Milton Keynes Central

Ridgmont

Aspley Guise

Bow Brickhill

Woburn Sands

Fenny Stratford

Bletchley

Leighton Buzzard

Cheddington

Tring

Berkhamsted

Hemel Hempstead

Apsley

Euston

Euston

> **Rugby** (via Northampton)

Journey: 31 min
Season: £2352
Peak: 2 per hr
Off-peak: 2 per hr

APSLEY is well-liked for its sense of identity. It has Victorian two-bedroom terraced houses at around £180,000 within walking distance of the station and a new large waterside development set round a marina on the canal where a swish two-bedroom apartment costs £190,000. **Boxmoor** is also worth looking at as a refuge from the modernity of Hemel Hempstead, to which it is now annexed. It still has a few little canalside cottages. You can buy older two- or three-bedroom cottages for around £190,000, or spend from £350,000 to £600,000 on a smart modern detached house with four bedrooms. Sunday afternoon walks might take you close to Watford to Cassiobury Park beside the Grand Union Canal, which leads into Whippendell Woods – 200 acres of beech, oak and hornbeam.

Bovingdon, to the south-west, is another antidote to Hemel Hempstead. The centre still has a village feel to it, with a green and a good medieval hall house. House prices are 10 per cent higher than in Hemel Hempstead, though there has been a lot of modern development. The market, held on Saturdays on the site of the old Bovingdon airfield, has more than 650 stalls, selling everything from home-made pies to hand-sewn clothes. "To tell you the truth, Bovingdon is a bit of a nothing place, but people who live there think they live in a village," is how one local cynic described it.

Journey: 29 min
Season: £2452
Peak: 4 per hr
Off-peak: 4 per hr

HEMEL HEMPSTEAD may not be to everyone's taste, just pre-dating Stevenage as a New Town, but it is very conveniently placed. The M1 and M25 both pass close to it, the train to London takes less than half an hour, and Heathrow is but 40 minutes away by car. It also still has rough Hertfordshire meadows on three sides of it. After all, the idea which underpinned the New Town concept was that people could combine the pleasures of town and country, and escape the overcrowded conditions of London. In the Nineties the centre was pedestrianised, making life easier for the footsoldiers of shopping. The town also has a shopping centre, sports centre, a ski slope, and an eight-screen Odeon. The old town grew up around the Norman church, with Regency and Victorian villas springing up along the Marlowes to take advantage of the distant views to the Chilterns. A two-bedroom cottage in the old town will cost £185,000. To the east you come to the sought-after area of **Leverstock Green**, where the housing is mostly post-Fifties. A four-bedroom detached home would cost between £325,000 and £400,000; a three-bedroom semi £250,000 to £320,000. There are also some very large houses set in half-acre plots in Longdean Park that fetch over £600,000. Ex-local authority housing tends to sell for a good deal less than private housing, so a two-bedroom house might be had for over £150,000.

The New Town has an all-dancing shopping centre with all the chain stores anyone could need. Large companies located here including Kodak and British Telecom. The British Standards Institute also has offices in Hemel Hempstead.

Potten End, to the north-west, is a dispersed Chiltern village with a green, a pond and the Red Lion pub. It borders on beautiful National Trust land that stretches along the spine of the Chilterns from Ivinghoe Beacon to Berkhamsted. You can buy a Thirties' detached house with a tile-hung bay window in a quiet suburban road for around £400,000. Old cottages, however, are thin on the ground. A substantial house with five bedrooms and half an acre of garden might fetch £600,000.

Chipperfield is expensive, too, though the centre has long-since been ribboned with developments built to accommodate fugitives from Watford. It is redeemed by its wooded common webbed with footpaths, and by the old village centre where the green is faced by an inn, a church and some little brick cottages. A four-bedroom detached house (most of the houses are this size or larger) would cost £500,000.

'Potten End borders on beautiful National Trust land that stretches along the spine of the Chilterns from Ivinghoe Beacon to Berkhamsted'

Journey: 32 min
Season: £2572
Peak: 4 per hr
Off-peak: 4 per hr

BERKHAMSTED is a prosperous old market town wedged in the

valley bottom, with the railway and canal running through some of the best countryside close to London. A general market on Saturdays and a flower-seller in the High Street provide constant charm and colour. The old castle, where Chaucer was clerk of works, is now little more than a few fingers of flint, but an increasing source of wonder to historians who have been studying fresh excavations. People are attracted by the thickly wooded common, towpath walks along the Grand Union Canal, and Berkhamsted Collegiate School, which includes the writer Graham Greene among its alumni.

On the steep valley slopes to the south are shoals of Victorian and Edwardian houses with large gardens, while the centre of town is packed with Victorian terraces. You can get a double-fronted, bay-windowed, three-bedroom 19th-century house for £320,000 within walking distance of the station. Canalside flats right in the centre sell for around £200,000 to £250,000 for two bedrooms. Detached three-bedroom houses built in the Sixties and Seventies cost £350,000 to £500,000. The large, individually designed, secluded houses in private roads run extravagantly from £700,000 to £950,000.

A bypass came to the rescue in the Nineties, removing much of the traffic from the centre. The busy shopping centre has all the chain stores, a Caffé Uno in the Victorian town hall, lots of restaurants and two fitness centres. There is a sports centre, and a golf course on Berkhamsted Common, the rest of which is mostly owned by the National Trust.

Little Gaddesden, to the north, is very desirable, perched on a ridge 600ft up in the Chiltern Hills. Most of the large houses and cottages face directly on to the beech woods and heathland of the vast Ashridge Estate, which is classified as an Area of Oustanding Natural Beauty. Physically the village is strung out in a linear settlement pattern; socially it is rather cliquey. You would pay £320,000 for a small two-bedroom cottage. There is a Church of England primary school, a church half a mile outside the village, and a village hall that hosts all the usual coffee mornings and clubs. The big house has been converted into a college which specialises in management courses. In nearby **Ashridge**, a discreet enclave of Twenties' and Thirties' houses with stockbroker-appeal, something with five bedrooms and three-quarters of an acre will cost over £950,000; a two-bedroom cottage £320,000 to £350,000.

Close by is **Aldbury**, a film-set village of thatched and timber-framed cottages that cluster round a large pond with stocks and whipping post. Even the smallest cottage here costs at least £200,000 and will usually sell by word of mouth. There is a general store and post office, two pubs – the Greyhound Inn and the Valiant Trooper – and a country club hotel with a golf course. Sightseers come to admire its good looks.

'The Walter Rothschild Zoological Museum, full of stuffed bears and other exotics, is typically eccentric – the family used to drive around in traps drawn by zebras'

Average: 43 min
Season: £2760
Peak: 4 per hr
Off-peak: 2 per hr

TRING station is one-and-a-half miles outside the town in a hamlet called simply **Tring Station**. The Rothschilds lived at Tring Park, and their stamp is everywhere. They gave open spaces, provided cottages, and in 1905 built the stockbroker-style, half-timbered Rose & Crown Inn. The Walter Rothschild Zoological Museum, full of stuffed bears, sloths and other exotics, is typically eccentric – the family used to drive around in traps drawn by zebras. Today Tring performs the dual role of commuter dormitory and market town. One defining feature sadly has been lost now that the thrice-yearly sheep auctions have stopped.

There are plenty of Victorian houses and new estates. A two-bedroom flat might cost £130,000; a two-bedroom Victorian cottage £180,000; a three-bedroom semi £230,000 to £300,000; a four-

Three-bedroomed
cottage, near
Tring

Journey: 48 min
Season: £2760
Peak: 3 per hr
Off-peak: 2 per hr

Journey: 44 min
Season: £2760
Peak: 4 per hr
Off-peak: 4 per hr

bedroom detached from £350,000. Tring does have a shopping centre, though people tend to use Aylesbury, Hemel Hempstead or Milton Keynes for more serious purchases. The Tring Nature Reserve's four reservoirs, which were used to store water in the 18th century, attract flocks of wintering ducks.

Two-and-a-half miles further north of Tring Station is **Ivinghoe**, a pretty village close to Ivinghoe Beacon from which you can gaze across to the chalk-hill white lion of Whipsnade Wild Animal Park. The centre of the village makes a pretty picture out of the older houses sitting sleepily on two sides of the green and the handsome watermill.

CHEDDINGTON is a quiet little village, best known for the fact that the Great Train Robbery took place at the railway bridge just outside. A farm with around 400 acres of dairy meadows could be expected to cost £5.6m. Prices are similar to Tring's and slightly higher than Leighton Buzzard's. You could buy a four-bedroom detached house for around £390,000 upwards; a three-bedroom late-Victorian cottage for £235,000 upwards.

LEIGHTON BUZZARD has swallowed whole the smaller town of **Linslade** on the west of the River Ouzel, which is where the station is located. It is prime commuter-land. Leighton Buzzard proper is an old market town with drunken timber and brick buildings, a pedestrianised main street, a twice-weekly market and a twice-monthly farmers' market. The main street is in the process of being pedestrianised. The smartest roads are Plantation Road (known as Bedfordshire's most beautiful mile) and Heath Road, studded with trees and a mix of Victorian and modern houses. Prices range between £125,000 for a two-bedroom terraced house to £500,000 for a large family house. In other parts of the town the standard price for a modern four-bedroom detached is £300,000. The town is well-padded in green belt.

Around the station in Linslade, which is more leafy than Leighton Buzzard itself, are Victorian terraces where two-bedroom houses sell for around £155,000, and three- to four-bedroom houses for around £175,000 to £220,000. There are two recently built estates, Billington Park and Sandhills. Billington Park has soaked up the grounds of a former RAF base and two-bedroom houses here cost around £140,000; three-bedrooms cost £175,000 to £200,000. At Sandhills, where building continues, a three-bedroom semi is £170,000.

Soulbury, two miles west, is one of the best examples of an open field village in north Buckinghamshire, and its proximity to the station makes it a favourite with commuters. The half-timbered and thatched houses around the green and church overlook the Ouzel valley. Other cottages are spread out between fields which are embroidered with footpaths, and there are a few modern properties at the village margin. You need a car to live here – there is no shop, post office or bus service, though there is a clubroom for the use of local societies. Houses rarely come on the market, and when they do they are expensive and will become more so when a new bypass is completed in 2005. A period three-bedroom cottage would fetch over £200,000; a four-bedroom detached house around £300,000 to £350,000.

'Between 1912 ands 1914 the suffragette Sylvia Pankhurst and her mother lived at Stewkley in a 16th-century cottage'

Further west in the Vale of Aylesbury is **Stewkley**, one of the longest villages in England, stretching a mile either side of St Michael's, its remarkably fine Norman church. Between 1912 and 1914 the suffragette Sylvia Pankhurst and her mother lived here in a 16th-century cottage. The village has a reputation for being rather superior and closed to outsiders whom it decides do not belong. A substantial five-bedroom house would cost over £450,000; an ex-council house with three bedrooms £180,000.

For a less rarefied atmosphere you could look southward to **Wing**, a busy, no-frills village with several shops, including a general store with a post office, a hairdresser and beauty salon, a fish-and-chip shop and two doctor's surgeries. Ascott House, bought by the Rothschilds in 1874, is close by, and village employment and activities have tended to revolve around the estate. Apart from the black-and-white estate cottages, there are rows of late-Victorian brick terraced cottages, plus the occasional thatched house and the usual modern estates on the fringe. A two-up-two-down Victorian terraced house might cost £140,000 to £165,000; a three-bedroom Seventies' detached £250,000; four-bedrooms £330,000.

The village has a highly-rated primary school, a secondary school, several football teams and a thriving adult education centre (upholstery and painting classes are particularly popular). The large green has footpaths and swings. The drawback is that the village is beginning to feel hemmed in by Milton Keynes and Leighton Buzzard. It is also used as a rat-run by commuters dashing for the Leighton Buzzard trains, though there is talk of a bypass by 2010.

One of the most beautiful villages in the area is **Mentmore**, a charming collection of mock-Tudor houses on top of a hill in old Rothschild country. The large village green is ringed with lime trees and offers breathtaking views in every direction. The big house is Mentmore Towers which caused a furore in 1974 when it was offered to the government and turned down. The contents were sold, important works of art went out of the country, and the house was bought by the Maharishi Foundation. In 1999 it came on the market again with an elastic price tag of £10m-£15m which dropped to £3m-£5m and it is now back in the hands of a private individual. A modest two-bedroom cottage on the crest of the hill in Mentmore village would cost over £200,000; a country house with a few acres £1.25m to £1.5m.

Journey: 50 min
Season: £2780
Peak: 4 per hr
Off-peak: 4 per hr

BLETCHLEY is the largest of the three towns gobbled up by Milton Keynes and is home to Bletchley Park, the war-time code-breaking centre, which is now open to the public daily. The town has a good shopping centre and an open-air general market is held three times a week. "The funny thing about it is that at the heart of it you will find a 16th-century thatched cottage with an acre of garden selling for around £550,000," says one local estate agent. "Where else can you find an acre of garden in the centre of town?" The rest of Bletchley has been developed in waves, reflecting the repeated housing booms of the last two centuries. You start with the thatched cottages, then come the grids of Victorian terraces selling for between £135,000 and £150,000, then the classic double bay-fronted Thirties' houses, built by Tranfield, some of which still have their sunburst stained glass.

Nearly 40 per cent of the town is council housing, which is why it tends to be looked down upon by some of its neighbours. The ex-council houses offer good value, however, with large three-bedroom semis selling for around £140,000. In the last building wave are the houses of the Eighties boom – typical mix-and match styles, with one-bedroom flats, small and large houses all mixed up together. A one-bedroom house costs just over £115,000; a four-bedroom detached with a garage over £190,000.

Padbury, to the west, is the classic chocolate-box village with half-timbered and thatched cottages, and a green swathed in leafy trees. The farms around were once owned by All Souls' College, Oxford. It has a butcher and a part-time post office in the garage, but the grocery stores have gone. There are tennis courts, a sports field and pavilion, and a village hall. Despite all this, old villagers complain that it is not the village it used to be, there has been such an influx of commuters and weekenders. Among the attractions for incomers is a highly-regarded local school for five- to nine-year-olds. People will wait years to get a house in Padbury, and pay £150,000 to £180,000 for a small semi-detached thatched cottage.

Neighbouring **Adstock** has timber, brick and thatched cottages built along narrow lanes giving it a feeling of cosiness and compactness, and there is a popular local pub, the Thatched Inn. A four-bedroom cottage with exposed beams and inglenook fireplace might sell for £400,000. For a vibrant village life, try **Thornborough**.

This is a long, thin village with a church, pub and green with pond, which is the scene of a great number of village events. There are fêtes, and a sports day followed by a barbecue in the evening. The Thornborough Sports Club caters for athletes and road runners and is a bit of a social hub. The primary school takes children up to eight years old and there is a post office which opens three days a week. When it rains the stream across the road swells and people come out to paddle. The resident ducks are none too fussy about where they lay their eggs; some of the drakes have been known to end up in village freezers. A circular five-mile walk round Thornborough watermill and the old canal is a favourite Sunday afternoon stroll. A five-bedroom detached house might cost £350,000 to £400,000; a three-bedroom, 18th-century stone-and-slate cottage £200,000 to £250,000.

> Branch line to Bedford via Fenny Stratford, Bow Brickhill, Woburn Sands, Aspley Guise, Ridgmont, Lidlington, Millbrook, Stewartby, Kempston Hardwick and Bedford St Johns

No through trains. Trains from Bedford to Bletchley, 1 per hr

Journey (from Aspley Guise): 65 min

Season ticket: £2832 (via Bletchley); £3140 (via Bedford as well)

This is the only remaining section of the old Oxford-Cambridge line and locals call it the Noddy Train because it is small and it rattles. The line is only 17 miles long, but is extremely busy since it serves villages that lack good local bus services and is heavily used by children on the school-run to Bedford. Commuters can change at Bedford for either St Pancras or Kings Cross Thameslink. Or they can go to Bletchley and change for Euston, which is most people's preferred choice. None of the stations along the line have car parks, nor are they manned. Information is Tannoyed from Bletchley to the individual platforms, and tickets are bought from the guard on the train. Season tickets to Euston, St Pancras or Kings Cross Thameslink are available from Bletchley or Bedford.

People living in the eastern suburbs of Milton Keynes tend to use the first two stations, **Fenny Stratford** and **Bow Brickhill**, rather than drive to Milton Keynes Central. Fenny Stratford is mainly Victorian, and you would have to pay over £130,000 for a three-bedroom house here. Bow Brickhill sprawls along a steep hillside reputed to have been a favourite haunt of Dick Turpin. Woodland has been cleared to make way for golf courses. It is an old village, with a beautician and a pub, The Wheatsheaf, but lies on a very busy road. Property is varied, from two-up-two-downs at around £150,000, to four-bedroom Sixties' houses at around £250,000 to £300,000.

House style in the South Midlands

The least attractive part of the region is Bedfordshire. It is blanketed in clay, which has been made into huge quantities of yellow and orangey-red bricks over the years. Industrial farming has done its worst and the clay-clogged, hedgeless fields only rarely erupt into pretty village scenes. Northamptonshire has long been under-rated by London commuters, though it is peppered with lovely limestone houses. Near Collyweston the houses are roofed in stone slates, with gabled bay windows and double stone chimney-stacks.

The stone turns pale and grey as you travel east. Pantiles for the roofs were brought from eastern ports up the rivers Welland, Nene and Ouse.

Woburn Sands has its own distinct identity, with a small High Street for day-to-day needs, and wonderful walks within five minutes of the centre in the Duke of Bedford's woodlands. There are a several fashion boutiques, restaurants, a butcher, doctor's surgery and medical centre, tennis courts, a cricket ground and a lower and middle school. You could buy a small late-Victorian house for £190,000, but a four- or five-bedroom Victorian house would be likely to fetch £350,000. Local activities include football teams, bowls and village fairs. **Aspley Heath** (within reach of Woburn Sands station) is where people from Woburn Sands aspire to move, since it has spacious houses set in large gardens with good views. It is known locally as millionaires' row, but you might sneak into a small cottage along here for £250,000.

'Aspley Heath is known locally as millionaires' row, but you might sneak into a small cottage here for £250,000'

Woburn itself (also within reach of Woburn Sands station) is a beautifully preserved Georgian town, best known for its proximity to Woburn Abbey and popular with golfers. It has a wine bar, several antiques shops and restaurants. Very few houses are freehold since the older they are, the more likely they are to be tied to the estate. The occasional four-bedroom modern house might come on the market for around £450,000; or you might find an ex-council three-bedroom semi for around £230,000. It does get cluttered in summer with tourists visiting the Abbey and its Wild Animal Kingdom.

For a sedate, select and expensive village, you would look at **Aspley Guise**. Middle-class Victorians regarded it as an "inland Bournemouth", but modern estate agents like to describe it as "the *Darling Buds of May* of Milton Keynes". It is very traditional. People smile and say good morning to each other, and they bother to keep the village tidy. There is a shop-cum-post-office, a hotel and the tiny railway station. People pay a lot to live here and then stay a long time. A two-bedroom Victorian terraced house would cost over £180,000; a modern four-bedroom house £350,000. Residents hunt and fish and go to church. The finest house in the village is Aspley House, believed to have been built by an assistant to Wren, or perhaps even by Wren himself. **Eversholt** (within reach of Aspley Guise), on the other side of the Woburn Estate, is typical of the

Duke of Bedford's estate in that the rows of cottages have no front doors. It is said that the Duchess didn't like to see people gossiping. A rectory with five or six bedrooms and four acres might cost over £1m.

Ridgmont is a typical Bedfordshire estate village with cottages built in two styles. There are two-up-two-downs with leaded lights that might sell for £250,000; and three-bedroom terraced houses, built in distinctive red brick in the late 19th century. A five-bedroom barn conversion recently sold here for £625,000. A by-pass is planned to relieve through traffic, but motorway noise can be a problem.

Lidlington is another estate village where the Duke of Bedford sought to muzzle the gossips by building houses without front doors. It has a general store and two pubs, one of which, The Green Man, doubles as the village post office on weekday mornings. Property prices are similar to those in **Millbrook**, which is little more than an old hamlet built for farm workers, with a pub and a golf course. The wooded valley near the church is supposed to have inspired John Bunyan's Valley of the Shadow of Death in Pilgrim's Progress. A two-bedroom cottage with a courtyard garden might be bought for £120,000; the odd four-bedroom modern house, built to plug the gaps, might fetch between £240,000 and £375,000. Watch out for cars going at break-neck speed as the lanes are sometimes used as a proving ground by car manufacturers.

Stewartby is dominated by its brickworks, which emits fumes the locals say they cannot smell. It was built as a model village in the Twenties by the Stewart family, owners of the brickworks, as a gesture of concern for their employees. The village was extended in the Thirties and Fifties, and a worked-out quarry was flooded to create a lake for watersports within a landscaped country park. A three-bedroom semi here would sell for around £175,000; a two-bedroom house for £120,000. **Kempston Hardwick**, the next station along the line, is given mainly to light industry and has very little housing.

At **Bedford St Johns** you have reached the southern suburb of Bedford and the nursery slopes of the local housing market. Here first-timers can start out with a three-bedroom Victorian terraced house at over £100,000, or a semi from £125,000. Something newly-built with two bedrooms and a garage starts at £120,000, with three it rises to £155,000. For Bedford itself, see page 104.

'Stewartby was built as a model village in the Twenties by the Stewart family, owners of the brickworks, as a gesture of concern for their employees'

> Continuation of main line

Journey: 41 min
Season: £3216
Peak: 6 per hr
Off-peak: 6 per hr

MILTON KEYNES CENTRAL The train service to Milton Keynes station is so good that it has a vast catchment area stretching all the way to Daventry (see, page 126). It has some of the newest rolling stock, makes an effort with punctuality, and the trains run so frequently that you hardly need bother with the timetable. Parking, however, is fairly chaotic, with vehicles silting up the side roads rather than paying for the privilege of the multi-storey car park.

To enjoy Milton Keynes properly, you need to think American. The grid pattern of wide boulevards in the centre, with one of the largest covered shopping malls in the country (three miles of shopfronts and 230 stores), plus the sea of car-parking, can make you feel as if the whole world has been turned into a supermarket. But the place is thoughtfully planned and very convenient. The 22,000-acre site, which includes Bletchley, Stony Stratford, Wolverton and 13 old villages, was conceived as a New Town in 1967 and was scheduled to contain a population of 250,000.

Housing is arranged in segments, with a mix of starter homes, three- and four-bedroom houses and retirement flats in each one, ensuring a full range of age groups and incomes. There is a large number of commuters, but many people are employed locally, too. Numerous major companies, including Abbey, Mercedes, Argos and Mobil, have moved here. The Open University gives it academic prowess, and the £19.6m lottery-funded theatre and art gallery creates a cultural life. Because the town is so young, the population is young with it.

Milton Keynes prides itself on offering cheaper housing combined with a fast commute to couples who cannot afford to live in London, but who want to maintain their jobs in the capital. English Partnership is selling plots for people to build their own new homes on, priced at over £200,000.

Much emphasis in the design of new housing has been put on energy-saving. Not all the housing is new, however. There are still places where you can find old thatched cottages (and new thatched houses, too, for that matter).

The sports centres are as new and ambitious as you would expect. The Stantonbury Campus offers indoor and outdoor leisure on a large scale. For watersports there is Willen Lake, and winter sports enthusiasts have a £60m ski-scape. Old fields have been retained to give green lungs to the town and provide playgrounds. The Great Ouse skirts the northern edge, as do the Ouzel and the Grand Union Canal which has canal boats slipping slowly along it. There are also several man-made lakes providing habitats for wildlife. North of the city centre is Linford Wood, a remnant of an ancient forest which is now laced with footpaths, bridleways, picnic sites and two wildlife reserves.

Areas are considered upmarket or downmarket according to how closely together the houses are built, and how spacious they are. Perhaps one of the most desirable is **Woughton-on-the-Green**, where the plots are large, houses are traditionally built, and the cheapest four-bedroom detached house would cost over £350,000. The **Bancroft Park** area is distinctive because the houses are built around a cleft in the landscape where an old ruin has been used to create a park. A three-storey, terraced town house here would cost around £170,000. **Willen** is also popular because it has a lake and a sense of space. Many of the houses have been built by the owners themselves, and one of these might now sell for around £350,000 (though the standard price for a four-bedroom house here would be less, at £300,000). In a typical mixed estate such as **Bradwell**, a two-bedroom late-Victorian cottage would cost £140,000; a two-bedroom new house slightly less.

One of the nicest villages in the area is **Weston Underwood**, built in greyish Cotswold stone (it lies in the northern part of the same ridge of oolite that gives the Cotswolds its character) and dating mostly from the 17th and 18th centuries. Ten miles further into Northamptonshire, the stone starts to turn red. Weston Underwood is entered through stone gates topped with pineapples. It remained in the ownership of the Throckmorton family until the Twenties, when it was sold. A small, three-bedroom stone cottage for sale would be a rare find, and would fetch over £300,000. The green, overlooked by the house once occupied by the poet William Cowper, is decorated with trees, seats and roses, and is *the* place to buy cream teas during August. There is a small zoological garden which specialises in exotic birds.

There are a few new houses, but villagers fight tooth-and-nail against development. Their cause is helped by the watermeadows around the Ouse, which make much of it unsuitable for building.

> 'Village people try to get to know new people, but the big problem is that many of them are mortgaged so heavily that they are both working and we don't see a great deal of them'

California-style home, Milton Keynes

Community spirit is strong, and is expressed through the fruit, vegetable and flower shows, and the playgroup. Local agriculture concentrates on cereals, but rape and flax are also grown. There are walks through the woods at Salcey Forest. "Village people try to get to know new people, but the big problem is that many of them are mortgaged so heavily that they are both working and we don't see a

great deal of them," says one of the older inhabitants. The local
shopping centre is at **Olney** – popular because it is as traditional as
Newport Pagnell (see below), but more rural. Property prices
therefore tend to run at 5–10 per cent higher. In the market square is
the red-brick William Cowper museum, occupying another house in
which the poet once lived with his friend Mary Unwin, who looked
after him during his lapses into insanity. The town is famous for its
pancake race, run every Shrove Tuesday from the market place to the
church. Traditionally, the winning housewife gets a silver cup and a
kiss from the verger.

Ravenstone, three miles west, is as pretty, expensive and exclusive
as Weston Underwood. The village green sprouts stone houses. **Stoke
Goldington** is the biggest in this clutch of villages, with new housing
stitched in between the old. Another handsome stone village is
Emberton, with 170 acres of country park and lakes along the River
Ouse. Houses in all of these villages sell so easily that the owners
often dispose of them privately. This entire belt is very convenient for
railway users, and only a short drive from the M1.

Five miles north of Milton Keynes is **Castlethorpe**. This is an
attractive stone village peppered with modern houses, but it is
affected by the railway line running through it. A two- to three-
bedroom cottage might cost £160,000 to £190,000; a four-bedroom
detached house around £300,000 to £350,000.

To the north-east of Milton Keynes is **Newport Pagnell**, on the
Rivers Ouse and Lovat. It has changed over the years from a lace-
making town to an industrial and commercial one. But it has
managed not to become forbidding, and new modern buildings are
sandwiched quietly between the old Georgian houses. The cinema
has been turned into a shopping arcade. A two-bedroom house in a
Victorian terraced house in the centre of town will cost around
£140,000. The most popular road is Lakes Lane, where the houses
back on to the common. A three-bedroom semi here will cost around
£220,000. There are also some huge six-bedroom houses that could
fetch up to £400,000. Green Park is the most popular of the new
estates. A modern four-bedroom detached house with a double
garage will cost over £225,000.

People living in the villages to the north of Milton Keynes might
use Wolverton station as an alternative to Milton Keynes Central.

Journey: 59 min
Season: £3216
Peak: 2 per hr
Off-peak: 2 per hr

WOLVERTON Stony Stratford is now part of Milton Keynes, but still
retains many original 18th-century buildings and seduces buyers
quite shamelessly. As a quaint old market town, with a market square
just off the High Street, it has quite a different character to the
modernity which has swallowed it. The George Hotel presents a
wobbly, black-and-white profile among the bakers, butchers and

building societies that surround it. Note that there are no superstores here. A Twenties semi with three bedrooms might cost £200,000 to £220,000, but a good three-bedroom, detached Georgian house would cost £300,000 to £320,000.

Wolverton has the local station and is packed with Victorian terraces, some of them reminiscent of Coronation Street. A three-bedroom house here would cost over £150,000, more than 10 per cent less than the equivalent house in Stony Stratford. A period, end-of-terrace, three-storey town house would cost £200,000.

To the west of Milton Keynes is **Upper Weald**, a hamlet of brick and stone. There are no shops, but you might find a small, period two-bedroom cottage for £170,000. Another worth mentioning is **Wicken**, for its stone houses, church and superb hotel with a Japanese restaurant. A 300-year-old, three- to four-bedroom stone cottage might cost around £460,000.

Further afield, on a hilltop in unspoilt countryside, is **Buckingham**, a typical market town where the stalls still appear on Tuesdays and Saturdays. It remains a pleasure to walk through its steep narrow streets and admire the old inns and almshouses. You might be able to buy a Victorian detached house with four bedrooms and a large garden for £400,000. There are a few modern estates on the edge of town, of which the most popular is Page Hill. The average price of a four-bedroom detached house here is £325,000. The town is very close to Stowe public school, once the home of the Dukes of Buckingham. The gardens, studded with follies by Vanbrugh, Kent and Gibbs, now belong to the National Trust.

'It remains a pleasure to walk through Buckingham's steep narrow streets and admire the old inns and almshouses'

Journey: 60 min
Season: £3400
Peak: 3 per hr
Off-peak: 4 per hr

NORTHAMPTON

It has to be said that Northampton is an unprepossessing town with a rugged commercial and light industrial bustle. Historically its prosperity came from the manufacture of boots and shoes, but in recent years it has widely diversified. There is a large brewing industry (the British headquarters of Carlsberg-Tetley); Barclaycard and Avon Cosmetics have a substantial presence, and more companies are moving in all the time. The 13th-century market square, in which an open-air market is still held, claims to be the largest in England. The Grosvenor Centre is a huge shopping mall with all the chain stores, while Peacock Place has the slightly more upmarket specialists. Schools include the highly-regarded private Northampton High School for Girls.

Northampton has developed over the years in a series of concentric circles. The Victorian workers' terraced houses at the centre can be picked up for between £95,000 and £200,000. In the next band come the more dignified, tree-lined streets of larger Edwardian terraces and semis, selling for £160,000 and upwards. Then the Twenties' and Thirties' semis, all pebble-dash and bay-windows, start from around £140,000. The north of the town is rimmed by an arc of Seventies' estates, where a three-bedroom house costs £145,000 to £180,000. The suburbs to the east contain the bulk of the new town development, and those to the south have the most modern estates. A detached four-bedroom house here might cost just from £185,000. This area is also closest to the M1 (Junction 15).

Northamptonshire has never been as fashionable as other counties north of London – people think of it as rather plain. There is little in the way of black-and-white building, and the villages close to Northampton tend to be built of dark brown ironstone with roofs of slate rather than thatch. To the north-west you will find some cottages built of cob (clay or earth bonded with straw), which require careful maintenance. When cob is whitewashed it often looks very much like stone.

To the north-east, towards Kettering and Oundle, you break into a belt of bleached limestone. Being closer to East Anglia, the houses here will sometimes be thatched in Norfolk reed. Or they may have Collyweston slates, which are not slate at all, but slivers of very dense, light-coloured limestone.

Due west is **Daventry**, another small market town that has kept its head. It was once a coaching stop on the road to Holyhead; today it has an international railfreight terminal with links to Europe through the Channel Tunnel. Commuters have long been attracted to it, not only from London, but also from Birmingham and Coventry, drawn by the M40 extension. There are plenty of no-frills Sixties' estates, where prices are 5–10 per cent lower than they are in Northampton.

Just to the south-west of Daventry is the village of **Badby**, whose 700-year-old woods are famous for bluebells and beeches. The Knightley Way footpath, which runs for 12 miles to Greens-Norton, touches the western edge of the woods, which are a designated Site of Special Scientific Interest. The village itself is built in stone and slate, though there is the occasional thatched roof. The local thatched pub, The Windmill, is one of three buildings in the village which date from before 1500. There is a post office and a general store, a primary school and a village hall where the Brownies, Guides, WI and Horticultural Society meet. Within a mile you can climb to the highest point in Northamptonshire, Arbury Hill, whence you can see the Malvern Hills. Four miles south-east of Daventry is the sizeable village of **Weedon Bec**, which has the frustrating disadvantage of having the railway running through it without a station to compensate. It has a similar range of housing and prices to Long Buckby (see page

'Daventry has plenty of no-frills Sixties' estates, where prices are 5–10 per cent lower than they are in Northampton'

Contrasting terraced houses, Northamptonshire

Schools in Warwickshire, Northamptonshire, Lincolnshire and Peterborough

Rugby has the public school which gave its name to the game. It now takes both girls and boys, boarding and day. It is not to be confused with Rugby High, the academically excellent grammar school for girls, which is down the road in Bilton. Another high-scoring school is Lawrence Sheriff for boys.

Warwickshire has two other high spots, Stratford-upon-Avon and Warwick (both within reach of Leamington Spa station), each with a matching pair of high-performing independent schools. Stratford-upon-Avon has the Stratford-upon-Avon Grammar for girls and King Edward VI for boys, while Warwick has King's High for girls and Warwick School for boys, as well as Myton comprehensive as a good local state school.

In Northamptonshire, Northampton itself has a good choice of public and private. The state schools include Guilsborough, Northampton for boys and Campion School (mixed); the non-selective schools include Bosworth Independent College and Quinton House; the independent schools include Northampton High for girls, Northamptonshire Grammar for both sexes and Wellingborough, which is co-educational day and boarding.

Oundle has the independent day and boarding Oundle School for boys and girls, and the Prince William co-educational comprehensive, to which children are bussed from all over the region. Good comprehensives include Southfield School for Girls and Bishop Stopford at Kettering.

King's School in Peterborough manages to be a kind of hybrid, because of the cathedral; it is a co-educational comprehensive with a good academic record and has boarding facilities for choristers.

Venture into Lincolnshire and you will find a host of high-performing grammar schools in Grantham and Lincoln and most of the towns throughout the area.

128), the next stop down the line. **Harpole** is closer to Northampton, and only just off the M1 at Junction 16. A vicarage-sized house here could cost from £500,000, though you might pick up a little Victorian terraced house for £155,000. Just along the road, on the south bank of the River Nene, is **Kislingbury**, a pretty stone village with some thatched roofs and relatively unspoilt, though there is some new housing. Prices are similar to Harpole. A four-bedroom, detached Victorian house in good condition will fetch around £335,000.

If you want town life, but find Northampton itself too depressing, then you might consider looking south-west to Towcester. It isn't as pretty as Buckingham and it has a large belt of new housing on one flank, where a four-bedroom three-reception-room house costs £250,000. The central focal points are the square and Town Hall. Towcester racecourse and Silverstone circuit are nearby. Off the main street, two- to three-bedroom Victorian terraced houses sell for £128,000, and there are a few large, detached Victorian houses that fetch £350,000.

Roade is perhaps plainer still, offering a mix of traditional Northamptonshire stone, Victorian terraced houses and Sixties' estates. It is popular with London commuters because they have a choice of station – Northampton or Milton Keynes – or they could opt to take the car down the M1. Property prices are slightly higher than those in Northampton.

East of Northampton you could look at **Earls Barton**, which has a church with a remarkable Saxon tower, thought to be the finest in the country. Built of plaster in four tiers, it has inaccessible doorways on the second tier. The village has blown up into a small town. It has the Barkers shoe factory with a shoe museum in the grounds. The fact that it is a whisker away from the A45 makes it very convenient for people working in Northampton or Wellingborough (see page 106), where the boys' public school is situated. A small, Victorian terraced house would sell for over £100,000; a detached house with four bedrooms would fetch £170,000 to £250,000.

Journey: 86 min
Season: £3440
Peak: 1 per hr
Off-peak: 1 per hr

LONG BUCKBY Having grown up around the railway, canal and A5, the attraction of Long Buckby is good communications rather than charm. With a strong Victorian core and a plethora of Seventies' estates, it stretches for one-and-a-half miles and contains a population of more than 5000. A four-bedroom detached house might cost £225,000, but something grander in a landscaped garden could reach £350,000. An old rectory in the area would cost £750,000, but it would be a rare find. The cheapest houses are Victorian cottages selling for around £100,000.

Journey: 60 min
(86 min Silverlink)
Season: £5228 all
operators; £4028
Silverlink only
Peak: 3 per hr
(Virgin); 1 per hr
(Silverlink)
Off-peak: 2 per hr
(Virgin); 2 per hr
(Silverlink)

RUGBY has never attracted architectural plaudits, but it has managed to develop a certain vigour in the last few years and at night it buzzes with restaurants, nightclubs and bars. The old industrial base has been replaced with a more commercial one. Commuters should be aware that Railtrack is committed to a multi-million pound improvement programme for the station. Rugby is best known for the boys' public school, used as a model for *Tom Brown's Schooldays*, where the eponymous ball game began in 1823 and whose former pupils include the poets Rupert Brooke and Matthew Arnold. A Home Of Rugby Football Visitor Centre has opened opposite the school and Gilberts rugby football manufacturers are still going strong.

Small houses for first-time buyers in the centre of town sell at around £100,000. There is also cheap property in the **Brownsover** area. If you can overcome the stigma attached to Brownsover, you could buy a three-bedroom semi for £130,000. The more upmarket areas are **Hillmorton** and **Bilton**, where you could find a dignified three-bedroom semi for £130,000, or you could pay £200,000 to £300,000 for four bedrooms on a new development. In Bawnmore Road, Bilton, property becomes more expensive, rising to £350,000. In Hillmorton Road, Hillmorton, there are some substantial houses built in the Thirties, some of which are very close to the town centre, for which you could pay up to £250,000 for a four-bedroom detached.

Living to the south of Rugby is thought to be slightly better than living to the north. Its most salubrious suburb is **Dunchurch**, a village two miles from the centre which has a dozen black-and-white timbered houses, as well as large, new, detached four-bedroom houses which sell for around £400,000. There are also some period two-up-two-down cottages that fetch around £160,000. Second best is **Clifton upon Dunsmore**, to the north, which again has a villagey feel to it, though the houses tend to be smaller. A two-bedroom terraced cottage will cost £130,000.

For a proper village you need to look south-east to **Ashby St Ledgers**, one of the last good Northamptonshire thatch-and-stone villages before the more industrial Midlands takes over. It is remarkable in that it was an estate village, built by Lord Wimbourne in 1912 and designed by Lutyens. Development was so tightly controlled that there are only 44 houses in all – the tradition was that two new houses were built every time the lord of the manor died. There is an old barn on the green that serves as the village hall. Since the Wimbournes left, the village has changed hands three times. There is a strong community spirit among the old villagers and a pub which strains at the seams. The half-timbered gatehouse next to the church is where Robert Catesby, one of the ringleaders of the Gunpowder Plot, is supposed to have met the other conspirators. Houses rarely come on the market, but you could expect to pay substantially more than local market values for the privilege of living here.

Birdingbury, southwest of Rugby, is another sought-after village. It has only about 150 houses, most of which are now occupied by commuters rather than the agricultural workers for whom they were built. Houses tend to be a bit more expensive because it is so close to **Leamington Spa** (see page 146). A two-bedroom period cottage might cost around £195,000. The River Leam meanders through the village, and there is a fishing club. There is a post office and a village store, but no pub, though villagers tend to use the Birdingbury Men's Club for meetings. Cricket and football are played at Marton, a mile away. There are too few young people in Birdingbury itself to make up full teams. The nearest school is at **Leamington Hastings**.

Sheer convenience makes **Kilsby** and **Barby** commuter habitats. Both are beside Junction 17 on the M1, and close to Rugby. Kilsby is unremarkable, but has a supply of four-bedroom, modern detached houses selling for around £240,000. Some properties are more lavish, built in stone with five bedrooms and selling for around £300,000.

Barby is smaller, with a stronger sense of village about it, and has a few old cob houses among the 19th-century and modern brick. A four-bedroom detached house here might sell for around £240,000. There are a few shops, a village hall, a school, and a claim to fame in that the MacLaren baby buggy was designed here in the Sixties by Owen MacLaren.

'In Ashby St Ledgers the tradition was that two new houses were built every time the lord of the manor died'

Aylesbury

Stoke Mandeville

Wendover

Great Missenden

Amersham

Chalfont & Latimer

Chorleywood

Marylebone

Marylebone
> **Aylesbury** (via Chorleywood)

Journey: 30 min
Season: £1776*
Peak: 6 per hr
Off-peak: 4 per hr
*Travelcard –
includes all
Greater London
tubes, trains and
buses. Commuters
can also take the
Metropolitan line
to Baker Street

CHORLEYWOOD The Victorian development of the railways created Chorleywood by making the lovely Chess Valley accessible from London. The M25 has done its best to make it inaccessible from anywhere. In theory it is possible to drive to Heathrow in 20 minutes. In practice the motorway is often blocked, but there are plans to widen it. Commuters tend to clog the lanes with their parking and leave the car park (£2 per day) empty.

Nevertheless, people enjoy the large 250-acre common with its nine-hole golf course and the wonderful views across the valley – so much so that they are willing to pay £300,000 for a two-bedroom cottage, or over £600,000 for a four-bedroom detached period house in what is known as the "station estate", a ring of Victorian and Edwardian houses built to take advantage of the first rail link with London. Berks Hill, South Road, Haddon Road and Hillside Road are all highly prized. The gated Loudwater estate once had the largest concentration of millionaires in the country. Prices are cheaper in the ring of Thirties' and Fifties' houses and outer ring of Seventies' and Eighties' homes. In Chalfont Lane, where large properties are set in a couple of acres, prices run from around £800,000 to £2.5m. There are a few small flats from £150,000 – a price which in Watford would buy a two-bedroom house – but first-time buyers in Chorleywood are young City types who can afford to start at £250,000. Whatever the price-range, the emphasis is on individuality; very rarely are two houses exactly the same. There are lots of stables and "No Galloping" signs on the roads. In addition to the easy half-hour journey into London, Chorleywood offers a lively

'Whatever the price-range, the emphasis is on individuality; very rarely are two houses exactly the same**'**

'Parents bemoan the passing of the schools into Hertfordshire control as this has taken them out of the grammar school system'

community, which makes good use of the public and club tennis courts, football and cricket pitches. The district beyond the village centre is very scattered. Houses trail up either side of the valley, leaving the shops in the bottom. This is inconvenient for elderly pedestrians, though there is a bus service which shuttles from one side to the other. Big shopping is done in Amersham and at the three-times-weekly market in Watford. Parents bemoan the passing of the schools into Hertfordshire control as this has taken them out of the grammar school system still retained by Buckinghamshire – the canny parents try to move to the Bucks side of the village to use the grammars all the same. Nevertheless, local schools retain a very high standard and reputation.

Journey: 34 min
Season: £1908*
Peak: 6 per hr
Off-peak: 4 per hr
*Travelcard – includes all Greater London tubes, trains and buses. Commuters can also take the Metropolitan line to Baker Street

CHALFONT & LATIMER Little Chalfont is a mini-town with a station, a strip of shops, four restaurants, a library and a number of very expensive houses in large grounds. "Too spread out to be matey," said one resident. Latimer is much prettier, with timbered cottages around a triangular green, but a two-bedroom cottage will cost at least £400,000. "It's the schools you see – the state schools are as good as the private," says one agent. The River Chess, flowing past Latimer House, offers trout fishing. Chenies, equally picturesque, was a typically feudal village owned by the Dukes of Bedford for 400 years until 1954. Be prepared to pay £400,000 in either village for even the smallest cottage. A couple of miles north-west of the station is Ley Hill, a particularly lively and friendly spot with golf and cricket on the common, a couple of nice old pubs and an infant and junior school. There are lots of local activities, including a dog club. The wooded countryside which surrounds all these villages attracts hearty backpackers who come to enjoy the spectacular walks.

Journey: 37 min
Season ticket: £2284*
Peak: 6 per hr
Off-peak: 4 per hr
*Travelcard – includes all Greater London tubes, trains and buses. Commuters can also take the Metropolitan line to Baker Street

AMERSHAM The old town of Amersham is anchored by a 17th-century market hall. The High Street, lanes and little courtyards offer a picturesque variety of architectural styles from timber-framed houses to Georgian brick, sometimes just façades on much older buildings. A plethora of old pubs recalls the town's history as a staging post on the coach road from London to Aylesbury, and traffic still comes to a halt in September when the annual charter fair is held. The smallest period cottage can cost from £250,000, with substantial houses up to £2.75m. The new part of the town, Amersham-on-the-Hill, was developed in the early 1900s when the Metropolitan Railway Company brought City merchants and West-End traders from Aldgate and Baker Street. As the last stop on the Underground, Amersham was considered the end of commuterland until motorways made more distant villages accessible. The modern housing includes ex-council flats from £130,000, three-bedroom

semis from £200,000, and four-bedroom family houses at £300,000. There are cricket, football and hockey clubs, a swimming pool, a film society and several riding stables and pony clubs. People often move here to take advantage of the local grammar schools – Dr Challoner's for boys in Amersham, and Dr Challoner's High for girls in Little Chalfont. **Chesham Bois** (the name derives from the Boyes family, owners of the manor in 1276, rather than the surrounding woods) feels itself to be set apart from the rest. It has five schools, a well-managed common, a village shop, and a powerful community heartbeat. The houses stand well apart from each other, some in an acre of land. Prices soar to £1.5m.

Chesham, only a short drive away, is also on the Metropolitan Line. The town is beguiling, cupped by the Chiltern Hills and brushed by the River Chess which flows, with an accompanying riverside walk, through beechwoods, past watercress beds and a trout farm. The shopping is good, with standard supermarkets and multiple stores, but also speciality shops, including a saddler, French baker and music shop. Sainsbury's brought with it the Elgiva Arts Centre as lucrative planning gain. Many of the shops front ancient buildings, some half-timbered 16th-century, others brick and plaster. At Christmas, the trees are cut on the Christmas tree farm and hauled by heavy horses, which is a sight to behold.

Journey: 45 min
Season: £2080
Peak: 4 per hr
Off-peak: 2 per hr

'The Lee has some of the grandest houses ever set around a tiny village green'

GREAT MISSENDEN

The narrow main street lined with houses and shops from the 15th to 19th centuries gives **Great Missenden** an intimate air and makes it an attractive small centre within easy reach of central London. It is also just a short stroll from the surrounding woods. High Street shops provide for day-to-day needs. Apart from a private tennis club, there is little entertainment for the young. "No youth club, no cinema, no transport. If you are under drinking age, forget it," said one. Roald Dahl is buried in the cemetery, and the former NatWest building is being turned into a museum dedicated to the author. A few born-and-bred residents live in the centre, where 19th-century cottage conversions with two or three bedrooms cost up to £500,000. There is a good deal of later development within walking distance of the centre. Prices range from £250,000 for a three-bedroom semi to £440,000 for a newly-built three-bedroom detached. There are also some handsome Edwardian houses set in mature grounds at around £750,000. For a Thirties' four-bedroom house in a couple of acres you might expect to pay up to £1.3m.

The surrounding villages have a pecking order headed by **The Lee**, a secluded community in the leafy uplands above Great Missenden. It has some of the grandest houses ever set around a tiny village green, and a picturesque pub. The rambling manor was for many years owned by the Liberty family, who did much to preserve the village. It is a conservation area so new development is frowned upon. There is "a little new money, but they keep the properties as they should". The area is favoured by captains of industry, writers and actors distinguished enough to need shelter from the public gaze. There is nothing under £400,000 here, and the average is £700,000 for a four-bedroom cottage.

Next in line is **Lee Common** (these villages are sometimes satirically nicknamed Lee Posh and Lee Common), separated from Lee by the Liberty Estate parkland where village shows and fêtes take place. The houses tend to be smaller, built for workers on the Liberty Estate, but it benefits from having a village shop and local primary school. A four-bedroom, semi-detached 19th-century cottage would cost around £450,000. For Thirties' houses overlooking green-belt farmland, look at **South Heath**. It has a sub-post-office-cum-stores, and a likely price-tag of £500,000 for a four-bedroom detached.

Journey: 51 min
Season: £2288
Peak: 4 per hr
Off-peak: 2 per hr

WENDOVER The beautiful National Trust countryside of the Chilterns attracts a lot of walkers to Wendover. The tables outside the bistro cafés make a picturesque setting for a refreshment stop. Part of the Icknield Way, Europe's oldest highway, runs through the broad High Street, which is cobbled and tree-lined and offers lively shops, restaurants, banks, a post office, and a library. There are many period houses, from Georgian all the way back to the enchanting thatch-and-timber row of Coldharbour Cottages, said to have been a gift from Henry VIII to Anne Boleyn. Infilling has been done carefully and blends well with the mature buildings. A two-bedroom cottage costs around £225,000. A new five-bedroom house costs £750,000. There is a first, middle and secondary school in the town and three golf courses in the neighbourhood, plus tennis, bowls and squash clubs, church societies and handsome old inns to gather in. Yet the town safeguards privacy by being too big for everyone to know everyone else's business.

At the turn of the century, **Weston Turville**, north-west of Wendover, was breeding Aylesbury ducks for the London market and making straw plait for the Luton hat industry. Its older properties are on the eastern edge of the village, but they are well outnumbered by the modern developments. Family houses range from three-bedroom semis at £235,000 to four-bedroom detached houses at £330,000 or more. There is a convenient post office and small parade of shops, several pubs, tennis courts and a golf club. The village has a combined first and middle school; older children go to grammar and secondary schools in Wendover or Aylesbury.

Journey: 55 min
Season: £2292
Peak: 4 per hr
Off-peak: 2 per hr

STOKE MANDEVILLE now is little more than a suburb of
Aylesbury. It has a general store, several pubs, a newly-opened
sports club and hotel, and a combined first and middle school, but
is largely dominated by the world-famous hospital and a lot of
Thirties' houses. These sell from £230,000 for a three-bedroom
semi to around £300,000 or more for a four-bedroom detached
house set in ample grounds.

Journey: 59 min*
Season: £2716
Peak: 4 per hr
Off-peak: 2 per hr
*Some services go
via Princes
Risborough

AYLESBURY Commercial development has overshadowed a good
deal of Aylesbury's ancient past. Its heart was cut out in the Sixties to
make way for office blocks, and large council estates were built on
the north side to accommodate London overspill. As if that wasn't
enough, the town has now been instructed to increase its population
by one third again. The payback is that lots of money and energy is
being poured into the town and the shops are to be re-vitalised and a
new civic centre and theatre created. Commuters prefer to live in the
surrounding villages. Farmhouses are the popular choice – there is no
equivalent of the Surrey stockbroker house here. For those who want
something more modern, a three-bedroom semi goes for £180,000, a
two-bedroom mid-terraced house for £130,000, a studio flat for
£70,000. Aylesbury Grammar School for boys and High School for
girls, and Sir Henry Floyd Grammar School have excellent
reputations; and there is an unusually good selection of hospitals in
the area. There is a big shopping mall, six-screen cinema, swimming
pool and the county museum with a special exhibition featuring the
author Roald Dahl.

'The future
of Dinton Hall,
where
Cromwell's
sword was once
kept, has been
a local hot
potato for
years'

Most of the surrounding villages have had their share of new
developments, but **Bishopstone** is still rural in nature in spite of the
busy roads. A timber-framed farmhouse costs around £500,000.
Dinton is blissfully peaceful and still has buildings made of witchert,
proper grass verges and no street lighting at night. The future of
Dinton Hall, where Cromwell's sword was once kept, has been a
local hot potato for years. At one time the hall was to become a hotel
with two golf courses, but it is now safely in private hands again.

To the north-west of Aylesbury, **Quainton** has all the ingredients of
the chocolate-box rural idyll: pretty thatched cottages, a broad village
green and a ruined medieval market cross, a restored windmill and a
group of 17th-century almshouses with dormers and Dutch gables.
Discriminating buyers will pay a premium to live here (it is in the
catchment of Aylesbury Grammar). Prices range from £180,000 for a
two-bedroom cottage to £300,000 upwards for a modern four-
bedroom detached. It is a horsey area.

Leamington Spa

Banbury

King's Sutton

Bicester North

Haddenham & Thame Parkway

Monks
Risborough   Aylesbury
        Little Kimble

Princes
Risborough

Saunderton

High Wycombe

Beaconsfield

Seer Green & Jordans

Gerrards Cross

Denham Golf Club

Denham

Marylebone

Marylebone
> Leamington Spa

Denham	
Journey:	26 min
Season:	£1520
Peak:	3 per hr
Off-peak:	2 per hr

Denham Golf Club	
Journey:	32 min
Season:	£1648
Peak:	1 per hr
Off-peak:	1 per hr

DENHAM and DENHAM GOLF CLUB If Denham had come straight out of the scenery department of the old Denham studios it couldn't be more picturesque. Only 18 miles from London, it is a patch of rural peace with a small green, a stream winding past wisteria-clad old brick and a village hall. It would be perfect, but for the pub visitors whose motors clog the lanes, accounting for the village's sobriquet as "the prettiest car park in Buckinghamshire". Several of the houses are well hidden behind high walls and wooded gardens, so the area is perfect ambassadorial territory, and a retreat for distinguished performers in both courtroom proper and courtroom drama. A three-bedroom semi will command £350,000. Larger houses go for £1.75m up to £5m. The other Denhams – **Higher, New** and **Denham Green** – are simply a few streets of Thirties' semis and bungalows, and Fifties' houses, where a three-bedroom semi can be had for £275,000. Denham Golf Club is little more than a railway halt for the club.

'A retreat for distinguished performers in both courtroom proper and courtroom drama'

Journey:	25 min
Season:	£1760
Peak:	5 per hr
Off-peak:	3 per hr

GERRARDS CROSS Because of its easy access to London by rail and road – M40, M25 and M4 all within spitting distance – the area around Gerrards Cross has the reputation of being one of the most expensive in the country. Definitely not for the first-time buyer, this is classic stockbroker belt with tree-lined roads and grand Victorian and Edwardian houses in half an acre or so for up to £2.2m. There are some modern infills but these, too, are big and luxurious. Five-bedroom detached houses go for £800,000 to £1.25m. Locals have fought and lost a battle to stop Tesco elbowing its way in – they feared the loss of their much-loved butcher, fishmonger and patisserie. The fashion boutiques specialise in the super-thin, there is a swimming pool and hot tub shop, BMW garage and excellent book shop. The population of commuters takes off early, leaving the centre

'Jordans is distinguished for the peculiarly English problem of cricket balls flying into gardens close to the cricket ground'

to its small-town trading, and the common to dog-walkers treading the paths once haunted by highwaymen. Properties south-east of the town should be visited several times in different parts of the day as noise from the motorways can be a problem in some roads. Golf and tennis are the main sports. Both private and secondary schools have high standards and are well liked.

South of Gerrards Cross is the village of **Fulmer**, with its wonderful foodie pub, The Black Horse, an infant school, well-kept gardens and resident famous name actress Angelina Jolie. Small, two-bedroom mid-19th-century cottages cost from £260,000. Further west is **Hedgerley**, which has two shops and pub, a strong community spirit, summer fête and active conservation group. The lanes are lined with three- to four-bedroom detached houses with large gardens, selling at around £600,000. Lots of walks can be had from the back door here.

Journey: 34 min
Season: £2032
Peak: 2 per hr
Off-peak: 2 per hr

SEER GREEN & JORDANS Seer Green hasn't a lot to say for

itself. Its old rural character has been changed by the station and the modern estate sitting in the middle. A two-bedroom cottage will cost £250,000 to £275,000. Its neighbours are more famous. **Penn**, to the west, is a long straggling village with a green surrounded by Georgian houses and 17th-century cottages in timber or brick. Views over the surrounding beechwoods are magnificent. William Penn lived here, a leading light in the Quaker Society of Friends. In the neighbouring village, **Jordans**, the Quaker connection continues with a barn built with timbers from the *Mayflower*. The village once hit the headlines because of the peculiarly English problem of cricket balls flying into gardens close to the cricket ground. This is a very cliquey area. Houses range in date from the 16th century to the 1940s, and are at a

Part 16th-century property, Beaconsfield

premium. A four-bedroom detached will command £750,000. Hopeful buyers need to be in the know to hear about a sale. Estate agents count themselves lucky to get hold of a property here. The charming village centre was designed by Fred Rowntree in 1919, with gabled brick houses set well back from a central green planted with silver birch and poplar. There is the bonus of a good primary school.

Journey: 31 min
Season: £2060
Peak: 5 per hr
Off-peak: 3 per hr

BEACONSFIELD has a dual personality and a dual population. The old town grew at the crossroads of the coaching routes to Windsor and Oxford, and is centred on a broad square and a pleasant green. Local people house-hunt in the old town for 17th- and 18th-century cottages, priced at £300,000 for a two-up-two-down terraced house. Commuters, and the many incomers who have arrived as a result of the several company relocations, prefer the convenience of the new town which has developed near the station since the 1920s. The average cost of a three-bedroom detached house is £550,000. Typical buyers are middle managers and young City strivers who move on up the scale to houses costing £3m to £5m. A good private school and state schools with high reputations add to the attractions. What used to be a strong community spirit is struggling to stay alive; it revives most energetically on 10 May for the annual fair. The Old Town has a posh furniture store, jeweller and the Loch Fyne fish restaurant and there is a very popular Tuesday market and monthly farmer's market.

Journey: 33 min
Season: £2312
Peak: 5 per hr
Off-peak: 4 per hr

HIGH WYCOMBE has left behind the wool and furniture industries upon which it was founded in order to embrace modern industries. The result is a myriad of housing from large Victorian piles to Thirties' semis and modern houses which fan out on either side of the valley within a spit of the M40. But the feeling is that it became overblown in the Eighties and that a "knock-down rather than expand" policy is a better one. Another swathe of new housing is planned on the old Ercol furniture site. One- and two-bedroom maisonettes start at £110,000, and there are plenty of starter homes for first-time buyers in the £130,000 bracket. At the upper end of the scale, a four-bedroom detached will cost £350,000. The smart places to be are on the fringes of the town in Downley, Daws Hill and Loudwater. There is a variety of schools with excellent reputations, including Wycombe High for girls, John Hampden and the Royal Grammar for boys, and the famous Wycombe Abbey public school for girls. A new arts complex was opened in 1993 with the Swan Theatre, which attracts celebrity shows acts and pre-London runs.

Sought-after villages are to the west and include **Lane End**, which has a pretty, cottagey High Street with a pond, and **Stokenchurch**, where 18th-century brick-and-flint houses start at £300,000 for two bedrooms. Both villages have basic shops and post office, and a range of modern housing from £180,000 for one-bedroom cottages to £275,000 for a family detached. Farms and smallholdings in this area can run into millions of pounds.

Journey: 54 min
(41 min peak)
Season: £2472
Peak: 2 per hr
Off-peak: 1 per hr

SAUNDERTON

Though Saunderton itself is not much more than a station surrounded by small housing estates, it is the most convenient station for some of the prettiest villages in the area. To the west in an area of outstanding natural beauty is **Bledlow**. A compact collection of thatched cottages with a few modern arrivals, it dozes beneath Wain Hill, site of one of the two huge turf-cut crosses in the county. No further building is allowed at present because of its conservation status. There is a village hall and a pub, but no post office or shop. Young residents take their children a mile down the road to Longwick junior or to secondary school in Princes Risborough.

Nearby **Lacey Green** is a sprawling village with a popular school, and an ancient windmill run by The Chiltern Society. Life is convivial and centres around the two pubs and busy village hall. A lot of new housing overshadows the few cottages, and the whole area is less cottagey than you might expect. If you can find something small with two bedrooms it will cost £195,000. Many houses are large, detached and swimming in ample grounds. A restored, period four-bedroom house would cost £825,000. The window dressing to look for is the superb view over the Vale of Aylesbury. Unlike other areas, where houses in outlying districts cost more than they do in town centres, prices in the villages around here vary little from those in Princes Risborough.

Journey: 43 min
Season: £2548
Peak: 4 per hr
Off-peak: 3 per hr

Converted barn, near Princes Risborough

PRINCES RISBOROUGH

A pleasant market town with the relaxed feel of an overgrown village, Princes Risborough High Street has a small market house in the centre and is an attractive place to shop and stroll. But it is abandoned for the capital each day by at least half its population. Human-scale architecture is here in plenty – there are no large modern estates, but a few mellow 16th- and 17th-century houses set along little roads and cul-de-sacs. There are some Victorian terraced houses, not always in the best locations, but costing from £225,000. Thirties' to Seventies' detached family houses cost from £230,000 for four bedrooms. Local schools take children through from toddler to late-teenage, and local clubs include tennis and bowls. The most prestigious area is **Whiteleaf**, right on the flank of the Chilterns. It has a few cottages and a pub and a regiment of expensive houses with large grounds and paddocks, for which you should expect to pay at least £650,000. These tend to be owned by business people who belong to the local golf and cricket clubs.

> Line to Aylesbury

Journey: 61 min
Season: £2596
Peak: 1 per hr
Off-peak: 1 per hr

MONKS RISBOROUGH No longer separated from Princes Risborough, but rather a suburb of it, Monks Risborough has a few relics of its medieval past and some pretty cottages, but now consists mainly of Sixties' and Seventies' semis and plenty of bungalows which attract retired people. An estate bungalow costs around £235,000; a roomy three-bedroom semi around £240,000.

Journey: 65 min
Season: £2616
Peak: 1 per hr
Off-peak: 1 every 2 hrs

LITTLE KIMBLE Many of the villages in this area sprawl rather than huddle, and Little Kimble is typical. Its straggling lanes contain a mix of properties from a few listed 17th- and 18th-century cottages to 1900s' and modern houses. The station house itself is a private dwelling. Prices for average-sized houses can be around 10 per cent above those in Princes Risborough, but there are also a few at around £650,000 with large grounds and paddocks (Kimble Races is an annual event). Although there is no focal point, there is a pub, an Indian restaurant and a village hall. With only 800 on the electoral roll, most locals would be able to call "I spy strangers" when prospective buyers come knocking. Local activities include the WI, a Country and Western club and a horticultural society which knows where to look for the rare wild orchids which bloom on the old rifle range. There is also the British Legion. Walks in the area take in Chequers and Ellesborough church, where successive prime ministers have offered the occasional photo opportunity.

'In Little Kimble, the horticultural society knows where to look for rare wild orchids'

AYLESBURY See **Marylebone to Aylesbury** line (page 135).

> Continuation of main line

Journey: 51 min	
Season: £2648	
Peak: 3 per hr	
Off-peak: 2 per hr	

HADDENHAM & THAME PARKWAY

Whichever way you look at it Haddenham is a pretty big village or a big, pretty village, now split into two, the old and the new. The Sheerstock estate of two-, three-, four- and five-bedroom houses, priced from £160,000 to £400,000, is the new. The southern end is the old. Here the green and duckpond make an acknowledged beauty spot, popular with television crews filming *Midsomer Murders* and Agatha Christie dramas. There are walls made of witchert (the Saxon word for white earth) topped rather surprisingly with Spanish tiles, enclosing little lanes leading to attractive Georgian and Victorian houses. Three-bedroom cottages cost around £300,000. This is a great place for people to retire to. Otherwise social life is divided into an energetic tennis-playing set who live on the new side, the old Haddenham agricultural and arts set and new people form the social sandwich filling. Lots of residents commute to London on the M40. There are plenty of local sports, arts and activity clubs, and a village hall where it all happens.

'Haddenham is an acknowledged beauty spot, popular with television crews filming Midsomer Murders and Agatha Christie dramas'

Thame is distinguished by an unusually wide high street, which the annual fair turns into a medieval parade ground against a backdrop of houses from the 15th century to the present. There are plenty of three- and four-bedroom houses at around £180,000 to £400,000. It has three primary schools and good sporting facilities – football, rugby, squash and snooker – and a sports and arts centre. Some commuters prefer to drive to Princes Risborough for the better choice of early and late trains into London.

West of the A418 between Thame and Aylesbury are three sought-after villages. **Cuddington**, which has a history of being elected best-kept village in Buckinghamshire, has a green and lots of old thatch. Two-bedroom cottages start at £300,000. **Chearsley** has a green, pub, shop and church, but no longer a school. There is a pretty set of thatched cottages and prices are high. **Long Crendon** is considered to be the *crème de la crème* of the area. Once the centre of the needle-making industry, it has a picturesque High Street running off the market square, an attractive green, a primary school and several interesting pubs. It is the sort of place that everyone dreams of calling home, and properties here attract a 10–20 per cent price premium. The majority of people who live in the area work in Oxford.

Journey: 62 min
Season: £3008
Peak: 4 per hr
Off-peak: 2 per hr

BICESTER NORTH

Bicester has a long history and the Bicester with Whaddon Chase Hunt dates back to the 1700s. Despite an old market square (triangle, rather) and some 16th-century gabled houses, it stopped being a period piece when the army depot was established in 1941. The town is mainly regarded as a modern provider of very large housing estates with an edge-of-town factory-outlet shopping centre. One-bedroom starter homes are priced at around £110,000; two-bedroom houses around £135,000.

Villages to the west of Bicester, including Steeple Aston (see page 175) and the **Bartons (Middle** and **Steeple)**, have returned to rural tranquillity following the decommissioning of the USAF base at Upper Heyford, but now fear that large quantities of new housing will fill the gap. Meanwhile, the stone-built village of **Kirtlington**, where Christopher Wren's father is buried, has retained is popularity because of its polo park and stud farm. It has a village green with a pond, a post office stores, a couple of pubs and a junior school. New developments here are stone-built in cottage style to blend with the older houses. The larger four-bedroom detached properties cost £300,000 to £350,000. Small houses start at £200,000. An 18th-century cottage with two bedrooms would be likely to fetch more. "People move here and don't move out again," says one local.

Villages north of Bicester are good value. For the price of a three-bedroom house closer to Oxford you will get four bedrooms in **Stratton Audley** (Stratton meaning enclosure on a Roman road, and Audley from the family which built the 14th-century moated castle). It is a tiny village where the houses group around the central green, but fears are mounting that the buffer which keeps its separate from Bicester – the land owned by RAF Bicester – will be sold off and used for new development. For £350,000 you could buy a substantial four-bedroom stone period house. Prices are about the same in **Stoke Lyne**, a similarly quiet Chiltern village set in undulating countryside where people are said to keep to themselves.

Just over the county border is **Marsh Gibbon**, with houses built of local stone rather than the brick and timber more usual in Buckinghamshire. A sprinkling of low-cost housing has been built here for sale to local families. The result is a busy little place with a village pond, a primary school and a younger than average age profile. A three-bedroom detached house might be found for around £350,000.

Launton, back in Oxfordshire, is growing rapidly into a dormitory of Bicester, though the intervening railway and bypass prevent it from being swallowed completely. It has a mix of old and young in both population and property. There are quite a few modern bungalows and new estates where a two-bedroom semi costs around £180,000. Young children go the local primary. Their older brothers and sisters, in common with those from all the surrounding villages, attend secondary school or sixth-form college in Bicester.

Journey: 81 min
Season: £3400*
Peak: 1 per hr
Off-peak: 1 per hr
* Also valid to
Paddington (see
Paddington to
Leamington Spa
line, page 175)

KING'S SUTTON

A few London commuters travel regularly from King's Sutton. Others prefer to drive to Bicester, which has a more frequent service. The majority of local residents work in Banbury or Oxford. Apart from the village green, which is dotted with thatched cottages and 18th-century stone houses, the property mix is almost exactly 50 per cent old stone houses, 50 per cent council brick, which residents say makes for a good community. They take advantage of the opportunities to get together through the Playing Fields Association, small tennis club and two churches. The local baker who called three times a week to bake fresh loaves for the village has been stymied by Eurobureaucracy, but there are still three village shops, one with a post office, and three pubs. Children go to the local primary school, then to Middleton Cheney Secondary. Despite the fact that several farms and barns have been sold off for conversion, there is still a farming presence. A Georgian five-bedroom house with a staff bungalow and paddock costs £500,000; a two-bedroom bungalow with a garden £170,000.

Neighbouring **Charlton** is a one-street village with a popular pub. Pleasant stone houses cost from £175,000 for a small two-bedroom cottage. **Aynho** has pretty cottages, too, plus one or two Georgian houses priced at around £450,000 for four bedrooms. Both Aynho and **Souldern** have been badly affected by noise from the M40, but

Local stone, ex-weaver's cottage, Deddington

those who don't mind say the A41 was bad enough anyway. There are some big properties around here, hidden away in a couple of acres, and for £500,000 you could find something quite special.

Deddington, a couple of miles south-west of King's Sutton, was equal in importance to Banbury until the canals and railways bypassed it. It is officially a town, but its atmosphere is villagey and it is most sought-after. Houses and small shops gather around the spacious market place. Side roads lead off, lined with honey-coloured stone houses and cottages, many of them Grade II listed. A busy social life revolves around the primary school, the church, a variety of clubs from football, bowls and badminton to yoga and nature conservation, and there are more than 100 cottage businesses. Residents work locally as surveyors, accountants and solicitors, and the area is also popular with pilots flying from Heathrow and Birmingham. "They put a pin in the map between the two and seem to hit Deddington," says one local. Commuters have tended to drive to Milton Keynes, half-an-hour's train journey from London, but now that the Banbury line has improved they don't need to. Otherwise the M40 is close enough for convenience and has unclogged the A423 between Oxford and Banbury. Prices range from £225,000 for a two-bedroom Victorian brick cottage to £275,000 for a Grade II listed 17th-century cottage of similar size.

> '**Deddington** is officially a town, but its atmosphere is villagey and it is most sought-after'

Journey: 80 min
Season: £3412*
Peak: 4 per hr
Off-peak: 2 per hr
*****Also valid to Paddington (see Paddington to Leamington Spa line, page 175)**

BANBURY has spent a lot of time burying its past in order to make

way for a bright new future which is now bursting upon it, complete with a re-vamped shopping centre, new industries and improved rail links. House prices shot up to Oxford and Home Counties levels when the M40 arrived and its strategic position halfway between Birmingham and London could be cashed in. The new commercial business parks and light industry lie to the east. Silverstone is 15 miles away, Eddie Jordan's Jordan Grand Prix is 10 miles away and the Benetton racing team is based nearby at Enstone. The older part of the town is late-Victorian or early-Edwardian, but most properties are post World War II. Small semis sell at £160,000, but on the more prestigious western side large Sixties' houses in well laid out gardens command £500,000. Parking at the station is easy enough.

The M40 has also had a mixed effect on the villages within five miles of Banbury. To the north-west, **Warmington**, which is very picturesque, **Shotteswell** and **Mollington** have all been adversely affected by noise; but **Wroxton**, a charming village with winding lanes, thatched cottages, grassy verges and a duckpond, has been made more accessible without suffering any serious damage. Just off the A422 to Stratford-upon-Avon (handy for a shot of Shakespeare), it preserves its tranquillity and yet is only a few minutes' drive from the motorway. It has a school and a couple of pubs, but no shop –

people nip over to Horley or do their main supermarket shopping in Banbury. A small semi-detached stone-and-thatch cottage with two bedrooms will cost about £270,000; a three-bedroom detached house £375,000 or more; a four-bedroom detached £500,000.

Generally, commuting professionals tend to prefer **Bloxham**, with the result that prices here are slightly higher than in neighbouring villages. There are several 16th- and 17th-century examples built in the local ironstone and buried down pretty lanes. The village has a parade of shops, a public school and good state schools. A couple of small estates of modern houses have brought more cars which clog the centre.

Shenington, too, is a popular and pretty village, full of lovely old golden stone houses. The presence of a rubbish tip not far away does deter some househunters, although most residents feel it isn't a problem. There is also a neighbouring airfield where noisy go-karting is held, but only a few times a year. The pub has seats outside on the verge of the green, and the primary school is a high-flyer. The charming cottages nearby fetch around £350,000 for three bedrooms, while larger five-bedroom houses go for around £650,000.

Sibford Ferris, a little further south, has delightful mullioned houses with broad grass verges and a mellow blend of stone and thatch. It also has a village shop and post office and a well-respected Quaker school. Two-bedroom cottages start at £200,000. The average price for a four-bedroom period house starts at £500,000. A large seven- or eight-bedroom Queen Anne or Georgian house with stables and three or four acres will weigh in at £1m.

Journey: 89 min
Season: £3720
(also valid to Paddington)
Peak: 2 per hr
Off-peak: 1 per hr

LEAMINGTON SPA The journey to Leamington Spa is much quicker than it used to be, making it a viable commuter's haunt. In the past the people who chose to live in this spacious spa town, with its Georgian and Victorian houses and attractive riverside walks, often came because of the development of light industry between Leamington and Warwick. The delightful Royal Pump Rooms, where rich and poor once took baths and needle showers, have been restored as an arts centre, and the town now teems with designer boutiques. One of the nicest parts of Leamington Spa is the tree-lined Beverley Road, offering a mix of Fifties' and Sixties' detached houses which sell from around £300,000 unmodernised, up to £425,000 restored. Northumberland Road is the most prestigious street, in which the price for a good-sized Twenties' house is £500,000, rising to £750,000 for the best.

Those who are willing to drive across five miles of farming landscape to Leamington station settle in **Harbury**, a lively village with a good community of mixed ages and a cosy, clustered centre near the church and pubs. There are frills of modern housing around it where small houses start at £180,000. Larger period cottages go for £400,000 to £500,000.

Neighbouring **Bishop's Itchington** is known in estate agency terms as Harbury's poor relation. A a two-bedroom terraced house here goes for £115,000; a detached house for £200,000. **Bishop's Tachbrook** has a little row of shops, but the few thatched houses are well outnumbered by Sixties' and Seventies' red-brick estates. A two-bedroom terraced house will be in the region of £120,000; a detached family house with four or five bedrooms about £245,000. The higher price reflects the bonus of easy access to the extended M40, which tends to attract young professionals.

'The delightful Royal Pump Rooms, where rich and poor once took baths and needle showers, have been restored as an arts centre**'**

Bristol Temple Meads

Bristol Parkway

Bath Spa

Freshford

Avoncliff

Bradford-on-Avon

Trowbridge

Chippenham

Kemble

Swindon

Didcot Parkway

Cholsey

Goring & Streatley

Pangbourne

Tilehurst

Reading

Henley-on-Thames

Twyford

Wargrave   Shiplake

Cookham   Marlow

Maidenhead

Furze Platt   Bourne End

Windsor &
Eton Central

Taplow

Burnham

Slough

Langley

Iver

Paddington

Paddington
> Reading and Bristol

Journey: 28 min
Season: £1476
Peak: 3 per hr
Off-peak: 2 per hr

IVER This is a lovely village of 16th- and 17th-century cottages clustered around the church, with tree-covered lanes and Iver Heath nearby. Train frequency has improved, but people often use Slough where there are six trains per hour to London. A country cottage with three bedrooms and a small garden will cost £180,000 to £250,000, rising with the amount of land. There are one or two blocks of exclusive flats where you will pay around £180,000 to £270,000 for two bedrooms.

Journey: 31 min
Season: £1604
Peak: 4 per hr
Off-peak: 2 per hr

LANGLEY is really an extension of Slough, with lots of new housing developments. At its heart is the very popular 15th-century pub, the Red Lion, a Norman church and a rare 17th-century church library. The 17th-century almshouses provide a monastic touch. Houses range from £185,000 for a three-bedroom semi on a new estate to £400,000 for a four-bedroom detached.

Journey: 18 min
Season: £1720
Peak: 6 per hr
Off-peak: 6 per hr

SLOUGH The huge trading estate – supposedly the largest in Europe – is the backbone to Slough, but it doesn't make it pretty to look at. Efforts have been made to improve the quality of life. The use of security cameras in the centre at night has created the conditions for nightlife to thrive. The twin peaks of shopping are contained in the Observatory and the Queensmere shopping malls, while The Village has the specialist shops. There is also a leisure centre and a sports centre, a 10-screen cinema and an ice-rink. There is a great mix of council housing and private modern estates. Windsor Meadows is particularly sought-after by airline staff because it is ideal for the M4 and Heathrow. A one-bedroom studio starts at around £95,000. On the whole, Slough vies with Reading to provide the cheapest properties in Berkshire. A small Victorian two-bedroom terraced house would cost £150,000; a larger four-storey town house might fetch £270,000. The large Asian population has settled in certain areas, particularly Chalvey.

The train service to Paddington is astonishingly good. There are several fast non-stopping trains an hour, and a handful of stopping ones. The station has a pavilioned roof reminiscent of a French château, and there is good parking.

The thing to watch out for in this area is how close you are to a Heathrow flight path. **Colnbrook**, two miles east, is affected by low-flying planes, but has a good old pub called The Ostrich Inn and you can pick up a listed, detached four-bedroom house or a barn conversion for £300,000 to £600,000. At the bottom end of the market, you could get a studio flat for £75,000 to £90,000. Two miles north, the landscape becomes suddenly rural and a village such as Stoke Poges feels very out-of-the-way. The poet Thomas Gray is supposed to have written his famous *Elegy* in the garden graveyard of the 13th-century St Giles Church, where he is buried. **Stoke Poges** is a cheaper version of Gerrards Cross, with a small parade of shops and a population peppered with both elderly and young stockbroker types. You might pay £425,000 to £599,000 for a four-bedroom period house in one of its tree-lined avenues. At the lower end of the market you could buy a three-bedroom house on one of the small Sixties' estates for £300,000. It's the kind of place where a couple of decades ago you could have built a new house in your garden and still have had an acre to spare. Sunday afternoon walks are taken at Langley Park and Black Park.

Modern estate houses, south Buckinghamshire

Branch line to **Windsor** and **Eton Central**

Trains to Slough: 3 per hr (peak)/2 per hr (off-peak)

Journey: 26 min

Season: £1892

No through trains. Change at Slough. See also Windsor & Eton Riverside on the **Waterloo to Reading** line (page 195)

> Continuation of main line

Journey: 29 min
Season: £1840
Peak: 4 per hr
Off-peak: 2 per hr

BURNHAM has quite a few modern shops but still manages to cling on to some of its 15th- and 16th-century charm. The centre is quaint and busy with a cobbler, two butchers and baker and a campaign is afoot to start a farmers' market. A three-bedroom period detached house might cost £300,000 to £350,000. North Burnham is the place to be. It leads to Burnham Beeches with its huge pollarded beech trees and winding lanes – a 600-acre remnant of a forest which once covered the Chilterns. Here a house with five bedrooms in an acre of land will cost £800,000 to £2m. The area attracts successful stockbrokers, bankers and the odd television presenter.

The northern flank offers some classic Buckinghamshire villages. **Farnham Royal** and **Farnham Common** are strung between Beaconsfield and Slough. Huge houses set in several acres cost £1m. Horse-riding is the popular pastime for wives left at home by day while their husbands are in the City. Both these little villages are right on top of Burnham Beeches.

For less expensive housing you have to look at somewhere like **Cippenham**, where Lovell Homes is building an ever expanding community of new homes. It has a Asda and other stores and everything from one-bedroom starter homes for £120,000 to three-bedroom detached homes for £250,000 to £265,000.

The station is used by those who work on the Slough Trading Estate as well as commuters to London. It has only a small car park.

Journey: 31 min
Season: £1956
Peak: 2 per hr
Off-peak: 1 per hr

TAPLOW This is where you start to find wonderful riverside villages with modest-sized cabin cruisers moored to the banks and anglers hunched beneath their green umbrellas. Taplow has lots of old cottages and a modern church with a distinctive copper spire. You can see Cliveden House, formerly the home of Lady Astor, in the distance on the cliffs above the river. Enormous houses with gardens running down to the Thames go for well over £1m, though in the village itself there are two-up-two-down Victorian cottages for around £250,000. There are also lots of flats. A one-bedroom converted flat in a large Edwardian house will fetch £150,000. People who live here might prefer to go to Maidenhead or Slough to pick up the faster train service and park the car more easily.

'In Taplow there are enormous houses with gardens running down to the Thames that go for well over £1m'

Journey: 33 min
Season: £2068
Peak: 4 per hr
Off-peak: 4 per hr

MAIDENHEAD is an old Thameside town with an ancient heart, small shops, and a High Street that is now fully pedestrianised. New facilities include a multiplex cinema, health club and restaurants. Just outside the centre you will find grids of reasonably pleasant turn-of-the-20th-century terraced houses. The ones with two bedrooms sell for up to £250,000. The modern developments are on the south-western outskirts, where three-bedroom semis cost £300,000 or more. The most sought-after areas, such as Maidenhead Bridge and Boulter's Lock, are close to the river. Here the houses are large, detached late-Victorian, with big gardens and wealthy owners who can afford to pay £600,000 to £700,000 for four bedrooms. A short walk along the Thames is Brunel's Sounding Arch, a remarkably long brick viaduct built in 1838.

Bray, scarcely two miles out of Maidenhead, is a tiny picturesque village on the lip of the Thames and one of the costliest places to live even in this expensive area. It combines closeness to London with a good train service. The narrow irregular streets are lined with timber-framed and Georgian houses. A two-bedroom village house will cost £300,000. Remarkably, there are two Michelin three-star restaurants here – the Roux brothers famous Waterside Inn, and Heston Blumenthal's Fat Duck. There is a clutch of resident television stars so the mere act of buying a pint in one of the two pubs can bring you up against Rolf Harris, and joining the local cricket team is likely to attract the interest of Michael Parkinson. There is hockey club and a tennis court here, too, and a post office.

Re-styled
Edwardian
house, near
Maidenhead

The Fisheries offers huge mansions in a woodland setting with a river frontage and prices running into millions. One of the things to watch for is the very occasional river flood. Just outside the village is Bray Studios, where the Hammer House of Horror films were made and short television dramas are still produced. Tourist coaches tend

to drive straight through because there is no tea-room, although tea is served on summer afternoons in the church hall. There are a few modern estates, but they are well-hidden. It is a conservation area and a regular regional and national winner of the Britain in Bloom competition. If you want to build anything new, or change the exterior of your house, you can expect heavy opposition.

Heading south you come to **Holyport**, an attractive village set around a large green with a pond with two pubs on it. This is the site of the annual village fair in early June. Cricket on the green has been stopped because too many windows got broken, but enthusiastic cricketers continue to play on their own ground elsewhere in the village. Holyport has some huge Tudor and Georgian houses, and small former estate cottages. A house with half an acre might cost £1m. The village is too spread out to have a strong sense of community, but there is an active preservation society. There are some council housing and new private estates, a handful of shops, and a primary school.

To the west is **Littlewick Green**, where the houses are built around the cricket pitch and the pub is called The Cricketers. This and neighbouring villages attract a lot of commuters – people running private businesses and staff from Heathrow. Another pretty village, still within the two- to three-mile belt around Maidenhead, is **Pinkneys Green**. It has some huge old houses that sell for over £700,000, and National Trust walks round an old brick and tile works. The first Girl Guide troop was formed here by Olave Baden-Powell in 1910. Another village worth considering is **White Waltham**. It is very rural, has a thriving primary school, a small airfield, and an active cricket club. Detached estate houses sell at £600,000 to £700,000. Then there is **Hurley**, on the Thames, with a lock, a 12th century pub and a working boatyard. A new two-bedroom cottage might cost around £279,000 to £325,000, a four- to five-bedroom period house £950,000.

> Branch line to Marlow via Furze Platt, Cookham and Bourne End

No through trains to Paddington from Marlow. There is one through train per hour from Bourne End, peak only; otherwise change at Maidenhead.

Journey: 55 min*
Season: £2236*
Peak: 2 per hr
Off-peak: 1 per hr
*From Marlow, changing at Maidenhead

The service connecting these stations to Maidenhead is nicknamed the Marlow Donkey. The train is very short and slow. The line follows the river and lifts its head out of the valleys to give good views. The area is close enough to London for people to commute by car, either on the M40 or on the M4.

Furze Platt station was built in 1937 to serve north Maidenhead, which had been taken over by light industrial development. A spread of new housing has followed in its wake over the last 20 years. At **Cookham** you are in prize countryside now grazed by commuters and television celebrities, swags of it owned by the National Trust. The snob address is Cookham Dean, up on the common, where house prices start at £250,000 for a two-bedroom semi and rise to £3m or more for a large riverside house. Cookham

Schools in Berkshire

Ascot has five girls' private schools: Heathfield, the Roman Catholic St Mary's School Ascot, Hurst Lodge, Marist Convent and St George's. For boys the dominant school is Eton, at Windsor, which can count 19 former prime ministers among its old boys, but there is also Presentation College, a good independent selective boys' school. In addition, there is Pangbourne boarding and day school for girls and boys, which has a strong naval tradition, and Wellington at Crowthorne for boys (girls in the sixth) with a strong army tradition. In Maidenhead there is Newland Girls' comprehensive.

Reading has Reading School, an unusual state day school for boys (some boarders) in that the working week extends into Saturday morning. For girls there are two independent schools, Queen Anne's boarding and day and The Abbey, as well as Kendrick Girls' Grammar. For boys there is Bradfield College public school and the Roman Catholic boys' boarding school, The Oratory.

Co-educational private schools include Leighton Park and Reading Blue Coat School (mostly boys). Little Heath at Tilehurst is a good co-educational comprehensive. Further out towards Thatcham, girls can attend Down House (boarding and day school) where first-year pupils spend a term at a château in the Dordogne.

Village is old and lovely, with chic restaurants and boutiques in the High Street. Stanley Spencer lived here, and the Spencer Gallery shows some of his works. There is a general store and an excellent butcher. The Cookham Rise area was expanded in the Fifties, close to the brick and flint station building. A three-bedroom semi here costs around £200,000; or you might find a small cottage at around £250,000. The riverside towpath provides walks and rides for ponies, but if you want to swim or do the gym then the nearest leisure centre is at Maidenhead.

The river village of **Bourne End** is just as expensive, and much of the social life revolves around sailing. The Upper Thames Sailing Club is here, and at Spade Oak Reach there is a marina with timber chalet holiday homes. These are almost impossible to get hold of and will cost around £550,000, including moorings. A more substantial, secluded riverside home, typical of the area, with six bedrooms, a boathouse and half an acre running down to the river, would sell for over £2m. A large proportion of the population commutes, but they tend to drive to Beaconsfield (see page 139) and get the train to Marylebone rather than suffer the Marlow Donkey.

Marlow is also prime commuter country. Its ancient High Street stretches down to the river and has a proper fishmonger, chocolatier, a Wednesday market and a monthly farmers' market. Burford County Combined School is a high-performer in the league tables. A two-bedroom Victorian cottage would fetch over £250,000; a three-bedroom terraced house £275,000; a three-bedroom Edwardian house £700,000 to £800,000. Large houses on the river rarely come up for sale and cost at least £2m. The west side of town is considered better than the east. At Marlow Bottom, two miles from the centre, is a huge modern estate with detached houses selling from £320,000. Since it is on the Berkshire, Buckinghamshire and Oxfordshire borders, parents can choose the local education policy that suits them. Nearby **Bisham** has the famous Compleat Angler restaurant and the Marlow Rowing Club, together with some pretty Tudor cottages, but it is rather spoilt by the heavy through-traffic into Marlow. The parish council has bought an orchard for people to play in and have picnics. Bisham Abbey is home to the National Sports Centre.

> Continuation of main line

Journey: 41 min
Season: £2424
Peak: 3 per hr
Off-peak: 3 per hr

TWYFORD is a typical small town surrounded by countryside. It has all the essential shops and is referred to locally as "the village". There are rows of Victorian terraces close to the station. Two-bedroom houses here sell for £175,000, three bedrooms go for around £230,000. The huge, tightly-packed new estate has starter homes at £125,000, up to four-bedroom detached houses at £450,000. The older, more established and expensive neighbour **Ruscombe**, with prices ranging from £350,000 to £800,000.

Waltham St Lawrence is two miles away, trapped in a rural world of its own. The price of this, in the form of a detached house with land, is over £700,000; a two-bedroom cottage is £300,000 to £400,000. Charming black-and-white cottages mix with modern houses. The village owns its own pub, The Bell, and has a general store with a post office. There is a good primary school within walking distance, as well as Brownies, playgroups, a cricket club and a silver band. The cricket team plays at **Shurlock Row**, which is rather smaller. It has a much-respected butcher and a good pub, the Royal Oak. Shurlock Row is also pretty, with a pond at the end of the main street. Prices are slightly lower than in Waltham St Lawrence.

For cheaper properties you have to look at the dense modern housing at **Woodley**, built on the aerodrome used by Douglas Bader. Here a three-bedroom detached house might cost over £235,000. At Charvil, a popular commuter dormitory, a modern three-bedroom terraced house could be had for £220,000.

> Branch line to Henley via Wargrave and Shiplake

Journey: 52 min*
Season: £2504
Peak: 2 per hr
Off-peak: 1 per hr

*From Henley, changing at Twyford. There is one through train to Paddington in the peak period (journey 48 min). For all other services, change at Twyford

'The hordes of people who now come to drink Pimms in the pink-and-white marquees give Henley an annual seizure'

Wargrave lies on a charming stretch of the Thames, and its narrow streets, trees and Georgian timber-framed houses on the river make it a rather prestigious place to live. Paul Daniels has a mansion nearby, which was seriously damaged by floods in 2003. You could get something with three bedrooms on a modern estate for between £365,000 and £500,000, but good secluded houses start at £600,000 and go up over the £1m mark. **Shiplake** is similarly expensive and exclusive. It has a number of new developments on which four- to five-bedroom detached houses cost £750,000.

The rowing regatta, held during the first week in July, has put **Henley-on-Thames** on the map. The first inter-university boat race was held here in 1829, and by 1839 it had become a recognised annual event, the story of which is told in the River and Rowing Museum. Hordes of people come to drink Pimms in the pink-and-white marquees and give the town an annual seizure. Though it remains pretty and rural, straddling the river by way of a lovely stone bridge, it has been affected by the influx of money. Two supermarkets have joined the good mix of small shops already here. The battle to keep open the old cinema (complete with organ rising up out of the floor) has been lost and it has now become a three-screen. The organ has moved to the Town Hall where it is used for concerts. Two-bedroom Victorian cottages sell for around £245,000; bigger terraced houses with no parking sell for around £300,000. Anything large with a river frontage would have a starting price of over £1m. Commuters often opt for flats with views of the river – two bedrooms might cost in the region of £300,000.

Hambledon, four miles away, is also worth looking at, if only to admire the cluster of houses around the huge chestnut tree with the village pump beneath. Film location hunters love it. The village has a church, general store and post office, cobbled pavements and a pretty little stream running through. Properties here rarely come on the market. A small cottage with no rear garden or parking might be picked up for £350,000.

Riverside residence, Henley-on-Thames

> Continuation of main line

Journey: 27 min
Season: £2776*
Peak: 9 per hr
Off-peak: 7 per hr
*Also valid to
Waterloo

READING is a significant shopping and business centre, and a university town. Its prosperity used to be based on beer (Courage), bulbs (Suttons) and biscuits (Huntley & Palmer), but now it has a much higher profile as the gateway to "silicon valley". Seven out of 10 American IT firms have bases here, including Microsoft and Oracle. The train service to London is superb – more than one every 10 minutes – as it is one of the busiest rail interchanges in the country (see also **Waterloo to Reading** line, page 206). Reading is also the terminus of the Kennet and Avon Canal, which was reopened in 1990 and offers some marvellous walks to the west.

Different areas cater for differing tastes. **Caversham Heights**, on the Thames, has a mix of detached houses, flat conversions and modern flats, and is very residential. The most expensive address is The Warren, up on a hill with river views. A two-bedroom flat in an Edwardian conversion with a mooring and garden sloping down to the river would sell for around £267,000. A large five-bedroom Edwardian house in three-quarters of an acre would sell for £800,000. Prices in this area have risen hugely. **Lower Caversham** offers mainly Victorian terraced housing with some modern infilling. A three-bedroom terraced house would cost £170,000; a modern two-bedroom flat on the river £225,000 to £280,000. **Caversham Park** village is made up of town houses built a couple of decades ago. Prices tend to hover under £170,000, which makes it attractive to young families and first-time buyers. **Emmer Green** is very Thirties, with a lot of open land and golf courses. A three-bedroom semi here would cost around £200,000.

West and east Reading are cosmopolitan, and prices are slightly lower. A one-bedroom flat would cost £105,000; a three-bedroom Victorian house over £200,000. To the south is **Lower Earley** (see page 206) and to the west **Tilehurst** (see page 158), both with their own railway stations. A three-bedroom semi costs from £160,000 to £300,000. **Whiteknights Road**, where the university is situated, has large Edwardian houses that sell for rather more.

The popular villages nearby include **Pangbourne**, **Goring** and **Streatley** (see page 158). **Sonning Common**, just inside Oxfordshire, is not beautiful in itself, but it lies in a sleepy, countrified area. It has a swag of shops, a bank and a vet. A two-bedroom detached bungalow might be bought for £220,000 to £250,000. Most of the villages to the south of Reading are not particularly outstanding in any way.

Journey: 57 min
(36 min by
changing at
Reading)
Season: £2776
Peak: 2 per hr
Off-peak: 2 per hr

TILEHURST is a western suburb of Reading. A three-bedroom semi costs between £160,000 and £300,000.

Journey: 62 min
(41 min by
changing at
Reading)
Season: £2776
Peak: 2 per hr
Off-peak: 2 per hr

PANGBOURNE, just five miles off the M4, is a riverside commuter haven where the Thames meets the Pang. This is where Kenneth Grahame, author of *Wind in the Willows*, lived and where the buffoons in Jerome K Jerome's *Three Men in a Boat* stopped off. Canoeists and boating tourists now cavort in the shallows. Its discreet Georgian charm, with its square, weir and meadow, has developed a certain hustle as the population has swollen to 2500. Local people say it is so busy that you can't cross the road in the rush hour, yet during the rest of the day it is so quiet you can lie down in it. There are old-fashioned shops – a butcher, baker – and it is known as an "eating village" because there are so many restaurants and take-aways. Pangbourne, the co-educational public school, stands on Pangbourne Hill. Prices are high. A modern semi in Kennedy Drive would cost £220,000; a Victorian terraced £250,000 to £275,000; a period detached house around £475,000. Flats with river views will fetch £200,000 to £250,000. Much larger houses go for anything between £750,000 and £1.5m.

Journey: 67 min
(46 min by
changing at
Reading)
Season: £2776
Peak: 2 per hr
Off-peak: 2 per hr

GORING & STREATLEY sandwich the Thames between them. Both are expensive and pretty, with enough shops to make life manageable.

A Victorian semi with three bedrooms will cost £350,000 upwards. Streatley doesn't have the frill of modern housing on its outskirts that Goring has, and it has the Swan on the towpath, which is a seductive hotel.

Journey: 72 min
(51 mins by
changing at
Reading)
Season: £2776
Peak: 2 per hr
Off-peak: 2 per hr

CHOLSEY is sprawly, so the prices here are lower. Its main feature, a pretty village green edged with listed cottages, has to face down the parade of modern shops on the other side. However, the shops and post office are useful, there is a good primary school and the parish magazine carries six pages of clubs and activities to join. It has a busy horticultural society, the Cholsey Silver band, and the Cholsey and Wallingford Steam Railway, which is run by volunteers. Agatha Christie is buried here. A three-bedroom house on a modern development would cost £200,000.

Journey: 45 min

Season: £3312

Peak: 4 per hr

Off-peak: 3 per hr

DIDCOT PARKWAY
Didcot itself lacks any romance and sadly the evening peak service which once pelted along at 95mph and completed the journey in 34 minutes has gone. It has about 25,000 residents and is soaking up new housing like a sponge. It is also being given a new heart in the form of an ambitious re-modelling of the town centre to provide shopping highlights, a Sainsbury's superstore, cinema and arts complex. Didcot West is about to tuck 3500 new houses under its wing. The most attractive part is **Northbourne**, which is old Didcot and still very beautiful. **East Hagbourne**, just outside, is distinctly special, displaying all the architectural eclecticism of the area – timber frame, thatch, zig-zag brickwork – clustered around the old village cross by the church. **West Hagbourne** is similar but quieter, with a village pond. Both are popular with staff at the Atomic Research Station at Harwell who can afford to pay from £300,000 to £380,000 for a three-bedroom 15th-century cottage.

'East Hendred is very horsey and a bit arty-crafty. Lots of four-wheel drives with stickers saying Canine Defence League'

Perhaps the village with the most charm and vigour is **Blewbury**, set against the Downs. Blewburton Hill to the east is crowned with an extraordinary prehistoric camp. The village has pretty old inns, a football club, a cricket green, brass band, church choir and a dramatic society. Once you get off the B4017 the prices are high. An early 16th-century cottage with four bedrooms and inglenook fireplace might fetch around £400,000 to £500,000, though you could pick up a four-bedroom modern house on a small new development for £200,000 to £280,000.

East Hendred, to the west, is a typical Downland village peppered with thatch and timber. It is close to the ancient Ridgeway, which enables you to walk at a giddy height for miles in either direction. "It's very horsey and a bit arty-crafty. Lots of four-wheel drives with stickers saying Canine Defence League," is how one local resident describes it. **Harwell**, by comparison, is plainer with plenty of workmanlike Victorian houses. An old three-bedroom farmer's cottage here can be had for £380,000 while four-bedroom modern houses cost up to £480,000.

16th-century thatched cottage, Blewbury

The combination of riverside with proximity to London makes some of these villages obvious film-star territory. **Shillingford**, on a bridge over the Thames, and **Warborough** both reek of money. **Wallingford** has a pretty shopping centre with a notable bookshop and lots of Georgian houses. On the river front they cost from £500,000 into the millions, back in the streets a Victorian three-bedroom terraced house will cost £250,000. The town is the fictional Cawston in the television drama *Midsomer Murders*.

Journey: 58 min
Season: £5308
Peak: 5 per hr
Off-peak: 4 per hr

SWINDON itself is architecturally brutal though wonderfully convenient for commuting, since the InterCity trains take a last breath here before sprinting on to the West Country. Big businesses such as Motorola, Honda and the Nationwide have their headquarters here. Professionals, bank managers and the wealthier shopkeepers huddle together in the **Old Town**, in Victorian and Edwardian houses on the south side of Bath Road. A three-bedroom terraced house at the cheaper end of the market here would cost £135,000. Four bedrooms in a more expensive road would fetch £260,000. **The Lawns**, near the lake and nature walks of Coate Water Park, is also sought after. Five-bedroom detached houses with gardens here cost £350,000. Or there is **Broome Manor**, with its golf course and a mix of modern Georgian, Regency and ranch-style houses selling at £400,000 and evoking the atmosphere of Dallas.

'People tend to flee Swindon for the chalk villages of the Marlborough Downs or The Vale of the White Horse'

On the whole, people tend to flee Swindon for the chalk villages of the Marlborough Downs or the Vale of the White Horse. The east is more popular, with villages such as **Liddington**, **Wanborough**, **Bishopstone** (which still has its watercress beds) and **Aldbourne**. These are cohesive, and tend to have primary schools and huge churches and pubs that are still free houses. A four-bedroom house could be bought for between £350,000 and £400,000 depending on position. Ex-council properties sell at around £150,000. Although they are only just off the M4, they have some prime hacking country right on the doorstep and are seriously horsey.

A walk across the Berkshire Downs connects us to the past as surely as any history book. The white horse is at **Uffington** – against the Ridgeway near Dragon Hill, where St George is supposed to have killed the dragon. It is worth remembering that the further you go from Swindon, and the nearer you get to **Hungerford** or **Faringdon**, the more attractive the villages are, and the higher the prices.

Country house, Swindon area

The National Trust owns much of the land to the north of Swindon, including the villages of **Coleshill** and **Buscot**. Here the infant Thames is hardly more than a stream running beneath the willows. Though **Lechlade** is idyllically pretty with a good collection of Georgian houses, it fills with boating people in the summer and, being 10 miles from Swindon, is a bit of a slog to reach at the end of a hard day. The

House style in the West

The great prize in the West is the Cotswolds, where the houses around the upper Thames, Cherwell, Evenlode, Windrush and Colne are built quite literally out of the landscape. They lie in the great belt of yellowy grey oolite which, when cut and dressed, makes each village street look as natural as an outcrop of stone.

Even the most humble cottages have a kind a church grandeur given to the them by the stone, and a decorativeness associated with wealth, including mullioned windows, arched doorways and drip-stones. The real money was made from the sheep dotted across the hillsides and the woollen industry of the 14th and 15th centuries. The roofs, usually made with layers of stone tiles and gabled windows to let the light into the top rooms, give that distinctive rhythm which brings tourists by the coachload to admire the scene.

South of Oxford you enter brick country, but there is also some clunch, taken from the Berkshire Downs, and around Aylesbury there is a chalk-and-clay mixture known as wichert. Many of the houses have lost the thatch they once had – a steep-pitched roof is often a clue to the fact that a house was once thatched. Flora Thompson's *Lark Rise To Candleford* is perhaps the best description there is of cottage life in this area at the end of the 19th century.

West of Swindon you reach the great sweeps of the chalk uplands with their ancient barrows, stone circles and white horses cut into the hillsides.

Eventually you come to the toffee-coloured stone of Bath, turned into the gracious 18th-century crescents and squares which make the city so attractive.

stone for St Paul's Cathedral was loaded here. **Fairford** is worth considering. It is a thriving community, has a few shops, active local societies, and a church with 500-year-old stained-glass windows. A small Cotswold house with two bedrooms might sell for £150,000 to £200,000. The old gravel pits at **Whelford** are popular with watersports enthusiasts.

Villagers driving in from the west of Swindon have to cope with a traffic problem on their way into the city centre. **Wootton Bassett** is a large market town with a good range of local shops, including a delicatessen. Hackpen Hill nearby has a white horse on its flank. The weekly market used to be so disorganised that an early photograph shows a large cow emerging from a solicitor's office. You can get studio apartments for £65,000, and ordinary little three-bedroom semi's for £145,000 to 175,000.

The **Somerfords** (**Little** and **Great**, divided by the River Avon), are popular because they border the Cotswolds and are closer to the prettiness of **Malmesbury** and its beautiful 12th-century abbey ruins than to the dead weight of Swindon. Great Somerford has a combined shop and post office. They have lots of local societies, from under-fives to the Somerford Stages amateur dramatics group. Great Somerford also has a primary school. An interest in horses is a useful social passport. The Vale of the White Horse Hunt is on the doorstep; there is polo at Cirencester Park, and endless bridleways and footpaths criss-crossing the Cotswolds. The price of a new detached house with four bedrooms, two bathrooms and a double garage is from £350,000 to £400,000.

Brinkworth has lots of good points including its foodie pub, The Three Crowns, and the gardening club and a quilting group called

The Bramble Patches. Set on a ridge, with wide-angle views, the village is notable for its extraordinary length – stretching to just over four miles. A period house with four bedrooms here will cost from £325,000 to £375,000.

Slightly to the east is **Lydiard Millicent**, typically north Wiltshire, with a pub, post office and green-belt buffer zone to insulate it from Swindon. A four-bedroom new detached house might cost £280,000. **Purton Stoke,** which has a pub and a village street that tapers into open countryside, is much nicer than its overblown neighbour **Purton**. A four-bedroom Victorian house at Purton Stoke might have a price tag of £395,000. A three-bedroom reconstituted stone cottage would cost £230,000.

To the south there are a few villages scattered in the sweeping chalk hills between Swindon and **Marlborough**, which actually lies closer to Pewsey station (see page 188).

> Line to Kemble

Journey: 78 min
Season: £5616
Peak: 1 per hr*
Off-peak: 1 every
2 hrs*
*More trains to
Swindon where you
can change.

KEMBLE is a very pretty Cotswold village, often commended in best-kept-village competitions in Gloucestershire. Planning controls are tight, so that even the council houses are built in local stone. The village has a school and a general store-cum-post office, though most people do their major shopping in Cirencester. The abiding local interest is reflected in the biannual flower and vegetable shows. Three-bedroom former estate-workers' cottages sell for around £180,000; Victorian railway cottages for more; four-bedroomed modern houses for £296,000 and above. Larger farmhouses can cost £600,000 to £1.35m for a five-bedroom coach house. "Location and rarity is everything," says one local agent.

To the east is a belt of desirable villages, all close to Cirencester and two good comprehensive schools. **Poole Keynes**, was little more than a farming hamlet with a medieval priory until the Sixties imposed modern housing. **Somerford Keynes** also has a lot of modern development but is socially very active. It has a thriving WI, plus bridge clubs, mothers-and-toddlers, and other groups. There is no shop, but the pub sells coffee and sugar, and bread is delivered three times a week. **Ashton Keynes** has a primary school, a petrol station, two shops and some lovely period houses close to the river. As you approach from South Cerney you will see some beautiful 17th-century cottages on the other side of the bridge. A large farmhouse in the countryside nearby would cost £600,000 to £750,000, while smaller houses are on a par with the rest of the area. **South Cerney** is close to the Cotswold Water Park – a collection of flooded gravel pits with water-skiing, sailing and fishing. A converted barn with four

Schools in Gloucestershire

There are highly selective grammar schools here for those who excel, but also good comprehensives and private schools. Villages between Cheltenham, Cirencester and Stroud are surrounded by choice. Cheltenham has the heavily oversubscribed Pate's Grammar for boys and girls, three impressive comprehensives, and strong private schools including Cheltenham Ladies' College, Cheltenham College for boys and girls, and Dean Close for both sexes. Stroud has

two grammars – Stroud High for girls and Marling for boys – and Archway School, a co-educational comprehensive. Westonbirt independent for girls is to the south near Tetbury.

Cirencester has two well-regarded comprehensives and Rendcomb College independent school for boys and girls.

Other good comprehensives are in Chipping Campden and Fairford.

bedrooms in this area would cost around £500,000. The village is marred slightly by the large quarry with its constant lorry traffic. At least six miles from Kemble, but well worth the journey, is **Down Ampney**, the most charming of the Ampneys (the others being **Ampney St Peter**, **Ampney Crucis** and **Ampney St Mary**), famous as the birthplace of Ralph Vaughan Williams and much admired for its beautiful gabled manor house, Down Ampney Hall. A tiny two-bedroom semi will cost £215,000; a modern stone family house £325,000. The larger country houses sell for up to £2m.

> Line to **Bristol Parkway**

Journey: 85 min
Season: £7152*
Peak: 2 per hr
Off-peak: 2 per hr
*Also valid at
Bristol Temple
Meads

BRISTOL PARKWAY The villages near here are perfect for commuters because the station is easy to reach and parking is plentiful. It also lies at the centre of a motorway network that can speed you north, south, east or west and link you with the major commercial centres of Wales as well as with Birmingham, Swindon and London. It is possible for a couple to live here and for one partner to work in Exeter and the other in London. It offers countryside, yet Bristol is on the doorstep. The station is on a spur that goes direct from Swindon, so you can be whisked to London in very little over an hour.

Only six minutes from the station are the pricey villages of **Almondsbury** and **Awkley**. They are out of earshot of all the motorways, and an old stone house with four bedrooms might typically cost £400,000. Though they are out of the way, they are now seen as useful locations because of the second Severn Crossing, linked to Junction 17 of the M5. **Hambrook** is also a village with instant appeal despite being within earshot of the M4 and M32. It has a couple of pubs, a hotel and Hambrook Common at its centre. Four-bedroom houses easily creep up into the £300,000 range.

'One partner can work in Exeter and the other in London'

Also within six minutes of the station is **Stoke Gifford** – almost an ex-village (with a serious rush-hour problem) now that it has attracted big organisations such as Hewlett Packard, AXA Sun Life and the Ministry of Defence. The village-proper is packed with old cottages, with those in Mead Road tending to be more expensive than the rest. A one-bedroom cottage will sell at around £125,000. A four-bedroom modern detached house will fetch £210,000 to £230,000. There is also a pair of Bovis housing estates, one being newer and much more popular than the other. The most sought-after roads are Touchstone and Fabian, where a three-bedroom detached house costs around £160,000.

It is impossible to ignore the lake of housing at **Bradley Stoke** on its doorstep, billed as the largest development in Western Europe. Builders took over a decade to build around 11,000 houses with primary schools, sports centres, pubs and supermarkets. Unfortunately it developed the nickname Sadly Broke during the recession in the early 1990s, but things have picked up and estate agents are now calling it Bradley Hope. The housing is pick-and-mix, with one-bedroom flats being sold for £95,000, three-bedroom houses at £160,000 to £240,000, and four bedrooms at £220,000 to £270,000.

'There is a village green where girls dance around the maypole in spring'

Much care was taken at Bradley Stoke to avoid the monotony of earlier new development grafted on to **Chipping Sodbury**. The old core remains a lovely old Cotswold town with a typically wide main street flanked with houses in Georgian brick and Cotswold stone. A 17th-century two-bedroom cottage costs around £160,000 to £300,000 for five bedrooms. The nearby villages of **Winterbourne**, **Frampton Cotterell** and **Coalpit Heath** blend one into the other, offering a mixture of old and new with a few working farms in the outlying areas. At the bottom of the market you could buy a three-bedroom ex-council house for £150,000. At the top end you could pay £450,000 for a four- to five-bedroom period cottage in half an acre. **Iron Acton** is also very pretty, with a village green where girls dance round the maypole in the spring, and two pubs.

If you are looking for a house around here it is worth remembering that in the area between Bristol and Wotton-under-Edge prices are affected by people who commute into Bristol. As you proceed beyond **Thornbury**, prices start to drop. On a bad day from this part, the journey to Bristol Parkway station could take 15 minutes, which many might consider too long.

> Continuation of main line

Journey: 77 min
Season: £5868
Peak: 3 per hr
Off peak: 2 per hr

CHIPPENHAM is a town that has been busy rediscovering its old heritage – paving the old market square with York stone, bringing back market day, re-erecting the Butter Cross and cherishing its Roman remains. It has all the basic shops anyone would need, including a new classical-style pedestrian shopping mall in Bath stone on the banks of the River Avon. It is a place for small family businesses, with a new business park on the western outskirts.

The set-piece village of **Castle Combe**, five miles away, is known as the prettiest village in England. In the 1960s, the arched bridge over the Bye brook, and little stone cottages with their steeply pitched roofs, were transformed to serve as a seaport for the film of *Dr Dolittle*. It is a bit of a goldfish bowl for tourists, but at least the visitors are expected to leave their cars behind at the top of the village. Residents become very attached and properties rarely come on the market. A thatched cottage could cost from £475,000. The pubs – the Castle Inn and the White Hart – make it convivial. The village hall opens as a post office for half a day a week and children go to the new primary school in the neighbouring village.

Quieter and just as pretty is **Biddestone**, slightly closer to Chippenham, which has the classic village centre with stone houses, duckpond, pubs and a recreation ground for football and cricket. An older three-bedroom cottage semi will cost around £275,000. To the north-east is **East Tytherton**, which is very small, has a village shop and attractive stone houses, and is close enough to the M4 to be favoured by those who prefer the car to the train. **Bremhill** is charming, too. A former resident, the vicar and poet Canon Bowles, kept the bells around the necks of his sheep tuned to thirds and fifths, and was a favourite visitor at Bowood House a few miles to the south. Bremhill has a post office-cum-general store, and a pub. A cottagey three-bedroom semi would sell at £250,000 to £300,000.

'At one time Box housed the workers building the Great Western Railway; now it harbours the occasional rock star'

People much prefer **Corsham**, which has a Cotswold stone heart and a delicatessen which proudly sells local produce. The new Heritage Centre concerns itself with the wool trade and stone quarrying. A handsome four-bedroom stone house and double garage sells for around £400,000 to £500,000 here. A restored Grade II listed house with five bedrooms could cost £500,000 to £600,000. Further towards Bath on the A4 is **Box**. At one time it housed the workers building the Great Western Railway for Brunel; now it harbours the occasional rock star and is considered ideal by those who want to be within easy reach of Bath, but also close to Chippenham railway station. Peter Gabriel's Real World Studios are here. The village has a general store which sells home-made quiches and pies, a chemist and a hairdresser, and two primary schools. There

Schools in Bristol, Bath and Somerset

Good independent schools for girls in the Bristol area include Badminton for boarding and day, Clifton High, Red Maids' School day and boarding, Redland High and Colston's Girls'. Boys' independent schools include Bristol Cathedral School (girls in the sixth), and Queen Elizabeth's Hospital day and boarding school. Co-educational independent schools include Clifton College boarding and day, Bristol Grammar day school and Colston's Collegiate. Good comprehensives include The Castle, Marlwood, The Ridings High School, Cotham School and Wellsway.

Bath also has its share of educational successes, including Norton Hill comprehensive, and three co-educational independents: King Edward's, Kingswood and Prior Park College. There is also the Royal High, an independent day and boarding school for girls.

are lots of local activities and the village fête, known as the Box Revels, usually lasts for a week. Two-bedroom stone cottages start from £145,000; larger houses will top the £450,000 mark. Local interests manage to be both horsey and cultural, and also sporting. Here you are in rugby country – thanks to the proliferation of boys' public schools and the huge success of Bath Rugby Club.

Marshfield, west of Chippenham on the A420, has a shop, butcher, doctor, pet and garden supplies. A three-bedroom terraced house on the High Street, in what was once the last staging post to Bath, would cost around £350,000. This long grey-stone street is dominated by the church tower and has some remarkable little almshouses dating from 1625.

Very few local sons and daughters can afford to buy homes in the villages they grew up in. First-time buyers are eased out into small towns such as **Calne** – an old woollen town with the site of an old Victorian bacon factory put down to grass in the centre. Two-bedroom flats cost from £85,000; a three-bedroom beamed house with an inglenook will weigh in at £350,000. Another possibility is **Compton Basset**. It has been made a conservation area because of its delightful chalk-stone cottages and 12th- and 13th-century church. A stock of surplus Ministry of Defence houses, which are eagerly snapped up by younger buyers, is kept at arm's length and known as Lower Compton.

Other villages worth looking at include **Cherhill** (pronounced Cheryl), towards Marlborough, which stands beside a huge Iron Age camp and white horse, and has its own primary school. Modern three-bedroom houses start at £170,000. Then there is **Heddington** – a small village with infant and primary schools and an international meditation centre called The Pagoda. It is very upmarket: a modern three-bedroom family house would sell for around £180,000. Another sought-after cluster of properties is at **Charlcutt**. The houses have breathtaking views of the countryside for 20 miles in all directions. Something with five bedrooms and a double garage will cost over £400,000. Although **Sandy Lane** straddles the A342, it is very beautiful and has some very lovely thatched houses. A two-bedroom cottage here might go for £275,000. Its population is mainly retired, and the residents tend to grow high beech hedges to guard their privacy. It is short of local activity, but contains a great deal of wealth. One London commuter from here prefers to travel by helicopter rather than by train. Unfortunately the village is used as a short cut by motorists heading off the M4 for Southampton.

South of Chippenham the showcase village is **Lacock**, but the jumble of timbered houses in the gorgeous twisted streets around the Abbey are all in the hands of the National Trust. The fringe offers the occasional dream house. A three-bedroom detached house costs around £425,000.

Part-time commuters might choose to live in some of the wonderful villages further south in the Avon valley, which are also served by the Melksham branch line to Bath (see below).

> Branch line to **Trowbridge,** via **Freshford, Avoncliff** and **Bradford-on-Avon**

Journey: 120 min
Season: £6028
Peak: 2 per hr
Off-peak: 1 or 2 per hr
*From Bradford-on-Avon. There are no through trains to Paddington. You must change at either Bath Spa or Westbury. There are through trains to Waterloo, but only off-peak.

FRESHFORD is favoured by retiring Bathonians. It is a strong little community, with its own shop and local railway station. Nipper trains drop you quickly into Bath, so there is no problem with parking the car.

Bradford-on-Avon is so expensive that it vies with **Bath**. Indeed, it is built of the same limestone as Bath, on hills falling so steeply towards the Avon that the winding paths between the houses give one the feeling of being in a Greek village. Across the arched stone bridge, and open to the public, is one of the biggest tithe barns in the country. Bradford attracts many tourists who come in summer to wander along the river and through the old shopping streets, have tea, buy second-hand books, and browse in the craft shops. It has a good swimming pool, rowing and sailing clubs, and an annual arts festival. There are also marvellous walks along the Kennet and Avon Canal.

The attraction of owning a house overlooking the tessellated rooftops of weavers' cottages, miniature 18th-century homes and narrow gardens bulging with hollyhocks is difficult to quantify. There is a definite ex-military and ex-naval presence here. Larger houses sell for hundreds of thousands of pounds, but it is occasionally possible to find a period three-bedroom terraced house on four floors, with a tiny garden, at around £210,000. On the outer roads, three-bedroom ex-council houses in reconstructed stone will sell for around £135,000 to £150,000. Towards the higher end of the market on the edge of town you could get a four-bedroom Victorian stone semi, with outbuildings in over half an acre, for around £450,000.

Broughton Gifford is much quieter, set in deep countryside with a village green faced by Gifford Hall, a 1688 village house. **Steeple Ashton**, like Bradford-on-Avon, was built on the profits of the wool industry. It has a post office which is run from the pub, church with no steeple and a swag of new housing. A five-bedroom executive house with a paddock would cost around £500,000. Just next to it is **Keevil**, a collection of rather exclusive cottages with a stone manor house. The sub-post-office-cum-general-store has closed but the primary school still thrives. A three-bedroom thatched cottage would cost over £380,000.

> Continuation of main line

Journey: 90 min
Season: £6028
Peak: 2 per hr
Off-peak: 2 per hr

BATH SPA People have been known to move to **Bath** and move out again within a couple of years – not everyone finds it easy to break into the social circles that centre on its elegant 18th-century squares and crescents. Its attractions are manifold: beautiful parks, specialist shops, some of them rather exclusive, and restaurants where the prices compete with Mayfair. The beauty of commuting from Bath, though, apart from its obvious physical splendour, is that you can live within walking distance of the station. Indeed you have to, otherwise the combined traffic and parking problems will sour your temper before the day has even begun.

The social hubs include the much-acclaimed international festival in June, the Theatre Royal, which is the starting point for many West End plays, Bath Rugby Club and, of course, the Pump Rooms, where balls are regularly held. The new Nicholas Grimshaw-designed multi-million-pound spa will add another life-enhancing experience. Various hotels, clubs and excellent restaurants rise and fall in the firmament as the right places to be seen at. Old Bathonians are extremely tight-knit. Public schools include King Edward's School, Kingswood School for boys and girls, Monkton Combe for boys and girls, and Prior Park College, which is a Catholic school for both sexes.

'It is possible to live outside the city in one of the villages, but driving into Bath is a problem'

The sought-after areas are the two hills to the north and south of the river. **Sion Hill** to the north is a sudden slope looking south over the city. This is where all the major crescents were built, including the Royal, for prominent figures in elegant 18th-century society. Very few of these houses are left intact: most have been split into flats. A lower-ground, two-bedroom flat in Royal Crescent, would go on the market at around £450,000. Between the roads full of architectural gems you find a mixed bag of houses, though nowhere are prices cheap. A five-bedroom Victorian bay-fronted semi in a quiet road might sell for £550,000.

To the south of the river is **Bathwick Hill**, with Widcombe and Lyncombe Hills, where a sister spa to the famous central spa was founded in the late 18th century. The architecture is equally fine, but the views are rather more rural than those from Sion Hill. Both attract businessmen, professionals and culture vultures, but people attach fiercely to their particular hill and would never swap.

Living in the centre of Bath only became fashionable again in the early Eighties. For decades previously the Georgian architecture was not cherished, and the buildings had blackened and become gloomy. In the late Seventies, for instance, you could buy a complete Georgian town house in The Circus for £7000. By 2000 it was worth £1m and now you could pay £2.5m to £3.5m for one. There is a tendency for the houses to have tiny gardens because they were designed in the belief that people would take their recreation in the parks. If you own a house in a square, you will often have the right to buy a key to the central garden.

Elsewhere, a modest little house close to the canal with a little garden, two reception rooms and two bedrooms might be found for £200,000. Three-bedroom ex-council houses sell at £150,000.

Georgian town house, Bath

It is possible to live outside the city in one of the villages, but driving into Bath is a problem. Parking adds an expensive premium to the season ticket, and traffic wardens are vigilant. To the south is the old Somerset coal-mining area, still with the occasional slag heap on the horizon. **Peasedown St John**, an early mining town, has been rediscovered and is now a popular commuter haven.

Norton St Philip has conservation status. It was built in local stone from the profits of the wool industry, and has some small modern cul-de-sacs stitched unobtrusively into the whole. It has a shop and post office, but is best known for its pub, the George Inn, which is one of the best-preserved medieval inns in the country. Pepys paid a visit with his wife in 1668, dined on 10 shillings and noted a plaque in the church to twin ladies who had only one stomach between them. **Hinton Charterhouse** is similarly unspoilt, but less self-sufficient, with the 13th-century ruins of Hinton Priory close by. The countryside is full of similar villages that you chance upon as you dip in and out of the valleys. But the farming crisis has affected them. In **Wellow** the local farmer no longer herds his cattle through the village at dawn and dusk. He has turned to arable and the barns have become houses. A small cottage will cost £200,000 at least. It no longer has a post office, but the postmaster from Hinton Charterhouse comes to the village hall twice a week to hand out the pensions, and the village shop is mostly run by volunteers. There are a lot of retired people, but also young families who use the primary school. Many people own horses, and there is a Trekking Centre.

To the west are the villages served by the Bradford-on-Avon branch line (see page 167). To the north is another magical stretch of countryside where time seems to have turned everything to stone. **Charlcombe**, **Swainswick** and **Woolley** lie in a U-shaped valley in a landscape which is almost Welsh, and which at its northen end becomes positively austere. It is expensive. In Woolley even a two-bedroom cottage would sell for £180,000 to £210,000; a four-bedroom house for over £400,000. To the east of the A46 is another stretch of villages which have that haphazard, ancient quality, including **St Catherine** and **Northend**. **Batheaston** is a favourite with commuters and the retired. Yet it manages to be a working village with post office, general store, two garden centres and a farm shop, Wednesday market, and a large council estate. It has 142 listed buildings altogether, which the Batheaston Society does its best to preserve. It has also been rescued from heavy traffic by a bypass. For breathtaking views across the watermeadows to the city you could look at **Bathford**, which has a busy village school and playgroup. Further north towards the M4, in villages such as **Upper Wraxhall** and **North Wraxhall**, prices drop considerably but you become a little separated from the spirit, social life and interests of Bath.

Journey: 100 min
Season: £7152*
Peak: 3 per hr
Off-peak: 2 per hr
*Also valid at
Bristol Parkway

BRISTOL TEMPLE MEADS Commuting from Bristol is never

easy. Parking is difficult, and the station is hard to get at, but a new commercial district is burgeoning alongside it, with new tower blocks taking the place of old eyesores. There are huge traffic problems. The M32 regularly clogs into four-mile tailbacks, and there is no integrated public transport system to relieve the pressure in a city where a lot of major companies – Lloyds TSB, British Aerospace and NatWest, for example – have their headquarters.

Culturally, however, it is rich, with the Bristol Old Vic, the theatre school and various pubs providing fringe theatre. The Hippodrome attracts the ballet and opera companies. Colston Hall is the rock venue, and the Watershed arts and media centre in the docks shows the arty films. Another big local interest is expressed through Bristol Rugby Club. The well-known public schools include Bristol Cathedral School, Bristol Grammar School, Clifton College, Colston's School and Queen Elizabeth's Hospital.

Clifton and **Clifton Village** are Bristol's Olympian heights, where the mix of Georgian, Regency and Victorian is very special and very expensive. Some of the houses are so large, with eight or nine bedrooms, that they have been divided into flats for upwardly mobile couples who will pay £250,000 to £275,000 for something stylish with two bedrooms, marble fireplaces, balcony, ceiling mouldings and a drawing room with shutters. Most of these huge old places have coach houses at the back to serve as garages. In Cliftonville, many of the 10-bedroom Victorian mansions overlooking The Downs have been converted into offices. It has good independent schools – Clifton High for girls and Clifton for boys. A four-storey Victorian house here would cost around £650,000 to £700,000. A four-bedroom Victorian terraced house in Cliftonwood would cost £375,000 to £400,000.

House prices in the rest of the city have been playing catch-up with remarkable speed though. An alternative to Clifton is **Redland**, which has a mix of Georgian, Victorian and Thirties, and a bohemian air. The closer to the city centre you get, the more you feel the presence of students from Bristol University. A one-bedroom first floor flat in a Regency terrace in Redland, close to Clifton Downs, would be priced at around £175,000. A mid-terrace three-bedroom Edwardian house, or a charming four-bedroom town house, could be had for £450,000. In **Southville** too, just across the bridge from Harbourside, Victorian terraced houses, once considered unfashionable, have shot up in value and desirability.

Bristol **Harbourside** is an area worth considering, if you haven't got a family. Huge new purpose-built Legoland-style developments are interspersed between old warehouse conversions. Isambard Kingdom Brunel's old stamping ground around the Floating Harbour is finally turning into a trendy area with bars and cafés. One-bedroom flats cost around £145,000 with a view. Three-bedroom town houses with a view are £385,000, without the view £285,000.

Waterfront apartments, Bristol

Evesham

Moreton-in-Marsh

Kingham

Shipton

Ascott-under-Wychwood   Charlbury

Finstock

Combe

Handborough

Oxford

Radley

Culham

Appleford

Didcot Parkway

Leamington Spa

Banbury

Heyford

Tackley

Paddington

Paddington
> Oxford and Evesham

For stations between Paddington and Didcot Parkway, see **Paddington to Reading and Bristol** line, page 148.

For stations between Paddington and Didcot Parkway, see **Paddington to Reading and Bristol** line, page 148.

Journey (from Radley): 58 min, changing at Didcot

Season (all three stations): £3312

There are one or two peak-hour trains from London in the evening but none in the morning. You have to change at Didcot Parkway or Reading

APPLEFORD, CULHAM AND RADLEY Appleford is little more than a halt with a string of bungalows threaded to the railway line beside a good pub. **Long Wittenham** is a village in two halves, old and new, and is convenient for those who want to use The European School at Culham, which was established for the children of people working at the research station there. **Radley** has more trains serving it than the other two halts, but it is a bit betwixt and between to be really sought after. Its main feature is Radley College, the boys' public school.

'Travelling on an Oxford train can be a bit like attending a literary tea party'

Journey: 57 min
Season: £3312
Peak: 3 per hr
Off-peak: 2 per hr

OXFORD can seem insufferably cliquey to some, but if you belong to the publishing, university, hospital or industrial scenes then it is not too much of a problem. It is, however, now very unfriendly towards the car and as it is virtually impossible to drive into the centre, drivers slip round the ring road to find the right point of entry. Park-and-ride is the way to do it. Travelling on the Oxford train can be a bit like attending a literary tea-party. As well as the city's obvious beauty, its schools are a great attraction to outsiders. Public schools abound: Magdalen College School, St Edward's, Radley College just outside, and Oxford High and Headington School for girls. Prices in Oxford have blossomed in recent years.

The nicer bread-and-butter houses for those making a start in Oxford lie in **Osney** or **Jericho**, both within walking distance of the station. Osney is almost moated by a combination of the Thames and the canal. Two-bedroom Victorian houses here sell for £230,000;

three-bedrooms houses for £270,000. Prices in Jericho are slightly higher, though the houses are small. Another area to consider is **Grand Pont**, where a Victorian house with three bedrooms would fetch £285,000 to £300,000.

For many, the only area to live is North Oxford, which is peppered with academics and successful professionals. It mushroomed in the 19th century after it was suddenly decided that dons should be allowed to marry. Huge Victorian houses on wide, tree-lined roads provided them with new homes, which now sell at around £850,000 to £1.2m. There are just not enough of them to meet demand. Houses get smaller and slightly cheaper towards **Summertown**, where Cherwell comprehensive is a much-respected school, as is St Philip and St James' first school. You could buy a family house here for around £500,000. **Wolvercote** village, a little further out, is particularly lovely, with The Trout Inn backing on to Port Meadow. Cheaper little brick-and-tile houses sell at around £200,000.

'For many the only area to live is North Oxford, which is peppered with academics and successful professionals'

Headington is popular with staff working at the hospital here, but it is the wrong side of Oxford for the station. Coaches heading for London (Victoria), stop here and many commuters use these instead of the train. **Old Headington** and **Old Marston** are both charming villages with crooked lanes and stone cottages that have been absorbed by the suburbs. Inhabitants tend to be rather rarefied. Pretty cottages in either might sell for £300,000 to £400,000. Oxford's equivalent of a stockbroker belt – large detached houses with the occasional tennis court or pony paddock – lies outside at **Hinksey**, **Cumnor** and **Boars Hill**. A Thirties' house with five bedrooms, three bathrooms, lofts, outbuildings, swimming pool and over two acres of formal gardens in a woodland setting could be bought for around £1.1m to £1.3m on Boars Hill.

Schools in Oxfordshire

Private schools tend to grab the limelight here, though there are some notable comprehensives. The latter include Lord Williams' at Thame and John Mason at Abingdon.

Oxford is the real educational powerhouse, with a clutch of independent schools. Girls' schools include the Oxford High (day), which tries to keep fees low, Headington for day-girls and boarders and Wychwood for girls, day and boarding. Boys have Magdalen College School and St Edwards, both for day-pupils and boarders.

Abingdon is the other bright spot. Here you find Radley College, high in the public school firmament, for which you need to put your son's name down at birth, and Abingdon independent boys' day and boarding school, both keen on rowing. For girls there is the independent School of St Helen and Katherine and Our Lady's Convent. Other girls' independent schools around Oxfordshire include Tudor Hall at Banbury and St Mary's at Wantage. A good comprehensive can be found in Didcot Girls' at Didcot.

> Line to Leamington Spa via Tackley, Heyford and Banbury

Tackley
Journey: 73 min
Season: £3312
Peak: 1 pr hr
Off-peak: 1 every
2 hrs*
*Change at Oxford

Heyford
Journey: 78 min
Season: £3312
Peak: 1 pr hr
Off-peak: 1 every
2 hrs*
*Change at Oxford

'The Steeple Aston Players put on productions of plays written by local people'

Since Oxford is so strangled by traffic and efforts to drive to the station are likely to be stressful, **Tackley** and **Heyford** come into their own with their local trains. **Steeple Aston**, a grey stone-walled village above the Cherwell, is definitely worth looking at. It has a village shop and post office, a choral society, football club and the Steeple Aston Players, who put on productions of plays written by local people. Commuters generally try to join in. The area is seriously horsey. A three-bedroom period cottage can be bought for £250,000. **Hopcroft's Halt** nearby is where the French highwayman Claude Duval clattered about on his horse. The American Air Force Base at **Upper Heyford** used to cause noise nuisance, but now that it has closed the great worry is that 1,000 new houses will be built there instead.

Then there are the **Tews** (**Great**, **Little** and **Duns**). Great Tew is particularly prized because it was a celebrated time-warp village (due to a neglectful previous owner it almost missed out on the 20th century). The combination of stone and thatch, post office and village stores, punctuated by greens and clumps of ornamental trees, seduced BBC location hunters when they were searching for somewhere to film *David Copperfield*. Even the overhead cables have been buried to keep the time-forgot atmosphere. Residents aren't antiques, however, and plenty of newcomers have arrived. A tiny two-bedroom cottage will cost £160,000 to £180,000.

For **Banbury** and **Leamington Spa**, see **Marylebone to Leamington Spa**, pages 145–146. It is possible to reach Paddington via the Oxford branch, but the direct route to Marylebone is much quicker.

> Line from Oxford to Evesham

This line takes you to what many people think is the most beautiful side of Oxford to live, where villages of golden stone rise up from the fields. The skip-hop service to **Charlbury**, **Kingham** and **Moreton-in-Marsh** (better served than **Handborough**, **Combe**, **Finstock**, **Ascott-under-Wychwood** and **Shipton**, which are sandwiched in between them) has become more frequent in recent years. There are now many more through trains that run from Evesham to Paddington and stop at these three stations. Otherwise you can get the local train and change at Oxford.

**Journey time: 75
min (65 min peak)**
Season: £4148
Peak: 2 per hr
Off-peak: 1 per hr

CHARLBURY

This area is a tapestry of extraordinarily lovely villages. You have to watch for those which are under the Oxford influence and hence more expensive than those further afield. **Charlbury** is very elegant and has a few business units in the stables of Cornbury Park, Lord Rotherwick's estate. Modern three-bedroom boxes can be bought for £250,000, or four-bedroom period cottages for £300,000 to £450,000. It is just too far from Oxford to be really expensive, or to appeal to the young, who say they can find nothing to do here.

Woodstock, which in Elizabethan times was the glove-making capital of the area, is slightly more expensive – its old stone houses lie closer to Oxford and it is only two miles from **Combe** station. In summer it swarms with visitors who browse through it on their way to Blenheim Palace, eat at the Bear Hotel and walk along the banks of the River Glyme. **Bladon**, just apart from it, is more attractive still. Its collection of ancient cottages is crowned by the elegant 15th-century chimneys of the old malthouse, and it is scarcely a mile from **Handborough** station. Sir Winston Churchill is buried here.

One of the best-liked small towns west of Oxford is **Witney**, which is rather less rarefied than some of the villages that surround it. Its fortunes were built on the blanket industry, which employed the waters of the Windrush and the wool from local sheep. It is a refreshing mix of old and new property, with greens at either end, raised pavements studded with limes, and modern shopfronts elbowing in between their Georgian neighbours. The central market place and the old covered butter cross give it a strong heart. Though it is only three miles from **Finstock** station, a lot of

Cotswold house, near Moreton-in-Marsh

commuters from here choose to drive. The town is just off the A40, which now links easily to the M40. There are long rows of old blanket workers' cottages that sell for around £210,000 each. A huge new housing estate has mushroomed on the western flank, on which houses sell for between £140,000 and £500,000.

Journey: 84 min
(76 min peak)
Season: £4420
Peak: 2 per hr
Off-peak: 1 per hr

KINGHAM The winding lanes, banked by streams and meadows overlooking the woodlands of the Evenlode valley, can make you feel quite isolated here. **Kingham** and all the villages around it are cut in fudge-coloured stone, with the occasional outcrop of council houses at the edge. People tolerate the longer commute to London from here because it is just out of reach of the Oxford influence and therefore cheaper. A handsome four-bedroom stone house could be bought for around £325,000; three bedrooms for £289,000; a smaller terraced house for around £210,000.

The **Wychwoods** (**Milton-Under**, **Shipton-Under** and **Ascott-Under**) are closer to Oxford and slightly more expensive. Ascott-Under-Wychwood has its own station, served by regional trains running from Evesham to Oxford. Many people moving to the area will aim for the catchment of the popular Burford comprehensive school. A stone house with beamed ceilings, stone-mullioned windows with leaded lights, Tudor fireplaces and five to six bedrooms might sell for around £650,000.

Bourton-on-the-Water, though a model Cotswold village with its own model village, pushes commuter tolerance a little since it is about 10 miles from Kingham station. But with it come the **Slaughters** (**Lower** and **Upper**), the Lower set upon a stream that wriggles through little stone bridges and the Upper being right on the banks of the Windrush. Locals tend to be farmers, retired couples or craftspeople who don't mind being miles from anywhere. The nearest shopping centre is **Chipping Norton**, an old market town where the huge old Bliss tweed mill has been restored to provide flats and houses alongside a leisure centre (priced at between £295,000 for a two-bedroom flat and £380,000 for a three-bedroom semi, plus service charges). It has a reputation for being wet and windy. Locals say it qualified for extra coal rations in the war because it was the coldest place in the region. The White Hart Hotel in the town centre is also being converted into apartments.

'Locals say Chipping Norton qualified for extra coal rations because in the war it was the coldest place in the region'

Journey: 91 min
Season: £4900
Peak: 2 per hr
Off-peak: 1 per hr

MORETON-IN-MARSH The perfection of towns such as Moreton-in-Marsh and **Stow-on-the-Wold** has meant torture by tourism. They seethe in summer and subside in winter. "The only people who live there are old dears in unmodernised houses who freeze every winter, or those involved in the tourist industry, or the very rich who can spend the hundreds of thousands necessary to buy one of the lovely big country houses," says one local resident. The area proved very popular with Londoners during the 1990s who swopped their Victorian terraced homes for the country, bringing higher prices with them. A little mid-17th-century cottage with three bedrooms would hit the market with an asking price of around £245,000. Large country houses can run into millions.

Terraced cottages, Broadway

In Stow-on-the-Wold antique dealers have a dominating presence but there is a butcher, bakery, a small supermarket, chemist and a Tesco. A two-bedroom cottage could cost £200,000 to £250,000, a three-bedroom terraced house on a new development £300,000.

Broadway and **Chipping Campden** are both beautiful towns, built mainly of stone. Chipping Campden attracts elderly people retiring from Birmingham, and it brims with local activities. The Chipping Campden Society looks after the historic buildings, many of which were built by affluent wool merchants in the 14th and 15th centuries. There are drama and football clubs, two primary schools and a comprehensive which brings in children from surrounding villages by the coachload.

Journey: 109 min
Season: £5276
Peak: 1 per hr
Off-peak: 1 per hr

EVESHAM Though not a great many people would choose to commute daily from Evesham, many might consider part-time commuting. Its tree-lined walks, lawns along the Avon and some wonderful old buildings give it obvious charm. It also has two golf clubs. Property prices are lower here than up in the Cotswolds. A three-bedroom Victorian terraced house might sell for £160,000; a three-bedroom modern detached house on an estate for £165,000. Two-bedroom cottages can be found in the surrounding villages for £175,000, with older four-bedroom detached houses costing over £225,000.

The Pershore side is particularly pretty, with picturesque black-and-white villages such as **Charlton**, **Cropthorne** and **Fladbury** (where the celebrated canoe club has sent members to the Olympics). Fladbury tends to attract Birmingham rather than London commuters. The three new housing developments draw a constant flow of people. It has an award-winning butcher, a new sports pavilion for football and cricket enthusiasts, and a church primary school for five- to eight-year-olds. The middle school is in the neighbouring village of Pinvin, and the secondary is in Evesham. Further north of Evesham is another black-and-white village, **Norton**. It was once ruined by traffic on the A435, but has now been rescued with a bypass. The **Lenches** (**Church** and **Atch**) are also popular on this northern flank.

For truly grand landscape, however, you should look to the west, in the villages beneath Bredon Hill. The **Combertons** (**Little** and **Great**) are especially lovely. **Great Comberton** has a heady mix of half-timbered farmhouses and thatched cottages, while Little Comberton has a village dovecote with walls over 3ft thick and more than 500 nesting holes. Another red-brick dovecote in the village is even bigger, with 1425 nesting holes.

'The area has proved popular with Londoners who swapped their Victorian terraces for the country, bringing higher prices with them'

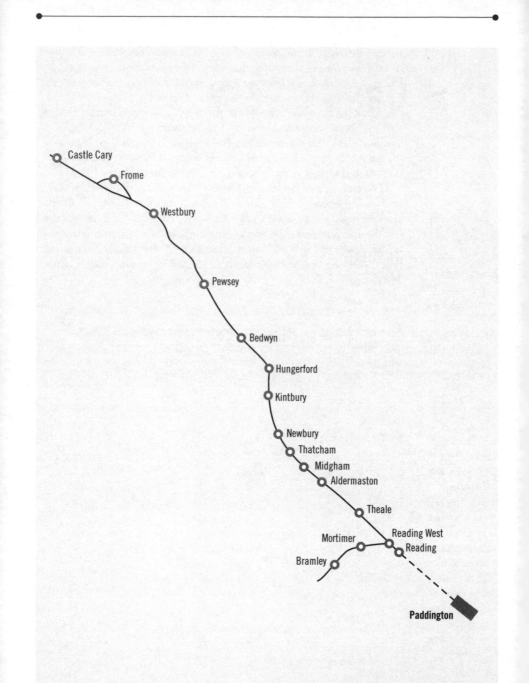

Castle Cary
Frome
Westbury
Pewsey
Bedwyn
Hungerford
Kintbury
Newbury
Thatcham
Midgham
Aldermaston
Theale
Reading West
Mortimer
Reading
Bramley
Paddington

Paddington
> Castle Cary

For stations between Paddington and Reading, see **Paddington to Bristol** line, page 149.

Journey: 33 min
Season: £2776
Peak: 1 per hr, 5 per hr changing at Reading
Off-peak: 3 per hr changing at Reading

READING WEST Reading offers fast trains and lies within striking distance of beautiful countryside. For a full description, see page 157.

> Branch line to Mortimer and Bramley

Journey: 50 min*
Season: £2792*
Trains to Reading (no through trains): 2 per hr
*From Bramley. It is possible to go via Basingstoke to Waterloo in the other direction. Season ticket valid in both directions, or £2780 via Basingstoke only

MORTIMER is the smaller and more rural of the two communities, with no mains gas and little street lighting. It is hoped that the 100 new houses planned will be screened from view. A minibus service to the station is a boon for commuters. A four-bedroom Victorian family house sells for £500,000; a two-bedroom terraced house for £220,000.

Bramley is a dormitory village which grew up around the railway in the mid-1890s and has had to swallow a lot of new houses in the last few years. It has a baker and a post-office-cum-store. A three-bedroom modern semi-detached house will cost £210,000, a larger four-bedroom detached £270,000.

'Reading offers fast trains and lies within striking distance of beautiful countryside'

> Continuation of main line

Journey: 43 min
Season: £2776
Peak: 1 per hr
Off-peak: 1 per hr

THEALE Since getting into **Reading** is a nightmare, many people prefer to use Theale station instead. It marks the beginning of the Berkshire farming belt beyond Reading, yet is more accessible and the fast trains stop here. The council has spent a considerable sum of money on restoring the town's Victorian image, reinstating cobbles and period lamp posts. Most of the main street, which has a baker, greengrocer and a few offices, is included within a conservation area.

Theale has accumulated large modern housing estates and an industrial area to the south and environmentalists are fending off the considerable pressure for more development. A large business park employs 10,000 people and accommodates major companies such as Vodafone, Thorn EMI and Walkers Crisps. Another is planned, together with a new hotel. A new two-bedroom house is likely to cost around £165,000; three bedrooms £190,000. A four-bedroom house (they are in short supply) could command £350,000. Some say Theale's name came from its brewery which made "the ale".

Journey: 51 min
Season: £2776
Peak: 2 per hr
changing at
Reading
Off-peak: 1 per hr
changing at
Reading

ALDERMASTON is a very pretty village on the Kennet and Avon Canal, with a main street of red brick and timber houses sandwiched between Elizabethan cottages. To outsiders, however, it is best remembered as the starting point for the Ban the Bomb marches, chosen by protesters because of its proximity to the Atomic Weapons Research Establishment. Despite the traffic that thunders through on the A340 to Basingstoke, the village has been well preserved. Until recently it was an estate village, and every third year on December 13 a candle auction is still held to determine the rent charged for a small piece of land called Church Acre – the end of the bidding is signalled by the extinction of a candle flame. Aldermaston Manor Hotel was once the big house, set in ample grounds. There is also a parish hall, a village green, a store and post office. Bowls and cricket are played.

The station itself is useful for shuttle services into Reading, from where fast trains to Paddington are plentiful. Newcomers to the village grazing the new Persimmon estate for purchases will find that a four-bedroom detached house can cost £349,000.

'To outsiders, Aldermaston is best remembered as the starting point for the Ban the Bomb marches'

Journey: 53 min	
Season: £2776	
Peak: 2 per hr	
changing at	
Reading	
Off-peak: 1 per hr	
changing at	
Reading	

MIDGHAM station is actually in **Woolhampton**, but was renamed Midgham station in 1873 because of the likelihood of confusion with Wolverhampton. Most people drive to Thatcham anyway because there is only a handful of parking spaces at Midgham station. It is a linear village, "big in land but not in people," is how one resident puts it. There is, however, a good food-lover's pub called The Coach & Horses. You could buy a three-bedroom period cottage for around £279,000.

At Woolhampton the River Kennet is the focal high point. The main street has half-timbered houses down one side and modern equivalents down the other, put up when the road was widened in 1931. The A4 and the railway thunder through making it too noisy to hear people speak. There are several shops, a post office, five pubs, and a fine watermill. A two-bedroom timber-framed cottage on the A4 recently struggled to sell at £210,000.

Journey: 41 min	
Season: £2776	
Peak: 2 per hr	
Off-peak: 1 per hr	

THATCHAM The old village of Thatcham, with the green at its centre, has swollen with new developments in the last couple of decades and more is yet to come. It has become a town, good for secondary shopping but Reading or Newbury (only two miles away) offer much more. Barratt and Redrow are busy building on former Ministry of Defence land with prices at between £159,000 and £300,000.The most sought-after new development is Dunston Park, within easy reach of the station and an established stamping grounds for professional couples and young families. Four-bedroom houses cost around £260,000 to £400,000. South Thatcham is less popular and sometimes less savoury (being close to the sewage works), so prices are lower. "Such a shame about the poo farm," says one agent. But lower prices mean good value and the average cost of a four-bedroom house here is around £230,000.

Thatcham station is served by the few through trains to London in the early morning. The snag is that you have to negotiate the level-crossing to reach the station. "If you are not careful, you can be stuck in your car at the crossing waiting for your own train to whoosh by," says one exasperated commuter.

Cold Ash, a little over a mile away, is particularly popular, straggling fetchingly down a hill into the Kennet valley. It has about 4000 residents, a community hall, a shop, a post office and some modern infilling. Property here sells quickly. A detached Twenties' three-bedroom house will cost £355,000.

The village of **Bucklebury** nearby, in an Area of Outstanding Natural Beauty, has some pretty cottages and a large common criss-crossed with footpaths. The Blade Bone pub has a copper-plated mammoth's shoulder bone on display, hence the name. Bradfield, the boys' public school, is close. A period cottage will cost from

If you are not careful at Thatcham you can be stuck in your car at the crossing waiting for your own train to whoosh by

£400,000 to £900,000, but anything larger with land attached will run up towards £1m. There is a curious little 17th-century painting of a fly and sundial in the local church, with the body and legs on one side of the glass and the wings on the other. *Tempus fugit* (time flies).

Journey: 49 min
Season: £2908
Peak: 2 per hr
Off-peak: 2 per hr

NEWBURY is a prosperous former market town with a good train service to London, and attracts commuters like flies to a honeypot. It has a mass of pretty downland villages within reach (*Watership Down* country) and is positioned on the edge of the so-called Silicon Valley. The centre is mostly 17th- and 18th-century with a good range of shops, including an old-fashioned pork butcher and pie-maker, and the Kennet and Avon Canal provides scenic richness. Many people feel, however, that new buildings have erased all sense of the brick-and-tile traditional country town. Vodafone has a massive presence. the firm was once spread between 48 office buildings here, but is now letting these out to new businesses and has moved itself into a huge new headquarters north of town. "Fifty years ago I can remember cattle and sheep being driven in, and the circus arriving by train and walking from it through the town. It's hard to imagine any of that now," says one elderly resident.

A great mix of people are attracted to Newbury. Computer companies have brought in the upwardly-mobiles; the racecourse (which has its own weatherboarded train station) attracts the punters; the much-contested bypass is being joined by a new underpass running north to south along the A34 to speed traffic further. Builders are busy catering for demand. Close to the centre you could find a three-bedroom restored Victorian house for around £275,000; spacious flat conversions in period buildings go for £350,000 to £400,000. A standard executive house sells at £400,000. In Garden Close or Tydehams, large houses built in the early 20th century in private grounds will sell for £700,000 upwards.

The once quiet nightlife has burgeoned as bars, nightclubs and health clubs have proliferated. There is also a recreation centre and a swimming pool and two new golf courses with a hotel have been built at **Donnington** just outside. The controversial bypass cuts a swathe across Enborne Chase, a beautiful unspoilt belt of land south of the town.

Villagers from as far to the north-west as **Lambourn** and as far south as **Hurstbourne Tarrant** will come in to use Newbury station. The National Hunt racehorse training centre is at Lambourn and there are 1400 horses in Lambourn and **Upper Lambourn**, both busy working villages. Stable-hands work from about seven in the morning until midday, when they rush to the village to shop before starting work again at about four o'clock. Lambourn itself has a few general stores, a farm shop, butcher, post office and saddler. The delicatessen is about to be replaced by an Indian restaurant. Upper Lambourn has little other than a pub. A three-bedroom semi will cost £210,000. You need a car if you live here though buses to Newbury and Swindon are becoming more frequent and a new shuttle to Hungerford station (see page 187) is planned to help commuters. Strings of 20 to 30 horses exercising in the narrow lanes across the rolling chalk hills can frustrate commuters driving to the station to catch the early morning trains, though gardeners love the manure they provide.

Eastbury, on the River Lambourn two miles closer to Newbury, is a lovely, but slightly more expensive village with a good pub, The Plough. Houses are built on the riverbanks, cleverly planted with shrubs and bulbs. It is a popular place to retire to. A five-bedroom Victorian house in four acres recently sold for £820,000; a period three-bedroom cottage would cost £300,000; a Sixties' bungalow £250,000. Neighbouring **East Garston** is another enchanting village of thatched houses, with three stables, a shop-cum-post-office and similar house prices.

'Strings of racehorses in the narrow lanes can frustrate commuters driving to the station'

Further east are two more good chalk villages, **West** and **East Ilsley**, just off the A34. East Ilsley, the slightly cheaper of the two, has a central square with a pond, and has resisted new developments apart from some sheltered housing for the elderly. Village life has changed dramatically over the years. This used to be the site of a twice-yearly sheep fair (the greatest sheep market in England after Smithfield, they say) and there were 13 pubs. Today only three pubs remain, and the place is largely inhabited by commuters. It has all the walks that the nearby Downs can offer, including the Ridgeway, along which Neolithic and Bronze Age man once commuted. West Ilsley is the pretty cousin, with a church at its heart, a village green, cricket pitch and pavilion, a pub, a racing stables owned by the Queen, and a good collection of cottages. Its social life tends to be dominated by the horse-racing fraternity. A four-bedroom period house set in half an acre would sell for around £550,000. Both villages have lost their post offices in recent years.

Stanford Dingley, set in the valley of the River Pang a good six miles to the north-east, is thought to be one of Berkshire's most beautiful villages. It has a classic mellow red-brick Georgian rectory, a 13th-century church screened by chestnuts, and two old inns called The Bull and The Boot. At The Bull a game called Ring The Bull is played, in which a ring dangling from the ceiling has to be swung on

Chalet-style house, Newbury

to a horn. "We're an active village," says the parish clerk. "We have barn dancing and hold summer fêtes, usually in someone's garden." The River Pang runs through some of the gardens, providing the setting for the annual tug-of-war in which the losers traditionally fell in the water, but damage to the banks has moved the event to another site. Houses rarely come on the market because people tend to stay put. A house with three or four bedrooms might be bought for around £450,000.

Yattendon, just north of the M4, has a picture-book village square surrounded by black-and-white 17th-century homes, backed up by Cromwellian red-brick houses. The partly-moated manor house, the church, rectory and malt house, all look immaculately cared for. Poet Laureate Robert Bridges's ashes are in the churchyard. Yattendon has a general store and post office, butcher, hairdresser, smithy, The Royal Oak Hotel and a restaurant. Socially it remains fairly feudal. There are tennis courts and a cricket pitch. The village fête is the main annual event. Property prices here are so high that an affordable housing scheme has been set up to provide 12 houses at lower cost for native villagers. A modern four-bedroom detached house might cost £425,000. A Seventies' house with four to five bedrooms and a good garden will fetch £600,000 or more.

> 'Prices are so high that an affordable housing scheme has been set up for villagers'

Much closer to Newbury, two miles north, is the village of **Bagnor**. It is scattered charmingly around a tributary of the Lambourn and remains fairly unspoilt, with a green, a pub called The Blackbird and a little theatre and restaurant called The Watermill, which attracts good productions. **Leckhampstead** also has a star quality setting, high above the Wantage to Newbury road, and wears its thatched cottages proudly around the small green.

Heading south you come to **Highclere** on the main Andover road, where houses range from £350,000 for four bedrooms to £500,000 for three bedrooms in a period cottage and half an acre. **Ecchinswell** is a handsome neighbour where a period four-bedroom cottage will cost £300,000 to £600,000.

Journey: 76 min
Season: £2940
Peak: 2 per hr
Off-peak: 1 per hr

KINTBURY is an unremarkable and yet endearingly compact and likeable village. It sits on the Kennet and Avon Canal deep in agricultural Berkshire, where its position attracts an element of tourism. There is a full range of house types and prices, from new developments for first-time buyers to executive detached houses. Locals fear that too many commuters who don't join in village activities are moving in and sending prices "through the roof". Anything with three bedrooms will now cost over £250,000 and even a starter home starts at £150,000.

Two miles away is **Inkpen**, a village strung out so thinly that you can't locate its centre (six hamlets have merged imperceptibly over the centuries). It is worth looking at, however, because of its position in the shadow of the Berkshire Downs. Steep winding lanes carry you hundreds of feet up to magical windy walks, and panoramic views from the gibbet on Walbury Hill.

Journey: 66 min
Season: £3020
Peak: 2 per hr
Off-peak: 1 per hr

HUNGERFORD
Being just off the M4, Hungerford is a favourite starting-place for house-hunters in the area. It is on the twee side of pretty, with a pleasant wide High Street stretching down to the Kennet and Avon Canal and the River Kennet. The tea and trinket shops of tourism are combined with upmarket interior design shops and day-to-day needs. It is the local antiques' capital, and has an antiques' arcade which is open on Sundays. Cattle graze the huge 180-acre common – given by John of Gaunt in the 14th century – which gives way to chalk downs and wooded hills beyond.

The community is close and tightly knit. As one villager says: "We have a cracking cricket team, a football team, choir, theatre club, band, good nursery school and so on. People get involved here. All the time something is happening, making it all tick." Ancient rituals are still observed. On the first Tuesday after Easter the Tutti men tour the town extracting kisses from all the women in return for oranges. There is also an arts festival and in December there is a pre-Christmas Victorian Extravaganza.

'Tutti men tour the town extracting kisses from all the women in exchange for oranges'

On the High Street you can buy two-bedroom terraced houses for £150,000 to £200,000. A larger four-storey Georgian house would start at £500,000. Standard four-bedroom houses on modern developments can be had for £350,000. But pressure on housing is a sensitive issue here. Plans to build 500 new houses were abandoned after every single person present voted against the plan at a public meeting.

The train service is good enough until about eight o'clock in the morning. After that the number of London trains dwindles to about one every hour or hour-and-a-half.

Black-and-white period house, Hungerford area

Within easy reach of Hungerford is the village of **Chilton Foliat**, a set-piece combination of brick, slate and thatch, with one shop and a pub. A three-bedroom thatched cottage on the main street would fetch £300,000. **Little Bedwyn**, on the Kennet and Avon Canal, is lovely, too. It has an outstanding 18th-century farmhouse in chequered brickwork, with a rare octagonal game larder. The farmyard, with timber-and-brick barns, is right in the village centre. A four-bedroom Victorian detached house will cost £425,000.

BEDWYN Above Bedwyn lie the great Saxon defensive ramparts of
Chisbury Camp. Down by the Kennet and Avon Canal towpath is the
1812 Crofton Pumping Station, which houses the two oldest steam
engines in the world that are still doing the job for which they were
designed. They are used to raise the water level in the canal. A large
four-bedroom Victorian house with a good garden in **Great Bedwyn**
will cost around £500,000.

Journey: 78 min
Season: £3108
Peak: 2 per hr
Off-peak: 1 per hr

PEWSEY Daily commuters have risen dramatically in number – at
least 100 hop on regularly now. The trains that serve Pewsey are
mostly InterCity services from the west. There are special commuter
trains each morning and evening. Otherwise it is always possible to
get a train to Newbury and change.

Journey: 65 min
Season: £4132
Peak: 1 per hr
Off-peak: 1 every
2 hrs

Pewsey is a pretty agricultural town between Salisbury Plain and
the Marlborough Downs. Some of the shops are still roofed in
thatch, and a statue of Alfred the Great stands in the centre,
overlooking the young River Avon and its resident ducks. It has a few
supermarkets, an estate agent, bank, bakery and so on, and its own
comprehensive school, playing fields and sports centre. The old
hospital has been converted and the grounds filled with new houses.
One of Wiltshire's six white horses was cut into the chalk hillside in
1785 and provides a potent local landmark.

Starter homes have doubled in price in the last three years, many
snapped up by investors, so that two bedrooms will now cost
£125,000 and will let at £500 per month. Just outside the town is a
Charles Church development where a modest four-bedroom
detached house will sell for £300,000. A four-bedroom thatched
cottage will cost rather more at £400,000 to £500,000

The pretty villages nearby include **Manningford Bruce**, two miles
away, where thatched cottages cluster around the church. A small
house here could be bought for around £175,000. The whole of this
area is classified as an Area of Outstanding Natural Beauty. A few
miles to the north-west you come to **Stanton St Bernard**. The Pewsey
Valley Riding Centre is here, and there are lots of weekend cottages
and larger country houses. A spectacular seven-bedroom converted
thatched barn in two acres with views of the Alton White Horse was
recently on the market at £1.25m.

Urchfont, though a little far from the station (nearly 10 miles west),
is also popular. It contains all the ingredients of the ideal village –
thatched cottages, good pubs, 16th- and 17th-century houses around
the greens, one of which is next to the church and has a duckpond.
There is also a William and Mary manor house. A thatched, 18th-
century, six-bedroom house off the green will cost £525,000.

One of the advantages of living to the west is that you are within
reach of **Devizes**, which is so attractive that it is a treat to go shopping

there. The market square is surrounded by houses which are older than their Georgian façades. The town has good small butchers and bakers, a Safeway and a Tesco, and a new shopping centre is planned. A small period terraced house will cost around £125,000; a three-bedroom period property £175,000 to £200,000. The Kennet and Avon Canal has a flight of locks, 29 over a two-mile stretch, rising 237ft to the town.

Less than three miles to the east of Pewsey is **Wootton Rivers**, where you pay a premium for prettiness. A two-bedroom thatched cottage here costs £320,000. There is only one street, running up from the bridge over the Kennet and Avon Canal, and a delightful pub called The Royal Oak. Along the towpath are the restored lock and lock-house.

The character of Wooton Rivers is so rural that even the churchyard seems merely an interruption in the farming landscape. The church itself is distinguished by a wooden belfry containing an unusual clock with a broomstick for a pendulum. Just to the north, for those in search of sylvan solitude, are the 2300 acres of Savernake Forest.

East Grafton, a few miles further east towards Hungerford, offers slightly larger houses. A five-bedroom period house with land and stables would command £800,000; a three-bedroom cottage £350,000. The A338 runs through it, but it keeps away from the village proper, where there is a large green and a Victorian church edged with thatched cottages.

To the north is **Marlborough**, the old halt for 18th-century stage coaches on the run from London to Bath. Today the town is dominated by the boys' public school (it now takes girls) and the tea rooms where they buy their sticky buns. Marlborough is an extremely popular place in which to live – it is close enough to the M4 at Swindon, it has a good range of small specialist shops (though Pizza Express and Caffe Uno have arrived) and is surrounded by spectacular countryside.

Georgian houses are the most sought after, though there are plenty of half-timbered houses hidden down the small back lanes off the broad open High Street. Two-bedroom Victorian terraced cottages sell at around £230,000; detached houses on newish estates £315,000 to £385,000; while a five-bedroom coach house in landscaped gardens recently went on the market at £1.4m.

There is a jazz festival each May and a fair each autumn, but there is no cinema. The church is strong. There is a choral society, civic society and railway society that has restored the old railway track to Swindon as a cycle path. The Scouts and Cubs have taken it upon themselves to clean the chalk outlines of the white horses in the area.

'Marlborough is dominated by the boys' public school (it now takes some girls) and the tea-rooms where they buy their sticky buns'

189

| Journey: 87 min |
| Season: £4936 |
| Peak: 1 per hr |
| Off-peak: 1 every 2 hrs |

WESTBURY

The train service is frankly thought to be better from Bath than it is from here. Westbury was once a charming small town with Georgian houses grouped around the market place and church (it still has a wonderful Victorian swimming pool), but it has been swamped by new housing. Blue Circle cement has replaced the old glove-making industry as the dominant local employer and its tall chimney throws sprinklings of unwanted dust over residents' windows. There are a few shops, including a butcher, greengrocer, bank and supermarket with post office. Two-bedroom starter homes can be bought for £117,000, and small three-bedroom semis for £140,000. High above Westbury stands the oldest white horse in Wiltshire, believed to have commemorated King Alfred's victory over the Danes in the 9th century.

Bratton, a couple of miles to the east, offers sleepy lanes where a small stream runs past some of the old cottages tucked into the hedgerows. The village has a store and a school. A beautiful four-bedroom Georgian house here would sell for around £575,000; a three-bedroom mid-terraced house for £175,000. **Edington** is similar, though more remote with a nice pub called The Lamb. This area is far from any large town so prices tend to be lower and commuting is rigorous. A thatched cottage might cost £249,000.

| Journey: 110 min* |
| Season: £4936 |
| Peak: 1 per hr |
| Off-peak: 1 every 2 hrs |
| *There are no through trains. London passengers must change at Westbury |

FROME

isn't quite in the best countryside close to Bath, nevertheless it has a distinct character with lots of stone buildings set on the steep eastern hillsides of the Mendips. The old market place is still here, though the cattle market moved out a few years ago. Its shopping centre is unimaginative, but the Black Swan art gallery is much admired and Sainsbury's has made its presence felt on the edge of town. The narrow, twisted streets are worth walking through just to admire. The most famous of them is Cheap Street, which is cobbled and has a watercourse running down the centre.

An old terraced cottage with three bedrooms will cost £155,000 in the conservation area just off the centre. New conversions in a

Late-Victorian house, near Frome

former hospital start at £95,000 for one bedroom, and £110,000 for two. Trains are not frequent from Frome as the station is on the loop served by trains from Weymouth.

To the west and south-west are several villages that teeter on the edges of the old stone quarries. When you look, bear in mind that there are plans to expand the quarries at Whatley and Leigh upon Mendip. Three miles north is **Lullington**, a very pretty little hamlet with a green and a church, but no shops, where an old stone house with three bedrooms might be had for £250,000.

Journey: 105 min
Season: £4936
Peak: 1 per hr
Off-peak: 1 every
2 hrs

CASTLE CARY This is long-haul commuting, but people do it.

Parking at the station is easy, and you can pick up the trains pelting back and forth to the Devon seaside. Castle Cary sits on the last few ripples of the Mendips before the relentless flatlands of the Somerset Levels. The town owes much of its prosperity to agriculture and the horse-hair weaving trade. There is still a weaver in the town, though the hair is imported from China. The remains of the old motte-and-bailey castle that gave the town its name are still here, and a small market is held on Thursdays.

The mellow, golden local stone is what makes people fall in love with the place. There are a few traditional shops, good private schools nearby, a thatched hotel called The George and a notable rectory just outside at **Ansford**, which was once the home of the Reverend James Woodforde, author of *Diary of a Country Parson*. New developments have arrived to the north and more are in the pipeline. A two-bedroom flat can be bought for around £90,000, a three-bedroom terraced house for £180,000, while a four-bedroom period house and garden will cost £400,000 to £500,000.

Commuters have to live close to the station out of necessity, because of the length of the journey. A clutch of villages within the five-mile belt include the stone-built **North** and **South Cadbury**, and **Yarlington**, which is a good agricultural working village with a mix of modern and old houses, priced very similarly to those in Castle Cary. To the north-west is **Ditcheat**, also a good working village. This is dairy country – rich, green and undulating – where much of the milk goes to butter and cheese-making factories.

‘Castle Cary sits on the last few ripples of the Mendips before the relentless flatlands of the Somerset Levels’

Reading
Earley
Winnersh Triangle
Winnersh
Wokingham
Bracknell
Martin's Heron
Ascot
Sunningdale
Windsor & Eton Riverside
Datchet
Sunnymeads
Wraysbury
Staines
Egham
Virginia Water
Chertsey
Waterloo
Bagshot
Camberley
Frimley
Ash Vale

Waterloo
> Reading

Journey: 33 min
Season : £1728
Peak: 6 per hr
Off-peak: 6 per hr

STAINES has been an important communications point ever since the Romans established a river crossing here on their route from London to the west. Not all subsequent bridges have been successful – three of them had collapsed by the end of the 18th century. The present one, opened by William IV in 1832, survives despite the heavy traffic from the A30 and M25. A surprisingly small station car park, accommodating only 50 or so cars, means that the surrounding roads are clogged by all-day parkers. Commuters often prefer to travel from other stations if they can. There is a wide range of housing. Large developments offer flats and houses from £160,000 for a studio, £250,000 for a two-bedroom flat, £230,000 to £270,000 for a three-bedroom semi and £450,000 for a four-bedroom detached. Staines is one of Surrey's three main shopping centres. The huge Elmsleigh shopping centre is re-opening in 2005 and is augmented by new arts entertainment venues, including a 10-screen Warner Brothers multiplex, health club and restaurants. The street market is on Wednesdays and Saturdays. The small roads leading off Laleham Road to the water are sought after and the riverside itself has become more fun with new lawns, walks, moorings and apartments along it. Two bedrooms and a patio could cost £450,000. There is a sailing and a rowing club.

Laleham, on the way to Shepperton, is the most favoured village, spread along a sizeable stretch of riverside. It has its own cricket club and a few basics, including a mini-supermarket, antiques shop and three pubs, and what one local calls a "cliquey atmosphere, but a nice clique. Everyone gets on well". In the village centre which is predominantly Victorian, three-bedroom semis can be bought for £300,000, a large four-bedroom detached house would cost £450,000.

'Three bridges at Staines had collapsed by the end of the 18th century'

'A cliquey atmosphere, but a nice clique. Everyone gets on well'

> Spur to Windsor & Eton Riverside via Wraysbury, Sunnymeads and Datchet

Journey: 44 min
Season: £1812
Peak: 2 per hr
Off-peak: 1 per hr

WRAYSBURY spreads itself rather wantonly and has several distinguishing characteristics. It has two stations – Sunnymeads, only a mile away (see below), still counts as Wraysbury – and three miles of water frontage. It is surrounded by gravel pits which have been landscaped into 60 acres of lakes, providing sanctuaries for wildlife and a magnet for birdwatchers and sailing clubs. Until recently 80 per cent of the houses were detached and individually built, though as a relatively new village it was rather looked down upon in its early days. Some roads are privately maintained by the residents, many of whom work at Heathrow which sends planes straight overhead. The M4 skirts the village without spoiling it, and counts as a convenience rather than a drawback. Wraysbury at one time was a weekend retreat for Londoners and there were many riverside shanties. These have given way to houses in the £350,000 to £800,000 bracket. There is a sprinkling of pre-Georgian cottages, a few Edwardian and Victorian terraces and some substantial small mansions. Modern three- and four-bedroom houses on a Barratt's development will cost £350,000 to £500,000. Surrounding Green Belt should provide protection against future development. There is a handful of local shops, including a pharmacy which makes its own aromatherapy remedies, a post office and a village green. One of the major features of life in Wraysbury is the number and quality of the local societies. These offer every option from cricket and fishing to history, drama, country & western and jazz, all of which are well attended and well organised. Opposite the village is the island where Magna Carta is believed to have been signed.

'Opposite the village is the island where Magna Carta was signed'

Journey: 46 min
Season: £1856
Peak: 2 per hr
Off-peak: 1 per hr

SUNNYMEADS, Wraysbury's second station, is on the boundary between Wraysbury and **Horton**, which is a rural village with a green, one shop and two pubs, both listed. It has proud historical connections with John Milton, who wrote some of his poems here, and with the Bowes-Lyon family. The local forge built the equestrian statue of George III, known as the Copper Horse, which stands on Snow Hill in Windsor Great Park. The snag is that the village lies directly in the line of most flights approaching Heathrow airport. The mix of properties ranges from a handful of listed houses to ex-council semis. A new block of apartments is being completed on the green, built as a replica of the old offices which stood there before. Flats here are selling at around £190,000 for two bedrooms. Bell's Lane is a leafy haven where a three-bedroom semi would sell at around £250,000, a detached house £285,000.

Journey: 47 min

Season: £1888

Peak: 2 per hr

Off-peak: 2 per hr

DATCHET

Only a mile from Windsor, Datchet has avoided being overshadowed and retains a village personality. Physically it is compact and shaped like a letter H with two cross-bars. The left of the H is on the river (one of the ports of call in Jerome K Jerome's Three Men in a Boat); the right is on the village green and the two cross-bars are High Street and Queens Road. The railway runs up the middle, regularly halting traffic at the level crossing (including Government ministers complete with police outriders on their way to see the Queen).

Until recently, most of the houses here were in the upper price bracket. In the last couple of decades, however, new estates aimed at first-time buyers have appeared. Studios and one-bedroom terraced houses cost between £90,000 and £140,000. Elsewhere, three-bedroom semis are from £275,000 to £325,000; detached houses with 150ft gardens and 45ft frontages over £375,000. Southlea Road is desirable and has some large 18th-century houses at £500,000 or more.

Datchet has always attracted London commuters and there is a large station car park. The other strong connection is with Heathrow: both ground staff and air crew favour the village for its pleasant atmosphere and easy access to the airport. Datchet's charms have also attracted its share of past and present celebrities, including Sir William Herschel, the astronomer, Sir Robert Watson-Watt, the inventor of radar, and now a clutch of ageing showbiz personalities. There is a post office, a Montessori, local primary and secondary schools. On the second Thursday of each month it holds a village market, selling home-made and home-grown foods and handcrafts. There is a local golf club with a long waiting list, a water-ski club, cricket (sometimes the village musters a showbiz eleven), sailing and a boatyard on the river which does daily hire.

Journey: 50 min

Season: £1908*

Peak: 2 per hr

Off-peak: 2 per hr

*£2004 if also
valid from Windsor
& Eton Central

WINDSOR & ETON RIVERSIDE

is Windsor's second station offering a slightly slower route to London than the shuttle from Windsor & Eton Central to Slough (which picks up the InterCity service from London to Paddington). Commuters from both stations benefit from Windsor's attractive mix of quaint old streets below the castle and smart new shops – everything from old family businesses to chain stores and branches of London department stores. It also has the 4800 acres of Windsor Great Park close by. Georgian houses cloak Castle Hill and pepper the centre of the town, which is composed mainly of Victorian terraces. A small cottage in need of improvement will start at £200,000; a three-bedroom house within walking distance of the town centre £325,000 to £400,000 and half as much again if very charming. The west and south of Windsor evolved in the Thirties and Fifties where semis now cost over £230,000.

Development is restricted by Crown lands and Green Belt. At Imperial Park, a large new estate on former Haileybury School grounds, apartments sell for £300,000 to £400,000, three-bedroom homes for £540,000 and six-bedroom detached houses for £920,000.

The most fashionable locations are in the conservation area around St Leonard's Hill, King's Road, Adelaide Square and Bolton Avenue. Newish four- to five-bedroom houses at King's Keep on Bolton Avenue sell for £475,000 to £550,000. It is expensive though and first-time buyers tend to gravitate to Bracknell or Slough. The Guild Hall in the High Street includes a marvellous bit of architectural deception by Christopher Wren. When the town councillors saw his plans in 1687, they apparently demanded more columns to support the upper floor (and their own combined weight). Wren obliged, up to a point. The new columns all ended slightly short of the ceiling.

Old Windsor, south-east of the town, was described in the *Domesday Book* as the third largest town in Berkshire. It had a wooden Saxon palace which deteriorated after William built his castle, when it was reduced to a village. Today it is a small town with parades of shops, a post office, bank and a convenient bus service into Windsor for major shopping. Large detached houses, some with river frontages, are a main feature of the market. The Friary is the road to aim for, where Victorian houses and modern infills in good-sized grounds cost around £500,000 to £650,000. The main road is fringed with Twenties-built houses from £220,000, one or two large enough to satisfy those who want a private estate close to London. These are the choice cuts in estate agents' windows, with price tags over £1m. Elton John occupies one. Two large housing estates provide less expensive homes, priced lower than their equivalents in Windsor where communications are better. Those who choose Old Windsor do so for its more rural atmosphere, fishing, boating and lively community spirit with plenty of sporting and social opportunities.

Eton is full of antiques shops, restaurants and schoolboys in wing collars and tailcoats. Inevitably, there is something of an us-and-them atmosphere. A three-bedroom Victorian house on the High Street could cost £550,000. Swanky luxury apartments have appeared at Eton Riverside new development selling at up to £1m.

'Eton is full of antiques shops, restaurants, and schoolboys in wing collars and tailcoats'

Dutch-style family house, near Egham

> Continuation of main line

Journey: 39 min
Season: £1816
Peak: 5 per hr
Off-peak: 4 per hr

EGHAM Although Egham technically is a small town it retains an unhurried atmosphere from its village past. The presence of Royal Holloway (London University's out-of-city campus college) means there are well-patronised bars, bistros and pubs, and a hungry market for student accommodation. Parents buy-to-let to students here. Among the new estates, first-time buyers can buy one-bedroom flats which cost from £130,000. Two-bedroom Victorian semis in the town centre start at £240,000. The town has a good mix of local shopping, including a butcher and a baker whose families have been serving the community for more than 100 years. There are plenty of sports and social clubs, and an active historical society.

To the west, **Englefield Green** is a prestigious address thought by some as rather twee. It comes with a green, traditional pubs and little high street of shops including a bakery. A two-bedroom terraced cottage will cost £250,000. To the south is **Thorpe**, a village bisected by the M25. Despite this apparent handicap, houses here are 15 per cent or so more expensive than their equivalents in Egham. The smallest two-bedroom Victorian semi will cost around £250,000, and there is a preponderance of large houses in spacious plots. A four-bedroom detached house built in the Thirties or Fifties will fetch between £280,000 and £330,000. There is a theme park just outside the village, but the traffic to it does not pass through the village itself.

Journey: 42 min
Season: £1928
Peak: 4 per hr
Off-peak: 4 per hr

VIRGINIA WATER, brushed by the M25, has seen two enormous new developments in the decade. Virginia Park and St Anne's Park are super-luxurious gated estates, each with a communal pool, gym, Jacuzzi, tennis courts and other Dallas touches. Their very presence has pushed prices up. A two-bedroom flat here will cost £365,000 (compared to £140,000 in the village). A five-bedroom detached house with a double garage will cost £1m. The grand estate lifestyle all began with the Wentworth Estate, built around the famous golf course by a speculative developer called Tarrant in the Twenties. Celebrities flourish in its prosperous atmosphere – the pantheon of names has included Russ Abbott, Bruce Forsyth, Nanette Newman and Brian Forbes. A five-bedroom family house on the Wentworth Estate will command upwards of £1.25m and more. Similar houses in half an acre in Lower Wentworth, which does not overlook the golf course, will fetch £750,000. The atmosphere is quiet and rural, the first breath of real countryside outside London, but there is little sign of rural hardship. There are two parades of specialist shops, boutiques, a delicatessen, and several excellent preparatory schools. Less expensive houses are few in number. For a two-bedroom Sixties' semi you would pay around £275,000, which represents a small premium over the next most prestigious area, Sunningdale. The stretch of water which gives the area its name is a great ornamental lake created in the 18th century by the Duke of Cumberland. He also built the nearby Fort Belvedere, later the home of Edward VIII where the abdication was signed.

> Line to Chertsey

Journey: 64 min
Season: £1928
Peak: 2 per hr
Off-peak: 2 per hr

CHERTSEY is reaping the commercial benefit of lying just inside the M25, an arbitrary boundary chosen by many London companies relocating their head offices. Developments have sprouted in the last decade to cope with the expansion. Very little remains of the famous Benedictine Abbey founded in 666. Henry VIII ordered the stones to be used in the rebuilding of his palace at Oatlands Park. But the handsome, seven-arched 18th-century bridge is still a landmark, and the town is finishing a 14-phase improvement scheme. There is a good selection of period properties which, foot for foot, offer better value than up-market Weybridge. Beside the park and woods of St Ann's Hill there are large detached houses with price tags which rise above £1.5m. Abbey Road is an equally prestigious address. Grove Road, by the football club, offers more affordable Victorian houses which cost £230,000 for three bedrooms. First-time buyers will find a wealth of one-bedroom modern flats at £130,000. Good schools include Sir William Perkins' girls' grammar, and there is a very highly regarded hospital, St Peter's.

Lyne and **Longcross** are the most sought-after villages in the area, graced with large detached houses (it costs 15–25 per cent more to buy into them). Bungalows in large garden plots cost £350,000 to £450,000. They lack properties of real character, but the agricultural smells and lack of a bus service are still enough to make country-lovers feel at home.

> Continuation of main line

Journey: 47 min
Season: £2140
Peak: 3 per hr
Off-peak: 2 per hr

SUNNINGDALE The development of the Southern Railway at the turn of the 20th century made Sunningdale accessible to London businessmen who wanted to build country mansions with golf and horse-racing right on their doorsteps. Several of these minor palaces still survive intact, but many were demolished in the Thirties and Sixties to make way for new development. Others have been converted into flats. It is a village of two parts, the old village around the church, and the busier shopping area near the station. Part of it lay within Surrey until 1991, when the whole was switched into Berkshire. The most sought-after houses are in Titlarks Hill (where Gary Lineker lives), leading to the golf course, and in Ridgemount and Priory Roads. Large houses in half to one acre sell for between £900,000 and £2m. Kenneth Branagh has completely rebuilt a house here. Sunningdale is not exclusively a playground for the rich, however. In the old village there are three-bedroom Victorian semis for between £285,000 and £375,000. Think twice before buying a house too close to the A30. When the M25 or M3 get clogged the traffic pours on to the other through roads and jams those, too. There is a good choice of state and private schools. Sport is plentiful, but rather exclusive. There are two top polo clubs, and golf at Wentworth and Sunningdale, which has the oldest golf club for women in the country.

Sunningdale offers country mansions with golf and horse-racing right on their doorsteps,

Sunninghill to the west is a large parish covering several communities, none of which has retained its original atmosphere. The area known as **Cheapside** is small and sweet with The Thatched Tavern which is memorable for its good food. Sunninghill has a busy High Street with 50 or so shops, but its identity problem is not helped by the fact that Ascot station (see below) is actually in Sunninghill, and most people prefer it to Sunninghill station. East-west trains stop at Ascot, and the car park has been considerably extended. Plentiful turn-of-the-20th-century houses sell to London commuters or to those with jobs or businesses in Camberley or Heathrow. You would pay between £285,000 and £350,000 for a two- or three-bedroom semi. The church is busy, as is the dramatics society, The Quince Players.

A couple of miles south of Sunninghill is **Windlesham**. It a village with a stout heart which has fended off new development recently and obtained lottery money to refurbish the amateur Windlesham Club and Theatre. Semis can be bought for £285,000 to £350,000. Yet it flirts with the rich and famous, too. His Highness Sheik Mohammed Bin Rashid Al Maktoum, Crown Prince of Dubai, owns a palatial residence here; Brian May, Queen guitarist, both lives and has a recording studio here; and the Duchess of York famously let Ruby Wax into her rented house here (and showed her the T-shirt shelves and fridge), but she has since moved on. A five- or six-bedroom Thirties' house standing in one or two acres in Westwood Road will fetch up to £4m.

Journey: 51 min

Season: £2268

Peak: 4 per hr

Off-peak: 2 per hr

ASCOT
Strangers expect Ascot to be a glamorous place to live, because of its high horse-racing and fashion profile. They are often surprised by its lack of character. Its main attraction is the racecourse, which was laid out in 1711 for Queen Anne. The shopping centre consists of rows of small exclusive retailers. The level of wealth, however, can almost be measured by the height of the hedges – and they are lofty here. Racehorse owners (those who own part-share of a horse rather than whole stables) pay a premium for four- to five-bedroom detached houses in Coronation Road and Kier Park. A seven- to eight-bedroom house on five acres would cost £2.25m to £2.5m; a period house with five bedrooms, an annexe, needing a little work, could be snaffled for £1m. You effectively buy into is a rich man's playground, close to Windsor and Heathrow Airport with golf at Hawthorn Hill and Wentworth, racing at Ascot and Windsor, polo at Smiths Lawn and the Royal Berkshire Polo Club, boating and sailing on the Thames. For the very rich there are some sizeable mansions. Not more than a mile away is Ascot Place and its several hundred acres, which changed hands for £20m. There are slightly smaller fry to be found. South Ascot has Victorian railway workers' cottages as well as larger Victorian semis which sell at £650,000 for four bedrooms. Property at Grand Regency Heights, a major new development facing the racecourse, sells at prices between £300,000 to £1m. Royal Ascot Golf Club is in the centre of the racecourse. There are also opportunities for squash, tennis and cricket.

'The level of wealth can almost be measured by the height of the hedges'

North Ascot is quite different in character from the Ascot that surrounds the racecourse. Concentrated building began here in the 1880s and has been spreading north and west of the racecourse ever since. A Victorian semi in North Ascot will cost £225,000 to £350,000; three-bedroom semis on infill developments start at around £225,000.

Parts of Ascot are in the parish of **Winkfield**, the largest in the county. It covers nearly 10,000 acres and contains communities which are described as settlements rather than villages with traditional focal points. Winkfield itself is semi-rural, with some listed buildings and small terraces with modern infill, and a new community hall regularly booked by local clubs and societies (from badminton to dancing). There is a real worry that it will lose its identity and become "just a place from which to get to other places". It has several parks and recreation areas, but no village green, though it still has an annual

May festival. A small terraced house sells for around £225,000 to £250,000. A wing in a Georgian-style 1860s house in ample grounds is priced at £500,000 to £800,000.

Most of the small communities in this area have their own local societies and, as this is partly Metropolitan Green Belt, the strongest voices belong to the residents' associations and conservation societies fighting against new development. Golf and polo are the favourite outdoor activities and there are numerous riding establishments. To avoid frightening the horses in the Cranbourne area you need to drive almost permanently in low gear.

> Line to Ash Vale via Bagshot, Camberley and Frimley

Journey: 68 min
Season: £2320*
Peak: 2 per hr
Off-peak: 2 per hr
(1 changing at
Ascot plus 1
changing at Ash
Vale)
*£2392 if also
valid via Ash Vale

BAGSHOT Once a wild heathland frequented by highwaymen (it was the perfect distance from London, reached by coach as dusk settled), Bagshot developed in the mid-19th century and is carefully maintaining its Victorian atmosphere. Lampposts are period-style, and new developments and refurbishments have to be in keeping. The area thrives because of the many London companies which have relocated here and to nearby Fleet. There is day-to-day shopping, good schools and plenty of opportunities for leisure. Connaught Park, a nine-year-old development on the outskirts, is often known as Terminal 5 because of the high concentration of airport personnel who live here. One-bedroom flats here sell for around £120,000; two-bedroom houses for £155,000. College Ride is highly prized for its gardens backing on to Windsor Forest and a tract of land recently made available by the Crown for public use is popular with walkers and bikers. Victorian and Edwardian house in a good position start at around £190,000 for two bedrooms.

'To avoid frightening the horses in the Cranbourne area you need to drive almost permanently in low gear'

Journey: 63 min
Season: £2392
Peak: 2 per hr
Off-peak: 2 per hr
(1 changing at
Ascot plus 1
changing at Ash
Vale)

CAMBERLEY
Before the mid-19th century when the Royal Military Academy was established at Sandhurst, Camberley simply did not exist. Large houses with between six and 12 bedrooms were built for officers, with more modest developments and shops following between 1880 and 1910. At first there were two areas, Cambridge Town and York Town, named after the two dukes who had been heads of the academy. But when the mail kept going to the university town instead of the military one, the whole area was united under the single name, Camberley. Most of the largest old houses have gone, demolished to make way for new cul-de-sacs. Those that remain will set you back by £600,000 to £800,000 for six bedrooms. A neo-Georgian detached house will cost £450,000 to £480,000. There are also some Victorian terraced houses which you can buy into for around £250,000. One disadvantage of living in Camberley is traffic noise from the A30 and M3. Attractions include good high street shopping plus the Main Square centre by the staion, and the Meadows shopping centre on the outskirts. The Camberley Theatre shows films in the auditorium and provides rehearsal space and there are good local comprehensive schools.

For something more rural and very desirable, you need to look west of Sandhurst to **Eversley**, where £400,000 will buy three bedrooms, or £1m will buy a six-bedroom house with nine acres.

Journey: 59 min
Season: £2392
Peak: 2 per hr
Off-peak: 2 per hr
(1 changing at
Ascot plus 1
changing at Ash
Vale)

FRIMLEY
is too modern to call itself a village. It is a one-high-street sort of a place, with all the basics and is particularly valued for its good schools. Most of the housing is contained on three large estates. Paddock Hill, for example, was built over a decade ago and offers one-bedroom maisonettes at £120,000, three-bedroom semis at £200,000 and Tudor-style four- and five-bedroom houses at £300,000 or more. A lively young population entertains itself at Bagshot's nightclub or at Basingstoke's bowling alley, ice rink and cinema, 20 minutes' drive down the M3. Five minutes from the centre is Frimley Green, which has a very old heart. The roads off the green have a mix of houses built in the Thirties, Seventies and Eighties. Houses with a country feel on the Guildford Road cost £400,000 up to £1m but you can pay much more for a period piece. Commuter parking is limited but most people either walk to the station or drive instead to Farnborough, whence the direct line to Waterloo takes only 40 minutes.

ASH VALE
See Alton section of the **Waterloo to Salisbury** line, page 210.

> Continuation of main line

Martin's Heron
Journey: 55 min
Season: £2284
Peak: 3 per hr
Off-peak: 2 per hr

Bracknell
Journey: 58 min
Season: £2320
Peak: 3 per hr
Off-peak: 2 per hr

MARTIN'S HERON AND BRACKNELL Nothing in Bracknell today suggests that in the early 19th century it might have been described as "a small thoroughfare hamlet adorned with many genteel residences and delightful villas". In 1948 it was incorporated as Berkshire's only New Town, planned for a London overspill of 25,000. It now has more than 52,000 inhabitants, all of whom must have chosen it for convenience rather than charm. The increase in commuter traffic was sufficient to require the building of a second station, Martin's Heron, over a decade ago. Property prices are relatively modest given that the journey to London takes less than one hour. One-bedroom flats can be found for £100,000 to £140,000; three-bedroom ex-council houses from £135,000 to £160,000; modern semis on private developments between £170,000 and £240,000, and four-bedroom detached houses at £250,000. Unkind critics attach the "concrete jungle" tag, but there is plenty of high-tech industry to keep a large proportion of the young population busy locally, with good sports facilities, every kind of club, a hands-on science exhibition in the Look Out Discovery Centre and a Coral Reef water complex with a pirate ship, water slides and erupting volcano.

Three miles west of Bracknell is **Binfield**, which has outgrown its status as a village to become a suburb of Bracknell. Historically it is notable chiefly for its connection with Alexander Pope, who lived here as a boy in the early 1700s. It is loosely knit with greens, has a few shops, including an art shop, curry house, chinese takeaway, fish-

Modern two-up-
two-down, near
Bracknell

and-chip-shop, some small businesses, the John Nike Sports
Complex (for dry ski-ing, ice-skating and tobogganing), as well as
the redoubtable Binfield Badger Group.

Modern estate housing includes Temple Park, overlooking the
golf course, and Foxley Field where prices start at £205,000 for a
two-bedroom detached, £225,000 for a three-bedroom detached,
£320,000 for a five-bedroom detached. A community spirit still
survives and young mothers, as well as the established older
residents, are involved in the two community centres, drama club,
Scout, Brownie and Guide groups, and line dancing. The local
primary school has a good reputation, with secondary age children
moving on to Bracknell and Wokingham.

'Nine Mile Ride was cut through the forest to enable ladies to
follow the chase from their carriages'

Journey: 65 min
Season: £2396
Peak: 3 per hr
Off-peak: 2 per hr

WOKINGHAM Despite centuries of doffing its cap to nearby royals
in Windsor Forest, Wokingham was not granted a coat of arms until
Coronation year, 1953. A relic of the royal hunt still survives in Nine
Mile Ride, which was cut through the forest to enable ladies to
follow the chase from their carriages. The town's Millennium effort
means that every public and private space should be covered in a
haze of bluebells in spring.

The old market town has expanded rapidly during the last few
decades, swelling its population from 9000 to around 30,000.
Strategically it is extremely well-placed, being served by the A329
London to Reading road and by the M4 which links it to Heathrow
airport, the West of England and South Wales. Bus services provide
links to Reading and Bracknell. The town centre is surrounded by
modern residential streets, many of which are still lined with old oaks
and other forest trees. On the west side stands the Woosehill
development, containing more than 2000 houses, as well as shops,
schools and community and health centres. Most of it went up in the
Seventies and Eighties. The mixed estate offers flats and one-, two-,
three- and four-bedroom houses at prices ranging from £115,000 to
£415,000. A relatively new addition is Keephatch Park, which has
five-bedroom detached houses at £500,000 to £550,000 and four-
bedroom houses at £280,000 upwards.

Lucas Hospital in Luckley Road, built in 1665 to provide a home
for 16 elderly men is Wokingham's prize Grade I listed building. The

'Wokingham has some attractive 16th- and 17th-century
houses, particularly in Rose Street and Shute End'

hospital is arranged around three sides of a quadrangle, with a chapel filling the right wing. Visitors are admitted by appointment. Elsewhere there are some attractive 16th- and 17th-century houses, particularly in Rose Street and Shute End. An 18th-century three-bedroom house in Rose Street with no garden could cost £240,000, but would be a rare buy.

The most expensive parts of town are in Murdoch and Sturges Roads, just to the south-east of the centre, where large Edwardian houses, with four or five bedrooms and big gardens sell at £700,000 to £1m. Priest Avenue and Rances Lane are also desirable, where three-bedroom houses in large gardens cost £320,000. Cheaper properties built in the Sixties are found around the Mulberry Business Park and along the Finchampstead and Luckley Roads. A three-bedroom semi here will cost around £200,000 to £220,000.

In the north, the large Emmbrook development was begun in the Thirties, with additions in the Sixties, Seventies and Eighties. Modest estate-type housing predominates, with prices starting £200,000 for a three-bedroom semi and rising to £220,000 for a four-bedroom detached chalet-style house.

'Wokingham is a good area for golf fanatics, who have five courses to choose from'

Wokingham is a good area for golf fanatics, who have five courses to choose from. It also has public playing fields, a sports centre, indoor swimming pool, and a small theatre. Shops include Tesco, Waitrose and W H Smith, but there is no major department store. Wokingham people tend to work and shop in Reading or Bracknell. Four weeks before Christmas the town seizes up for the winter Carnival, and each February it turns out for the half marathon which attracts over 1750 entrants.

Winnersh	
Journey: 69 min	
Season: £2456	
Peak: 3 per hr	
Off-peak: 2 per hr	

Winnersh Triangle	
Journey: 71 min	
Season: £2492	
Peak: 3 per hr	
Off-peak: 2 per hr	

WINNERSH AND WINNERSH TRIANGLE has been built on old Windsor Great Forest land, starting in the Twenties and gathering pace in the last three decades. There is a supermarket, a large health club and DIY store for Sunday Black & Decker fiends. The new 12-screen cinema has upset older villagers who have described it as "a warhorse with neon signs". The Winnersh Triangle sounds dangerously exotic, but it's not a place where boats disappear without trace – rather it's a large business centre. Traffic-hum from the A329M and M4 is a constant reminder of the quality of the road communications.

'The rhododendron drive to the next village of Barkham still survives, though it has been hacked about a bit by new development'

The most famous former resident of Winnersh was John Walter II, son of the founder of *The Times*. He built a Georgian mansion called Bearwood, which his son replaced with the present mansion, now a boys' private school. Walter also built the "model" estate of **Sindlesham** with its church, pub, school, dower house, cottages and farm and now a golf course. The rhododendron drive which he planted to the next village of **Barkham** still largely survives, though it has been hacked about a bit by new development. The model estate itself is now part of Winnersh and rather swamped, but Sindlesham manages to charm. Along the Reading Road are some good-value late Sixties' and Seventies' houses. The village is generally cheaper than Wokingham. A three-bedroom terraced house would cost £225,000. There are also some half-timbered houses

To the north lies **Hurst**, a "proper" village with a duckpond and green, much the nicest on this side of Reading. It has a shop and a butcher, post office, primary school and strong cricket club. The most desirable four-bedroom cottages here sell for £500,000 to £600,000, but there are cheaper properties, too.

Journey: 74 min	
Season: £2512	
Peak: 3 per hr	
Off-peak: 2 per hr	

EARLEY Despite the name – Earley derives from the Anglo-Saxon words for eagle and wood – there is nothing at all rural on the horizon here. There are three parts to Earley: Maiden Erlegh, Lower Earley and Earley proper. By some calculations Lower Earley is the third biggest housing estate in Europe, clamped to the southern underbelly of Reading, right beside the M4. Prices range upwards from £120,000 for one-bedroom to £450,000 for five bedrooms, but many residents describe living here as awful. The provision of

facilities has not kept pace with new houses. Old Earley has the oldest and most expensive properties – older in this context meaning turn-of-the-20th-century. Prices range from £140,000 for a two- or three-bedroom Victorian terraced house to £300,000 for a three-bedroom semi and £550,000 for a large five-bedroom house. Maiden Erlegh Park is a belt of ancient woodland with a lake, kept as a community nature reserve.

The area is nicer than the less appealing parts of Reading, but still rather a suburban sprawl. The centre of Reading is about 15 minutes away by car, and the "village" – a misnomer if ever there was one – is enlivened by a large hall of residence for students of Reading University, mostly overseas mature students.

Journey: 78 min*
Season: £2776
(also valid to
Paddington)
Peak: 3 per hr
Off-peak: 2 per hr
*Waterloo only.
For faster services
see Paddington
to Reading and
Bristol line,
page 157

READING For Reading main entry, see **Paddington to Reading and Bristol** line, page 157.

> Salisbury and Southampton

Journey: 24 min	
Season: £1896	
Peak: 5 per hr	
Off-peak: 3 per hr	

WEST BYFLEET is a large village that has expanded over the years to become inseparable from Woking. Property prices are high because of its closeness to London. A modern three- to four-bedroom town house will be unlikely to cost less than £300,000. An older detached house would be at least £450,000.

Journey: 26 min	
Season: £2132	
Peak: 10 per hr	
Off-peak: 10 per hr	

WOKING is a busy but unremarkable commercial town, hoping to catch attention with the planned new Woking Galleries designed by the creators of the London Eye. The rail service is very frequent, even if available seats may be few, and it is conveniently placed for access to the A3, M3 and even the M25. The north side of the town is mostly given over to council houses and the south tends to be more sought after. A neo-Georgian three-bedroom house on a small development would start at around £240,000; a new four-bedroom detached would cost £400,000. Hook Heath is where the wealthy gather, in mini-mansions on large plots which sell for over £750,000. For lower prices, but a vast range of choice, you could look at Goldsworth Park, where 8000 homes have been built over the last three decades and a two-bedroom terraced house costs £165,000 to £180,000. New developments by the station come with concierges and private gyms.

Horsell, on the outskirts and separated by the canal, tends to be slightly more expensive than Woking proper. The novelist H G Wells lived in Woking for a time, and in *The War of the Worlds* he described the Martians landing on Horsell Common. A Thirties' detached house with three bedrooms would cost around £450,000.

For a vintage Home Counties village there is **Chobham**, two miles to the north-west and no weakling in the Best Kept Village stakes. Lorries have been banned from the High Street, which is very much a conservation area with antiques shops, eateries and a pretty hump-backed bridge over the Bourne brook. Chobham Common is a precious green lung in this part of Surrey, providing wooded bridleways for pony-lovers. People from outside the village run the football and tennis, but the cricket, Brownies, Guides and WI are domestic affairs. The village is greatly sought after, so a small period cottage will cost at least £230,000. For a larger period house, perhaps with a paddock, you must expect to pay £900,000.

Journey: 36 min
Season: £2236
Peak: 3 per hr
Off-peak: 3 per hr

BROOKWOOD has the edge on Woking because people prefer the idea of living in a village, no matter how built-up it has become. The strangest fact about the station is that is was built originally to serve the enormous cemetery (created to take 1854 London typhoid victims), not for the convenience of commuters. Small cul-de-sacs of fairly new houses abound. A three-bedroom Thirties' detached house would cost around £280,000.

> Fork to Alton

Journey: 38 min
Season: £2328
Peak: 3 per hr
Off-peak: 2 per hr

ASH VALE is usually considered a rather unfashionable address, though it has the attraction of affordable prices for first-time buyers. It consists mainly of Victorian terraces arranged in grids around the railway station. A two-bedroom terraced house would start at around £165,000.

Journey: 42 min
Season: £2384
Peak: 3 per hr
Off-peak: 2 per hr

ALDERSHOT is an army town with a pretty rough feel to it at night. There are 10,000 soldiers and their families living here. The good thing is that it has terrific sports facilities, including games pitches, a new gymnastics academy, ski slope and an Olympic-sized swimming pool. Victorian terraces went up in Aldershot like mushrooms in a cow pasture. You could buy a two-bedroom terraced house now for around £145,000. In the nearby dormitory of Fleet (see page 212), the same house would cost £10,000 more. Aldershot's terraces are surrounded by lots of army married quarters built in the Thirties and Sixties. Prices rise a little on the Farnham side of town, where a three-bedroom detached house will cost around £250,000. New growth is planned on huge swathes of ex-army land.

Journey: 48 min
Season: £2476
Peak: 3 per hr
Off-peak: 2 per hr

FARNHAM is something of a refuge from Aldershot, having a lovely Georgian heart with the castle at its centre. People living anywhere between the two towns will always say they live in Farnham. The south side is more upmarket than the north. It has more of a country feel, even though it is very well-connected to London by train and the A3. A three-bedroom detached Thirties' house in a quiet road will cost £600,000; a more spacious five-bedroom house over £750,000. There are some modern apartments on the south side, where a three-bedroom unit will cost £225,000 to £275,000.

Journey: 58 min
Season: £2500
Peak: 2 per hr
Off-peak: 1 per hr

BENTLEY is an attractive hamlet which has become more sought after since the new bypass put the A31 further east. There are one or two discreet modern estates, and a small Charles Church development of large four-bedroom houses with double garages, selling at around £315,000. Smaller three-bedroom period terraced cottages may be bought for around £275,000. Novelist Jane Austen's brother was once curate of Bentley; Robert Baden-Powell, founder of the Boy Scouts, lived in Pax Hill house; and a director of the White Star Shipping line, owners of the *Titanic*, lived at the big house, Jenkyn Place. It is has a primary school and shop and strong sense of community, one reason why it was made the subject of the BBC Radio 4 programme *The Village*. The station is just under a mile from the village, near Alice Holt forest.

Journey: 65 min
Season: £2592
Peak: 2 per hr
Off-peak: 2 per hr

ALTON is a handsome little market town whose square still fills with stalls every Tuesday. The station building is painted in the old Southern Railway livery of green and cream. The community of 17,000 is essentially a rural one, though it has drawn commuters with the lovely countryside that surrounds it and has occasionally been highlighted by agents for its fast growing property prices. You might find a mid-terrace Grade II listed house with two bedrooms, beams and an inglenook fireplace dating from 1800, for around £185,000. Newer three-storey town houses with three bedrooms start at £225,000. A new development on the fringe of the town has five-bedroom houses from £415,000.

Period five-bedroom thatched houses in the lanes will cost from around £600,000 to £650,000. One of the most sought-after villages is **Chawton**, a mile away, though the stone-and-thatch cottages only rarely come up for sale. Chawton's main claim to fame is that the novelist Jane Austen lived in a small cottage with her parents and wrote most of her novels here in the early 19th century. Her nephew, Edward Knight, lived in the manor house. The cottage is now open to the public.

Old manor house,
Alton area

> Continuation of main line

Journey: 39 min
Season: £2416
Peak: 3 per hr
Off-peak: 3 per hr

FARNBOROUGH It is socially advantageous to have some connection with flying if you live in Farnborough. This is where the Royal Aircraft Establishment was based, and where the Farnborough Air show is held biannually. The heart of the town has been fairly unceremoniously ripped out. There is now a shopping centre which is being spruced up, a good leisure centre and some small Victorian terraces, suitably priced for first-time buyers at around £170,000 each. Further out, the housing is of Sixties' vintage: three-bedroom semis from £200,000; four-bedroom detached houses from £250,000.

Journey: 49 min
Season: £2448
Peak: 3 per hr
Off-peak: 2 per hr

'Fleet divides into quarters, each one conveniently date-stamped'

FLEET The army's huge presence in Fleet has reduced and ex-army land is going to be developed for housing. The train service to London is good, and it is popular with commuters. Another great attraction is Fleet Pond, whose 133 acres of freshwater lake, woodland, heath and reedbed are fiercely protected by the Fleet Pond Society. Fleet itself divides neatly into quarters, each one conveniently date-stamped. If you have a taste for the Twenties, you'll find a good selection of Arts-and-Crafts houses with three-bedroom semis in the £250,000 range. If you prefer the architecture of the Fifties and Sixties, closely-packed in leafy roads, then you'll find a range of choice at between £240,000 and £300,000. The other two quarters are modern, built in the last few decades, with many of the three- or four-bedroom houses aimed squarely at that archetypal creature of the Eighties, the yuppy. You could pay £285,000 for four bedrooms; £400,000 to £500,000 for a house with five bedrooms and three or four reception rooms. Creatures of the Nineties and Noughties are here, too: more than 2500 new houses have been built in the last 20 years and another 1200 are planned.

Journey: 54 min
Season: £2488
Peak: 3 per hr
Off-peak: 2 per hr

WINCHFIELD Around the station there is scarcely a village to speak of. Little more than a mile away, however, is **Hartley Wintney**, practically two centuries removed from Fleet. It has old coaching inns with archways leading into cobbled yards, five village ponds and five village greens with ancient oaks, and the second oldest cricket ground in England. The centre is full of antiques shops and has an art gallery which specialises in English watercolours. "Very Hampshire," says one local. There is a butcher, a bakery and two coffee shops and a market on Wednesday mornings. Social highlights include productions by the local dramatic society, and there are all the usual clubs and societies – WI, Scouts, Brownies and so on. High prices follow the 17th- and 18th-century architecture. Council houses are tucked out of sight. A classic four-bedroom cottage overlooking the cricket ground might cost £500,000. A modern four-bedroom house would be in the range of £340,000, while a two-up, two-down Victorian cottage on the common might be had for £270,000.

Journey: 58 min
Season: £2532
Peak: 3 per hr
Off-peak: 2 per hr

HOOK is modern-day Commuterland as opposed to Metroland, with a major Tesco and hundreds of new houses arranged in estates. The London-bound trains are frequent, and it is very close to Junction 5 of the M3. Four-bedroom detached houses start at around £245,000, rising to £350,000 for one from the up-market builders Charles Church. There is a big helicopter base a couple of miles away at RAF Odiham. Thomas Burberry, of raincoat fame, had a house here called Crossways, the site of which is deluged with modern developments.

Journey: 40 min
Season: £2728
Peak: 5 per hr
Off-peak: 5 per hr

BASINGSTOKE The station car park is capacious and there is a good selection of fast trains. Some actually start from here; others come through from Bournemouth and Weymouth. Thirty years ago Basingstoke was a comparatively sleepy market town with a few local engineering firms and a population of 25,000. Now it is a London overspill town with a population of 150,000 and more than 400 companies, including the Automobile Association, IBM, Sony Broadcast and Sun Life Financial of Canada. The shopping centre, refurbished, has all the usual chain stores. Basingstoke Leisure Park has a 10-screen cinema, 10-pin bowling rink, aquadrome, championship-size ice-rink and golf driving range. The old town is the place for wine bars, pubs and restaurants and The Haymarket Theatre. It is also the place for two-up-two-down Victorian terraced houses, priced from £150,000, and four-bedroom Thirties' houses at £300,000. In the quiet of Cliddesdon Road, large, detached five-bedroom Victorian and Edwardian houses sell for over £600,000. Further out, you come to the council estates and more sedate private bungalows. The modern estates are on the outskirts. North Chineham is one of the most popular because it has matured over a decade and has a shopping centre with a Tesco superstore. Three-bedroom semis can be bought for £210,000; five-bedroom detached houses for £350,000. Hatch Warren is very similar.

'Watercress beds are a particular feature of the local countryside'

Watercress beds are a particular feature of the local countryside. Old Basing, Mapledurwell, St Mary Bourne and Whitchurch all have them. One of the best-known villages, only four miles to the south-west, is **Dummer** – a small linear village that found itself besieged by the world's press at the time of Prince Andrew's wedding, being the home of his then parents-in-law. Perhaps because of its exposure it is rather a tight-knit community. A two-bedroom period cottage costs at least £225,000. A larger Georgian pile with land costs from £750,000. Very close to Basingstoke's eastern flank is **Old Basing**, where brick cottages are prettily arranged around the church, the

River Lodden, and what remains of Basing House. The house was a glamorous Tudor mansion which became the focus of a two-year siege by the Roundheads during the Civil War and was eventually destroyed. Some of the stone was salvaged and used to build houses in the village. There is a strong village spirit and, says one local, "the place is alive with horses". A two-up-two-down period cottage would cost at least £200,000. Two villages nearby, **Mapledurwell** and **Upton Grey**, are the stuff of an adman's dream, with Range Rovers carelessly parked outside idyllic thatched cottages. "Actually Mapledurwell is more Land Rovers, Upton Grey more Range Rovers," says one insider. Upton Grey has a duck pond, willow trees, some 17th-century cottages, village shop and post office. Prices vary from over £350,000 for a thatched cottage to around £750,000 for a new four-bedroom house.

'Actually Mapledurwell is more Land Rovers, Upton Grey more Range Rovers'

> Fork to Salisbury

Journey: 54 min
Season: £2792
Peak: 2 per hr
Off-peak: 1 per hr

OVERTON used to be rather pretty and had a defined role as a venue for sheep fairs and silk mills. Now it is where the paper for our banknotes is made. It still retains a certain appeal, though it has become extremely corpulent with new housing estates pushing at its seams. There are some thatched cottages, shops, pubs and restaurants, and a gun shop. A 17th-century, four-bedroom house in the centre will cost around £400,000. Family houses on the new developments cost up to £300,000; large individual houses over £450,000. Winchester Street is the poshest bit.

'On the doorstep is the wonderful rolling chalk downland that envelops the River Test, the landscape used in *Watership Down*'

Journey: 60 min
Season: £2792
Peak: 2 per hr
Off-peak: 1 per hr

WHITCHURCH is an old silk-mill town on the River Test. The mill on Frog Island is now restored and sells extremely expensive bespoke silk-lengths. But Whitchurch, too, has grown fleshy with huge council estates and private developments designed for those who made money in the Eighties. At Lynch Hill Park, for instance, there are huge mock-Tudor and mock-Georgian houses selling in the £300,000 to £350,000 bracket. At the lower end of the market are two-bedroom terraced houses at around £170,000. To the west of the town, newly-built four-bedroom houses fetch around £350,000. On the doorstep is the wonderful rolling chalk downland that envelops the River Test, the landscape used by the author Richard Adams in *Watership Down*. An 18th-century brick-and-flint farmhouse in this area would start at £500,000.

Journey: 65 min
Season: £2940
Peak: 2 per hr
Off-peak: 2 per hr

ANDOVER had the stuffing knocked out of it in the Sixties and is now a town of shopping malls and modern housing. However, it is well-placed for the M3/A303 magic carpet to the West Country and it sits plum in the middle of some of Hampshire's prettiest countryside. Not even Andover's best friend would call it a cultural oasis, but there is the theatre at Cricklade College, home to drama and music societies. One of the most prominent new shopping centres is the Chantry, which takes up much of the old upper High Street. In the tapering market place there is a general street market on Thursdays and Saturdays and a farmers' market once a month.

In the few Victorian streets that remain, you might buy a three-bedroom terraced house for around £150,000. Some of the most popular properties are the Twenties' and Thirties' semis which sell from around £180,000 for three bedrooms. The west of the town is where the newest housing is to be found. At Weyhill, for example, you could buy a four-bedroom detached family house for £225,000.

The chalk hills around Andover hold some of the loveliest villages in the country. All those along the Bourne Valley, from **Hurstbourne Tarrant** to Longparish, have a definite social cachet. Hurstbourne

'The chalk hills around Andover hold some of the loveliest villages in the country'

Tarrant sits in the valley bottom with Hurstbourne Hill casting a steep green shadow in the background. Stage-coaches used to change horses here before tackling its merciless incline. William Cobbett visited on his *Rural Rides* in 1830 and his initials are carved on a brick in the garden wall of Rookery Farm, where a former owner used to put out plates of food for hungry travellers. Jane Austen's parson brother also lived here and she visited frequently. To move here now you have to pay through the nose, though, fortunately, new low-cost housing is allowing some local people to stay. A two-bedroom period cottage could cost £250,000; a four-bedroom period house £500,000.

St Mary Bourne is further east along the sparkling chalk River Bourne – often called the Swift by locals, especially when it is in full spate. The village is a wonderful muddle of brick-and-flint, oak beams, wattle-and-daub and thatch. It has 15 listed buildings and a lovely Norman church with a black marble font. There is a thriving village primary school, five pubs, a village hall and shop, plus all the usual village societies. Some of the local families have lived here for centuries, as an 1842 tithe map has proved. "Our main worry," said the parish clerk, "is that new people moving in want to throw a glass dome over the place and don't want it to change, even though the demands of the village are changing." A two-bedroom thatched cottage will cost from £180,000; a modern four-bedroom house £400,000 and up.

Longparish, at the lower end of this exclusive corridor, is indeed a very long parish, threading along three-and-a-half miles of winding lane and the meandering River Test. Some of the field walls and the thatched cottages are built of clunch (chalk stone), with some modern estates sandwiched in between. The big flints in the fields are known as "Hampshire diamonds"; the other white specks are sheep. Property prices are higher than those in St Mary Bourne.

Ludgershall, to the north-west, offers housing even cheaper than Andover's, if you can bear the development going on all around you. "There are hundreds of houses going up. It's out of control," said one villager. A three-bedroom terraced house built in the Twenties will cost around £160,000; a two-bedroom terraced house around £140,000. Further west are **North Tidworth** and **South Tidworth**, both of which offer outstanding value for money but have rather transient populations. The army, which has a strong presence in the area, has been shedding staff, with the result that you might pick up a two-bedroom flat for £80,000, or a three-bedroom house for £150,000. **Shipton Bellinger** is very ordinary and again dominated by the army. Three-bedroom semis fetch around £170,000 to £200,000. Closer to Andover itself is the rather more cosy community of **Penton Mewsey**, where you might buy a four-bedroom period house for around £480,000.

'The big flints in the white fields are known as "Hampshire diamonds"; the other white specks are sheep'

To the south-west is **Monxton**, with the Pill Hill brook gambolling through it under a small bridge. It is a very compact village with some timber-frame and thatched cottages, a small green, a pub but no shops. Jujitsu, badminton, line dancing and drama classes take place in the village hall and incomers are welcomed. A small thatched terraced cottage would be likely to cost over £200,000; a four-bedroom modern house over £375,000. **Abbotts Ann**, close by, is also pretty. Its status has risen to rival the villages of the Test or Bourne valleys and it has a newly-opened village shop with a baker who bakes fresh bread daily. You could buy a thatched cottage with three or four bedrooms for £375,000 to £475,000; a four-bedroom detached modern house for about the same.

Stockbridge, further south, has enormous cachet. It lies in breathtakingly lovely countryside and is a great angling centre for some of the best and most expensive fishing in England, along the River Test. The Grosvenor Hotel, with its huge overhanging porch, houses the exclusive Houghton Fishing Club. The wide main street, edged with Tudor and Georgian houses, a superb butcher and other good shops, belies the village's size for there are very few back streets. Stockbridge Down, a mile away, is dotted with ancient earthworks, and up in the hills are the Iron Age forts of Woolbury Camp and Danebury Ring. A two-bedroom, period terraced house with a small garden in Stockbridge costs £225,000 to £260,000; a more substantial Georgian terraced house around £400,000. Half a dozen new six-bedroom detached houses carry a value of £500,000 or more. An oddity close to Stockbridge is **Leckford**, an estate village of tied thatched cottages owned since 1928 by the John Lewis Partnership. All the properties are occupied by retired former employees of John Lewis, and all the gables and woodwork are painted John Lewis green.

Journey: 75 min
Season: £3084
Peak: 2 per hr
Off-peak: 1 per hr

GRATELEY

GRATELEY proper is an old-fashioned farming village. Many of the period properties have been in the same families for years and few come on to the market. The range of property is wide, however. You could pay just around £180,000 for a two-bedroom Victorian slate-roofed terraced house; over £425,000 for a four-bedroom period house if you were lucky. The Andover side of the village is best. There is a newer area of development around the station, where there are starter homes and council houses. To the south, **Over**, **Middle** and **Nether Wallop** are attractive villages with some nice period properties, but surrounded by a sea of post-war council estates. A four-bedroom white-washed thatched cottage at Nether Wallop will cost £400,000.

Journey: 83 min
Season: £3344
Peak: 2 per hr
Off-peak: 2 per hr

SALISBURY

SALISBURY The city of Salisbury is full of visual treats, architectural nooks and crannies, gabled houses, half-timbering and Chilmark stone. Unlike Winchester (see page 221), which grew out of medieval clutter, it was built on a grid pattern and so has a greater sense of space and order. At the heart of Salisbury is the confluence of the rivers Avon and Nadder, spanned by medieval bridges. Another remnant of medieval life is the open-air market on Tuesdays and Saturdays. Shops in the city centre tend to be small and specialised, with Waitrose and Tesco kept out of sight on the edge of town. The Salisbury Playhouse is the main theatrical venue, with the Salberg providing productions on the fringe. The Arts Centre has celebrity lectures.

The top of the property pyramid in Salisbury is Cathedral Close – once home to the novelist Henry Fielding and now to the former prime minister, Sir Edward Heath. Situated beside the river, it is regarded as one of the most beautiful closes in England, dating from the late 18th century when graves were pushed to one side and some remarkable houses were built for the city's more important residents. One of the buildings, Mompesson House, is now in the hands of the National Trust. The close is perfectly quiet, shut away behind locked gates at night and as expensive as Chelsea or Westminster. A 48-year lease here can cost £900,000; a rare freehold could well top £2m. There are some other good streets near the Cathedral, overlooking Queen Elizabeth Gardens. In this area you might pick up a four-bedroom turn-of-the-20th-century terraced house with a 60-ft garden for around £550,000 upwards. A short distance away is Fisherton Island, a small group of detached houses built in the Sixties which also command high prices – around £500,000 for four bedrooms. It is also possible to buy into one of the oldest streets in Salisbury, Guilder Lane, where a brick-and-timber cottage with two bedrooms might cost £195,000. Popular schools include Cathedral School, The Godolphin, Bishop Wordsworth's Church of England School and South Wilts Girls'.

'On the edge of Salisbury Plain, the magic of a country walk might be exploded by a training exercise'

At the lower end of the market are hundreds of turn-of-the century terraces fronting directly on to pavements. Beware the terrible parking problem. You might get a two-bedroom terraced house for just over £170,000. But in the gentrified streets, identifiable by the hanging baskets, you could pay £180,000, and in St Anne's Street over £300,000. On the city outskirts, areas such as Shady Bower offer flats at around £210,000 and modern four-bedroom houses at £385,000. For a more villagey feel, look to the leafy lanes of Milford, where four-bedroom detached houses fetch around £250,000.

Outside Salisbury, the Wiltshire chalk downlands and the five valleys of the Avon, Wylye, Nadder, Ebble/Chalke and Bourne provide the setting for some very attractive, unspoilt villages. Some are subject to flooding in bad weather. Those to the south tend to be more popular. Those to the north are on the edge of Salisbury Plain, where there is a massive military presence and the magic of a country walk might be exploded by a training exercise.

Going south you come to **Fordingbridge**. This is rather far for regular London commuters, but people's fondness for it is such that it acts as a magnet for the villages between it and Salisbury. Its best asset is the River Avon, crossed by a seven-arched medieval bridge and overlooked by a statue of the painter, Augustus John, who once lived here. It has shops for day-to-day needs, as well as a bookshop, antiques shop and china shop. It is ideally placed for people who like to hack across the New Forest and for anglers with rods on the Avon. Inevitably, it is also popular with retired people. There is a real mix of housing, from the often flimsily built, but sought-after houses of the New Forest, for which you could pay £190,000 for two bedrooms, to huge Twenties' set-pieces in 20 acres of ground from £1m. Pony paddocks are very expensive here. On one of the several

Schools in Wiltshire

Salisbury gets all the accolades. The Godolphin is an independent day and boarding school for girls, and there are two grammar schools – Bishop Wordsworth's for boys and South Wilts Girls' – both of which get excellent results. Other strong independent schools include St Mary's at Calne for girls, Dauntsey's in Devizes for girls and boys and Marlborough College in Marlborough for girls and boys.

There are good comprehensives including those in Wootton Bassett, Corsham and Sheldon.

modern developments you would pay £230,000 for a three-bedroom detached house; up to £350,000 for four bedrooms.

Nearby is **Breamore**, pronounced "Bremmer", a typical Wiltshire brick village. "It's a horsey, hunting, shooting village. Brilliant," said one happy local. Breamore House, the home of the Hulse family, is an Elizabethan manor overlooking the Avon valley, open to the public. There is a good choice of period houses, but catching one as it comes on the market is like finding a hen's tooth. Villages slightly to the west within this group, such as **Rockbourne** and **Martin**, are also very rural and pretty, and a two-bedroom period thatched cottage here will cost £230,000. Rockbourne and **Damerham** operate one of the first federated primary schools in the country, sharing teachers and facilities. Its reputation is good.

Closer to Salisbury's southern edge, yet with the advantage of being near to Fordingbridge, is **Downton**, a village that once depended on lace-making, flour-milling and paper-making. It has an authentically ancient atmosphere, especially in the lovely main street, The Borough. A two-bedroom semi-detached period house in the village will cost £225,000. It is a large village, with a population of 2500, so it has better amenities than most, including shops, a medical centre, a bank and a library. Villagers usher in the spring with the annual May Cuckoo fair.

Even closer into Salisbury, beside the city's watermeadows, is **Britford**, a sleepy collection of brick cottages and farmhouses on the River Avon. It has a school and a common, but there are no shops and it has to share its vicar with other villages. Residents have a reputation for being rather reclusive and rarefied, particularly those who occupy the large houses on the lower road along the river bank. "People who live there really think they're something," carped one neighbour. A good period house with four bedrooms would cost well over £400,000. Nearby is **Odstock** and its neighbours **Nunton** and **Bodenham**, where the social life is rather more robust. People who have moved away find themselves drawn back for the annual fête, to join in the river raft races and dance the night away. Odstock has a school and a pub popular with doctors from the nearby hospital. Prices are similar to Britford's.

The Chalke Valley is also a good hunting ground. **Bowerchalke**, though very much a one-road village, occupies a beautiful position in an Area of Oustanding Natural Beauty surrounded by the Downs, just before the countryside tips over into Dorset. It has a mix of brick-and flint, cob and green sandstone, and with some modern houses, too. Everyone knows everyone else. There is no pub and it has lost its battle to keep its shop, but there is a playgroup. Incomers are not always a bad thing, as one villager recalls. "Everyone used to inter-marry. The IQ of the village was saved by the arrival of the

'Villages retain their sense of remoteness and yet have easy access to the city'

bicycle." There is a trout farm and a small stream running through, and endless walks. Houses here and in the neighbouring village of Broad Chalke are usually easy to sell. A 19th-century two-bedroom cottage will fetch £220,000; a modern four-bedroom house in vernacular style £400,000. **Broad Chalke** is on the Ebble where it meets the Chalke, and it regards itself as the capital of the Chalke valley. It lies between two chalk ridges, Here Path and Ox Drove Road, which both provide challenging walks. There is an ancient pub, and shops which include a butcher who makes his own faggots. The village school is still going strong, and there is a doctor's surgery. One of the most successful of its many clubs and societies is the Wilton and District Youth Band. Owners of some swimming pools in the village allow their neighbours to use them. South Street is particularly pretty because of its thatched cottages.

The town of **Wilton**, three miles west of Salisbury, is spoilt by its position on the A30 and A36, though it has a good market square peppered with antiques shops, and some nice old houses. A two-bedroom cottage could be picked up for around £170,000. This is where Wilton Carpets are made. Much of the town is owned by the Pembroke estate. The nearby Wilton House, built by the Earl of Pembroke, is open to the public.

The next spoke in the wheel of valleys around Salisbury is the Wylye Valley. The villages here both retain their sense of rural remoteness and yet have easy access to the city along the A36. **Codford St Mary** and **Codford St Peter** are rather strung out along the road and have plenty of modern houses, but they have one of the only village theatres in the country. A four-bedroom house would cost around £300,000; a three-bedroom Thirties' semi around £145,000.

Thatched cottage, Chalke Valley

To the north of Salisbury, the Woodford Valley is given particular charm by the River Avon. There is a dearth of smaller cottages so this is not first-timer country. A four-bedroom period family house, possibly with a paddock, is likely to fetch over £600,000. There are people here whose families have lived in the area for centuries; many of the newer arrivals have military connections. **Lower Woodford**, **Middle Woodford** and **Upper Woodford** are all strung out along the river, so there is no strong sense of community. There is no shop or post office, though there is a pub and they share a primary school. The football team and cricket team have also withered on the vine. Heal House, where Charles II sheltered after the Battle of

Worcester in 1651, opens its gardens to the public. Lower Woodford has a pub, next to some thatched chalk cottages. **Great Durnford** also lies in this exclusive belt and is similarly expensive.

Further north, a couple of miles from Stonehenge, is **Amesbury**. This is in the neighbourhood of three army camps – Larkhill, Tidworth and Bulford – and the army personnel help to keep the first-time-buyer market ticking over. A mass of new developments has sprung up in the last three decades alongside the older brick-and-flint cottages, and more growth is likely. On the new estates you would pay around £130,000 for a two-bedroom house, £170,000 for a three-bedroom semi, £235,000 for a four-bedroom house. Older three-bedroom cottages fetch around £185,000. There are a handful of select roads such as Countess and Stonehenge, where large detached houses built in the early part of the 20th century sell for close to £300,000.

Just to the east of Salisbury is **Laverstock**, separated by the River Bourne. Large riverside houses appeal to the local bank-manager class. In addition to the primary school, there are three secondary schools which have good reputations. A modern detached house with four bedrooms will cost around £300,000.

> Fork from **Basingstoke** to **Southampton**

Journey: 59 min
Season: £2828
Peak: 1 per hr
Off-peak: 1 per hr

MICHELDEVER The countryside really takes over here. Micheldever has a good collection of thatched cottages arranged haphazardly by the Dever brook and around a triangle of grass with a seat and a tree on it, known as the Crease. Duke Street is perhaps the prettiest for terraced cottages: two bedrooms will cost around £220,000. There is an old-fashioned village school, a store and a pub. The station is a couple of miles from the old village, but has had a whole new community spring up around it. There are Fifties' and Sixties' estates and bungalows, where a family-sized house might cost £260,000. The area has been earmarked for new town development. The main road at one end of Micheldever does tend to impinge on the rural dream, but most people hear the A33 and M3 only as a low growl on quiet nights.

Journey: 57 min
Season: £3112
Peak: 4 per hr
Off-peak: 4 per hr

WINCHESTER Its beautifully simple Norman Cathedral, boys' public school and streets lifted straight from a Jane Austen novel give Winchester a compelling appeal. Winchester society is a force to be reckoned with. Much of it revolves around a tightly-knit farming set, for whom the sporting weekend is essential. It has several fashionable hunts and shooting estates, and the Houghton Club on the River Test provides some of the best trout fishing in the country. The shopping centre is much as you would expect, rather upmarket, with pricey toy shops – the kind that sells hand-made rocking horses – and clothes shops dedicated to posh frocks, plus an antiques market in King's Walk. New park-and-ride has eased parking problems. There are lots of pubs and restaurants. Art exhibitions are held at the Guildhall Gallery, the Winchester Gallery and the Heritage Centre; concerts at the Guildhall and in the Cathedral. Chesil Theatre and John Stripe Theatre are busy with amateur theatrical productions, while the Theatre Royal attracts national and international stars.

Little Minster and Great Minster, right by the Cathedral and close to Winchester College, are two of the best addresses in the country outside London. Tourists are the main drawback. Flocking through to see where William the Conqueror claimed his crown, and where King Canute and Jane Austen are buried, they can't help pausing to look at the beautiful 18th-century houses, too. Small terraced houses in Cannon and Colebrook Streets are also extremely sought after, though life here can be inconvenienced not only by seriously difficult parking, but also by film units seeking period backdrops. A tiny flat-fronted terraced house could cost between £250,000 and £300,000; a larger, imposing Georgian house £400,000 to £700,000. At the lower end of the market, two-bedroom Victorian terraced houses fetch between £200,000 and £250,000, rising to £400,000 for three- to four-bedroom semis. The area down by the watermeadows in St Cross is popular with young professional families. Here you can buy two-bedroom Victorian terraced houses, or two-bedroom flats in converted houses at around £250,000. Two more areas that are within walking distance of the city centre and are coming up are Hyde, where you would have to pay £320,000 for a three-bedroom Victorian terraced house, and Fulflood, which is slightly cheaper.

Some people prefer the comparative peace of some of the avenues away from the city centre, such as Chilbolton and Bereweeke Avenues, where houses range from Victorian to Sixties and a four-bedroom detached can be bought for £500,000. Just outside Winchester is a large modern development known as Badger Farm. One-bedroom flats here cost £130,000; two-bedroom terraced houses £160,000; four-bedroom houses £250,000 to £300,000.

The neighbouring villages compete to be the most beautiful and socially spirited. The particularly desirable area to the north-east contains **Itchen Abbas**, a village described by Charles Kingsley in *The Water Babies*. The Pilgrims' Way runs through it, as does the River Itchen. There is no shop, but the village does have a primary school, foodie pub, the usual local societies and a new village hall. A four-bedroom period house here would cost £480,000. For cricket you must follow the river down to Easton, another pretty village with a

'Little Minster and Great Minster, right by the cathedral and close to Winchester College, are two of the best addresses outside London' mix of thatch and half-timber, Victorian and modern, with the snarl of the M3 in the distance. **Avington** is also in this select group. Most of its old brick-and-flint cottages are protected within a conservation area. Its flagship is Avington Park, a fine Carolean mansion set in ancient parkland with a lake, which is open to the public. You could expect to pay £275,000 for a two-bedroom thatched cottage in any of these villages.

'New Alresford attracts day trippers because of the Watercress Line'

New Alresford attracts day-trippers because of the Watercress Line, an eccentric railway which offers a half-hour return journey through Hampshire farmland, chalk cuttings and hills. Antiques and curio shops have sprung up as a result. Nevertheless, small two- and three-bedroom Georgian terraced houses around the centre can be bought for £350,000. To the south is **Old Alresford**, with a fine church and village pond. A four-bedroom detached family house costs between £350,000 and £450,000.

To the north-west is **Crawley**, where there are some picturesque thatched cottages by the village duckpond. It has the kind of star quality that earns it regular appearances on scenic calendars. As an old estate village it was planned as a whole, and some of the architecture is flamboyant. You could pay £400,000 for a detached bungalow or £350,000 for a semi-detached period cottage with three bedrooms. A larger detached house with grounds could reach £1m to £2m. Prices have risen rapidly.

Sparsholt is rural and convivial, and provides the opportunity of walks from the back door into 1000 acres of hills and woodland in Farley Mount Park. The village is particularly proud of its church-

House style in Surrey and Hampshire

A wonderful mixture of styles is packed between the metropolitan hard edges of south-west London and the retirement haven of the south coast. Through the sandy heaths of Surrey, the collectors' items are the houses designed by Edwin Lutyens in gardens by Gertrude Jekyll. Lutyens's architecture combines formality with naturalness, texture with geometry.

Then comes Hampshire, where stockbroker belt meets Georgian good manners and beautiful villages laze in the folds of the chalk valleys around Winchester and Andover. You have to marvel at what can be done with a stone as soft as chalk.

Around Petersfield there are farm walls made of clunch (chalk stone). When it is combined with flint and arranged in a chequerboard pattern or horizontal stripes, it turns humble cottages into architectural curios.

Where the chalk gives way to the poor soil of the New Forest, you find a range of brick-and-timber, brick-and-flint, thatched and even cob houses. Particularly pretty are the one-and-a-half-storey thatched houses, known as "bun" cottages, with steep roofs that look as if they have risen like loaves of bread.

The New Forest itself often disappoints. The original houses were small and low, and now would be considered scarcely habitable. Those that still stand have often been changed and extended beyond all recognition. The exceptions lie in wealthier villages such as Beaulieu and Bucklers Hard in the south, where shipbuilders' oak went into the houses.

Bungalow-itis is ever-present along the coast, but makes a strangely natural partnership with the old defence fortifications around Southampton.

controlled primary school, though the influx of new home-owners tend not to use it. There is a village shop, post office and a new hall, funded partly through the efforts of the local community, where country and salsa dancing is a regular event. Property prices are similar in most of the villages throughout this area. Due south of Winchester the M3 has snaked its way across Twyford Down to join the M27, leaving the old M3 a bizarre sight in a conservation area with the former motorway bridge surrounded by grass.

Journey: 77 min
Season: £3112
Peak: 2 per hr
Off-peak: 1 per hr
changing at
Winchester

SHAWFORD is bisected by the M3, so one of the major factors governing prices here is whether properties have been affected by it or not – hundreds of home-owners filed for compensation. You would pay £230,000 for a two-bedroom Victorian or Edwardian terraced house away from the main road – 10 per cent less if it's in the traffic zone. Towards Compton there are some huge individual houses, built on large plots, that sell for £1m to £2m, though some of these are affected by the motorway.

Journey: 78 min
Season: £3196
Peak: 3 per hr
Off-peak: 2 per hr

EASTLEIGH strikes a commercial note after Winchester. It was built around the railway and still has a railway works as well as a clutch of companies such as Pirelli, Norwich Union Healthcare and B&Q. It also has the headquarters of the Royal Yachting Association. In the early days the social divisions between railway employees were underlined by their choice of address. Drivers and inspectors lived in the north; everyone else in the south. Today the north is still the better side of town, and properties here sell for slightly more. Its basic stock-in-trade is a mass of late-Victorian terraced houses, fronting the pavement and selling at between £170,000 and £180,000.

Bishopstoke and **Fair Oak** were once older villages, but they now behave more like comparatively prosperous suburbs of Eastleigh. Bishopstoke has modern estates where you might buy a three-bedroom house for less than £200,000, or a four-bedroom detached house with two en-suite bathrooms and double garage for £350,000. Fair Oak is slightly more up-market, with its old village square still intact.

Modern development, Chandler's Ford

Journey: 89 min
Season: £3416
Peak: 1 per hr changing at Eastleigh
Off-peak: 1 per hr changing at Southampton Airport Parkway

CHANDLER'S FORD The stockbroker belt is at Chandler's Ford, parts of which consider themselves to be more Winchester than Eastleigh. Much of it is modern. The Hiltingbury area, developed in the Sixties, has three-bedroom semis at between £185,000 and £220,000; three-bedroom detached houses at £260,000; chalet-style houses at £300,000. The Oakmount area, which followed in the late Sixties and early Seventies, has two-bedroom maisonettes now costing around £120,000 and three-bedroom terraced houses at £150,000. In the Eighties came Valley Park. You can buy a five-bedroom house for around £320,000 here, though you might think they were rather tightly packed.

The expensive side of Chandler's Ford is **Hocombe**, built in the Thirties when little heed was paid to land values. Large four-bedroom houses with spacious sitting and dining rooms spread themselves over extensive gardens and change hands at £500,000 to £550,000. This is where the IBM executives from Hursley tend to congregate. Also on the northern side are two good comprehensive schools, Toynbee and Thornden, which themselves are an attraction to the area. Layers of new housing continue to be added, especially now that the M3 slicing past it offers easier access to the rest of the country.

> Fork to Fareham via Hedge End and Botley

It is also worth considering **Hedge End**, **Botley** and **Fareham**, strung below Eastleigh, because they now have direct train services into London, supplemented by services which involve changing at Winchester.

Hedge End can be reached with a journey of 88 minutes (season ticket £3196). While Botley can be reached in 91 minutes (season ticket £3196). Botley has some good 16th- and 17th-century houses and sits at the head of the tidal reach of the Hamble. The National Trust has bagged a few acres along the river to preserve them for the future. Fareham takes 98 minutes (season ticket £3196). Beyond that Gosport looms like an ugly giant.

> Continuation of main line

Journey: 68 min
Season: £3468
Peak: 3 per hr
Off-peak: 3 per hr

SOUTHAMPTON AIRPORT PARKWAY This station is really here for the convenience of Southampton International Airport. The train service as a result is fast and frequent, but the station car park is rather expensive. Many of the houses are close to the railway line. A three-bedroom Victorian terraced house would cost between £150,000 and £160,000.

Journey: 74 min
Season: £3468
Peak: 1 per hr plus 2 changing at Southampton Airport Parkway
Off-peak: 1 per hr changing at Southampton Airport Parkway

SWAYTHLING is an area of Victorian terraces and ex-local authority housing with lower prices than at Eastleigh. A two-bedroom house might cost £105,000. Many workers from the nearby Ford factory have their homes here, and it can seem as if nearly all the 19,500 students from Southampton University have their digs here, too.

Journey: 79 min
Season: £3468
Peak: 1 per hr plus 2 changing at Southampton Airport Parkway
Off-peak: 1 per hr changing at Southampton Airport Parkway

ST DENYS This is one of the older parts of Southampton and a happy hunting ground for first-time buyers. Turn-of-the-20th-century terraced houses and semis sell for between £115,000 and £145,000.

> Branch line to Hamble via Bitterne, Woolston, Sholing and Netley

**Journey: 110 min
(from Hamble)***
Season: £3468
**Frequency: 1 per
hr to Southampton
Central or to
Fareham**
*No through trains

BITTERNE, Woolston and Sholing float on the skyline like a sea of chimneypots. This is probably the cheapest part of Southampton, composed mainly of turn-of-the-20th-century terraced houses, but with some Thirties' housing stitched in, too. It lies on the east side of the Itchen River, crossed by a tollbridge which can seem a bit of a bother. A three-bedroom terraced house costs around £140,000; a three-bedroom Thirties' semi about £190,000, possibly with good views thrown in. Houses backing on to the river cost substantially more.

Netley is given a certain status by its pebbly shoreline on Southampton Water. It leads to the Royal Victoria Country Park, a marvellous place for picnics, and a vantage point for watching the ferries and tankers chugging across to the Fawley oil refinery on the other side of Southampton Water. Netley also has the remains of the Royal Victoria Military Hospital, where Florence Nightingale nursed casualties from the Crimea. Large four-bedroom family houses, built in the early Eighties, might cost around £400,000. More modestly, a small two-bedroom terraced house would fetch around £190,000. Part of the old military hospital has been converted into flats, selling at around £230,000 for two bedrooms.

Hamble (together with the village of Warsash on the other side of the Hamble River) is used as the setting for yachty television series. It is one of the most concentrated yachting centres in the country, positively bristling with marinas and boats for hire. It is very smart, though in spite of all the visible wealth it still retains the atmosphere of a village. There is a green and a church, and a huge common that leads down to the water. It was a working fishing village until 1914. Some pioneering aviation work was also carried out here, and in World War II the Americans used it as a base to prepare for the D-Day landings. Property prices can break the £1m barrier, but you could find an ordinary three-bedroom semi for around £250,000.

> Continuation of main line

Journey: 75 min
Season: £3468
Peak: 4 per hr
Off-peak: 3 per hr

SOUTHAMPTON CENTRAL Southampton is a busy modern city that has managed to attract some sizeable organisations, including Price Waterhouse, Skandia Life and the Marine and Coastguard Agency. Its increasingly aggressive commercial face, unrivalled shopping and proximity to the sea and the New Forest are all major assets. It can also offer five museums, numerous cinemas, nightclubs and discos, an art gallery, the Mayflower Theatre and Southampton University, which has its own gallery, theatre and concert hall. Southampton Football Club moved to new premises at St Mary's in 2001; there is first-class cricket at the Hampshire's new Rosebowl county ground and horse-racing at Goodwood, a 30-mile run east on the M27. Participation sports include golf, plenty of tennis, athletics, swimming and diving in a new complex at The Quays. There is also a choice of health and fitness clubs. Southampton Airport provides flying lessons for those with strong stomachs and the money to match. But the principal leisure activity is still sailing. There are clubs, moorings and dinghy schools all around the coast.

'A good vantage point from which to watch the ocean-going liners sail into port'

Ocean Village is the place for weekending sailors. It's a mixture of docklands architecture, frivolous shopping, bars and restaurants – the Port Grimaud of southern England, where a lot of the early property buyers turned out to be interested in investment only. A two-bedroom apartment with a berth for the boat costs £205,000 or more; a town house might cost £245,000, rising towards £280,000 if it has a berth.

Old Southampton is considered to be rather special. The old town stretches from Bargate in the north to Town Quay in the south

Schools in Hampshire

People move to Winchester just for the schools. Winchester College independent boys' boarding school (with some day-boys) has a formidable academic reputation. Girls have St Swithun's independent boarding and day school, which still teaches lacrosse. Among the co-educational comprehensives are Perins and Westgate. The latter takes both boarders and day pupils, and provides an evening meal for children of working parents.

At Petersfield there is the progressive school Bedales, an independent co-educational day and boarding school, as well as Churcher's College, a co-educational independent day school.

At Hook there is an independent, Lord Wandsworth (mixed) boarding and day. At Farnborough there is Salesian College, an independent Roman Catholic school for boys, and Farnborough Hill Roman Catholic girls day school. Good comprehensives are at Ringwood and Yateley.

Southampton also has some popular schools. King Edward VI is a selective entry co-educational independent; St Anne's is a comprehensive for girls, with priority given to practising Catholics; St Mary's College is an independent, selective school for both sexes.

Portsmouth's best include the Grammar, a co-educational independent day school to which the hand-picked brightest children will travel from miles around; and Portsmouth High independent day school for girls.

– a good vantage point from which to watch the ocean-going liners sail into port. The medieval town wall is another reminder of the city's long maritime history. (It was not until the 18th century that it became a fashionable resort.) There are new developments of luxury flats and listed warehouses converted into apartments on the seafront. You can expect to pay around £395,000 for four bedrooms. Inner Avenue is one of the best places to look for older town houses. A two- or three-bedroom house within walking distance of the city centre would cost between £160,000 and £200,000. For cheaper housing you could look at **Shirley**, where a two-bedroom turn-of-the-20th-century terraced house would fetch just over £150,000.

Further out from the town centre is **Bassett**. This has become rather chic because of its proximity to Southampton Common, the university and two good schools – King Edward VI independent school and The Atherley independent school for girls. A three-bedroom Thirties' semi here might cost £250,000; a three-bedroom detached house around £300,000. There are some larger, rather distinctive, four-bedroom houses which sell for over £400,000.

North of Southampton is **Chilworth**, which is considered irredeemably smart. Wealthy businessmen are attracted to the individually built large houses with anything from half an acre to two acres of ground. Smaller three- or four-bedroom houses start at around £500,000, with prices rising inexorably over the £1m mark as you enter the mini-mansion market.

Journey: 86 min
Season: £3468
Peak: 1 per hr*
Off-peak: 1 per hr*
*Change at
Southampton
Central

MILLBROOK A surprising number of people cannot resist living along the coast to the west, or in remote parts of the New Forest, even though it means taking this sweeper service into Southampton. Millbrook, still in the Southampton suburbs, is mainly ex-local authority and a Fifties' three-bedroom terraced house can be picked up for around £125,000.

Journey: 90 min
Season: £3468
Peak: 1 per hr*
Off-peak: 1 per hr*
*Change at
Southampton
Central

REDBRIDGE By Redbridge you are hitting mixed housing estates, where a modern one-bedroom flat might cost around £92,000 and a two- to three-bedroom semi around £130,000.

> Branch line to **Romsey** and **Dunbridge**

Journey: 95 min (from Romsey)

Season: £3480

Frequency: 3 per hr from Romsey; 1 every 2 hrs from Dunbridge*

***No through trains. Change at Southampton Central, Southampton Airport Parkway or Salisbury**

ROMSEY scores high marks for quality of life. It is a classic English market town with a strong agricultural base. A general market is still held twice a week just off the market square (overlooked by a statue of Lord Palmerston). The silent simplicity of the Abbey, which is essentially Norman, gives the centre of the town a tremendous architectural and spiritual uplift. It has a lavish leisure centre and small specialist shops, with Southampton near enough for major purchases. It also has its own newspaper and local theatre, The Plaza, bought by the amateur dramatics society and used by the Romsey Art Group. In the centre of town a restored two-bedroom Victorian terraced house costs around £200,000. The small farms and older country houses dotted along the Test Valley start at over £600,000 and run into millions. Broadlands, once the home of Lord Mountbatten and now occupied by his grandson, Lord Romsey, is nearby.

Michelmersh, where TV presenter David Frost has a house, is a rather sought-after village which spreads itself out through the lanes like the fingers of a hand. Part of it is a designated conservation area. Its exclusivity is guaranteed by some of the country's best – and most expensive – trout fishing on the Test nearby. It also contains a brickworks that still produces hand-made bricks. You could buy a four-bedroom house for around £500,000, but prices vary enormously depending on position and age.

Mottisfont is another of the area's wonderful surprises, owned mostly by the National Trust. It is a stop-off point for ramblers on a trail that runs from Totton, close to Southampton, along the chalk downs to Inkpen Beacon. You will need at least £650,000 to be in the running for one of the handful of houses left in the open market. Mottisfont Abbey, with its gardens of old-fashioned roses beside the River Test, also belongs to the National Trust. It has a tea room and licensed restaurant.

'Mottisfont Abbey, with its gardens of old-fashioned roses beside the River Test, belongs to the National Trust'

> Continuation of main line

Journey: 82 min
Season: £3508
Peak: 2 per hr
Off-peak: 1 per hr

TOTTON likewise is part of the Southampton sprawl, being joined to the city by a causeway across the River Test. It offers a wide variety of new estates, with four-bedroom, double-garaged detached houses priced at over £300,000. The Woodlands side of Totton, which faces on to the New Forest, is distinctly more up-market. Here you could pay £500,000 for a three-bedroom house with a paddock; £350,000 for a modern bungalow with two double bedrooms.

'This was the closest the local landowners would allow the railway to come to Lyndhurst'

Journey: 87 min
Season: £3508
Peak: 1 per hr
Off-peak: 1 per hr

'Lyndhurst has proper shops, including a marvellous butcher'

ASHURST NEW FOREST station was the closest to Lyndhurst that the powerful local landowners would allow the railway to come. Lyndhurst, known as the capital of the New Forest, is exquisitely pretty, but seizes up with tourist traffic in the summer. People come to visit the church, with its stained glass by William Morris and Burne-Jones, to admire Swan Green with its cordon of thatched cottages, and to visit the New Forest Museum and Visitor Centre. The Forestry Commission has its local headquarters here in The Queen's House, a former royal hunting lodge. Lyndhurst has proper shops, including a marvellous butcher, and a fruit and veg shop.

Property prices in the New Forest are high, despite the fact that the scarcity of building materials means that the quality of the older houses is often rather poor. Prices in Lyndhurst start at around £190,000 for a two-bedroom terraced house and rise effortlessly to £600,000 in sought-after Pikes Hill Avenue. A newish development in the centre provides cheaper property, with three-bedroom detached houses at around £230,000 and four-bedroom versions around £260,000. An owl and otter park set in 2000 acres of woodland, is nearby.

Journey: 91 min
Season: £3716
Peak: 3 per hr
Off-peak: 2 per hr

BROCKENHURST is blessed because it receives the fast trains from Weymouth. They stop here, at Southampton Central, Southampton Airport Parkway and Winchester, then go non-stop to Waterloo. This is a pretty, vibrant village with some gracious old houses set in half-an-acre or so, for which you might pay £600,000 and more, and some new estates within walking distance of the centre where you could pay £350,000 for four bedrooms. Brockenhurst teems with tourists in the summer.

'Beaulieu is the most exclusive village in the area... Lymington is an extremely expensive, but rather quaint yachtsman's playground'

Beaulieu, four miles to the east, is the most exclusive village in the area, where people compete for invitations to Lord Montagu's drinks parties. A three-bedroom thatched cottage costs £500,000 upwards; a six-bedroom house with a couple of acres on the Beaulieu River, fit for the occasional stray pop star, sells for several million. The Beaulieu Motor Museum is a great attraction.

The village of **Pilley Bailey**, known locally as Pilley, is a little less expensive. It is very small, with a pub, a church and a shop. A two-up-two-down cottage here would fetch around £250,000. The whole of this area is very close to the sea, and in particular to **Lymington**, an extremely expensive, but rather quaint yachtsman's playground. A 150-year-old cottage close to the river with three

New Forest Thirties-style house

bedrooms will cost at least £325,000 here. A fast shuttle train links it to Brockenhurst.

As rail services have improved, commuters are now prepared to move even further down the line to **Bournemouth**, attracted by its pine-cloaked valleys, sandy beaches and breezy clifftops. It is also a commercial success story, attracting big insurance companies to relocate and establishing its name as a major conference centre. The journey to London can be done in 107 minutes, an annual season ticket costs £4108, and there are three peak trains per hour.

Incomers are drawn by the purpose-built leasehold flats in blocks with sea views along the Eastcliff, each of which has its own price hierarchy. A middle-market block will yield up a one-bedroom flat from £160,000; two-bedrooms for £230,000; three-bedrooms £300,000. You will be extremely lucky to find a freehold house facing full frontal to the sea; should such a rarity come on the market, you could expect to pay £650,000 to £700,000 for three bedrooms, a roof terrace and cliff top access.

'Commuters are now prepared to move even further
down the line to Bournemouth'

Portsmouth & Southsea
Portsmouth Harbour
Fratton
Hilsea
Bedhampton
Havant
Rowlands Castle
Petersfield
Liss
Liphook
Haslemere
Witley
Milford
Godalming
Farncombe
Shalford
Chilworth
Guildford
London Road
Clandon
Worplesdon
Waterloo

Waterloo
> Portsmouth

Journey: 32 min
Season: £2180
Peak: 3 per hr
Off-peak: 1 per hr

WORPLESDON, sandwiched between Woking and Guildford, is a main-road village with the A322 cutting straight through it. The station is at least a mile from the centre, but it is close to some rather nice private roads running off Goose Rye Road. Large Twenties' and Thirties' detached houses here sell for £600,000 upwards. A four- or five-bedroom gabled and dormered house with a detached granny-annexe will fetch around £850,000.

Sutton Green, a mile south-east of the station, is semi-rural. Sutton Place, one of the finest Tudor houses in the country, is owned by an American foundation which uses it to exhibit works of art. A two-up-two-down turn-of-the-century cottage costs around £275,000; a four-bedroom detached house of the same period is over £600,000.

Journey: 36 min
Season: £2324*
Peak: 4 per hr
Off-peak: 4 per hr
***Also valid via London Road (Guildford). See page 237**

GUILDFORD Even though it is so close to London, Guildford offers rich pickings for shoppers and culture vultures alike. The steep, cobbled pedestrianised High Street has a wide variety of boutiques and specialist shops, and the Friary shopping mall has all the major chain stores. The Roof Garden Food Court on the top floor is the place to snatch a snack. Architectural highlights include the Guildhall with its famous 1683 projecting clock, and one of the country's few modern cathedrals, designed by Sir Edward Maufe with a very plain interior. The Yvonne Arnaud Theatre attracts London-bound shows on their way to the West End, The Electric Theatre is a leading studio theatre, and the nine-screen cinema keeps film buffs happy. The Guildford Philharmonic Orchestra is also widely respected. Athletes head for the Spectrum leisure centre, which has an athletics track, ice hockey, an ice-rink and 10-pin bowling.

It is possible to live right in the centre of the town. A one-bedroom flat over the High Street shops costs around £150,000; a purpose-built, three-bed, two-bathroom flat just off the High Street around £350,000. There are some streets of old houses around Guildford Museum, near the remains of the 12th-century

235

castle at the bottom of the High Street. Most have been converted to business use, but the occasional three-bedroom terraced house comes up for around £325,000.

On the north side of town, in the **Woodbridge Hill** area, are the typical bay-fronted, net-curtained, respectable mind-you-own-business streets of provincial England. The houses are solid, with good-sized rooms, but even though it is convenient for the hospital, the Cathedral and the university, nobody rushes to live here. A three-bedroom Thirties' detached house will cost around £280,000; a three-bedroom semi £220,000. Cornhill Insurance has its headquarters here. Much more popular is Fairlands, where housing of the Sixties and Seventies has bedded down and matured nicely, and where a good community spirit has evolved around the school, the doctor's surgery and so on. It even has its own free local news magazine. It is a good place to look for a bungalow: three bedrooms for £270,000 to £290,000. A three-bedroom semi-detached house will cost slightly less.

On the north-eastern fringe is **Burpham**, no longer a village but a sea of modern houses, designed with enough breathing space to make them palatable. There are four developments: Weybrook Park, Weyley Farm, Merrow Park and Bowers Farm. A tiny studio costs just under £105,000; a three-bedroom semi £230,000; a large four- or five-bedroom house between £425,000 and £450,000. There are also some large early-20th-century houses with five bedrooms and four reception rooms which sell for over £500,000. Nearby **Merrow** is now a suburb of Guildford. It has a golf course and leafy private roads where houses built in the Thirties have the occasional bungalow wedged in between. Both bungalows and houses, with four to five bedrooms, tend to sell in the £575,000 range.

Small modern estate house, Guildford area

The south of the town is particularly well-heeled and attracts successful local professionals. In White Lane are some large houses, built in the Twenties and later, with big gardens and views across to the North Downs. The likely price for one of these would be over £1m. Further to the south-west is Loseley Park, an Elizabethan country house which is open to the public and whose farm produces the well-known dairy products that bear the Loseley name. A very popular village to the south-east is **Cranleigh** (see entry for Ockley on the line to Horsham, page 280). Closer to Guildford's southern flank is **Bramley**, which is well-liked and rather expensive. Its exclusivity is expressed by the presence of a posh car dealer and well-subscribed golf club. Another attraction is the girls' private school, St Catherine's, which is the sister school to Cranleigh School for boys. A modest three-bedroom semi here will cost £325,000. A four-bedroom detached house with a large garden and driveway could go for well over £550,000.

'Its exclusivity is well expressed by the presence of a busy posh car dealer'

To the west of Guildford is **Wood Street**, a large linear village surrounded by farmland, with an ample village green, church and post office. The council housing is discreetly tucked away and there is quite a lot of property built between the Thirties and the Sixties. For £280,000 you might pick up a three-bedroom Edwardian semi, or a more modern three-bedroom detached house with a large garden backing on to fields.

> Waterloo to London Road (Guildford) via Clandon

Journey: 47 min
Season: £2056
Peak: 4 per hr
Off-peak: 2 per hr

CLANDON West Clandon and East Clandon both command very high prices. The station is at West Clandon, a linear village, part of which is protected as a conservation area, part devoted to council housing. Until 1900, East Clandon was solely an estate village attached to Hatchlands Park, a National Trust house with splendid Robert Adam interiors and gardens by Repton and Gertrude Jekyll. A Fifties' four- or five-bedroom house in either village will cost over £750,000.

Journey: 52 min
Season: £2196
Peak: 4 per hr
Off-peak: 2 per hr

LONDON ROAD (GUILDFORD) London Road is Guildford's second station. For a description of Guildford, see page 235.

> North Downs line east to Shalford and Chilworth

Journey: 43 min
Season: £2532
Peak: 2 per hour*
Off-peak: 1 per hour*
*Change at Guildford

SHALFORD is a one-street village of period houses and cottages with a green. Two-bedroom Victorian terraced houses start at £250,000. Five- or six-bedroom houses can cost £600,000 or more. Shalford Mill, an 18th-century tile-hung watermill on the River Tillingbourne, is now in the hands of the National Trust.

Journey: 48 min
Season: £2532
Peak: 1 per hour*
Off-peak: 1 every 1.5 hours*
*Change at Guildford

CHILWORTH spreads itself rather uneasily along the A248, a bland mix of houses and bungalows built in the Thirties and Fifties. Cars tend to park along both sides of the road as few of the houses have garages. Chilworth has its own primary and middle school, and an old gunpowder factory on the banks of the Tillingbourne. A three-bedroom Thirties' semi would cost £300,000 at the better end of the village; £275,000 at the other.

> Continuation of main line

Journey: 43 min
Season: £2356
Peak: 3 per hr
Off-peak: 2 per hr

FARNCOMBE is the poor man's Godalming (see below), of which it is really now a suburb. It does have its own recognisable centre, however, graced by the presence opposite the playing field of 10 early 17th-century red-brick almshouses, still administered by the Worshipful Company of Carpenters. A four-bedroom Victorian semi-detached house in Farncombe sells for around £275,000; a Twenties', detached three-bedroom house for £300,000; a modern two-bedroom terraced house for £200,000 or slightly less.

Journey: 46 min
Season: £2368
Peak: 4 per hr
Off-peak: 2 per hr

GODALMING Forever prosperous, Godalming thrived first on the wool trade, then as a coaching stop on the London to Portsmouth road, now on café culture. Since the 1870s it has been the home of Charterhouse, the private school for boys and girls. The High Street contains a wonderful collection of 16th-, 17th- and 18th-century buildings, and in the centre is The Pepperpot, a distinctive colonnaded building with a clock tower. Godalming was further distinguished by being the first town to replace gas street lighting with electric. Its shopping is typically small-town, with one or two specialist shops and a Sainsbury's on the edge. There are good walks along the River Wey that runs from Godalming Wharf to the Thames at Weybridge, complete with locks and weirs. For autumn colour the place to stroll is the National Trust's Winkworth Arboretum. The two most fashionable areas of Godalming are **Busbridge** and **Charterhouse**. Busbridge has quiet leafy streets lined with properties spanning every period from Victorian to the Thirties, and a famous water tower converted into an eccentric house. A three-bedroom detached house here will set you back £500,000, though you could pay up to £1m for a large house with half a dozen bedrooms and a capacious garden. Charterhouse is similar, though the houses tend to be larger. The tail-end of Mark Way is a private road where some of the older houses were built in such enormous acreages that strips of garden were sold off for building plots in the Fifties. A four- or five-bedroom house set in a third of an acre will cost at least £550,000. At the lower end of the market are some two-bedroom terraced houses on small modern developments that sell for around £200,000.

> 'At Dunsfold the church is set apart on a mound next to a 1000-year-old yew tree'

The nearby village of **Dunsfold** is lovely if you can afford it. The houses, some of them dating from the 15th and 16th centuries, are gathered around an open common, with a pub, small shop, nursery school, and church picturesquely set apart on a mound next to a 1000-year-old yew tree. Even a tiny two-bedroom period farmworker's cottage here will fetch over £250,000. Larger houses start at £500,000.

Journey: 50 min
Season: £2384
Peak: 3 per hr
Off-peak: 1 per hr

MILFORD has been rather carved up by main roads (including the A3), but there are compensations in the pretty rambling-and-riding countryside that surrounds it. The village sprawls around the shops and church and provides a broad range of properties. You might pay just under £200,000 for a two- or three-bedroom ex-council house; £260,000 for a modern three-bedroom semi; £250,000 for a Thirties' semi; £500,000 and over for a four- to five-bedroom Victorian or Edwardian family home.

Elstead, three miles to the west, is more rural, with some bracken-covered Surrey commons within walking distance. The architect, Sir

Schools in Surrey

Guildford has a highly-valued independent boys' day school, Royal Grammar, which creams off the top 10 per cent of the ability range in the area if it can. There is a choice of three independent schools for girls: Guildford High day school, St Catherine's day and boarding and Tormead day school. The two co-educational comprehensives of note are Guildford County and George Abbot.

Other good independent schools are scattered throughout the county. They include Charterhouse for boys (girls in the sixth) and Prior's Field for girls at Godalming, and Cranleigh School for boys and girls at Cranleigh, Caterham for both sexes and Woldingham for girls at Caterham, Dunottar Day for girls and Reigate Grammar for both sexes at Reigate, The Royal School for girls at Haslemere, the Lingfield Notre Dame for boys and girls at Lingfield, St John's for boys (some girls) in Leatherhead, Notre Dame Senior for girls and the Yehudi Menuhin for the musical at Cobham.

Good comprehensives can be found at Dorking, Redhill, Leatherhead and Oxted.

Edwin Lutyens, spent the early part of his career working in the area, which contains a number of his houses. Elstead itself has one good example, Fulbrook, built in 1896. The village also has a pretty watermill, a 12th-century bridge, a green and a couple of pubs, but the fight is on to slow the traffic with 20mph speed limits and plenty of sleeping policemen. A one-bedroom flat in a converted Edwardian house will cost just over £150,000; a Victorian two-up two-down terraced house just over £250,000; a two-bedroom Thirties' semi £250,000. A large detached house, built in the early part of this century and backing on to the commons, will cost £600,000 upwards.

Journey: 54 min
Season: £2396
Peak: 3 per hr
Off-peak: 1 per hr

WITLEY is spread out over several miles, with housing estates from the various 20th-century building booms linking arms around the half-timbered and tile cottages of the old village centre. You could pay anything from £225,000 for a two-bedroom terraced house to well over £750,000 for an early 20th-century detached house with five bedrooms. Witley Common, 500 acres of National Trust land, is a great local asset.

The station is a mile to the south at **Wormley**. This is a quiet residential area where a detached house built in the Twenties, shielded from the road by a bank of trees and a long driveway, is likely to cost over £500,000. On a hilltop eminence is King Edward's private school for boys and girls.

Hambledon, a mile to the east, is a more conventional village. It lies in a hollow surrounded by hills and woods, with good views of the Hog's Back. The village has a pretty green with a cricket pavilion and pond. Just off the green, one of the oldest houses, Oakhurst Cottage, is kept by the National Trust as a 17th-century museum. The village school is now a nursery, the shop closed but has since been revived by the community and is staffed by volunteers, and the old workhouse is now luxury housing. Houses rarely come on the market, and the tiniest of cottages is likely to fetch £300,000. A 17th-century Grade II listed house with three bedrooms set in half an acre starts at £500,000; grander houses would fetch over £1m.

'Chiddingfold green hosts a spectacular bonfire night party with 400 torchbearers'

Chiddingfold, two miles south of Witley station, is also tailored to the traditional image of a perfect English village. The green in the centre hosts a spectacular bonfire night party with 400 torchbearers. It is overlooked by the oldest pub in Surrey, the Crown Inn, and by an 11th-century church. Other events on the green include a summer fête. Shops include a newsagent, chemist, general stores, post office, hairdresser, butcher and there is a fishmonger who calls weekly. A new company has started here which exports curry sauces round the world. In the reign of Elizabeth I there were a dozen glassworks in the village, the profitability of which can be seen in the lovely half-timbered houses of the period. The church is notable both for its Chiddingfold glass windows and for the huge collection of lichens in the churchyard, which are an attraction to botany students from all over the country. The large 16th- and 17th-century houses on the green would break the £1m barrier if they ever came on to the market. There are a couple of small modern developments where you might buy a four-bedroom modern detached house for £400,000.

Journey: 51 min
Season: £2528
Peak: 5 per hr
Off-peak: 4 per hr

HASLEMERE has a reputation for being recession-proof. This is rich commuter territory, surrounded by National Trust land and with a pretty High Street stiff with half-timbered 16th-century buildings. The shops are intimate and intriguing. One of the town's best-known features is the Dolmetsch Workshops, founded by the Swiss Arnold Dolmetsch, who helped to revive an interest in early musical instruments, including the recorder. Replicas are still made, and the public can visit the workshops by appointment. There is a festival of early music every July. Another attraction is the Haslemere Educational Museum, which contains displays of British birds, geology, zoology, local history and so on – the mummy with one toe exposed is a big hit with schoolchildren.

There are very few houses in the centre. In Lower Street you might find an artisan's Victorian two-bedroom cottage for £230,000. In Petworth Road you might get a large detached Victorian house with walled gardens for £800,000. Ubiquitous Thirties' semis spread outwards from the centre, selling for £250,000 and upwards depending on the street.

A lovely address to aspire to is Tennyson Lane, named after the poet who lived here. The huge Victorian and Edwardian mansions have large grounds with views of Blackdown Hill (National Trust), and are within 15 minutes' walk of the centre. The larger ones sell for vast sums, though some of the smaller interlopers, slipped on to remnants of gardens, might be had for £750,000. Scotlands Lane is similar, though the houses are later (Twenties' and Thirties') and the road itself is not so quiet.

On the Wey Hill side of town you find the Victorian terraces, with banks and building societies, small supermarkets and chip shops complimenting the large Tesco. A two-bedroom terraced house here will sell for just over £220,000. There is some new development: on the Deepdene estate you might buy a two-bedroom terraced house for £180,000, a three-bedroom semi for just over £240,000 or a four-bedroom detached house with a garage from £370,000.

North of Haslemere is the 900-ft high Gibbet Hill which, if you are up to the climb, gives lofty views over the Weald and the South Downs. To the west is the open heathland of Frensham Common with Frensham Great and Little Ponds. Both have sandy (and rather dirty) beaches. They were created in the 13th century to supply fish to, among others, the Bishop of Winchester.

Between these two beauty spots lies **Hindhead**, which was once rather fashionable – Sir Arthur Conan Doyle, George Bernard Shaw and Lloyd George lived here. But it has had its nose put out of joint by the A3, which regularly comes to a standstill here, though vital bypass plans should be acted upon soon. There are still some huge houses that sit snugly behind their shields of greenery, but there's little point considering them unless you have upwards of £700,000 to spend. You could buy into a modern development by the A3 for £300,000. Hindhead Common, 1100 acres of heath and woodland, is a major local attraction.

Although it has a proper little shopping centre, **Grayshott** is still at heart a village where those who can afford it retire for peace and quiet. "It's a lovely little village, everyone pulls together. It sounds corny I know. We have local village clear-up days," said one happy local. A two-bedroom Victorian house will cost £220,000 to £250,000; a large Thirties'-built house with several acres and a pony paddock around £750,000. **Grayswood**, on the lip of Haslemere, is less exclusive, but still in the top drawer. Twenties' and Thirties' detached houses come onto the market priced at around £350,000 for three bedrooms; and two-bedroom Victorian semis for £240,000.

'The Surrey/Hampshire boundary looms large in people's minds because there is intense rivalry between the two counties'

Seven miles south, beyond the Blackdown Hill, is **Midhurst**, a market town on the River Rother whose attractions include the Cowdray Park polo ground. It is in many respects a rather plain town, but at least the shops have not been completely homogenised and there are some very attractive houses. Next to the church, for example, is a Queen Anne terrace with likely price-tags close to £350,000. The parklands of some of the largest houses in the town, such as Heatherwood, Elmleigh, Guillards Oak and Heathfield Park, have been developed as small housing estates. The average price for a four-bedroom detached house (of which there is a great number) is £350,000. Heathfield Park also has some pseudo-Georgian three-bedroom terraced houses, priced at around £275,000. Another good area is Close Walks Wood. A dozen or so houses have encroached into the woodland and fetch around £650,000 for four bedrooms. Elsewhere in the town you could find an ordinary three-bedroom, turn-of-the-20th-century terraced house for around £200,000.

Journey: 66 min
Season: £2556
Peak: 3 per hr
Off-peak: 1 per hr

LIPHOOK The Surrey/Hampshire boundary looms large in people's minds because there is intense rivalry between the two counties. Liphook just falls into Hampshire. It is cheaper than Haslemere because it is further south. A bypass has recently relieved it of the A3. The Square, where six roads converge, is a conservation area dominated by the 17th-century Royal Anchor Hotel. Builders have been busy. Loseley Park, built roughly a decade ago, is a network of terraced and detached houses. A three-bedroom terraced house costs £185,000; a four-bedroom detached £300,000. Victorian three-bedroom semis in Liphook fetch between £190,000 and £250,000. The old army barracks has been developed by Barratt and Westbury and a two-bedroom flat here will cost £160,000; a five-bedroom house over £400,000

Journey: 72 min
Season: £2644
Peak: 3 per hr
Off-peak: 1 per hr

LISS is sliced in two by the railway and River Rother. It is very mixed and not greatly sought after, though it does provide a good range of houses. One-bedroom modern flats start at £95,000. Two-bedroom Victorian terraced houses cost £180,000; three-bedroom modern detached houses £240,000. There are some large Victorian properties at Liss Forest, an extension of the village where a four-bedroom house costs £400,000 or more. On the outskirts, four- or five-bedroom period houses with a few acres start at £750,000.

Four miles north-west is **Selborne**, an idyllically pretty village slightly handicapped by a main street too narrow for the volume of traffic. The house of the 18th-century naturalist Gilbert White is an attraction to tourists, as are the beech hanger and meadows (now owned by the National Trust) which he described in his classic 1789 book *The Natural History of Selborne*. It also contains an exhibition dedicated to Captain Oates, companion to Captain Scott on his ill-fated expedition to the Antarctic, and his family. The High Street is lined with picturesque brick-and-limestone cottages, some thatched, some early Victorian, though it turns into something of race track during rush hours. A small, late-19th-century stone cottage here sells for around £220,000. A four-bedroom cottage on the hillside, with large grounds and lovely views, could fetch £600,000. There is a small amount of modern housing. The price for four bedrooms and a double garage is around £340,000.

'The High Street is lined with picturesque brick-and-limestone cottages, some thatched'

Journey:	64 min
Season:	£2740
Peak:	4 per hr
Off-peak:	3 per hr

PETERSFIELD

PETERSFIELD The countryside to the west of Petersfield is a designated Area of Outstanding Natural Beauty which is often referred to as Little Switzerland or the Hampshire Alps. A line of hangers, or hanging beechwoods, follows a meandering escarpment from Binstead, just to the the west of Alton, to Petersfield, where it connects with the South Downs and rises to a 900-ft peak at Butser Hill. Butser is within the Queen Elizabeth Country Park, four miles south of the town, which is the place for picnics, pony rides and even grass skiing.

With this remarkable landscape to hand, and with Winchester and Chichester only half an hour by car, it is not surprising that Petersfield is a very desirable, and hence expensive, place to live. (Beyond Butser Hill to the south, property prices drop rapidly as you move outside commuting range.) Petersfield owed its initial prosperity to wool, leather and its usefulness as a coaching stop on the road to Portsmouth. Its charm comes from the grouping of ancient buildings around The Square, a former market place. Running off it is Sheep Street, lined with 16th- and 17th-century houses. A small two-bedroom house here would cost around £250,000. The Spain is a kind of unexplained opening in the original street plan, now containing some good Georgian houses. Petersfield was once a predominantly agricultural town, but is now popular with retired couples as well as with commuters to London and

Fifties' detached
house, Petersfield

Portsmouth. Just a short walk from the High Street is a pond and 69 acres of heath. Here there are boats for hire, a cricket pitch and golf course, as well as lonelier spots where you come across Bronze Age burial mounds. The Heath every October is the scene of the Taro Fair, once a horse fair, but now a throng of roundabouts and stalls. The best addresses in town are on The Heath. Imposing Victorian or Edwardian detached houses, with possibly eight bedrooms, several reception rooms and a billiards room, sell for between £750,000 and £800,000. Typical residents are successful local solicitors and retired naval officers.

On the outskirts are some substantial houses built in the Twenties. Four bedrooms will cost from £500,000. Major new developments have appeared, including town-centre flats which start at £145,000 for one bedroom. Herne Farm is still under construction and offers one-bedroom flats at £110,000, to five-bedroom detached houses at £450,000. The Village, built in the centre of the town, is of "olde worlde" design and colourfully painted. A three-bedroom house here costs £300,000; four bedrooms £330,000 or more. Stoneham Park, built in the Seventies, has two-bedroom houses at £150,000; four bedrooms at around £300,000. The Gallifords is similarly priced.

Surrounding Petersfield are some beautiful villages. Two miles north is **Steep**, a trickle of houses across a hillside which they share with the co-educational private school Bedales. There are dramatic views of the beech woods, to which you can walk by taking a route across the common, past the primary school and up into the hangers. A notable feature of village life are the social events at Bedales, which include plays in the Olivier Theatre, concerts and talks. There is also an art gallery open to the public.

You could buy a small period cottage in Steep for around £220,000; a three-bedroom Victorian semi for £320,000; a four- or five-bedroom detached Victorian house for up to £600,000. A one-off five-bedroom detached modern house with an acre of garden could start at £800,000. The Petersfield bypass is a sore point in the village because of its close proximity.

Sheet, one mile north-east of Petersfield, exudes an historic charm. An ancient horse chestnut tree stands on the village green close to the Queen's Head pub, with the church and a terrace of old cottages nearby. Two former mills set off some of the larger houses very nicely. The village sustains a large primary school, which also serves the extensive Thirties' housing estate. Prices have risen since the bypass drained away the traffic. A two-bedroom period cottage will cost around £230,000; a three-bedroom Thirties' detached bungalow £280,000. A four-bedroom Georgian house might fetch around £600,000.

'A notable feature of village life are the social events at Bedales'

To the south-east of Petersfield is **South Harting**, recognisable from a distance by its octagonal copper church spire seen against the backdrop of Linch Down. Beneath it, in the graveyard, lies novelist Anthony Trollope. The main street, running uphill to the church, has thatched and timber-frame cottages, hairdresser, post office and carpet shop. There is a primary school and villagers have secured the future of the village shop by owning it outright. A three-bedroom half-timbered cottage in South Harting costs just over £280,000; a three-storey Georgian house with four bedrooms around £600,000. The village hall is the meeting place for all the local clubs and societies, including the Harting Society and a four-days-a-week playschool. There is football and cricket on the recreation ground. Uppark, the house restored by the National Trust after a devastating fire, is a mile away up the hill.

To the west is **West Meon**, which suffers from traffic on the A32, and its sister village **East Meon**, both lying in the shadow of the Downs. West Meon has a primary school, a post-office-cum-store, a butcher, clubs and societies. A 16th-century four-bedroom thatched cottage in need of modernisation might cost a little under £500,000; a Seventies'-built three-bedroom semi around £250,000. East Meon is the prettier of the two, with the River Meon flowing beneath a sequence of little bridges. There are one or two 14th-century houses, plus some Tudor and Georgian, and a working forge. A four-bedroom Georgian house would cost over £650,000; a newly-built four-bedroom house in The Meadows £540,000. Leydene Park is a new development a few miles south with giddy views of the south coast, tennis courts and five-bedroom detached houses for over £750,000.

> '*Rowlands Castle is a village for IBM executive types where you need a really new four-wheel drive to pick up the children from school*'

Journey: 87 min
Season: £2888
Peak: 3 per hr
Off-peak: 1 per hr

ROWLANDS CASTLE has all the appearances of a traditonal

English village with a crescent of green at the centre, flanked by cottages and Georgian and Victorian houses. A large country house, Deerleap, stands behind a flint wall opposite the green, and has in its grounds the remains of the castle which gave the village its name. The place is stiff with money and retired naval officers. "This is a village for IBM executive types, where you need a really new four-wheel drive to pick up the children from school," is how one local observer put it. There is a long waiting-list of people eager to pay the not inconsiderable fee to join the golf club. The village has its own primary school, shops, five foodie pubs on the green, vet, doctor's surgery, football and cricket pitches, tennis and cricket clubs. Huge detached houses built in the Twenties and Thirties with an acre of garden sell for around £500,000 in Links Lane, which is the smartest address. Bowes Hill is also smart, with four- and five-bedroom houses of the same period priced between £400,000 and £600,000.

Nearby is Ditcham Park, the private school for boys and girls, which has a liberal tradition, but is not as fashionable as Bedales. Rowlands Castle is strung between the ancient Forest of Bere and Stansted Park, the family seat of the Earl and Countess of Bessborough, which is open to the public.

Journey: 77 min
Season: £3032
Peak: 4 per hr
Off-peak: 3 per hr

HAVANT, too, is fairly sedate. It lies inland from Langstone Harbour, which is a popular sailing and watersports centre with good moorings and sailing clubs. The town is also well placed to take advantage of the cultural riches offered by Chichester, 10 miles to the east. Another major attraction is the old shore path (part of which is the Solent Way) to Warblington and Emsworth, running past Hayling Island and a much-prized area of marsh and mudflats designated as a Site of Special Scientific Interest. The older part of Havant is now masked by modernity, notably by the Meridian shopping centre, with library and multi-storey car park en suite. A short walk away is The Parchment, so called because the modern flats and mews houses here are built on the site of an old parchment-making works. A two-bedroom flat will cost £125,000; a four-bedroom house with two bathrooms £250,000. More up-market areas are Meadowlands and Wade Court, both within half a mile of the town centre. Individually designed detached houses with four and five bedrooms, built in the Twenties and Thirties with plush gardens, sell for between £385,000 and £500,000.

'A major attraction is the old shore path to Warblington and Emsworth running past Hayling Island'

Two miles to the east is **Denvilles**, a comforting Thirties' suburb with new accretions where three-bedroom detached houses with large gardens sell for around £230,000 and humble three-bedroom semis can come as cheap as £175,000. A four-bedroom detached house on a Seventies' estate would fetch between £210,000 and £230,000. There is also a huge council estate, Leigh Park, built in the Fifties to house Portsmouth overspill.

Journey: 95 min
Season: £3032
Peak: 2 per hr
Off-peak: 1 per hr

BEDHAMPTON is, with Denvilles (see above), one of the prime residential areas of Havant. It was developed in the Fifties as a series of bungalow estates where something with three bedrooms will now cost £230,000 to £260,000. There are three-bedroom semis for around £220,000 and detached houses for £250,000.

Housing developments cling on to Havant for several miles around, and to the north they don't let go until you get beyond Clanfield. Within this built-up area are former villages such as **Cowplain**, where there are 20- and 30-year-old estates and bungalows. A three-bedroom detached house on a Sixties' development might cost £225,000; a bungalow the same. **Denmead** village proper is greatly sought after, though it stands in a sea of anywhere-modernity. It has shops, pubs and a village green. A late 1880's cottage with three bedrooms and a bit of land could fetch £325,000. There are also plenty of small new developments, popular with young families because of the local school. Prices are similar to those in Waterlooville (see below).

Waterlooville is a very modern quiet suburb, around 80 per cent of which was built during the last two decades. Off Tempest Avenue, which runs from one end to the other, is a run of cul-de-sacs with mixed housing in each. A studio apartment costs £75,000, a three-bedroom semi £170,000 and a four-bedroom detached house £250,000. **Purbrook** has an air of retirement about it. The streets are quiet, the population is older, and there are some 19th-century houses between the bungalows. A two-bedroom bungalow costs £225,000.

'The navy dominates Portsmouth. Along with IBM it is the biggest employer, though it can sometimes create a them-and-us feeling in the city – particularly when hordes of American seamen come ashore and head straight for the nightlife in Southsea'

Journey: 99 min
Season: £3196
Peak: 3 per hr
Off-peak: 2 per hr

HILSEA is really north Portsmouth (see below). Streets of houses built in the Thirties fan out around the station. A three-bedroom semi costs between £160,000 and £200,000.

Journey: 87 min
Season: £3196
Peak: 3 per hr
Off-peak: 3 per hr

FRATTON is the home of Portsmouth Football Club, known to friend and foe alike as Pompey. It is very Coronation Street, like much of Portsmouth. Flat-fronted two- to three-bedroom terraced houses sell for £105,000.

Portsmouth &
Southsea
Journey: 91 min
Season: £3196
Peak: 3 per hr
Off-peak: 3 per hr

Portsmouth
Harbour
Journey: 95 min
Season: £3196
Peak: 3 per hr
Off-peak: 2 per hr

PORTSMOUTH & SOUTHSEA AND PORTSMOUTH HARBOUR
The navy dominates Portsmouth. Along with IBM it is the biggest local employer, though it can sometimes create a them-and-us feeling in the city – particularly when hordes of American seamen come ashore and head straight for the nightlife in Southsea. The dockyard has been home to the Royal Navy for 500 years, and the fleet is still serviced here. It is not only a good place for spotting modern warships, there is also an impressive collection of historic ships, including *HMS Victory* and the *Mary Rose*, which attracts tourists all year round. On top of the naval traffic there are the constant comings and goings of the Cherbourg, Le Havre, Caen, St Malo and Santander ferries into Albert Johnson dock. In the Mountbatten Centre, the city has one of the best leisure centres in southern England, which also doubles as a conference and

'Fogeys might prefer to browse among the bay-fronted Victoriana of North End'

trade show venue. Portsmouth Grammar School is the local private school that takes both boys and girls.

Portsmouth Harbour station is close to **Old Portsmouth** and the ferries to Gosport and the Isle of Wight. An 18th-century four- or five-bedroom house in Old Portsmouth would cost around £350,000. Quaint little cottages of the same period cost between £200,000 and £250,000. Gun Wharf Quays is a new marina here with smart shops, restaurants, a nightclub and Jongleurs comedy club, where a one-bedroom flat costs £200,000, and four-bedroom town houses £400,000. North of Portsmouth Harbour is **Port Solent**, a product of the high-earning, fast-living Thatcher years. The marina is the centrepiece, with surrounding houses, shops, restaurants and a sailing school. A two-bedroom flat will cost £260,000; a three-bedroom town house with a berth £320,000.

Throughout the city, first-time buyers compete for two-bedroom Victorian and Edwardian houses, priced at around £115,000. A third bedroom puts the price up to around £125,000. Second- and third-time buyers attracted to newish houses, could look in **Anchorage Park** in the north of the city, where a studio costs £100,000; four-bedroom detached houses £250,000. Fogeys might prefer to browse among the bay-fronted Victoriana of **North End**, an area undergoing gradual gentrification. A three-bedroom terraced house here would cost around £135,000.

Southsea has the feel of a seaside resort, with two piers, a shingle beach, permanent funfair, ballroom and the King's Theatre. It is packed with shops, restaurants and pubs. The Pyramids leisure centre is a wonderland of fun pools, water chutes and so on. Running back from the seafront are plenty of Victorian and Edwardian houses. You would pay around £160,000 for three bedrooms; up to £190,000 for a three-and-a-half bedroom corner house.

Edwardian family home, Portsmouth

Eastbourne
Hampden Park
Polegate
Berwick
Glynde
Lewes
Cooksbridge
Plumpton
Wivelsfield
Haywards Heath
Balcombe
Brighton
Hove
Portslade
Shoreham-by-Sea
Lancing
Worthing
Preston Park
Hassocks
Burgess Hill
Arundel
Amberley
Pulborough
Billingshurst
Christ's Hospital
Horsham
Littlehaven
Faygate
Ifield
Crawley
Three Bridges
Gatwick Airport
Horley
Salfords
Earlswood
Godstone
Edenbridge
Nutfield
Redhill
Reigate
London Bridge
Victoria

Victoria/London Bridge
> Arundel and Brighton
and on to Eastbourne, Lewes and Worthing

Many peak and all off-peak services from Brighton to London Bridge go on to Blackfriars, City Thameslink, Farringdon and Kings Cross Thameslink. The season ticket prices quoted for London Bridge are valid across London to Kings Cross Thameslink (but not on the Underground).

To Victoria
Journey: 28 min
Season: £1740
Peak: 3 per hr
Off-peak: 2 per hr

To London Bridge
Journey: 34 min
Season: £1740
Peak: 2 per hr
Off-peak: 2 per hr

REDHILL has outstripped its older neighbour **Reigate** (see below), though it only began to sprout in about 1841 when the railway arrived. It is now heavily commercialised. There is a huge new shopping centre, The Belfry, anchored around a large Marks & Spencer, as well as the Harlequin theatre and a sports centre, The Donyngs, with saunas, Jacuzzis, swimming pool and gym.

Redhill is slightly cheaper than Reigate. There is an abundance of Thirties' semis and detached houses with bay windows and steep cottage-style rooftops. Buy-to-let investors have been snapping up flats and pushing up prices. One-bedroom flats now cost £125,000, two-bedroom flats £175,000 to £220,000. You can get little two-bedroom cottages for around £200,000, three-bedroom terraced houses for £210,000 and three-bedroom semi-detached houses for £200,000 to £250,000. Something more sumptuous, with five bedrooms backing onto the golf course, could be bought for £575,000.

> North Downs line east to Edenridge

To London Bridge
Journey: 32 min
Season: £1740
Peak: 1 per hr
Off-peak: 1 per hr

NUTFIELD is little more than a ribbon town which has grown up along the A25, with the pedigree of a 13th-century church on the High Street. You can buy a three-bedroom semi for £385,000. But a new four-bedroom detached house could cost £500,000 to £635,000. **South Nutfield** (where Nutfield station is situated) has a school, a general store and a post office. The local watering hole is the Station

251

Hotel. An early-20th-century semi here might cost £240,000; a modern four-bedroom house costs £390,000. The most exclusive address is The Avenue.

<table>
<tr><td>To London Bridge</td></tr>
<tr><td>Journey: 46 min</td></tr>
<tr><td>Season: £1740</td></tr>
<tr><td>Peak: 1 per hr</td></tr>
<tr><td>Off-peak: 1 per hr</td></tr>
</table>

GODSTONE is right on the A25 with a one-way traffic system that turns the centre into an alternative bottleneck when the M25 is blocked. It is no longer the rural backwater where William Cobbett spied double violets as large as small pinks. But it still has the neat gardens he admired, the green, the pond and the White Hart Inn where he stayed. A two-bedroom Victorian cottage in a quiet pocket at the centre might be priced at £235,000. A Grade II listed four-bedroom 15th-century house would cost £480,000.

<table>
<tr><td>To London Bridge</td></tr>
<tr><td>Journey: 50 min</td></tr>
<tr><td>Season: £1740</td></tr>
<tr><td>(also valid</td></tr>
<tr><td>Edenbridge Town)</td></tr>
<tr><td>or £2034 via</td></tr>
<tr><td>Tonbridge</td></tr>
<tr><td>Peak: 1 per hr</td></tr>
<tr><td>(3 per hr changing</td></tr>
<tr><td>at Redhill or</td></tr>
<tr><td>Tonbridge)</td></tr>
<tr><td>Off-peak: 1 per hr</td></tr>
<tr><td>(3 per hr changing</td></tr>
<tr><td>at Redhill or</td></tr>
<tr><td>Tonbridge)</td></tr>
</table>

EDENBRIDGE has two stations, the other being Edenbridge Town on the Hurst Green to Uckfield line (see page 287). The stations are a mile apart, and the two railway lines hold the worst bit of town in a pincer-grip between them. The area is a depository for factories and former council estates. The best parts of town are in the north and south. Buy-to-let investors are busy putting pressure on the lower rungs of the market. First-time starter flats cost around £90,000 to £135,000; two-bedroom flats from £120,000 to £180,000. Large houses on the golf course built by Rydon Homes are popular and sell at £300,000 for three bedrooms or £550,000 for five bedrooms.

Although Edenbridge is not one of the gems of Kent, it does have its attractions. It is an hour from London and the same from the coast. Gatwick is only 30 minutes away, but not so close that aircraft noise is a worry. The town has a seemingly endless High Street, a string of beautiful half-timbered houses by the River Eden and a restaurant in a restored mill. The south-eastern portion of the town, towards Hever, is more pleasing, especially where it turns into the hamlet of **Marsh Green**. The south-west end of town, towards Haxted, is also inviting. **Haxted** has a large watermill and the stables next door have been turned into a restaurant, which serves Dover sole and roast pheasant inside by candlelight or outside on the terrace by the millpond in summer. On the northern flank of Edenbridge is a large industrial estate and a very large council estate called Spittals Cross, where many of the houses with thin slit windows and flat roofs are now in private ownership. Wits say that Edenbridge is a tale of two towns, offering a spectrum of urban blight to rural delight within one-and-a-half miles. There are all the usual sports: cricket, football, tennis, badminton, rugby, hockey, bowls and golf.

The villages surrounding Edenbridge are much more scenic than the town itself. They have a number of fine timber-framed houses from the 16th century, built on the proceeds of the iron industry which collapsed in about 1700. The magnificent half-timbered old houses of **Chiddingstone**, often used for film locations, are in the hands of the National Trust and are let to tenants. The Castle Inn is a popular eating place.

> North Downs line west to Reigate

To Victoria
Journey: 42 min
Season: £1740
Peak: 3 per hr
changing at Redhill
Off-peak: 1 per hr
plus 1 per hr
changing at Redhill

REIGATE is Redhill's older brother, tucked under the North Downs, with rows of quiet residential streets and a shopping centre with a significant Safeway. Sunday afternoon walks are taken on Reigate Heath, 130 acres of open space on the edge of the town, where there is a restored windmill which is used as a church. Education is shared with Redhill. There is a Roman Catholic/Church of England co-educational comprehensive, St Bede's, which prepares students for A-levels and Oxbridge entrance. East Surrey College offers degrees in art, design, science and computing.

Reigate has a greater quantity of properties at the top end of the market than Redhill. The most exclusive areas are High Trees Road and just off Reigate Hill. A large family home on Pilgrims Way with ample gardens would cost more than £1m, but a two-up-two-down in the town centre could be bought for rather less, at £220,000.

> Continuation of main line

To London Bridge
Journey: 35 min
Season: £1740
Peak: 2 per hr plus
2 per hr to Victoria
Off-peak: 1 per hr

EARLSWOOD It is hard to find a dividing line between Earlswood and Redhill. Many of the people who live here work at the nearby East Surrey Hospital. There are also plenty of commuters, travelling to both Croydon and London. The conversion of the Royal Earlswood Hospital into luxury apartments, now re-selling at £250,000, has improved the situation and there is a beautiful common with two lakes for boating and fishing. A two-bedroom flat would cost £140,000; a three-bedroom early-20th-century semi-detached £235,000.

To London Bridge
Journey: 42 min
Season: £1996
Peak: 2 per hr plus
2 per hr to Victoria
Off-peak: 1 per hr

SALFORDS is nice in parts, but has the disadvantage of straddling the A23. It has a village shop-cum-post-office and a newsagent. People tend to head for Redhill, Horley or Hookwood for their major shops. There is a primary school, but older children have to bus to Horley or Redhill for secondary schools. Long-suffering parents spend a lot of time chauffeuring their children about because there is not much for them to do in the village itself (the Scouts' group is at neighbouring Sidlow). The nearby aerodrome is a thorn in the side. Night-flight training programmes for light aircraft and helicopters are a regular irritation. A three-bedroom semi with a long garden here might cost £250,000; a two-bedroom bungalow about the same. Larger properties in leafier roads lie to the east.

To Victoria
Journey: 33 min
Season: £1996
Peak: 4 per hr
Off-peak: 1 per hr

To London Bridge
Journey: 46 min
Season: £1996
(also valid to
Victoria)
Peak: 2 per hr
Off-peak: 1 per hr

HORLEY
Compared to the two commercial bullies, Reigate and Crawley, that lie on either side of it, Horley is a mute backwater. "A lot of people think it is too quiet," says one resident. It does, however, have a swimming pool at the Horle Anderson Centre, in additon to cricket, hockey, bowling and football clubs. Gatwick Airport is a big local employer. The two main thoroughfares are the A23 and a modest high street. The local comprehensive, Oakwood School, is well-liked. In the sea of Thirties' semis you could pay between £220,000 and £250,000 for three bedrooms. There are also some Victorian terraces where three-bedroom houses start at around £180,000. The modern Langshott estate, with over 700 houses on it, won awards for landscaping and design when it was built. A five-bedroom detached house here would cost over £350,000. The area is earmarked for another armful of new housing.

The village of **Charlwood** struggles admirably to hang onto its rural image, despite the fact that Gatwick Airport is only a few miles away. The recent government announcement that Gatwick will not expand towards the village has lifted a black cloud, though the parish council remains vigilant. Villagers lovingly nurse the large number of listed buildings, which include a Grade I listed Norman church. There is a newsagent, which also sells fruit and groceries, a post office, a soft furnishings shop, a pine shop and a builders' merchants. The village has a school for the under-sevens. People living here have the choice of commuting either from Horley or from Gatwick, where the service is fast and frequent. A brick-built two-bedroom cottage might be bought for £185,000; a third bedroom puts the price up to around £200,000.

Grade II listed
house,
Charlwood

Smallfield, to the north-east, has been greatly affected by the development of Gatwick. Aircraft noise is a problem, and the very presence of an airport has allowed more industrial development than would otherwise have been the case. It has a burgeoning population, with a good mix of young and old, yet it is straggly and has no real centre. Local shops include a greengrocer and butcher, local events take place in the new Centenary Village Hall. There is an annual flower show, a carnival each July and dinner-dances in the church and school hall. Prices are similar to those in Horley. A three-bedroom semi-detached house near The Plough pub recently sold at £217,000 and a detached three-bedroom house at £250,000. Modern four-bedroom detached houses cost around £300,000.

GATWICK AIRPORT

To Victoria
Journey: 30 min
Season: £2124
(except Gatwick
Express); £2860 all
operators
Peak: 5 per hr
Off-peak: 8 per hr

To London Bridge
Journey: 29 min
Season: £2124
(also valid
Victoria)
Peak: 2 per hr
Off-peak: 4 per hr

GATWICK AIRPORT Gatwick Express trains whistle into London from here at a frequency of one every 15 minutes, making it a popular choice for commuters in a hurry. People living in the villages to the west might prefer it to stations on the nearer, but much slower **Victoria to Waterloo/Horsham** line (see page 277).

THREE BRIDGES

To Victoria
Journey: 43 min
Season: £2236
(£2880 Gatwick
Express included)
Peak: 4 per hr
Off-peak: 2 per hr

To London Bridge
Journey: 33 min
Season: £2236
(also valid
Victoria)
Peak: 3 per hr
Off-peak: 3 per hr

THREE BRIDGES Some of the better parts of Crawley such as **Pound Hill** and **Copthorne** are close to this station. One-bedroom flats cost about £122,950; three-bedroom detached houses about £250,000 (see Crawley, page 256). Three Bridges, so-called because of the bridges that cross Gatwick Brock nearby, was a village in its own right before Crawley was first thought of. It contains some Victorian terraces that sprang up around the railway station, but the bulk of it was built in the early Fifties when more than 2000 houses were put up for 4800 newcomers. Prices here are about the same as those in Crawley.

'Three Bridges, so-called because of the bridges that cross Gatwick Brock nearby, was a village in its own right before Crawley was first thought of'

> Main line from Three Bridges to Arundel

To Victoria
Journey: 47 min
Season: £2236
(£2880 Gatwick
Express included)
Peak: 3 per hr
Off-peak: 2 per hr

To London Bridge
Journey: 57 min
Season: £2236
(also valid
Victoria)
Peak: 2 per hr
Off-peak: 1 per hr

CRAWLEY is not much loved by anyone and can't avoid the nickname Creepie Crawley. A few years ago the young here felt they had nothing. "There isn't even a Miss Selfridge," whined one. Now there is a Miss Selfridge, and two nightclubs as well. But the great plus here for the young is that the recession never made its presence felt – unemployment has hardly touched it. Jobs at Gatwick Airport are plentiful, and the factory estates and business parks that have grown up around it include every kind of industry from light manufacturing to pharmaceuticals and foodstuffs.

It was developed after World War II for people moving out of London and was the only New Town in the south of England. The design was originally anchored around nine neighbourhoods (now there are 13 with one at planning stage), each with a population of 6000. Each area was to have its own shopping parade, primary school, church, pub, community hall and playing fields. The first new-towners arrived in 1949, when Gatwick Airport was no more than a war-time runway on boggy ground on the town's outskirts, a far cry from the noisy, air-polluting monster that it has become.

People moving to the area would probably choose to live in one of the neighbouring villages, or closer to Three Bridges station, and go into Crawley only to take advantage of County Mall, the enormous covered shopping centre, and the new Crawley Leisure Park which has a fitness club, bowling, restaurants and a 15-screen Cinema. Other attractions include Tilgate Park with its rare and domestic animal collection, and the 18-hole municipal golf course.

For £175,000 it is possible to get one of the original three-bedroom semis put up in the New Town's early days. Studio flats cost around £90,000 and one-bedroom flats £120,000. The original neighbourhoods are still identifiable. West Green, for instance, was one of the first, and it still has rows of brick terraces and some older labourers' cottages. The less popular neighbourhoods are changing as people buy ex-council properties. They include Broadfield, Bewbush, which was hastily built to accommodate second-generation Crawley families, and Langley Green.

'Jobs at Gatwick Airport are plentiful, and the factory estates and business parks that have grown up around it include every kind of industry from light manufacturing to pharmaceuticals and foodstuffs'

To Victoria

Journey: 59 min

Season: £2236

(£2880 Gatwick

Express included)

Peak: 2 per hr

Off-peak: 2 per hr*

To London Bridge

Journey: 60 min

Season: £2236

(valid Victoria)

Peak: 2 per hr

Off-peak: 1 per hr

To London Bridge

Journey: 54 min

Season: £2612

(£2880 Gatwick

Express included)

Peak: 2 per hr

Off-peak: 1 every

4 hrs*

To Victoria

Journey: 64 min

Season: £2612

(£2880 Gatwick

Express included)

Peak: 3 per hr

Off-peak: 2 per hr*

To London Bridge

Journey: 66 min

Season: £2612

(valid Victoria)

Peak: 2 per hr

Off-peak: 1 per hr

*Changing at

Gatwick Airport

IFIELD is on the outskirts of Crawley, but at least there is a conservation area which contains the old village green, St Margaret's Church and the Plough Inn. The old Ifield Watermill on the millpond is open in the summer and the miller's house is now a pub called The Mill House. A larding of new houses was added in 1956. You can buy a three-bedroom Fifties' semi at £190,000 and two-bedroom cottages from £195,000. A grander period family house might be bought for £550,000.

FAYGATE This little station is only served in the rush hours. Property is a little more expensive in Faygate than in Crawley because people like the intimacy of scale offered by the village, but in truth the semi-rural atmosphere is negated by the dual carriageway screeching past. A two-bedroom Victorian semi costs £250,000; a five-bedroom modern country house £775,000.

LITTLEHAVEN was once a separate village, but is now essentially a part of Horsham, with modern estates providing the putty between the two. The older houses are in Rusper Road, but much of the property for sale is modern, with three-bedroom semis sensibly priced at around £220,000. Wise advice from one seasoned commuter: "The station platform is only four carriages long so you have to make sure you're in the right bit of the train or you can't get off."

House style in Sussex

The tile-hung cottages of Sussex with their hipped roofs, rich timbering and modest proportions, give the most sought-after villages their texture and colour. Set against the drama of the North and South Downs, often tucked into folds or valleys, their russets and terracottas glow in the landscape.

The tiles themselves are hooked over battens, often fastened only every third or fourth course with nothing more than oak pegs. Baking in the kiln caused them to become slightly distorted, so they form a pleasingly uneven line with small variations in colour. Line them up, row upon row, and you get a decorative kind of architectural needlework. Vary the shapes by introducing diamonds and fishtails, and the humblest of cottages looks as prettily feathered as an exotic bird.

Architectural deceit is something to watch for in this part of the country. For here it was that mathematical tiles were invented – tiles to look like bricks – in the 18th century. The theory is that this was done as a means of avoiding brick taxes, but it may have had more to do with vanity. Brick was *the* fashionable building material of the time. The deceit continues as mathematical tiles often fool modern housebuyers who believe them to be brick. The key to their detection is the absence of lintels and arches over windows and doors.

East and West Sussex are also counties which have provided great wealth and pleasure. This is where William the Conqueror built some of the first Norman castles and established the feudal system. Later royals used the seaside towns as their favoured watering holes, hence all the Regency froth and finery of Brighton. The town was transformed with squares and crescents by the Prince of Wales in the early 1800s.

To Victoria
Journey: 56 min
Season: 2612
(£2880 Gatwick
Express included)
Peak: 3 per hr
Off-peak: 3 per hr

To London Bridge
Journey: 69 min
Season: £2812
(also valid
Victoria)
Peak: 2 per hr
Off-peak: 1 per hr

HORSHAM is a busy little Sussex town which manages to combine its old character as a smugglers' haunt and late-18th-century garrison town with plenty of interesting little shops and local businesses. It has a population of 45,000, which is expanding fast. It is in a marvellous position with a good train service to London, but with house prices lower than they are across the border in Surrey. Chichester and Guildford are close enough for theatres, though Horsham has its own small theatre, and the sea is 20 miles away over the South Downs. You can go to the races at Goodwood, show jumping at Hickstead, hunt with the Crawley and Horsham Pack, and there are golf clubs at Pulborough, Mannings Heath, Pease Pottage, West Chiltington and Ockley. It also has Christ's Hospital public school for boys and girls, where there is a separate railway station (see opposite).

Some of the houses in the town are collector's items. Walk down Pump Alley and into the Causeway, for example, and you find a street that is much as it was 300 years ago. These houses with bulging walls and uneven roofs very rarely come on the market. For something more family-friendly, such as a detached five-bedroom house near the station with access to good schools, you could pay at least £750,000. A small, modern two-bedroom house would cost around £190,000. There are council estates to the east and west of the town.

Local villages also maintain strong links with the past. **Slinfold**, to the east, has a good collection of Georgian houses hemmed in by tall hedges and walls, strung out along a very pretty winding lane. It still has a village shop and school. A six-bedroom, three-bathroom period house with country views can set you back by £825,000. Closer to Horsham, separated from it by the A24, is Broadbridge Heath, which has a sports centre and a Tesco. Field Place at **Broadbridge Heath** was the birthplace of the poet, Shelley, and is occasionally open to the public.

Further south is **Itchingfield**, which has an intriguing priest's house attached to the tiny church; and **Southwater**, which is little more than a dormitory to Horsham and free-fire zone for new housing. Moving west you come to **Nuthurst**, a delightful village with 16th-century houses and a timber-framed inn. A modern five-bedroom detached house here recently sold for £525,000. **Lower Beeding** is small, elongated and has a post-office-cum-shop. The big house, Leonardslee, has rhododendron gardens that are open to the public from April to October. The countryside lapses back into heathland here in St Leonard's Forest, which covers 12,000 acres of old Royal hunting ground, once thought to have harboured dragons and to which (within living memory) pigs were driven up from Brighton to snuffle for acorns. To the south-west is **Cowfold**, which has lost some of its character through being a junction for the A272 and A281, but it is still well-liked. An old, two-bedroom terraced cottage here might be bought for £170,000.

North of the forest is **Rusper**, an enchanting village with an ancient church dating from the 13th century, a high street lined with black-and-white timber buildings and two pubs, The Plough and The Star, which are centuries old. A pretty, five-bedroom 16th-century cottage with an eccentric topiary garden recently sold here for £900,000. On this side of Horsham you have to beware the noise of aircraft from Gatwick Airport.

> '**The countryside lapses back into heathland here in St Leonard's Forest**'

> '**Christ's Hospital is a much sought-after area, with a disproportionately large railway station**'

To Victoria
Journey: 59 min
Season: 2612
(£2880 Gatwick
Express included)
Peak: 1 per hr plus
1 per hr to London
Bridge
Off-peak: 1 per hr

CHRIST'S HOSPITAL, hardly distinct from Horsham, is dominated by the public school, fondly known as C H by local people, which disgorges pupils in their distinctive blue and bright yellow uniform. Around Christ's Hospital has grown a low-level brick settlement, largely 20th-century, which looks to neighbouring Southwater for small-time shopping. It is a much sought-after area, with a disproportionately large railway station. A two-bedroom ex-farmer's cottage in need of work recently sold for £220,000; a three-bedroom semi in good order would be more likely to cost £250,000. New houses are planned because the station is so handy.

BILLINGSHURST

To Victoria
Journey: 66 min
Season: £2800
(£2880 Gatwick
Express included)
Peak: 2 per hr plus
1 per hr to London
Bridge
Off-peak: 2 per hr

BILLINGSHURST feels more like a small town than a large village. It has some fine 15th-century houses beached on a shore of modern developments and is very much divided by the A29, which follows the route of the old Roman road, Stane Street. Commuters love the place, because it is more intimate than Horsham or Crawley yet has the fast rail links. "Our looks and intelligence distinguish us from other villages," says one resident. On the large new Penfold Grange development, a three-bedroom detached house will cost £250,000. **Wisborough Green**, two miles away, is literally a film-set village, regularly used by film directors as a backdrop. It has a cricket green that borders the A272, a village shop-cum-post-office and two inns. A lovely 16th-century four-bedroom cottage with seven acres and stabling would be priced at £675,000. You need to remember that stations south of Horsham are much less well served by trains to London.

PULBOROUGH

To Victoria
Journey: 73 min
Season: £2800
(£2880 Gatwick
Express included)
Peak: 2 per hr plus
1 per hr to London
Bridge
Off-peak: 2 per hr

PULBOROUGH This is where the Arun valley becomes spellbindingly beautiful, and houses backing onto it are extremely sought after, though beware flooding. "The wetlands, the bird sanctuary, the downland walks, make it an absolutely glorious place to live, full of sunny corners," says one local resident. This rather belies the fact that Pulborough is under a lot of development pressure, and local conservationists are battle-scarred. Local societies do their stuff, with Cubs, Brownies, rugby, cricket and plenty of vigorous football on offer. The greenfingered work hard on the allotments and join the horticultural society. The village has two butchers, a supermarket, a new village hall and good schools. In the jumble of brick, flint and thatch you might find a 16th-century three-bedroom cottage with inglenook fireplaces for £350,000.

Many of the villages on the felted slopes of the South Downs are particularly lovely. **West Burton** and **Sutton**, for instance, are very small and rural, no more than a handful of cottages and a pub. A pretty four-bedroom cottage here might cost £750,000.

Period town house, Petworth

Nutborne, just to the north-east, is another little hamlet with a pub, The Rising Sun, and local vineyards. You might find a two-bedroom cottage here for £300,000 or a small manor for £900,000. Further west you come to what local people tend rather dismissively to call the "Surrey part of Sussex", meaning that it is more suburban in character than the wilder countryside to the east. A four-bedroom cottage in comparatively manicured **West Chiltington** costs £550,000 to

£600,000. It is close to the shops at **Storrington**, a village that long ago burst its boundaries with new houses, but which offers a reasonable range of shops and two ponds with ducks and swans. The River Stor has not burst its boundaries since 2000, but ask about flood risk if you are buying a house here. Dying here also poses problems because the graveyard is full. In recent years people had been under pressure to be cremated, but thankfully a field has now been consecrated to take the overspill.

The star in the west is **Petworth**. The town stands at the gates of Petworth House, begun by the Duke of Somerset at the end of the 17th century and surrounded by hundreds of acres of National Trust land. The old timber-frame houses in the tangle of narrow streets around Petworth's square attract lots of tourists in the summer. The large car park is full by breakfast-time, much to the annoyance of the local shoppers.

Petworth is also an antiques centre, with more than 30 antiques shops. There aren't many other shops, though there is a gunsmith for the sporting fraternity. Villagers feel oppressed by the traffic coming through on the A285 and A272; a by-pass has been talked of since 1935 and has now developed into grand ideas for an underground tunnel through which cars could mole in order to avoid the town. A 17th-century commercial premises ripe to be turned back into a four-bedroom house was recently on the market at £350,000. Commuters have the choice of using the faster line into Waterloo from Haslemere, which is 10 miles away.

Fittleworth, closer to Pulborough, is a more mixed kind of village where neighbours find it difficult to get to know each other. It has its own shop, church and inn, a very good primary school and is close to marvellous riding country in Bedham Woods and on the Downs. A four-bedroom house set in 15 acres would cost £985,000.

> 'A bypass has been talked of since 1935 and there are now grand ideas for a tunnel,

To Victoria
Journey: 81 min
Season: £2880
Peak: 1 per hr
Off-peak: 1 per hr

AMBERLEY is another of the many villages in this area that have hung onto their character. It is protected from heavy traffic on a side road off the B2139.

Flint-and-thatch cottages with old-fashioned cottage gardens cluster around Amberley Castle, once the residence of the Bishops of Chichester and dismantled by Parliamentarians during the Civil War. A footpath to one side leads to Amberley Wild Brooks, protected water meadows visited by migrating birds. The village has a shop-cum-post-office. A shortage of five-year-olds means that it is struggling to keep the primary school going. A two-bedroom thatched cottage with an inglenook fireplace will be priced at £365,000; a larger chocolate box cottage at £470,000. House prices remain on the steep side in several other popular villages further from the station, such as **Houghton** and **Bury**.

To Victoria
Journey: 82 min
Season: £2880
Peak: 2 per hr plus
1 per hr to London
Bridge
Off-peak: 2 per hr

ARUNDEL is a busy old town on the River Arun, dominated by its castle which is often described as Windsor in miniature. The High Street, winding steeply between the river and the castle, has plenty of antiques shops, but none of the standard chain stores. There is a butcher and two bakers, a general stores, a fine-wine-cum-deli and a walking-stick shop. Chichester is only 10 miles away with its attractions for yachtsmen and theatre-goers, athough Arundel has its own Priory Playhouse for smaller-scale productions; Goodwood racecourse is a mere three miles up on the Downs, and there are plenty of golf courses. The sea is three miles to the south, and there is a good beach at Climping. The River Arun has to be watched; it is tidal, and one of the fastest flowing rivers in the country after the Severn. The Arundel Wildfowl Trust, founded by Sir Peter Scott, runs special events for children during the school holidays.

You could buy a two-bedroom cottage for £200,000. For a building in traditional brick-and-flint, you will have to pay a premium. For three-bedroom houses the price jumps to £250,000-£300,000. People either opt for old Arundel, which climbs steeply up the hill, layer upon layer towards the castle, or they look at the larger Fifties' houses on the slightly cheaper Chichester side. These have large gardens and garages, are within walking distance of the town and are rather more suburban. A four-bedroom house in this neighbourhood will cost between £350,000 and £400,000.

The villages of **Burpham** and **Wepham** lie to the east, on the way up to the top of Harrow Hill where the views are wonderful. Both are popular, and a thatched two-bedroom semi with small garden would cost £300,000. **Slindon**, to the west, is the kind of village people wait years for a chance to move into. Not only because of its beauty, but because the involvement of the National Trust means that very few houses are still freehold. A period house with five bedrooms and a small paddock could cost close to £695,000.

> Main line from Three Bridges to Brighton

To London Bridge
Journey: 38 min
Season: £2560 also
valid to Victoria
(£2880 Gatwick
Express included)
Peak: 1 per hr
Off-peak: 1 per hr

BALCOMBE Its position on a railway line set deep in an Area of Outstanding Natural Beauty has gilded the house-price lily in Balcombe. Commuters have a strong presence there. They usually begin by sending their children to the local nursery and primary schools, but switch them into the private system later. The village has an old quarter and a modern quarter, and its great good luck is that the new estates have been planned well enough to avoid any feeling of claustrophobia. Just off the village centre in the old quarter, Victorian semis with three bedrooms, three reception rooms and a garden sell for £340,000 as soon as they appear on the market. A five-bedroom swanky new house with six acres out of the village could fetch over £1m.

The village is described by the parish clerk as "happy, friendly and caring". Strangers are soon spotted by vigilant members of the Neighbourhood Watch. Among the myriad clubs and activities is a Care Group which arranges to take people to hospital, collect prescriptions and so on; and a Christmas Tree Society to aid the needy. There are societies to cover the needs of every age group from mixed Cubs to pensioners, plus tennis, cricket, football and badminton clubs. The actor Paul Schofield lives here.

Balcombe is close to **Ardingly** (the last syllable rhymes with eye) Reservoir where people sail, windsurf and fish at weekends. Mostly it is used by students from Ardingly College, the independent school for boys and girls which sits on the bank. The hill-ridge village of Ardingly is best known for the National Trust's Wakehurst Gardens. These are leased by the Royal Botanical Gardens at Kew and for the South of England Showground. The three-day agricultural show every June makes it the agricultural capital of Sussex. The grounds are also used for antiques shows and Pony Club displays. Ardingly's village hall is heavily booked with ballet classes, mother-and-toddlers, playgroups and horticultural society meetings. A Thirties' semi with three bedrooms in a quiet cul-de-sac within walking distance of all these activities sells at around £300,000.

To Victoria
Journey: 46 min
Season: £2800
(£2880 Gatwick Express included)
Peak: 5 per hr
Off-peak: 2 per hr

To London Bridge
Journey: 42 min
Season: £2800
(also valid Victoria)
Peak: 2 per hr
Off-peak: 4 per hr

HAYWARDS HEATH
This is prime commuter country, close to the M23 and the M25, fed by fast trains to London, yet sufficiently far south for trips to the sea. Successful local businessmen and airline pilots from Gatwick also help to put prices up. The town feels hugely superior to Burgess Hill, which is three miles away and probably has slightly better shops, though Haywards Heath has both a Marks & Spencer and a Sainsbury's. Property prices are high. A simple one-bedroom flat costs around £115,000, rising to between £130,000 and £180,000 for a two-bedroom flat. A detached four-bedroom house with two bathrooms is likely to cost around £550,000. Better parts of town are in the conservation areas at Lucastes and Lewes Road. Also popular is Muster Green, where the large Victorian and Edwardian houses have ample gardens around an open space which has much of the character of a village green.

You can throw money at houses in the Haywards Heath area. Villages such as **Wineham** are very popular. Here, a three-bedroom period cottage might cost around £350,000. **Lindfield** has all the ingredients of the perfect village: a high street with tile-hung Sussex houses, five pubs, a junior and primary school, a pond with ducks, a large open common and a historic parish church. It is in two halves. One half remains Elizabethan. The other half consists of ex-council housing. Stockbrokers' houses are slipped into the lanes round about. A Victorian house with four- to five-bedrooms could be bought for £485,000, a three-bedroom Victorian semi with a long garden will cost £350,000.

Further north still, **Horsted Keynes** is another village that mutated during the Fifties. You drive through the centre thinking how lovely the village green is, then turn a corner and confront a mass of cheap housing. The pretty bit is still very popular and commands higher prices than Haywards Heath. A mid-terraced two-bedroom cottage with a little garden will cost £235,000. About a mile away is the privately-run Bluebell Railway, a great delight for steam-train enthusiasts. **Paxhill Park** is popular for its golf course, but lacks a real village spirit.

To the west is **Scayne's Hill**. It has been sliced in two by the A272, but has some dignified Victorian houses. A two-bedroom bungalow might be snapped up for £265,000. **Fletching** is tiny, but has a lovely collection of 16th-century houses and a couple of pubs (see page 291).

Less than two miles to the east of Haywards Heath is the tall spire of **Cuckfield** parish church, which German bombers used as a landmark during World War II. Beyond it you negotiate a tortuous bend, then climb the beautiful 15th-century high street, lined with medieval cottages. At the brow of the hill the spell is broken and medieval England dissolves into Victorian and modern. A Fifties' three-bedroom semi here could be bought for £199,950.

Since the village was once a staging post it is well-endowed with pubs; there are five altogether, for a population of 3000. Cuckfield is extremely active and shows its independence in eccentric ways. A fight with the district council over the ownership of the playing fields resulted in the village declaring independence and producing its own passports, currency and stamps. It still holds mock elections for a mayor every year, and residents pay one penny to vote. The Independent State of Cuckfield is the eccentrically named local pressure group which does much charity fund-raising and has fought off plans for a rubbish

Unusual tile-hung cottage, Wivelsfield

tip. Cuckfield has its own museum, library and local beauty spot, New England Wood.

To the west are the more remote hamlets of **Bolney** and **Warninglid**. Both had strong connections with the medieval iron industry, and are rather beautiful, and kept scrupulously tidy by elderly inhabitants. A four-bedroom house with Tudor features will cost £550,000.

To Victoria
Journey: 52 min
Season: £2800
(£2000 Gatwick
Express included)
Peak: 2 per hr
Off-peak: 1 per hr

To London Bridge
Journey: 51 min
Season: £2800
(also valid
Victoria)
Peak: 3 per hr
Off-peak: 2 per hr

WIVELSFIELD station is actually two-and-a-half-miles away on the edge of Burgess Hill. The village is split, with the older part gathered around the church and school, and the newer part on the east of the B2112 at Wivelsfield Green. Property prices are similar to those in Burgess Hill (see below). People tend to pass through it on their way to Haywards Heath or Lewes. The influx of London and Brighton commuters since the war has doubled the population to nearly 2000, but the old village families are still involved in agriculture and Young Farmers' events are well attended. It has a post-office-cum-village store which stretches to delicatessen food and French bread, a hairdresser and garage. The primary school is popular though the Victorian buildings are worn and torn. Older children move on to Haywards Heath comprehensive and a tertiary college at Chailey. There are lovely tiled cottages in some of the older roads, such as Church Lane. A three-bedroom semi would come to the market with a £270,000 price tag.

To London Bridge
Journey: 55 min
Season: £2800
(also valid
Victoria)
Peak: 2 per hr plus
2 per hr to Victoria
Off-peak: 2 per hr

BURGESS HILL was an intimate little place until a few decades ago. In 1951 its population was just 8000. Since then it has been overwhelmed by new estates built to soak up London overspill. The population has shot up to 29,000 and is still climbing as big companies, including British Oxygen and American Express, move in. A new relief road and link to the A23 unlocked pockets of building land for thousands more new houses, but a grass buffer to the west of town called the Green Crescent provides a protective belt of sorts. The old Sixties' shopping centre, The Martletts, has been redeveloped in a Nineties' mould. There is a Waitrose and Tesco, but otherwise the shopping is unimaginative. Cultural treats can be had at the cinema and the Burgess Hill Theatre (venue for local dramatic and choral societies), and muscle tone can be developed at the Triangle Leisure Centre. The comprehensive school is oversubscribed; the fee-paying alternative for girls is Burgess Hill School.

The town is downmarket of Haywards Heath and probably offers the lowest property prices to be found in this expensive mid-Sussex belt, though prices are still rising fast. Two-bedroom houses start at around £160,000; three-bedroom houses at £175,000; four-bedroom houses at £250,000. Silverdale Road, Keymer Road and Folders Lane are where you find the most expensive older houses, with company directors and airline pilots settling at around £500,000. A few very old farmhouses still survive on the former commons.

To London Bridge
Journey: 58 min
Season: £2800
(also valid
Victoria)
Peak: 2 per hr
(plus 2 per hr to
Victoria)
Off-peak: 2 per hr

HASSOCKS likes to think of itself as a village, but it is actually town-sized with a population of 6000, including quite a high proportion of retired people. It snuggles up to **Hurstpierpoint** and **Keymer**, though the people of Hurstpierpoint regard themselves as quite separate. The small shopping parade meets basic needs, but for serious food shopping people go to the Waitrose or Tesco at Burgess Hill. Hassocks is not architecturally distinguished. It grew up around the railway in the 19th century, with new developments appearing in the Thirties and Fifties. But it does sit under the wing of the South Downs, so there are magnificent views of the Jack and Jill windmills on the crest where you can also take lonely windblown walks.

You would pay around £275,000 for a three-bedroom modern detached house, but older properties go for much more. For example, a three-bedroom Thirties' detached house with a large garden would set you back £360,000. Hassocks has primary and secondary schools which are thought to be good. There is a Beacon Club for the mid-teens, but not much for older teenagers to do. The old Sussex game of stoolball is still played here, kept alive by the Stoolball Association. It is a form of rounders, invented by milkmaids who wanted a recreational use for their three-legged milking stools. There is an amenity association which looks after conservation, plus drama and horticultural societies.

'There are magnificent views of the Jack and Jill windmills on the crest of the Downs'

Ditchling, just to the east, is one of the most rarefied spots in this part of Sussex, luxuriating in a dramatic valley beneath the spine of the South downs, though it is hammered by traffic heading for Brighton. During the last 100 years it has attracted a succession of artists and calligraphers, originally drawn by a Roman Catholic artistic community that included Eric Gill, which settled on the Downs. A small house in its own plot in need of refurbishing might cost £300,000 and more; a Victorian semi with three bedrooms would sell at £230,000. Houses at the cheaper end of the market can stick because people moving to Ditchling want something rather more special. Over the years it has attracted many famous inhabitants, including the actress Dame Ellen Terry and singer Dame Vera Lynn. It has a few basic shops, tea shops, an art gallery, a good primary school and a Museum of Local Life. It is particularly proud of its choral society. Nearby is Ditchling Common, offering nearly 200 acres of walks; and Ditchling Beacon, over 800ft high, where a fire was lit to warn of the approach of the Spanish Armada.

The illustrator Raymond Briggs lives in the nearby hamlet of **Westmeston**, which is another beautiful quiet retreat at the foot of the

Downs. Residents recently raised money to have the unsightly overhead wires buried underground; the village pulse can be taken in the new Parish Room where events are held. There is no shop or post office, but there is a public telephone box. The nearest primary school is in Ditchling and there are secondary schools in Lewes, Chailey and Hassocks.

To London Bridge
Journey: 65 min
Season: £2880
(also valid Victoria)
Peak: 2 per hr
(plus 2 per hr to Victoria)
Off-peak: 2 per hr

PRESTON PARK is a part of Brighton that particularly attracts commuters because of its railway station. Teeth have to be gritted when Brighton and Hove Albion are playing at home. A four-bedroom three-storey Victorian house might cost £525,000. It is much leafier than the Victorian streets of North Laines and Westhill, which are both close to the station in Brighton proper.

To Victoria
Journey: 51 min
Season: £2880
Peak: 2 per hr
Off-peak: 2 per hr

To London Bridge
Journey: 56 min
Season: £2880
Peak: 2 per hr
Off-peak: 4 per hr

BRIGHTON is metamorphosing into London-on-Sea, developing an increasingly sophisticated and cosmopolitan air, playing up its strengths as a conference centre and weekend retreat. It is short on domestic gardens and garages, but the frivolity of the Royal Pavilion, the beautifully landscaped parks and the backdrop of the Sussex Downs make it an enviable place to live. The Brighton Festival in May is England's biggest arts festival. There is a plethora of restaurants and the Theatre Royal attracts many plays on their pre-London tours. There has always been a theatrical crowd in Brighton – Lord Olivier once lived here – attracted by the Regency terrace houses of Montpelier with their canopied bow fronts and panelled drawing rooms. Brighton has always been the place to have a flat, and the various building booms of the last few decades have provided plenty of opportunities, both in purpose-built blocks and in large houses that have been converted. There is also now a boating crowd, drawn by the marina.

Commuters tend to live within walking distance of the railway station, which is central, within half a mile of the seafront, though parking is tortuous. The shops, seafront and residential areas are so closely knit that many people don't have cars at all. There are various interlocking conservation areas which househunters might aim for. **North Laines**, **Westhill** and **Clifton** are close to the station, all now rather gentrified with little boutiques and antiques shops. In the Clifton Conservation Area, a three- to four-bedroom Regency house with distant sea views and a sun room sells for around £800,000. The young like the new two-bedroom American style apartments appearing on the market which can be bought for around £250,000. Millionaires' Row is at **Roedean**, just beside the girl's private school and opposite the marina. Large mansions line up to catch the sea breezes and sell for over £1m. A six-bedroom Victorian semi could be bought for £470,000. If you think about buying anything facing the sea, however, consider the havoc wrought by salt-laden winds on your exterior paintwork.

> Fork from Plumpton to Eastbourne

To Victoria
Journey: 58 min
Season: £2800
(£2880 Gatwick
Express included)
Peak: 2 per hr
(plus 1 per hr to
London Bridge)
Off-peak: 1 every 2
or 3 hrs

PLUMPTON The railway line divides Plumpton into two parts, Plumpton proper and **Plumpton Green**. The latter consists of modern estates close to the railway station, with the National Hunt racecourse to the south. A roomy three-bedroom Victorian semi in need of refurbishment, with a large garden, could cost £290,000. The old village is anchored to Plumpton Place, a 16th-century moated manor. It has a general store-cum-post office, a couple of garages and a primary school, and is the home of the East Sussex Agricultural College. There is wonderful riding over the Downs if you have your own horse. The wildflowers on the Downs are prized by honey farmers. **East Chiltington**, with The Jolly Sportsman pub, is deliciously unspoilt. Here you could pay £190,000 for a two-bedroom terraced house or £1.7m for a seven-bedroom country house with outbuildings and nine acres.

To Victoria
Journey: 61 min
Season: £2800
(£2880 Gatwick
Express included)
Peak: 2 per hr
(plus 1 per hr to
London Bridge)
Off-peak: Nil

COOKSBRIDGE The desirability of Cooksbridge is reduced because it sits on the main road to Lewes and on the railway line, both of which can be noisy. Prices lag behind a little. A three-bedroom end-of-terrace house could be bought for £180,000, but potential is king and a four-bedroom chalet bungalow on a good plot recently sold for £500,000.

To Victoria
Journey: 68 min
Season: £2880
Peak: 2 per hr
(plus 1 per hr to
London Bridge)
Off-peak: 2 per hr

LEWES Large parts of Lewes, the county town of East Sussex, are still medieval in style, particularly along the main street, which follows the route of an ancient causeway. The passages winding away from the street are an irresistible invitation for shoppers to explore. Bookshops, antiques shops and 15th-century timbered cottages lean against colour-washed houses. The Bloomsbury connection (Vanessa Bell and Duncan Grant used to live here, and Virginia Woolf lived at Rodmell, two miles away) has left an arty-crafty atmosphere and the town is always alive with exhibitions and craft shows. It has its own coterie of resident artists, several of whom work in studios at the Star Brewery.
Property is more expensive than in the surrounding areas. A two-

Schools in in East and West Sussex

The ample arms of the North and South Downs give Sussex's schools the most beautiful settings, with huge acreages and lofty views down to the sea. At Crawley in West Sussex, occupying a 19th-century mansion with a monastery and abbey attached, is Worth School, the independent boarding school for boys. Not far away is Burgess Hill independent day and boarding school for girls.

Haywards Heath offers a choice of popular private and state schools. These include Ardingly, the co-educational boarding and day school, and Warden Park, the co-educational comprehensive.

At Horsham, choices include the comprehensives Millais for girls and Tanbridge House co-educational, as well as nearby Christ's Hospital independent boarding school for both sexes (where the fees are means-related) and Farlington independent girls' boarding and day school. East Grinstead has the Sackville and Imberhorne co-educational comprehensive schools.

Brighton has attracted a rash of independent schools. These include the girls' day school Brighton & Hove High, and the independent, co-educational, day and boarding school Brighton College. Roedean boarding school for girls is nearby, as is Lancing College boarding and day school for boys and girls, which has a commanding position set in 550 acres on the top of the Downs.

Eastbourne has the Moira House independent boarding and day school for girls and Eastbourne College independent boarding and day school for boys (with girls in the sixth), set in wonderful cloisters around a cricket square. Another school spoken highly of in East Sussex is St Leonards-Mayfield, near Crowborough, an independent Roman Catholic school for girls.

bedroom terraced house costs over £190,000. It would probably have a mean garden or a small courtyard since the town is tight for space. Parking is like playing sardines. The tiny cobbled streets just off the High Street have a particular cachet, and houses here don't often come on the market. A four-bedroom period house in Bull Lane, however, recently sold for £600,000. The local council has hung onto its large stock of council housing rather than sell it off or pass it on to housing associations. There are some bland modern private estates which generate little interest among incomers.

Shopping is adequate. Lewes has Boots, Safeway and Tesco, and Eastbourne and Brighton are not far away. The local private school is The Old Grammar School. The great social occasion of the year is the huge Bonfire Night party which commemorates the burning not of Guy Fawkes, but of a batch of Protestant martyrs.

There are some extraordinarily lovely Downland villages around Lewes. **Kingston**, in the south, has a street of distinguished old houses and a modern estate where four-bedroom homes sell for around £325,000. The village is something of an enclave for Sussex University professors. Then there is **Rodmell**, which seduced the Bloomsbury Group with its mix of flint-and-thatch and tile-hung cottages, folded into the Ouse valley. A three-bedroom cottage will cost £315,000. Neither of these villages has shops. Any house with views of the Downs sells for 15-20 per cent more.

To the north is **Barcombe**, which has prices to match its beauty. A three- to four-bedroom barn conversion near the river at Barcombe Mills recently sold for £385,000. It is really a village of three parts.

There is Barcombe Cross, which has tile-hung houses and shops, a pub and a 16th-century Forge House. Then there is Barcombe Mills, on the River Ouse, where people go for picnics. And then Old Barcombe, by St Mary's Church, abandoned by the population during the plague. **Ringmer** is more of a dormitory to Lewes, where houses sell briskly on the prettiness factor. Three-bedroom semis fetch about £190,000 to £200,000; a large four-bedroom detached farmhouse around £500,000. The centrepiece is the village green, fringed with old cottages overlooked by the parish church, where cricket is played in the summer.

To Victoria
Journey: 77 min
Season: £2880
Peak: 1 per hr to London Bridge only
Off-peak: 1 per hr changing at Lewes or Brighton for Victoria or London Bridge

GLYNDE consists of little more than the big house, Glynde Place, The Trevor Arms pub, a post office and village store, an 18th-century church and a grassy bank that becomes a cloud of daffodils in spring. Mount Caburn, one of the highest points along the South Downs, looms above. The Glyndbourne Opera House, which draws the dinner jackets with their picnic hampers between May and August, is on the parish boundary with Ringmer. Much of the local property is in private ownership and leased to villagers.

To Victoria
Journey: 93 min
(75 min peak)
Season: £2880
Peak: 2 per hr
(plus 2 to London Bridge plus 1 per hr changing at Lewes or Brighton)
Off-peak: 1 per hr changing at Lewes or Brighton

BERWICK is best known for having a church decorated with murals by Duncan Grant and Vanessa Bell; they are so vivid that they caused an outcry when they were painted in the Forties. Unfortunately it draws coach parties in the summer, as does Drusilla's Zoo theme park. Houses close to the station were built during the Thirties, many of them offering good views of the Downs and Arlington reservoir. A three-bedroom semi sells at around £220,000; a four-bedroom detached house for £260,000 to £300,000.

To Victoria
Journey: 83 min
Season: £2880
Peak: 2 per hr
(plus 1 per hr to London Bridge)
Off-peak: 2 per hr

POLEGATE is really the outer rim of Eastbourne. It is a village that billowed during the Thirties and again during the Eighties. The single High Street has everything from a greengrocer to a hairdresser. Thirties' and Fifties' semis sell at £150,000 to £160,000. It is a very popular because of the station. A one-bedroom flat can cost £92,500, a two-bedroom flat £125,000. Polegate sprawls in its egalitarian way towards Hampden Park, and there is no distinct division between the two.

To Victoria
Journey: 100 min
Season: £2880
Peak: 2 per hr
(plus 1 per hr to
London Bridge)
Off-peak: 1 per hr

HAMPDEN PARK There are expensive and cheap sides to Hampden Park, which glories in all the variations on the theme of suburban mock-Tudor that you could imagine. In a good area three-bedroom terraced houses sell for £125,000; detached houses for around £300,000 to £400,000. There is nothing in the Victorian department. This is where Eastbourne has its industrial estate, and all the hangar-sized stores such as B&Q, and a 24-hour Tesco have been put here, too.

To Victoria
Journey: 89 min
Season: £2880
Peak: 2 per hr
(plus 1 per hr to
London Bridge)
Off-peak: 2 per hr

EASTBOURNE is still very much a holiday resort and retirement town. Attractions such as Fort Fun and the Treasure Island theme parks resound in summer to the shrieks of holidaying children, who then make for the beautiful Victorian pier to gorge themselves on ice-cream. Adults can indulge with a trip to the Winter Gardens, Devonshire Park or the Royal Hippodrome theatres. There are also nightclubs and cinemas. Healthier pursuits include stupendous cliff walks over Beachy Head and those vast switchbacks of chalk, the Seven Sisters.

To live within walking distance of the station you have a choice of Edwardian and Victorian houses, or some Thirties' detached. Prices vary enormously depending on size. You could pay £235,000 for three bedrooms; up to £380,000 for a mock-Tudor with five bedrooms. The cheaper flats start at over £90,000. One of the most prestigious addresses is The Meads, a conservation area that attracts professionals and couples who have retired early. A five-bedroom semi here might cost £550,000. You can expect to pay a premium price if you want to live near any of the three golf courses: The Royal, The Downs or The Willingdon. The hip new area is Sovereign Harbour marina development.

Thirties' Tudor-style house, Eastbourne

271

> Spur from **Preston Park** to **Worthing**

There are some other stations along this route, but the London trains don't stop at them.
For Preston Park, see page 267.

To Victoria
Journey: 67 min
Season: £2880
Peak: 2 per hr
(plus 1 per hr to
London Bridge)
Off-peak: 2 per hr

HOVE is much more sedate and "respectable" than its neighbour Brighton, though the two are now officially joined at the hip by the Brighton and Hove City Council established in 1997. Its image has been that of a haven for the elderly, and indeed it does have plenty of sheltered housing and low-level flats. However, as part of its campaign to attract a younger set, Hove has built up a sporting image with a big complex offering everything from martial arts to synchronised swimming. The King Alfred Leisure Centre is being redeveloped to create shops, restaurants and 400 new homes.

Hove suffered in the Thirties when some of its most important houses were demolished and replaced with 10-storey blocks of flats. Nevertheless, there are still some classic, sweeping Regency curves to be found in the Brunswick area; some good Sussex cottages near the King Alfred Centre; and some fine Victorian and Victorian

Georgian terraced house, Hove/Brighton area

Gothic houses in The Avenues, Willett Estate and Cliftonville. Property tends to be cheaper on the outskirts, where the modern estates are located. A two-bedroom Victorian garden flat just off the seafront could cost £215,000; a Regency balcony flat with sea views £335,000; three-bedroom family houses start at £250,000 and good family houses away from the sea can hit £800,000. The up-market sedate addresses are Tongdean Avenue, Tongdean Road and Dykeroad Avenue, with the new millionaires'

'Just as Hove has had a complex about Brighton so Portslade has one about Hove'

272

row at the west end of town where Fat Boy Slim and the McCartneys have houses backing onto the beach. A whole house on the sea will start at £1m.

While Sussex County Cricket Club still calls Hove home, Brighton and Hove Albion FC has been moved into temporary quarters at the Withdean Stadium in Brighton while the powers that be contemplate its future. There are two golf clubs – the West Hove and the Brighton and Hove. And there is also, of course, the beach. In the last few years this sedate old lady of a town has developed a certain sparkle by acquiring a galaxy of restaurants along Church Road which are good enough to lure foodies from Brighton and the surrounding area.

To Victoria
Journey: 72 min
Season: £2880
Peak: 2 per hr
(plus 1 per hr to
London Bridge)
Off-peak: 1 per hr

PORTSLADE Just as Hove has had something of a complex about Brighton, so Portslade has one about Hove. It might not look particularly impressive as you drive through, but if you turn off the main road you will find some 16th-century flint cottages and a church dating back to 1100. Portslade's recent history is not very distinguished. Two decades ago it was known locally as "Nappy Valley" because it offered a mass of housing cheap enough for young couples to buy and breed in. Housing is still relatively inexpensive. Two-bedroom terraced houses sell for over £155,000, three-bedroom terraced for £175,000 and three-bedroom Thirties' semis for £195,000 to £225,000.

Villagers have succeeded in protecting from development a field in the centre, so there is a green of sorts for people to walk on. More recently, money has been spent on restoring Portslade's main streets. They have been re-paved, Victorian-style street lamps have been installed and the Victorian red-brick water tower which used to supply an isolation hospital has been renovated. American Express has sponsored the installation of a camera obscura, which gives a wonderful panoramic view of the South Downs.

To Victoria
Journey: 74 min
Season: £2880
Peak: 2 per hr
(plus 1 per hr to
London Bridge)
Off-peak: 2 per hr

SHOREHAM-BY-SEA Shoreham is a Victorian seaport which still imports two million tonnes of cargo each year. The High Street, with the River Adur at one end, has basic shops for day-to-day needs, and the Holmbush Centre has brought Marks & Spencer and Tesco. The town is free from hotels and bed-and-breakfasts and does not feel like a seaside resort. There is a sandy beach at low tide, and a popular pit-stop for wildfowl in the Widewater, a lagoon behind a man-made shingle bank. Shoreham Airport (whence the first commercial flight was made in this country) operates charter flights and is the base for several flying schools. Across the river on the shingle spit is the site of what was once Bungalow Town – a colony of wooden huts, made largely from disused railway carriages, which was

Bay-fronted
bungalow,
Shoreham-by-Sea

occupied by the London Music Hall fraternity. Some early films were made there, but most of it was destroyed in World War II to prevent its use as a beachhead.

Commuters gravitate towards North Shoreham and the town centre where a two-bedroom ground floor flat sells at around £139,000. A two-bedroom bungalow with a sun room would fetch around £165,000. For a three-bedroom semi in Shoreham Town or Beach, you would have to pay £200,000 to £250,000 . There are two secondary schools, the most popular being Kings Manor Comprehensive on the border of Shoreham and Southwick; the boys' public school at Lancing is nearby.

A colony of wooden huts, made largely from disused railway carriages, was occupied by the London Music Hall fraternity

To Victoria
Journey: 81 min
Season: £2880
Peak: 2 per hr
(plus 1 per hr to
London Bridge)
Off-peak: 1 per hr

LANCING Old north and south Lancing have blended into one, and the once pretty High Street has been spoilt by tasteless development. Many people commute to Gatwick and Brighton from here, but few to London. There is still a smattering of thatch-and-flint among the Thirties' terraces. A two-bedroom flat will cost £115,000 to £140,000, but a period cottage with three bedrooms is likely to be nearer £270,000. The boys' public school Lancing College, which takes girls in the sixth form, stands in 550 acres on a spur of the Downs overlooking the sea. There are several primary schools which feed the state secondary school, Boundstone Community College.

To Victoria

Journey: 80 min

Season: £2880

Peak: 2 per hr

(plus 1 per hr to

London Bridge)

Off-peak: 2 per hr

WORTHING has been increasingly popular with commuters over the last decade, absorbing house-hunters displaced by high prices from the Surrey commuter belt, and Brighton and Hove. To be within walking distance of the station and shops you would need to live in one of the Edwardian terraces north of the town centre and obtain a resident's parking permit. Spacious three-bedroom houses sell for £215,000. Bed-and-breakfasts are concentrated in the centre, near the four large hotels, nightclubs, theatres and cinema. The shopping centre is surprisingly varied, with specialist stores. Don't imagine a town full of little old ladies in fluffy hats: the largest segment of the population is the 16 44 age group, and the adult education centre is very well subscribed. Big businesses, including Beechams Pharmaceutical, have settled here, too. Worthing is proud of the fact that it is the home of bowls. One small warning: the seafront can get rather smelly when the seaweed is churned up from the Bognor Regis beds.

Horsham

Warnham

Ockley

Holmwood

Dorking Deepene

Dorking West

Gomshall

Betchwoth

Dorking

Boxhill &
West Humble

Waterloo   **Victoria**

Victoria/Waterloo
> Horsham

To Victoria
Journey: 45 min
Season: £1680
Peak: 2 per hr
(plus 3 per hr to Waterloo)
Off-peak: 1 per hr

BOXHILL & WEST HUMBLE Just beyond the M25, London suddenly lets go and gives way to one of the best-known beauty spots in the south-east. Box Hill itself rises to nearly 400ft above the River Mole and affords panoramic views of the surrounding chalk downland and glimpses of the South Downs. It has become very popular in spite of the fact that the approaches to it are given over to caravan sites. Big houses with big gardens attract the interest in Box Hill, though for many it is more a place to visit, than to live in.

West Humble is no more than a handful of houses at the foot of Box Hill. Norbury Park is close by. There are three working farms and Bocketts Farm, a rare breeds farm open to visitors.

To Victoria
Journey: 48 min
Season: £1740
Peak: 2 per hr
Off-peak: 2 per hr

To Waterloo
Journey: 40 min
Season: £1740
(also valid to Victoria)
Peak: 3 per hr
Off-peak: 2 per hr

DORKING is an ancient market town shot through with antiques shops, some new buildings and a couple of delicatessens. It prides itself on its variety of restaurants, from Thai to French. Reigate Grammar and St John's at Leatherhead are the two popular local public schools. Guildford is close enough for smart shops and the theatre. The web of villages that surround it have much to offer. Property prices in and around Dorking are fairly constant. A three-bedroom semi with work to be done sells for around £280,000. One in better condition will fetch around £320,000. One-bedroom flats sell for about £120,000.

Five miles west is **Shere**, a village with a stream bubbling through it that is so pretty that British Gas used it to illustrate the rural idyll in an advertising campaign. The square is picturesquely framed with old houses; it has a 12th-century church, several shops, a post office, tea-rooms and a couple of antiques shops. Social activities abound, including a gardening club, youth and old folks' organisations. For the time being it retains its village school. The dramatic society is shared with **Peaselake**, which backs on to Hurtwood Common, one of the many Surrey commons that are covered in golden broom and gorse, with shelter-belts of pine. The village has a green with a war memorial, and is very leafy. Another popular village is **Abinger Hammer**, which has a green, a working blacksmith and an insatiable

277

passion for cricket. The full Australian team was invited to play here, and the villagers managed to make the return match, too. There is also an annual celebrity match. Men swap their white flannels for green tights when the annual medieval fair comes round to Abinger Common. Opposite the pub is a clock tower from which a little man emerges every hour to strike the bell with a hammer, hence the name of the village.

'The poor soil made it unsuitable for farming, so it became a refuge for smugglers and squatters'

Nearby is **Holmbury St Mary**, which has a green and a post office that opens only in the mornings, but it has lost its school. This was once considered to be one of the most remote places in Surrey. The poor soil made it unsuitable for farming, so it became a refuge for smugglers and squatters and only began to be recognised as a village in the 1850s. Then it became popular with weekenders who built the first large Victorian houses on Holmbury Hill, from where there are magnificent views over the Weald. By far the most remote spot here now is Coldharbour. Designated an Area of Outstanding Natural Beauty, it clings to the side of the 960-ft high Leith Hill, from where, on a clear day, you can see the Channel. It is a mountain in the middle of Surrey. The narrow winding roads that lead up to Coldharbour are often cut off in winter. There is no school, though it has a pub, a church and good-neighbourly residents who take elderly villagers into Dorking.

To the east is **Brockham**, with 18th-century houses overlooking the green, pubs, a primary school and 16th-century church. You can easily spend £350,000 to £1m on a large house here, but there are some superb smaller ones which start at around £200,000. The main event of the year is the bonfire on Guy Fawkes night, which draws thousands of people from miles around. **Leigh** (pronounced Lye) is also an extremely popular small village with a 16th-century priest's house on the green, and a weatherboarded pub. **Newdigate** is tucked right away from the main roads and has an excellent farm shop, a blacksmith and a new estate of executive homes.

'Holmbury St Mary was recognised as a village in the 1850s. Then it became popular with weekenders who built the Victorian houses on Holmbury Hill, from where there are magnificent views over the Weald'

> North Downs line west to Gomshall via Dorking West

**Journey: 54 min
(from Gomshall)
Season: £2264
Peak: 2 per hour*
Off-peak: 1 per
hour*
*Change at Redhill
or Guildford. There
are no through
trains**

DORKING DEEPDENE is a good-quality residential area, close to the station yet set in beautiful woodland. It takes its name from the Deepdene Estate, which was owned by the Howard family. Large detached houses in Deepdene Wood sell for around £750,000 to £1m; three-bedroom semis for £225,000 to £250,000. **Dorking West** is partly residential, partly commercial, with new business parks springing up. A small terraced house costs around £220,000; a semi £250,000 to £300,000. **Gomshall** is an expensive village marred by traffic. A Victorian two-bedroom semi costs just under £280,000.

> North Downs line east to Betchworth

**Journey: 48 min
(from Betchworth)
Season: £1740
Peak : 1 per hour*
Off-peak: 2 per
hour*
*Change between
Dorking and
Dorking Deepdene
using footpath link
or at Redhill. There
are no through
trains**

Sitting on the banks of the River Mole, surrounded by the North Downs, **Betchworth** is something of a local beauty spot. It has some 17th-century houses inhabited by retired High Court judges and diplomats who can play golf at nearby Betchworth Park. A four-bedroom detached house is likely to cost £500,000; a two-up-two-down further out at Peeble Hill starts at £250,000.

> Continuation of main line

**To Victoria
Journey: 55 min
Season: £1840
Peak: 2 per hr
Off-peak: 1 per hr**

HOLMWOOD Note that after Dorking the rail service is not as good; the last train leaves Waterloo at 7.20pm. Some villages have been badly affected by the A24 cutting south. **Beare Green** straddles it, and now consists mainly of houses built during the Seventies and Eighties. These sell for less than those in Dorking, of which it is effectively a dormitory. The **Holmwoods** (**North** and **South**) are also staked out along the A24. North Holmwood retains its green and pond, but has been submerged by new housing. The surrounding countryside is lovely, with 600 acres of common for pony treks and long walks. Just to the north is a memorial to Alfred Gwynne Vanderbilt, a member of the American millionaire family, who sacrificed himself by handing his lifejacket to a woman passenger when the *Lusitania* sank in 1915.

<table>
<tr><td>To Victoria</td></tr>
<tr><td>Journey: 59 min</td></tr>
<tr><td>Season: £1840</td></tr>
<tr><td>Peak: 2 per hr</td></tr>
<tr><td>Off-peak: 1 per hr</td></tr>
</table>

OCKLEY Ockley's prettiness is being spoilt by traffic on the A29, but it has some strong points, including a cricket pitch (visible from the main road), a conventional green with old houses around it, and its own school. This whole area lies close enough to Guildford for commuters to take advantage of the fast trains into Waterloo (see page 235) as well as the local theatre and shops. Others commuters choose to jump a station by driving to **Clandon** (page 237), where it is easier to park.

Cranleigh, strung between Ockley and Guildford, would meet many people's idea of the perfect small town. This is where the first cottage hospital was established. The main street has a story-book intimacy and, despite a population of 12,000, the town still thinks of itself as a village. It has a cricket green, food shops, gift shops, shoe shops, delicatessens and a gun shop (the green wellington fraternity has a strong presence here). A three-bedroom period cottage might cost between £300,000 and £500,000; a larger old house with three

Modern family house, Horsham area

acres and a tennis court could fetch over £700,000. Modern houses sell for less: four bedrooms for around £450,000. The area is wealthy and popular with executives in insurance, banking and oil, owners of successful local companies, TV personalities and ageing rock stars. Cranleigh School is the local boys' public school; the sister school, St Catherine's, is at Bramley near Guildford (see page 237).

To Victoria
Journey: 65 min
Season: £2280
Peak: 2 per hr
Off-peak: 1 per hr

WARNHAM
A sign warning that deer may cross the road is the first thing you see as you approach Warnham and its deer park. The old farming community has now been largely replaced by commuters to Guildford, London and Horsham, who are attracted by the green, pubs and old houses. A small semi in need of modernisation might sell for £250,000. Larger detached houses start at around £330,000 and rise to over £1m.

To Victoria
Journey: 56 min
Season: £2612*
Peak: 3 per hr
Off-peak: 3 per hr
*£2880 Gatwick
Express included

HORSHAM
For Horsham main entry, see **Victoria/London Bridge to Arundel** line, page 258.

To London Bridge
Journey: 69 min
Season: £2812
(also valid to
Victoria)
Peak: 2 per hr
Off-peak: 1 per hr

Victoria/London Bridge
> East Grinstead and Uckfield

To Victoria
Journey: 38 min
Season: £1376
Peak: 2 per hr
(plus 3 per hr to
London Bridge)
Off-peak: 2 per hr

OXTED is everything that most people would want a small town to be. It is safe for children and pleasant to live in, but not so pretty that it suffers invasion by tourists. It has a population of around 14,000, and all its vital organs are centralised within walking distance of each another, including the station, cinema, shops and Tandridge Leisure Pool (which has a gym). The cinema has a wine bar and shows all the new releases, and the atmosphere is cosy enough for parents to allow their children to go unaccompanied. The town is also reasonably safe to walk around in after dark.

There are two main shopping streets, Station Road West, which is lined with mock-Tudor shops, and Station Road East. There is a Cost Cutter and a Safeway, by they don't seem to have knocked the established shops for six yet. Old Oxted is the prettiest part of the town, where the 14th- to 16th-century cottages have pleasantly weathered pantiled roofs. Much of the rest is classic Thirties' development.

A huge number of residents commute to London or Croydon; otherwise people work in local shops or in the factories at Hurst Green. The wealthier residents live in the private

16th-century cottage, Oxted

wooded roads of Rockfield Road and Icehouse Wood, where large detached houses cost at least £750,000. Nearly all the gardens in the town are large by London standards, most extending to half an acre or more. Even the few modest two-bed Victorian terraced houses, selling at £200,000 to £250,000, have 100ft gardens.

Teenagers looking for a good night out head for East Grinstead or Croydon, where there are nightclubs. Older funsters go into London for theatres, or to country restaurants

Teenagers looking for a good night out head for East Grinstead or Croydon, where there are nightclubs. Older funsters go into London for theatres, or to country restaurants. There are golf courses nearby at Tandridge and Limpsfield.

Limpsfield and **Limpsfield Chart** are five minutes away by road. Both villages are occupied almost exclusively by newcomers, and both are split by the A25. A car is essential for living here. Limpsfield is olde worlde and expensive, its main street eye-catchingly lined with stone cottages. There are a few shops, a pub, a very good bookshop and a highly-rated restaurant, The Old Lodge. Limpsfield Chart is also attractively set in National Trust landscape. The Chart is a stretch of common land which tumbles over the edge of the Weald, offering superb views as you head south and containing remnants of a Roman road. In spring the woods are carpeted with bluebells. A grand four-bedroom house on the common overlooking the North Downs, with tennis court and two acres of garden, could sell for over £1m.

A stretch of common land tumbles over the edge of the Weald. In spring the woods are carpeted with bluebells

The village of **Tandridge** is less expensive, with Sixties' and modern housing added to the mix. Three-bedroom Victorian houses and artisans' cottages cost over £300,000. Tandridge has a pub and a primary school, and the feel of a proper village even though it is only two miles from the M25. The north is the nicest part, with a lovely church and steeple standing on a little hill.

To Victoria
Journey: 42 min
Season: £1376
Peak: 2 per hr
(plus 3 per hr to
London Bridge)
Off-peak: 2 per hr

HURST GREEN is more mundane and sprawly than Oxted and it is cheaper. It is a popular choice for people moving out of London looking for varied house types at low prices. On the 1960s Home Park estate, for instance, you could buy a two-bedroom house from £175,000, or three bedrooms for £200,000. There is a Wates estate, where one-bedroom starter homes on Barnfield Way cost around £135,000, and a couple of council estates with some ex-council houses for sale. The town is segmented, and some of the segments are nicer than others. The Green itself is picturesque and is framed by older houses. The advantage residents have here over those in Oxted is that they are more likely to get a seat on the train. A detached three-bedroom house nearby could fetch around £300,000. Other parts of Hurst Green harbour the odd factory or two. All the segments have infant and junior schools, churches, post office and shops. Between Hurst Green and Edenbridge lies Staffhurst Wood, famous for its bluebells.

> Fork from Hurst Green to East Grinstead

To Victoria
Journey: 49 min
Season: £1560
Peak: 2 per hr
(plus 2 per hr to
London Bridge)
Off-peak: 2 per hr

LINGFIELD and Dormansland (see page 286) are glued together by Lingfield racecourse. Lingfield is the larger and older of the two villages, with a population approaching 5000. There has been very little new development, so the marvellous collection of 15th-century, Tudor, Jacobean and Georgian properties remains intact, and many of the buildings are scheduled as ancient monuments. Modern interlopers include the occasional Thirties' house and a small Eighties' estate.

The area is very popular with people who need to be close to Gatwick Airport. Pilots, air hostesses and ground staff live here; so do many business travellers. There are excellent communications. The M25 is only eight minutes' drive away and the M23 is also close by. Lingfield has a typical range of village shops, including two small supermarkets, a post office, butcher and baker. Next to the pond, at the heart of the village, is a strange stone structure roofed with iron bars. This is the so-called "cage", built in 1473 and thought to have been used as a lock-up for poachers and drunkards.

House prices cover an enormous range, from a two-bedroom flat at £130,000 to a five- or six-bedroom detached family house in a

'Lingfield's marvellous collection of 15th-century Tudor, Jacobean and Georgian properties remains intact'

couple of acres for £750,000 to £1m. There is no such thing as a typical Lingfield house to extrapolate average prices from, but a three-bedroom terraced house might go for £180,000; a three-bedroom detached for £275,000. Houses at the top end of the market might come with their own equestrian facilities, though the racecourse, one of the first in Britain to have an all-weather surface, has not attracted many trainers or jockeys to live in the area. The style is more Pony Club and conspicuous wealth. The village has a primary school. Older children are bussed to Oxted.

To Victoria
Journey: 52 min
Season: £1560
Peak: 2 per hr
(plus 2 per hr to
London Bridge)
Off-peak: 2 per hr

DORMANS
Dormansland is slightly smaller than Lingfield, with a population of around 4000 if you include Dormans Park. It has a post office, hairdresser, couple of pubs, church and primary school. Houses are largely Victorian with a smattering of modern and small council estates. **Dormans Park**, which is actually closer to the station than Dormansland itself, has a curious history. It grew up when wealthy Victorians used to come down from London for the Lingfield races. A number of little summer houses were built around the Dormans Hotel (now disappeared), where many of them liked to stay. The summer houses grew grander, and Dormans Park became the sort of place where the playboys of the time liked to entertain their mistresses. Nearly all the houses are large, detached villas in sizeable plots surrounded by countryside. A six-bedroom affair with a paddock and outbuildings might sell for £1m. The area is rather secluded and has no local facilities of its own.

To Victoria
Journey: 55 min
Season: £1600
Peak: 2 per hr
(plus 2 per hr to
London Bridge)
Off-peak: 2 per hr

EAST GRINSTEAD
The town of East Grinstead itself retains the characteristics of the market town it once was, though it now has a relief road and other modern appendages. It is in two parts: the old town, which includes much of the High Street, and London Road, which contains the new major shops. It is becoming more of an industrial and commercial centre, with offices springing up. East Grinstead draws in people from the surrounding villages for their regular shop, though large or specialist items have to be sought in Croydon or Crawley. The Kings Centre provides a swimming pool and sports complex for hearties, while The Atrium has a nightclub, pub and two cinemas for night owls. The Chequer Mead Art Centre has a 320-seat theatre. One of East Grinstead's attractions to commuters is that its station is at the end of the line, so there is no danger of going to sleep and missing your stop.

There are some pretty old buildings in the centre of the town, including 14 hall houses in the High Street. Particularly handsome is Sackville College, a Sussex sandstone almshouse with high chimneys, quadrangle and gardens, which is now converted for sheltered housing. Otherwise there is a wide range of housing, mainly on new estates which have sprung up in the last 20 years. Cheap starter homes and flats cost between £100,000 and £120,000. A larger modern mock-Georgian four-bedroom house will fetch over £300,000.

Two manor houses outside the town are put to strangely contrasting uses. Saint Hill Manor, to the south, is the headquarters of the Church of Scientology. Gravetye Manor is one of the best small country-house hotels and restaurants in Britain. For fishing, sailing and walking there is Weir Wood Reservoir. To the south is Ashdown Forest, where the countryside becomes very beautiful. Here you come up on to the High Weald, where you find some of the last remaining heathland in the south-east.

> Fork from Hurst Green to Uckfield

New services now go to London Bridge, not Victoria

To London Bridge
Journey: 45 min
Season: £1740
(also valid at
Edenbridge)
Peak: 2 per hr
Off-peak: 1 per hr

EDENBRIDGE TOWN For main entry see Edenbridge on the **North Downs** line east from Redhill, page 252.

To London Bridge
Journey: 50 min
Season: £1740
Peak: 1 per hr
Off-peak: 1 per hr

HEVER is one of the area's tourist attractions, popular with visitors en route to Hever Castle, where Henry VIII courted Anne Boleyn. The village is unspoilt and is an extraordinarily small place to command its own railway station. Consequently, a house here will cost around £150,000 more than a similar property in Edenbridge. For a detached four-bedroom house you will have to pay in the region of £600,000. There is no cheap property in Hever, but the least expensive are the former labourers' cottages from the Astor estate. These have been sold and, as the locals put it, "tweed up" by their new owners. The village has a church, a few houses, a golf course and the Henry VIII pub. Beyond a massive stone gateway you enter the drive to Hever Castle and its strange mock-Tudor village, which is hired out for conferences. In high summer, plays and concerts are held in the Italian gardens; in winter a Christmas Fair raises money for the local church and school.

Hever's Church of England primary school has such a good reputation that it reverses the usual demographic trend. Instead of children being bussed from village to town, children from Edenbridge are brought to Hever. Locals, however, have had to fight to keep it from being closed. Village life is lively, though there are no shops and the nearest post office is three miles away in Edenbridge. Horticultural shows and WI markets are held in the village hall. Although Hever proper is small, the parish has 800 on the electoral roll and is quite far flung. As there is absolutely nothing for teenagers to do, it is probably just as well that the population consists of solicitors, commuters, retired people and minor landed gentry.

To London Bridge
Journey: 55 min
Season: £1740
Peak: 1 per hr
Off-peak: 1 per hr

COWDEN is a very pretty village cushioned amid the quiet leafy lanes that wind through the Weald. Its main street has a curious symmetry, with a housing estate at each end and a pub in the middle, and it contains the village's oldest houses, many of which date back 400 years. Buses do exist, but you would be seriously inconvenienced without a car. There are no shops. It pays to get on with the neighbours because the same people are likely to belong to the same societies – the horticultural society, British Legion, WI, among others – and to turn up to the same events. There is no school, and teenagers have little to do except gatepost-hang. A modern four-bedroom house designed in the Kentish farmhouse style, with a small garden and double garage, might cost £500,000.

'Buses do exist, but you would be seriously inconvenienced without a car'

To London Bridge
Journey: 60 min
Season: £1740
Peak: 1 per hr
Off-peak: 1 per hr

ASHURST is very rural and slightly reserved. You may have to spend six months waiting on the platform with the other six passengers at Ashurst station before they get round to acknowledging you. Though the village is small it has a smart new village hall where keep-fit groups, yoga, IT tutorials and the pre-school group strut their stuff. Property in Ashurst is more expensive than nearby Eridge (see opposite), but houses in both villages rarely come up for sale and you'll have to move quickly if you want to buy. There is a bus service of sorts but, as ever in this area, car ownership is practically essential.

'Groombridge Place was used for the film *The Draughtsman's Contract*... the gardens are open to the public in summer'

The larger villages of **Langton Green** (see page 297) and Groombridge are also close to Ashurst. **Groombridge** straddles the county boundary with the new, modern dormitory village forging into Sussex and lovely Old Groombridge lingering in Kent. The old part, including the 16th-century terraced cottages, the Crown Inn which faces the triangular green, the 17th-century moated manor house, Groombridge Place, and its 200-acre estate, was marketed in 1992 with an asking price of £3.25m. The big house (chosen by the director Peter Greenaway for his film of *The Draughtsman's Contract*) is now used mostly at weekends. The gardens are open to the public in the summer.

To London Bridge
Journey: 60 min
Season: £1740
Peak: 2 per hr
Off-peak: 1 per hr

ERIDGE is a very small village best known for its huge park, which is scored with footpaths. It has a church, but has lost its store and post office. Much of Eridge was once part of the Abergavenny estate. Some of the old estate cottages occasionally come on to the market.

To London Bridge
Journey: 65 min
Season: £1740
Peak: 2 per hr
Off-peak: 1 per hr

CROWBOROUGH is one of those strange areas that are sedate and suburban to the core, with a serviceable High Street that has Woolworths, Boots, Safeway and Waitrose. It began as a series of big hilltop hotels built around a golf course. Later it became a popular retirement haven and then, in the early Fifties, there was an explosion of housing estates which turned it into a commuter dormitory with a population of 23,000. The only cinema closed down a few years ago, but there is a leisure centre with swimming pool, badminton and squash.

The Warren is the smartest part of town, built to the north and looking down over Ashdown Forest. Homes in the Warren are mainly detached houses with four or five bedrooms, priced in the £400,000 to £1m bracket. Most of the larger houses once stood in extensive grounds, but have since had smaller houses or flats built around them. This infilling has spoiled the previously rather gracious character of the area.

On the new estates a one-bedroom starter home costs £90,000, a three-bedroom house £190,000. Much of the building in and around the town centre is Victorian, and the least attractive streets are those near the station and the industrial estate. Further out are a number of former 16th- and 17th-century farmhouses. Sir Arthur Conan Doyle lived at Hurtis Hill, and when he died in 1930 he was buried in his back garden overlooking Crowborough Common and the golf course. His body was later exhumed and re-buried in Minstead Churchyard in the New Forest. The house has since been turned into a residential home, Windlesham Manor, but the town still fills up with Sherlock Holmes fans for the annual Conan Doyle festival.

Rotherfield, nearby, has at its core a conservation area studded with listed buildings, antiques shops and Victorian terraces. A small cottage costs around £235,000.

'Crowborough fills up with Sherlock Holmes fans for the annual Conan Doyle festival'

To London Bridge
Journey: 75 min
Season: £1740
Peak: 2 per hr
Off-peak: 1 per hr

BUXTED is mostly modern, but nevertheless quite attractive. It has a population of around 4000, and real shops that sell clothes and food rather than antiques. Property prices are slightly higher than those in Uckfield.

To London Bridge
Journey: 80 min
Season: £1740
Peak: 2 per hr
Off-peak trains: 1
per hr

UCKFIELD is a rapidly expanding "strip" town. The population currently stands at around 13,000, but new houses are going up all the time. Older properties are mainly Victorian – a three-bedroom semi of this period will cost around £225,000. Locals describe the rail service as abominable, and suggest that it would be quicker to travel by pram. For a smallish town there are a lot of facilities, including a leisure centre, cinema, library, bowling green and the nearby Piltdown golf club. It is also surrounded by lovely countryside, ideal for walking or cycling. To the north-west the country lanes wind into Ashdown Forest. Here there are also some rather grand houses – five bedrooms, paddock and enormous garden would cost over £750,000.

Because of the shortcomings of the local rail service, many London commuters prefer to drive the 12 miles to Haywards Heath (page 263) and use the faster service from there. Uckfield used to be a notorious bottleneck on the A22 to Eastbourne, but has been bypassed. Fortunately all public car parks in the town are free – a mercy for people from the surrounding villages who have few shops of their own – but the council is considering introducing charges.

The beautiful villages nearby are **Fletching**, **Nutley** and **Barcombe Cross**. Fletching is the most desirable. It has no new estates and is set in the Ashdown Forest, making it ideal for walks and pony rides. This is like villages used to be, with a close-knit community and a good village centre with beamed pubs. Many of the houses are picture-postcard trim. Three-bedroom houses, some with half an acre of land, sell for around £400,000 to £500,000.

Little Horstead, to the south, is popular with golfers because of its proximity to Horstead Place, a large country estate with hotel and golf complex.

‘Locals describe the rail service as abominable, and suggest that it would be quicker to travel by pram’

Hastings ○—○ St Leonards Warrior Square
          ○ West St Leonards
          ○ Crowhurst
          ○ Battle
          ○ Robertsbridge
          ○ Etchingham
          ○ Stonegate
          ○ Wadhurst
          ○ Frant
          ○ Tunbridge Wells
          ○ High Brooms
Tonbridge ○   ○ Leigh   ○ Penshurst
          ○ Hildenborough
          ○ Sevenoaks

Cannon Street   Charing Cross

Charing Cross/Cannon Sreet
> Hastings

All trains are to Charing Cross except where otherwise specified.

Journey: 31 min
Season: £1808
Peak: 5 per hr
(plus 3 per hr to
Cannon Street)
Off-peak: 4 per hr

SEVENOAKS has been a commuter town ever since the railway arrived in 1862. Recently it has developed a reputation for wealth – a survey showed more cars per head of population than any other town in England. The concentration of private schools is another reliable money indicator. There is Sevenoaks School for boys and girls, Walthamstow Hall for girls, and a clutch of prep schools. The childrens' fathers are surveyors, accountants, solicitors and other successful professionals. The shops are good, and there is a Sainsbury's and a Tesco, though many locals prefer shopping at Blue Water or Tunbridge Wells. Outsiders flock into Sevenoaks for the quaint little shops in Dorset Street, Bank Street and Well Court. Other attractions include the Stag Cinema and Stag Theatre, the swimming and sports centres, an abundance of golf courses, and The Vine, the pitch on which the first-ever nationally reported cricket match was played. Sevenoaks Cricket Week happens every July, and if the sound of ball on bat is not music enough to your ears, then there is the Sevenoaks Summer Festival of music, drama and art. Nearby are the wooded walks of the North Downs Way, the lakes and grassland of the Sevenoaks Wildfowl Reserve, and Knole, one of the largest private houses in Britain, set in a vast deer park, where Vita Sackville-West spent her childhood.

Some of the most expensive addresses are on the Wildernesse Estate, where small mansions were developed on two-acre plots during the Thirties. Many of these now have smaller modern

'A survey showed more cars per head of population in Sevenoaks that in any other town in England'

293

houses squeezed in beside them, often bought by what estate agents refer to as New Money. A five- to eight-bedroom house here will cost £1m to £3m with a swimming pool and all the trimmings. The **Kippington** area is also popular, offering a mix of Victorian, Thirties and post-war housing priced in £800,000 to £1m. Throughout the town you can buy ordinary four-bedroom family houses of varying periods at prices between £450,000 and £650,000. One of the quaintest streets is Six Bells Lane, where tiny one-bedroom 18th- and 19th-century cottages cost around £180,000. There is a snag here, however. If the cottages score points for charm, they lose them on parking difficulty. The large houses around The Vine cricket ground harbour a few flats, the cheapest of which sell at around £250,000. There are more flats in a purpose-built block also overlooking The Vine, where a really spacious apartment with views would cost over £300,000.

Journey: 38 min
Season: £2144
Peak: 3 per hr
(plus 2 per hr to
Cannon Street)
Off-peak: 1 per hr

HILDENBOROUGH is something of a poor relation to its wealthy neighbours. It has the occasional shop and garage, but no real centre, and the B245 makes it a place to drive through rather than to stop in. For affordable housing, however, it's worth a look. A two-bedroom house will cost around £150,000; three-bedroom £200,000 to £250,000.

Journey: 40 min
Season: £2304
Peak: 5 per hr
(plus 3 per hr to
Cannon Street)
Off-peak: 6 per hr

TONBRIDGE has none of the glamour of Tunbridge Wells, to which it gave its name, though it does have the remains of a motte-and-bailey castle on the banks of the River Medway in the town centre. It is a busy one-street town with quite a few businesses and small industries. It also has the private Tonbridge School for boys and two grammar schools for girls. A studio flat in Tonbridge will cost £100,000; a two-bedroom terraced house £125,000 to £150,000; a three-bedroom detached £200,000 to £250,000.

> North Downs line west to Leigh and Penshurst

Journey: 53 min
(from Penshurst)

Season: £2304
from both stations

Peak: 2 per hr*

Off-peak: 2 per hr*

***Change at**
Tonbridge. There
are no through
trains

Leigh (pronounced Lie), is very much a dormitory village. It has a huge green canopied with conker trees, and traditional tile-hung and weatherboarded Kentish houses. There is a post office stores and a hairdresser. The primary school flourishes, and organised activities range from the mothers'-and-toddlers' group to the cricket club. Leigh is popular with London solicitors and bankers, which explains the arrival of a new development of executive houses. A five-bedroom period property with four reception rooms, granny annexe, tennis court and swimming pool costs £1m or more.

Penshurst nearby is an attractive, straggly Kentish village with some nice old tile-hung cottages and its own primary school. The heavy influx of commuters here has resulted in a certain them-and-us feeling. Commuters are often referred to as "invisible parishioners", so slight is their involvement in village activities. At least membership of the village football and cricket teams is growing again. When Penshurst's general store closed, Lord de L'Isle of Penshurst Place opened up a post office and grocery store in the village garage for the convenience of the elderly. Unfortunately Penshurst Place and Hever Castle bring tourists as well as patronage, which can be an irritant in summer. Activities include amateur dramatics, bridge, dancing and stoolball (a cross between rounders and cricket, played with a round wooden bat). Property is now so expensive that it is beyond the means of local young people. A two-bedroom cottage might cost £200,000, a five-bedroom period stone house £1m, a substantial Queen Anne house over £1.5m.

Chiddingstone is also a show-stopping village. The main street, with Chiddingstone Castle at one end, is owned by the National Trust (the castle made an excellent Toad Hall in the film of The Wind in the Willows). Prices are on a par with Penshurst.

> Continuation of main line

Journey: 49 min

Season: £2472

Peak: 3 per hr
(plus 1 per hr to
Cannon Street)

Off-peak: 2 per hr

HIGH BROOMS, dominated by out-of-town retail stores, is the industrial face of Tunbridge Wells. It consists of a steep hill lined with streets of Victorian terraces, most of them built in brick from the old Tunbridge Wells brick company, whose workers lived here. It is within reach of the more elegant part of town, but property prices are low enough to attract young commuters. A two-bedroom terraced house will cost around £140,000; a three-bedroom semi around £170,000. On the eastern side are Sherwood Park and Home Farm, two areas where new housing estates burgeoned during the Eighties. A two-bedroom house here will cost £140,000; four bedrooms £220,000.

Journey: 52 min
Season: £2472
Peak: 3 per hr
(plus 1 per hr to
Cannon Street)
Off-peak: 2 per hr

TUNBRIDGE WELLS is to Kent what Bath is to Somerset. The

gracious crescents and elaborate terraces, designed by Decimus Burton to serve its image as a fashionable 18th-century watering hole, still give it an air of great prosperity. Beau Nash was master of ceremonies at the wells from 1735, and you can still take a foul-tasting sip from the dipper at the Pantiles. For a more complete re-creation of the past there is "A Day At The Wells", one of those sight, sound and smell museums that aims to leave as little as possible to the imagination. Modern Tunbridge Wells caters for recreational tastes of every kind. There are a couple of art galleries, theatres, a cinema, a lively arts centre and two golf courses, plus a rugby club and Kent County Cricket Ground. It is a shopper's paradise, with a huge range of specialist shops, kitchen shops, chocolate shops, tea-rooms, antiques shops and bespoke jewellers. In the Royal Victoria Shopping Mall you find all the chain stores. It is also rich in good primary and secondary schools.

Undoubtedly one of the best addresses in Tunbridge Wells is Nevill Park, a private road with lodge gates at each end, 10 minutes' walk from the station, where large and sumptuous houses dating from the 1800s to the present day overlook the town from a ridge. On one side is the green expanse of Tunbridge Wells Common; on the other is Hungershall Park where a grandly-proportioned house with five bedrooms, three reception rooms and

Stable block conversion, near Tumbridge Wells

perhaps a Victorian conservatory at the back might cost between £700,000 and £1m.

You will need a similarly deep pocket if you want to consider one of the 21 exquisitely-designed houses by Decimus Burton in Calverley Park. A house here might cost around £2m to £3m. In Calverley Park Crescent, where shops were originally designed into the ground floors beneath heavily-gardened balconies, you could find a home for around £350,000 to £600,000. The imposing private houses built along Mount Ephraim are also sought after, though 70 per cent of them have been turned into flats. A three-bedroom flat with grand reception rooms will cost between £275,000 and £325,000. There are some smaller ones costing around £225,000.

Ordinary family houses are to be found in Royal Chase and Culverden Down, behind Mount Ephraim and only a short walk from station and shops. Many of them were built during the various building booms of the 20th century. A four- to five-bedroom, tile-hung Thirties' house in three-quarters of an acre will cost £600,000 to £650,000.

Those of more modest means head east to the tightly-knit area of terraces and semis, where a three-bedroom semi with no garage will cost between £175,000 and £225,000.

The reputation of the local schools is another major factor in the town's popularity. They include the boys' grammar school, Skinners, Tunbridge Wells Boys' Grammar, Tunbridge Wells Girls' Grammar and two comprehensives. All are close to St John's Sports and Indoor Tennis Centre and swimming pool.

Tunbridge Wells is surrounded by rich riding country, well provided with bridleways and livery stables. The Eridge and South Downs Hunt and the Pony Club are both vigorously attended. **Langton Green**, two-and-a-half miles to the west, is a favourite with local businessmen. It has its own village shops, pubs, some old village houses and cottages, plenty of new housing and a popular mixed prep school, Holmwood House. A four-bedroom detached house here costs between £400,000 and £500,000, a two-bedroom cottage £175,000. Immediately to the north of Tunbridge Wells is **Pembury**, which has a bypass and offers a large volume of middle-

'You will need a deep pocket if you want to consider one of the exquisitely-designed houses by Decimus Burton in Calverley Park'

'Tunbridge Wells is surrounded by rich riding country, well provided with bridleways and livery stables'

range modern housing. A three-bedroom detached house here costs around £250,000, but you need to avoid the roads used as peak-time rat runs. See also Penshurst, Leigh and Chiddingstone on the **North Downs** line (page 295).

Journey: 60 min
Season: £2472
Peak: 2 per hr
(plus 1 per hr to Cannon Street)
Off-peak: 1 per hr

FRANT The most striking feature of this hilltop village is its green. Surrounded by superb timber-frame and Georgian houses which now sell for more than £1m a piece, it makes a perfect setting for village cricket. A modern four-bedroom house in Frant would fetch around £400,000 to £500,000. The village has its own shop, a bowling green and a well-attended primary school, though the rural idyll is marred slightly by lorries using the village as a cut-through. The station is actually at Bells Yew Green, where for years the stationmaster ran a wellie-warming service for homebound commuters. Post-journey comfort these days is more likely to be found at the Brecknock Arms, just around the corner.

Lamberhurst is definitely a village worth looking at. A new by-pass is saving it from the hammering of the A21 and the welcome quiet it provides should push property prices up by 10 per cent. Lamberhurst has some good oak-framed houses, antiques shops, a village store-cum-post-office, and a vineyard. Two-bedroom cottages sell for around £175,000; three bedrooms up to £250,000. This is too much for some local people, so affordable housing is being created in a new development in the old slaughter yard.

Journey: 60 min
Season: £2560
Peak: 2 per hr
(plus 1 per hr to Cannon Street)
Off-peak: 2 per hr

WADHURST is a narrow, busy and attractive village set in an Area of Outstanding Natural Beauty in the High Weald. It is big enough to have around 30 shops, including a couple of banks, butchers, doctors, dentists, solicitors and so on. Lying on the borders of Sussex and Kent, it offers the choice of two different county education systems. Some people choose Wadhurst's own Uplands Community College, which combines the role of good comprehensive school with adult education and sports centre. Others shuttle their children into Kent to take advantage of the old-fashioned grammar schools in Tunbridge Wells. Lots of teenagers ride and there is a local livery stable.

'Lying on the borders of Sussex and Kent, Wadhurst offers the choice of two different county education systems'

A two-bedroom village house, old or new, will cost around £170,000, a one-bedroom flat in one of the small modern developments around £140,000. Three-bedroom terraced houses built in vernacular style fetch £200,000 or more; five-bedroom executive houses with 2,400 sq ft of space are around £400,000. A decent period house with four bedrooms and a garden will cost around £275,000; something more lavish with five bedrooms, tennis court and swimming pool will be around £750,000.

Journey: 71 min

Season: £2680

Peak: 2 per hr

(plus 1 per hr to

Cannon Street)

Off-peak: 1 per hr

STONEGATE itself is tiny and is becoming increasingly desirable. It is something of a drive-through village with a good primary school and several modern executive developments. Victorian three- to four-bedroom semis sell at around £300,000; four-bedroom Edwardian detached houses at £535,000. Neighbouring **Ticehurst** is attractively set around a central square in a conservation area. Three horse chestnut trees guard the bus stop in the old village pump shelter. Shops include a village store, bakery, butcher, haberdashery, dry-cleaner and greengrocer. There are also estate agents and a handful of pubs. Ticehurst has its own primary school and a good choice of local societies. Prices are about the same as Wadhurst because, while it is more out-of-the-way, it is closer to Bewl Water. A small semi in a cul-de-sac will cost £155,000; a weatherboarded two-bedroom cottage £190,000; a three-bedroom bungalow £275,000. A big house in the village will cost from £700,000.

Journey: 76 min

Season: £2680

Peak: 2 per hr

(plus 1 per hr to

Cannon Street)

Off-peak: 1 per hr

ETCHINGHAM is popular because it is reasonably good to look at and has the convenience of its own railway station. The village winds up the hill from the railway, offering a sprinkling of traditional weatherboarded properties among the 18th-century houses and a Fifties' estate. There is also a modern development opposite the village hall. Etchingham has a general store, post office and a butcher that has been in the same family for generations. There is a much-loved primary school, and the Etchingham British Legion Club where people meet for billiards and darts. A small semi in the village might cost between £170,000 and £190,000; a three-bedroom detached house down one of the lanes would be around £250,000 to £300,000.

'Half a mile away is Bateman's, where Rudyard Kipling lived and wrote Puck of Pook's Hill'

Burwash is more attractive than Etchingham and is well-known for its striking High Street of white weatherboarded and tile-hung houses, tea-rooms, brick footpaths and lime trees. Not so well-known is its warmth and friendliness. Prices are higher than those in Etchingham, for though it is further from the station, it is prettier. On the edge of the village are some five- and six-bedroom modern houses, each one set in half an acre of garden, selling for £500,000. Half a mile away is Bateman's, where Rudyard Kipling lived and wrote *Puck of Pook's Hill.*

To the north-east, back over the border into Kent, is **Hawkhurst**, a village in two halves. Housebuyers would probably avoid the half that contains the junction of two main roads in favour of an area known as The Moor in the neighbouring valley. This has a large village green, playing fields and small shops and cottages. A two-bedroom terraced house will cost around £180,000; a three-bedroom semi £175,000 to £180,000; a four-bedroom detached modern house £300,000. A four-bedroom period house in one of the lanes will fetch over £400,000. Both Hawkhurst and its much smaller neighbour, **Sandhurst**, are within the catchment area of Cranbrook School, one of the most highly respected schools in Kent, run on traditional grammar school lines. Hawkhurst is also the setting for the private school, Marlborough House.

Journey: 80 min
Season: £2680
Peak: 2 per hr
(plus 1 per hr to
Cannon Street)
Off-peak: 1 per hr

ROBERTSBRIDGE Considering the prettiness of the

countryside that surrounds it, Robertsbridge is surprisingly unprosperous. There is no major town or city centre close enough to attract regular commuters, and those who come here tend to want to escape. Hastings, it has to be said, does not offer much of a diversion. Robertsbridge's lovely village high street has now been relieved of through-traffic by a bypass. It has a sub-post office, part-time bank, butcher, chemist, greengrocer, general store and two hairdressers. The new village hall hosts regular meetings of the archaeological society, playgroups and dancing classes. There is also football, stoolball for women and, especially, cricket. The Gray-Nicholls factory makes bats out of locally-grown willow, as well as the round wooden bats for Sussex stoolball. A three-bedroom cottage will cost £170,000 to £175,000, a three-bedroom modern house £220,000 to £230,000, and a larger country house with extensive grounds £400,000 to £500,000. Its most famous former resident was the late thinker and journalist Malcolm Muggeridge. Current residents include the mild-mannered members of a commune who live in the beautifully-restored TB sanatorium. They are very self-contained, make their own clothes and educate their own children. The women distinguish themselves by always wearing headscarves.

Journey: 77 min
Season: £2800
Peak: 2 per hr
(plus 1 per hr to
Cannon Street)
Off-peak: 2 per hr

BATTLE is as self-contained, charming and spirited as any market

town in England might have been before the 20th century came along to ruin it. Its most famous asset is the remains of Battle Abbey, on the site of King Harold's defeat by William the Conqueror in 1066. A spectacular bonfire is lit on the playing fields on Guy Fawkes night, big enough to rival the one in Lewes (see page 268). The town has a High Street full of shops and inns, some of them timber-framed or weatherboarded, and there are some nice old tea-rooms for connoisseurs of the sticky bun. A first-time buyer could find a two-bedroom period cottage in need of renovation for just under £120,000. Three-bedroom semis come at between £180,000 and £200,000; four-bedroom detached houses at £200,000 to £240,000.

In the lanes around Battle are some rather grand houses in the £500,000 to £1m range. A converted oast with 30 acres and a barn for conversion would be likely to fetch in excess of £700,000. Of the neighbouring villages, **Sedlescombe** is particularly pretty with a traditional village green fringed with brick and tile-hung cottages. It has a post office, tea-room, pub, hotel, restaurant, good primary school and societies on every night of the week. Villagers have recently built a new village hall. **Catsfield** and **Ninfield** are so popular that most of the house-moves involve people already living there. Social trends have been reversed here because a new shop and a new pub have opened. For rural tranquillity there is **Penhurst**, a picturesque hamlet in deep Sussex countryside. Prices in all the villages are roughly similar to those in Battle itself.

Journey: 92 min
Season: £2800
Peak: 1 per hr
(plus 1 per hr to
Cannon Street)
Off-peak: 1 per hr

CROWHURST The station makes Crowhurst an extremely sought-after village. The electrification of the line was followed by an influx of buyers from outside the area (two-thirds of people looking for property at that time were from London). You can now expect to pay £185,000 to £225,000 for a three-bedroom semi; anything from £400,000 to £1m for an older detached house. As you come down the hill from Bexhill you see the remains of the old medieval manor house next to the Norman Church. There are some lovely tile-hung houses and the oldest yew tree in the county, which may have been here to welcome William the Conqueror. Crowhurst has often been voted "Best Kept Village", though the judges have criticised it for the clods of mud left by the herds of cows that plod through for the morning and evening milkings. The Plough Inn runs an annual pumpkin show, providing plantlets to people on a specific date so that all the competitors start level. The village has a post

Grade II listed
terrace cottage,
East Sussex

office, primary school, clubs, sports groups from tennis to cricket, horticultural society and a busy drama group. Tesco at Hollington sends a bus to Crowhurst each week, and there is a shopping and recreational complex at Glyne Gap, between Bexhill and Hastings.

WEST ST LEONARDS AND ST LEONARDS WARRIOR SQUARE

West St Leonards
Journey: 98 min
Season: £2880
Peak: 2 per hr
(plus 1 per hr to Cannon Street)
Off-peak: 1 per hr

St Leonards Warrior Square
Journey: 87 min
Season: £2880*
Peak: 2 per hr
(plus 1 per hr to Cannon Street)
Off-peak: 2 per hr
***Also valid to Victoria via Eastbourne**

Though the stations are only three minutes apart, many trains do stop at both. St Leonards was created by James Burton and his son Decimus in the 19th century as a bit of early speculative development. It was conceived by them as a dignified residential area, but time has taken its inevitable toll. A string of fish-and-chip shops and restaurants overlook the sea front. Conservationists are beginning to pamper some areas, such as Victorian Southwater which has attracted lottery funding. People from South London and Tunbridge Wells tend to move here for the sea air and the comparatively low prices, though the serious retirement area is to the west, at Bexhill-on-Sea. Recovery from the Nineties' recession was slow. Studio flats start at only £25,000, with smarter one-bedroom units at up to £65,000. A sea-view can affect prices in boom time, but in a time of glut it tends not to make much difference. Three-bedroom houses of any period tend to cost between £120,000 and £180,000. There are also some very large six-bedroom Victorian houses in more salubrious areas such as Upper Maze Hill and The Green.

HASTINGS

Journey: 89 min
Season: £2880*
Peak: 2 per hr
(plus 1 per hr to Cannon street)
Off-peak: 2 per hr
***Also valid to Victoria via Eastbourne**

has never quite caught the limelight in the way that Brighton has. Much of it has a slightly down-at-heel look, though the population still swells with trippers and holidaymakers during the summer. There are good walks along East Cliff across the gorse-covered valleys to Fairlight. Hastings sea front is much like any other, with a fine pier built in 1872. The castle ruins now tell the 1066 story in audio-visual style. The White Rock Theatre does a good line in variety shows, concerts and plays, and there is a cinema. The High Street shops and the new £50m Priory Meadows mall draw shoppers from the neighbouring villages. You can buy fresh fish from fishermen pulling their boats up on to the beach.

Much of the housing is Victorian. Commuters usually prefer to live within walking distance of the station, close enough to the William Parker comprehensive if they have families. A two-bedroom house in this area costs around £110,000; four bedrooms around £160,000. One-bedroom flats in a converted house come at around £65,000. A view, or even a squint of the sea, will add a small premium. A two-bedroom top floor flat with a sea view costs around £90,000.

One of the smartest areas is **St Helen's**, close to Alexandra Park, where a three-storey, four-bedroom Victorian house will cost £160,000 to £180,000, and a three-bedroom semi with 100ft garden over £150,000. For modern properties people look to **Parkstone**. A two-bedroom bungalow here will sell for over £150,000; a four-bedroom detached around £210,000. Prices in other parts of Hastings have fallen steeply and the properties have become populated by immigrants and DHSS claimants. If you don't mind it being in need of repair, you might get a little Victorian house for as little as £110,000. The most expensive area is probably the **Old Town**. Some people find it too claustrophobic, with tourists pressing their noses against the windows in summer, but others find the innate charm of the close ancient streets well worth the extra money. Here you might pay £85,000 to £90,000 for a two-bedroom flat; up to £180,000 for a four-bedroom Edwardian terraced house.

'Much of Hastings has a slightly down-at-heel look, though the population still swells with trippers and holidaymakers through the summer'

'If you don't mind it being in need of repair, you might get a small Victorian house for as little as £110,000'

Charing Cross/Cannon Sreet
> Canterbury
(via Tonbridge and Ashford)

All trains are from Charing Cross unless otherwise specified.

TONBRIDGE For Tonbridge main entry see **Charing Cross/Cannon Street to Hastings** line, page 294.

Journey: 48 min
Season: £2420
Peak: 3 per hr
(plus 2 per hr to
Cannon Street)
Off-peak: 3 per hr

PADDOCK WOOD Londoners have always been attracted to Paddock Wood. Those with happy memories of hop-picking settled here after the war. More recently there has been a steady trickle of suburban refugees from Bromley and Orpington. Paddock Wood now is a town with little romance, large enough to support a department store, a Waitrose supermarket, a sports and leisure centre and some light industry. Its comprehensive school has a good reputation and doubles as an adult education centre. Property prices have risen to match the surrounding area, with three-bedroom semis at between £190,000 and £250,000. Four-bedroom detached houses cost £190,000 to £310,000. It would be misleading to describe all the property here as cheap. The convenience of the journey into London means that a large detached house with land and old Kentish oasts can fetch £750,000 upwards.

> Branch line to Maidstone West via Beltring, Yalding, Wateringbury and East Farleigh

For train
information see
page 306

Close to Beltring station is the Hop Farm Country Park. It contains the largest group of Victorian oast houses in the world, and runs many events and craft fairs throughout the year. Beltring itself is not an identifiable community and has no more than a few houses. Nearby **Laddingford** is a village on the River Teise, with a trout stream, a good pub called The Chequers and a clutch of

Journey: 75 min
(from East
Farleigh)

Season: £2420

Frequency: 1 per
hr*

*Change at
Paddock Wood.
There are no
through trains. It is
also possible to
travel to Charing
Cross via Strood in
the opposite
direction

detached and semi-detached houses with generous gardens which sell from £180,000 upwards.

Yalding is a lovely old village served by winding country lanes, with several shops, a post office, a working forge, a beautiful 14th-century bridge over the River Beult and a Church of England primary school. The village has now recovered from the severe floods of October 2000 when streets were deluged by 3ft of water. A three-bedroom house with a handkerchief garden will cost £200,000 upwards; a newish four-bedroom detached house, £340,000 (add £50,000 to £100,000 for a period version).

The prettiness of **Wateringbury** is marred by the busy A26 Tonbridge to Maidstone road which thumps through it. It has some shops, a post office and a Church of England primary school. You would have to pay over £240,000 for a four-bedroom detached house; over £450,000 for a period detached house with land. The village has a few fine stone-built Georgian houses and creeping modern development.

East Farleigh is much quieter than Wateringbury (though it is increasingly used as a rat run to Maidstone) and just as attractive with a five-arch 14th-century bridge pinning the centre together. It has a county primary school and a shop-cum-post-office run by villagers from a Portakabin in the pub car park after the loss of their post office in 1995. Again, small cottages are expensive – at least £135,000. A spacious three-bedroom bungalow might cost £250,000; a four-bedroom house, £340,000.

For **Maidstone**, see **Victoria to Ashford International Line**, page 314.

> Continuation of main line

Journey: 53 min

Season: £2520

Peak: 2 per hr
(plus 2 per hr to
Cannon Street)

Off-peak: 2 per hr

‘Goudhurst is a
classic English
village with
half-timbered
cottages and a
duckpond’

MARDEN has some pretty Kentish weatherboarded houses, genuinely useful shops, including a butcher, greengrocer and post office, and a primary school. Three-bedroom semis sell for around £150,000 or more. You might find a small, three-bedroom, period terraced cottage for £250,000, but a larger four-bedroom Georgian house will fetch £400,000 at least.

Just over four miles to the south is **Goudhurst**. It is set on a hilltop surrounded by orchards, cornfields and hop gardens and has lovely views across the valleys of the Low Weald. This is a classic English village with half-timbered cottages, a duckpond and a church which is spectacularly lit at night. It is a self-sufficient community with its own primary school, shops and a tea-shop for the summer visitors. A small terraced house can be bought for £180,000; a period house with land £450,000. Just over two miles to the south, there is a huge forest known as the Bedgebury Pinetum which has one of the world's finest collections of conifers.

Journey: 56 min
Season: £2520
Peak: 3 per hr
(plus 2 per hr to
Cannon Street)
Off-peak: 3 per hr

STAPLEHURST has a little light industry and a large Mazda
warehouse by the station. It is a plain village in comparison with some of the jewels of the Kentish landscape which lie to the south. But the vibrant community spirit (from a football club to a bellringers' society) helped it to become Kent Village of the Year in 2003. With 6000 residents it is large and has its own primary school, four pubs, three churches and a full range of shops. Three-bedroom semis on Sixties' estates sell for around £170,000; four-bedroom detached houses are at least £300,000. Period properties carry the expected premium, with a three-bedroom cottage selling at over £325,000.

'Cranbrook is an enchanting town of weatherboarded houses with a well-preserved smock mill at one end'

Cranbrook has a special appeal for Londoners worried about schooling. Cranbrook School for boys and girls has a reputation sufficient to add a premium to property prices within a catchment area which stretches just over six miles. The school is a state school though fees are charged for boarding, so parents will sometimes choose to live outside the catchment for the cheaper house price (a £1m house can sell for £200,000 less outside the catchment) and pay for their children to board. Cranbrook is an enchanting town of weatherboarded houses with a well-preserved smock mill at one end. New houses are being slipped in all the time. The town used to be cut off in winter because of the deep mud on the roads, and this has given it a lingering feeling of insularity. Small two-bedroom houses, old or new, start at just under £150,000. Three-bedroom semis cost £160,000 to £210,000; period farmhouses on the outskirts from £500,000 to over £1m.

A mile up the cramped lanes from Cranbrook is **Sissinghurst**, a pretty one-street village of weatherboarded and half-timbered houses with a pub and primary school, close to Sissinghurst Castle (National Trust), where Vita Sackville-West and her husband Harold Nicolson created their wonderful gardens. **Benenden** is just over seven miles from Staplehurst (15 minutes by car) and is popular with commuters. It is a perfect Kentish village set around a green (cricket is played in summer) beside the King William IV and The Bull pubs. There is a handsome range of brick and weatherboarded cottages and old hall houses, close to the parkland of Benenden, the girls' public school. A Grade II listed 15th-century house with five bedrooms, cottage and barn here could cost £895,000.

Journey: 67 min
Season: £2600
Peak: 3 per hr
(plus 2 per hr to
Cannon Street)
Off-peak: 2 per hr

HEADCORN is very popular with commuters, not least for its large station car-park. It is big enough to support a busy shopping centre which includes a Sainsbury's and restaurants, though serious shopping means a trip into Maidstone or Ashford. Other assets include a primary school, village green, a flower farm and vineyard, an aerodrome and the Lashenden Air Warfare Museum. Well-heeled commuters pay over £400,000 for a house with an acre or two on the outskirts. Medieval timber-framed cottages are silent reminders of the past. A timbered farmhouse with 20 acres and an oast might cost £700,000 to over £1m. Within the village itself, a period four-bedroom house will fetch around £400,000 to £450,000. There are also some new developments where a four-bedroom detached might be bought for £350,000. A three-bedroom semi right in the centre will cost £235,000.

Smarden, three miles to the east, is a beautiful well-kept village with listed cottages grouped around a 14th- to 15th-century church. There is a post office, a butcher and an art gallery. The mobile library calls once a week and there is a primary school. The village teems with activities, including a cricket club and gardening club. It tends to be popular with families. Large, family-sized period houses with perhaps two acres cost from £450,000 upwards. A three-bedroom semi-detached period cottage costs £200,000; a two-up-two-down terraced cottage, £150,000.

Biddenden, three miles south of Headcorn, is favoured because of its proximity to Tenterden, a stylish Wealden town that has become something of a local antiques centre. It has a newsagent, butcher, pub and hairdresser. This is where you find Kent's oldest commercial vineyard and can buy the locally made ciders, wines and apple juices. An 18-hole international golf course, Chart Hills, designed by Nick Faldo, is nearby. A three-bedroom terraced house looking onto farmland could cost £160,000; a five-bedroom detached house with an inglenook fireplace and rural views £400,000 or more.

Journey: 75 min
Season: £2600
Peak: 2 per hr
(plus 2 per hr to
Cannon Street)
Off-peak: 2 per hr

PLUCKLEY The countryside around Pluckley will be familiar to anyone who watched the television serialisation of H E Bates's *Darling Buds Of May*. The influence of the Dering family, previous lords of the manor of Surrenden Dering, is evident here. Kentish ragstone was used for many of the older houses, most of which have distinctively-arched Dering windows. The village has managed to stay small, with a population of just over 1000 served by two shops, a hugely admired silversmith, four pubs, a church and a Church of England primary school. Leisure opportunities include cricket, tennis and Pluckley Pantomime Unlimited. Houses are expensive. The smallest detached cottage can fetch £225,000. A new interloper could be bought for £295,000. A period country house with three acres on the outskirts will cost £500,000 or more.

Bethersden, a couple of miles south of the station, is another pretty conservation village of listed weatherboarded and tile-hung houses. It clusters around a post office and general store, a butcher, a church, three pubs, and primary school. Bethersden is cosy and comfortable in character rather than smart like Smarden. A two-bedroom Victorian brick semi costs about £140,000. A four-bedroom detached house with a half-acre garden £250,000.

ASHFORD INTERNATIONAL For Ashford main entry see Victoria to Ashford International line, page 313.

Journey: 64 min
Season: £2720
(also valid to
Victoria)
Peak: 3 per hr
(plus 3 per hr to
Cannon Street)
Off-peak: 3 per hr
(plus 1 per hr to
Cannon Street)

> Branch line to Rye via Hamstreet and Appledore

Journey: 107 min
(from Rye)
Season: £2880
(also valid to
Charing
Cross/Victoria via
Hastings)
Frequency: 1 per
hr*
*There are no
through trains.
All services
change at Ashford
International

HAMSTREET is a large and expanding village which has had some of its tranquillity returned thanks to the arrival of a bypass. It has a green and a duckpond by the village hall and is built on land reclaimed from Romney Marsh. There is a primary school, doctor, dentist, post office, general store and an antiques shop. New houses are being built. A small terraced house might cost £130,000. A four- to five-bedroom house in a third of an acre will fetch £300,000 or more. Just to the north are the Hamstreet Woods, a linked series of five woods in a nature reserve famous for its nightingales.

Appledore is a delightful village and one of the best places to slip off the main road to enjoy the eerie flat landscape of Romney Marsh just to the east. It has lovely old black-and-white houses and a particularly attractive main street, church and three pubs. Unfortunately Appledore has lost its primary school, due in part to the incomers' preference for private education. The result is that village children are now bussed three miles to Wittersham. The village has an old forge, a bric-a-brac shop and antiques shop and small general store. The Royal Military Canal, built in the 19th century as a second line of defence inland from the Martello towers, runs along the margin of the street. Houses sell very quickly here, with buyers always waiting for an opportunity. A little period three-bedroom terraced house will cost £130,000 or more; a four-bedroom detached house £450,000; an old farmhouse with land and stables over £500,000.

Rye is regarded as one of the most picturesque towns on the south coast. Two miles into the mouth of the River Rother, it was once a flourishing port huddled behind protective sea walls. Now its cobbled streets and Tudor, Stuart and Georgian houses attract hordes of summer tourists. It is an intimate place in which to live and most people seem to know what everyone else is doing. There are plenty of shops selling food, antiques and souvenirs, but going to the cinema means a trip into Hastings. Rye has all the usual clubs and societies, including the Rye Players, who perform a Christmas pantomime each year, and the Rye Medieval Association organises an annual Medieval Week. Well-known local residents used to include John Ryan, the creator of *Captain Pugwash*, and Spike Milligan who had a house nearby in Udimore. A two-bedroom Victorian terraced house in Rye will cost £150,000 or more. The picture-postcard streets include Church Square, Watchbell Street and steep and cobbled Mermaid Street, where houses rarely sell and are much sought after at over £500,000. The rail journey is arduous and many residents prefer to drive to Ashford and hop on the train there.

> ‘Two miles into the mouth of the River Rother, Rye was once a flourishing port huddled behind protective sea walls’

> ## Line from **Ashford** to **Canterbury**

Journey: 86 min
Season: £2720
Peak: 1 per hr
(plus 1 train to Cannon Street)
Off-peak: 1 per hr
to Victoria*
*Or change at
Ashford
International for
Charing Cross

WYE is possibly the most sought-after village in the Ashford area. Not only does it have the station, but it has the remarkable Bridge Street in which many of the medieval houses are reached by stone steps. Their purpose originally was to raise the buildings above the stream that once ran down the middle of the road. The Great Stour does still run through the village and is overlooked by the Tickled Trout pub. Houses here sell at a premium as the countryside around is so beautiful and the area feels tucked away. A three-bedroom period house with half an acre of garden could cost £375,000.

The village has shops enough for anything you're likely to need. There are also two banks, a garage, a primary school and The Wife of Bath restaurant. The Department of Agricultural Sciences of Imperial College at London University is based in the former Wye College and introduces an unusually young, cosmopolitan element. The college has an annual rag week and celebrates Bonfire Night with a torchlight procession to the Crown, a chalk image cut into the Downs. There are good walks along the North Downs Way, which passes through the village, and in the Wye Nature Reserve. The latter contains a deep wooded hollow which is known as the Devil's Kneading Trough.

Journey: 92 min

Season: £2760

Peak: 1 per hr
(plus 1 train to
Cannon Street)

Off-peak: 1 per hr
to Victoria*

*Or change at
Ashford
International for
Charing Cross

CHILHAM

CHILHAM The central square of 14th- and 15th-century black-and-white houses in Chilham is an irresistible draw for tourists, film crews and wealthy house-hunters. The church is known for its roughly chequered flint tower. The gardens at privately-owned Chilham Castle – a Jacobean mansion with a 12th-century keep – were laid out by the 17th-century botanist John Tradescant. The mulberry trees here are said to be 500 years old. There is a post office and general stores, but many find shops geared to tourists rather than residents. Properties rarely come up for sale in Chilham, but, if you are lucky, you might snatch a family-size house for £375,000. On the outskirts a compact modern house, on one of the small-scale new developments, might come up for resale at £230,000. It is a village with a strong community spirit. There is football, cricket and tennis, and in May the square is closed for a huge fair at which the villagers dress in period costume. Chilham also has the considerable advantage of being only five miles from Canterbury.

Old Wives Lees, a mile to the north, is a cheaper alternative, known to locals as Old Wives Knees. There is plenty of modern development here. A three-bedroom older house might cost £200,000.

Journey: 96 min

Season: £2760

Peak: 1 per hr
(plus 1 train to
Cannon Street)

Off-peak: 1 per hr
to Victoria*

*Or change at
Ashford
International for
Charing Cross

CHARTHAM The River Stour, which divides before it enters the village, was for centuries the source of power for the local paper mills – one of which is still in production. Chartham is not as smart as Chilham. It has a mix of old houses – some of the nicest are by the little green and the 13th-century church – as well as Victorian and modern estates built on the sites of old orchards and St Augustine's hospital. A three-bedroom end-of-terrace in Chartham would cost around £160,000; a four-bedroom house £275,000. It is quite a large village served by a handful of small shops and its own primary school.

Petham, three miles to the south-east, also has a mix of old thatched cottages, turn-of-the-century and new houses in a lovely setting. It has a church, a primary school and a garden centre. A four-bedroom cottage in the heart of the village might cost £260,000; a four-bedroom converted barn £335,000.

Journey: 88 min

Season: £2760
(also valid
Canterbury East)

Peak: 2 per hr
(plus 1 train to
Cannon Street)

Off-peak: 2 per hr
(plus 1 per hr to
Victoria)

CANTERBURY WEST For Canterbury main entry see **Charing Cross to Canterbury** line via **Rochester**, page 235.

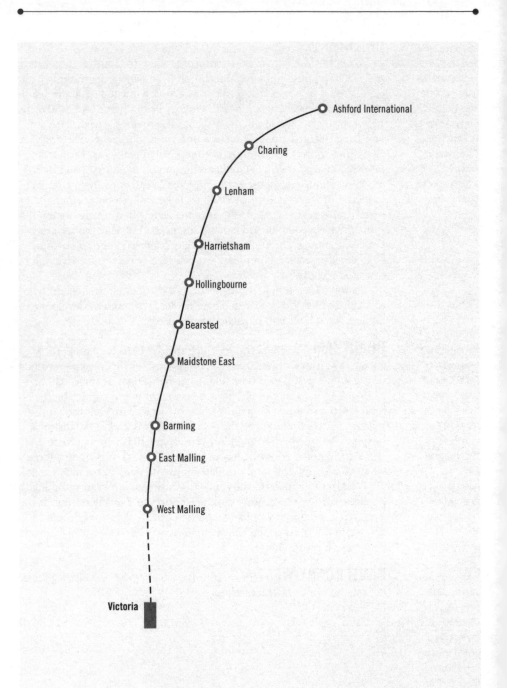

Ashford International

Charing

Lenham

Harrietsham

Hollingbourne

Bearsted

Maidstone East

Barming

East Malling

West Malling

Victoria

Victoria
> Ashford International
(via Maidstone)

WEST MALLING Considering its closeness to London, West
Malling is surprisingly unspoilt. The old High Street, in parts Tudor
and Georgian, opens out into what was once the market square.
There is a Tesco, a delicatessen, bakery and a store which sells
everything from plimsolls to vests. Cake decorating, knitting and
sewing are practised in the local craft centre. The village has two
primary schools and a 900-year-old abbey. As always, there are a
number of local stalwarts who keep the social wheels turning,
running the conservation society and fending off new development.
The fields that cushion the village from Maidstone are guarded with
particular vigilance. The local airfield, a former World War II fighter
station, has been turned over to housing with a business park known
as Kings Hill. Four- and five-bedroom houses here range from
£270,000 to £500,000. The M20 is close enough to be audible from
the nearby woods. A four-bedroom period house in the main street at
West Malling is unlikely to cost less than £400,000, though you might
pick up a two-bedroom modern box for as little as £160,000.

Journey: 49 min
Season: £2260
Peak: 2 per hr
Off-peak: 2 per hr
plus 1 per hr to
Cannon Street

EAST MALLING is much smaller than West Malling and its
property prices are slightly lower. The old heart is picturesque with
a church, pub and village green, but ex-council estates tend to
dominate. The East Malling Research Station, which develops new
fruit varieties, is based in Bradbourne House, a Queen Anne-style
mansion. A three-bedroom, Victorian terraced cottage might
cost £200,000.

Journey: 55 min
Season: £2260
Peak: 2 per hr
Off-peak: 1 per hr

BARMING lies on a beautiful stretch of the River Medway. It was
crossed by a 1740 wooden bridge until the county council
condemned it and had it removed. To outsiders it may seem like a
suburb of Maidstone. To those who live here, however, it is very
definitely a village. The old centre has been swallowed by new

Journey: 59 min
Season: £2260
Peak: 2 per hr
Off-peak: 1 per hr

development, yet it is still extremely popular. A two-bedroom terraced cottage will cost over £180,000; a three-bedroom modern semi around £200,000. The post office-cum-general store sells everything from wine to plants.

Journey: 57 min

Season: £2420
(also valid
Maidstone West)

Peak: 2 per hr

Off-peak: 2 per hr
(plus 1 per hr to
Cannon Street)

MAIDSTONE EAST Maidstone looms rather brutishly on the Kentish landscape – particularly if you approach it from the pretty southern villages. Nevertheless, it is a friendly and workmanlike hilly town where people manage to have the time to say good morning. Its focus is the River Medway, with the Archbishop's Palace (used as a place of rest on journeys to Canterbury) on the bank. It is a county town rather than a cultural centre. The remains of some 14th-century collegiate buildings are now occupied by the Kent Music School. The Maidstone Museum and Bentlif Art Galley are in Chillington House, a 16th-century manor. The Corn Exchange is a cultural focus too – home of the Hazlitt Theatre and a venue for concerts, dances and conferences.

Maidstone has always had a commercial and agricultural bias. In earlier centuries it supplied hops, linen, paper, ragstone and gin to London. Today it is particularly strong on shopping. The Chequers Centre has a host of major high street names, all gathered together under a single roof. The Royal Star Arcade has more upmarket specialist shops; Starnes Court is a Victorian-style arcade of designer-shops set around a courtyard. A new shopping centre is being built on the site of the old Fremlin brewery. Beside the river on Lockmeadow there are Tuesday and Saturday markets for furniture, bric-a-brac and agricultural produce. Mote Park, being the former parkland of an old country house, is a popular venue for boating, fishing and football. The new treat though is the Maidstone Millennium River Park with paths trailing the River Medway. The Maidstone Leisure Centre has rock-climbing as well as leisure pools and health-and-fitness equipment. The town has the benefit of four Kentish grammar schools, two for boys and two for

Detached period
house, near
Maidstone

House style in Kent

Medieval England is clearly reflected in Kent's many hall houses. They were built with great arched, interlocking timbers, each one carefully notched and marked like a huge rustic modelling kit. Beneath the common roof the entire household would huddle around a central hearth (chimneys didn't appear until the late 16th or early 17th centuries).

These days, hall houses can be hard to recognise because they have been divided into smaller rooms or had upper floors inserted, but the magisterial timbers soon give them away. You can see beautifully restored examples of early houses at the Weald and Downland Museum at Singleton in West Sussex.

Timber for these old buildings was felled from the great woods which stretched across the Weald (Anglo Saxon for wooded country). The use of intricate brick- and tilework, made from the local terracotta clays, developed in the 17th and 18th centuries when it was most lavishly applied to the houses of high clergy at Canterbury. Alec Clifton-Taylor described the tile-hanging of Kent in his book *The Pattern of English Building*: "A good tile-hung wall is a creation of infinite subtlety, an agglomeration of shallow and slightly irregular convexities, seemingly held in place, under the right conditions of light, by a fine mesh of shadow."

Weatherboarding is another familiar sight in the Kentish villages, looking strangely ephemeral for a building material. Cranbrook, built upon the wealth of the Flemish clothworkers who settled here, is like a toy-town made of wood. The clothworkers also left behind them a string of cloth halls and weavers' cottages.

girls, plus a Mid-Kent College of Higher and Further Education. Much of the housing in Maidstone is Victorian. There are terraces of small artisans' cottages where you might pay £150,000 for three bedrooms. The houses get larger as you move further away from the centre. A four-bedroom terraced house with three reception rooms and a walled garden could cost as little as £180,000.

The huge new Grove Green estate is densely built, but popular. You could buy a three-bedroom semi for around £190,000, or a four-bedroom detached for £295,000.

To the south-east is **Sutton Valence**, a pretty hilltop village with views over the Weald of Kent. It is marred by the busy A274 running through it, but is favoured because of Sutton Valence School, a private school for girls and boys aged four to 18. There is also a local primary. The village has lost some of its shops, but still has a post office and hairdresser. At the centre is an enclave of old houses – some black-and-white half-timbered and some weatherboarded. On the outskirts, a good address might cost £550,000, a two-bedroom period cottage in need of renovation £200,000. In the churchyard there is a memorial to John Willes, the man who introduced round-arm bowling to cricket.

Due south of Maidstone, and hardly separate from it, is one of those lovely English villages that everyone would love to call home. **Loose** owes its attraction to its position on the steep valley slope of the fast-flowing Loose stream. Old mills litter the wooded streambanks, which are overlooked by the church and The Chequers pub. The 15th-century half-timbered Wool House is now administered by the National Trust and open to the public on written application. The Loose Viaduct, designed by Thomas Telford in 1830, has helped the village to keep its olde-worlde charm by removing large volumes of traffic. The village has a primary school, a post office-cum-shop and antiques shop. You might find a four- or five-bedroom house for £400,000. On the outskirts a two-bedroom beamed cottage could cost £200,000.

To the north is **Boxley**, set in an Area of Outstanding Natural Beauty with the North Downs Way and the Pilgrims Way running close by. The village has a good pub, The King's Arms, but no shop. The Channel Tunnel rail-link unfortunately carves its way close to the village, but trains are hidden by cut-and-cover. A couple of miles away, at the top of Detling Hill, is the Kent County Agricultural Showground. This is where White Horse Wood has been planted to mark the Millennium.

> '**The Channel Tunnel rail-link unfortunately carves its way close to the village, but trains are hidden by cut-and-cover'**

BEARSTED, insulated from Maidstone by a belt of green, is a very popular village, though in recent decades it has become rather bloated with new development. The older part, to the north of the A20, has a core of 17th-century houses around a large green on which is one of the earliest cricket pitches in the county. The poet Edward Thomas lived by the green, close to where the shops now stand – there is a butcher, bakery and chemist, a newsagent and two pubs. The infant and junior schools in the area are thought to be excellent. Baroness Orczy also lived here, and the Scout troop is known as The Scarlet Pimpernels after her successful novel. A Grade II listed terraced cottage with two bedrooms near the green could cost £240,000. A family-sized house would reach £400,000 or more.

Journey: 62 min
Season: £2420
Peak: 2 per hr
Off-peak: 1 per hr
(plus 1 per hr to Cannon Street)

A disadvantage of Bearsted is that the old and the new sides of the village are rather split, each having its own village hall. Some villagers on the Madginford side, to the south of the Ashford road, feel that the north side grabs the limelight. The new estates to the south have their own supermarket and parade of shops. A two-bedroom house on the Grove Green development is priced at around £140,000.

The first pocket of rural life on Maidstone's eastern flank, but closer to Bearsted, is **Otham**. Here there is a 900-year-old church, a few ancient half-timbered houses, and a tradition of parish life which is maintained. A four- or five-bedroom family house might cost you £450,000. The WI hall also does duty as a village hall and nursery school. There are some pretty walks up the valley around the River Len, where you could keep in training for the egg-and-spoon race at the annual fête. In the Len valley is **Downswood**, an area of high-density modern housing estates set in farmland, with four shops, where you might buy a three-bedroom semi for £185,000 or a four-bedroom detached for £230,000.

Journey: 67 min
Season: £2420
Peak: 2 per hr
Off-peak: 1 per hr

HOLLINGBOURNE is one of the prettier villages in this part of

Kent, though it lies in the path of the Channel Tunnel rail-link which
has been buried underground in order to minimise disturbance. The
High Street is lined with half-timbered houses. A small two-bedroom
terraced cottage costs £130,000; a four-bedroom detached house at
least £320,000. The upper village clusters around the Elizabethan
manor house, with the shops kept in their place at the lower end.
There is a primary school, a football team and an architecturally
admired early council housing estate built just after World War II.
Hollingbourne church contains the 300 year-old embroidered
Culpeper cloth. The North Downs Way passes through the village
and affords some breathtaking walks.

This is also the station for Leeds Castle. The castle was built in
1192 in the middle of a lake formed by the River Len, and presented
by Edward I to his wife Eleanor of Castile. It was given to the nation
in 1974 and is now a venue for conferences, open-air concerts,
balloon events and so on. Prices in **Leeds** are similar to those in
Hollingbourne. It merges into the neighbouring village of **Langley**,
where there is a shooting ground and a golf course, and where you
can spot deer in the woodland. A three-bedroom semi will cost
around £190,000.

Journey: 71 min
Season: £2540
Peak: 2 per hr
Off-peak: 1 per hr

HARRIETSHAM is split by the A20 and has been heavily

developed. Homeowners can find themselves living with both railway
noise and road noise from the M20. It has a store, post office, Indian
restaurant, pub and Church of England primary school. A three-
bedroom modern semi will cost around £160,000; a four-bedroom
house with a generous garden £400,000. Among the older properties
you might stumble across a strange anachronism – a cottage with a
flying freehold on a bedroom in the house next door.

Journey: 74 min
Season: £2540
Peak: 2 per hr
Off-peak: 1 per hr

LENHAM is a large working village with a population of around

3500. It combines a pretty central market square, surrounded by
Wealden hall houses and Georgian-fronted buildings, with a strong
industrial base on the village edge. In the Seventies the Lenham
Storage Company set up Freightflow, one of Britain's first
international customs depots. This brings a lot of trans-continental
lorries to, but not through, the village. A new parish hall has been
built on the outskirts and is heavily used by organised groups ranging
from badminton to British Legion. There is a delicatessen,
ironmonger, hairdresser and some little antiques shops, as well as a
pub and the Dog & Bear Hotel. It has its own primary and secondary
schools. Because of the changes in farming methods, ramblers often
now find themselves prairie-walking rather than following the ancient
footpaths, but the village's saving grace is that it lies just at the foot of

the North Downs, which is a designated Area of Outstanding Natural Beauty. Prices don't vary much in the villages between Maidstone and Ashford. Small cottages start at around £160,000, with prices rising to £700,000 or over £1m for the largest period properties. For a three-bedroom semi on a modern estate you would have to pay around £175,000.

Journey: 79 min
Season: £2540
Peak: 2 per hr
Off-peak: 1 per hr

'A modern library has replaced the old pig slaughterhouse'

CHARING At the heart of Charing is the old Archbishop's Palace, once used by Archbishops of Canterbury, but now a private house. The green – a favourite place to sit in summer – overlooks the market place, where a modern library has replaced the old pig slaughterhouse. The main street with its Elizabethan and Georgian-faced houses is a whole town in miniature. It has two butchers, an interiors shop, two grocers, a watchmaker, post office and doctor's surgery. Charing likes to be thought of not just as a pretty village but as a hard-working one, too. A two- or three-bedroom period cottage here could cost £275,000; a large, family-size period house would start at £400,000 and a four-bedroom modern detached house £300,000. The village has a primary school and a host of clubs and societies. The WI holds a weekly market in part of the Archbishop's Palace.

Journey: 87 min
Season: £2720
(also valid to Charing Cross)
Peak: 2 per hr
Off-peak: 1 per hr
See also Charing Cross to Canterbury West line, page 309

ASHFORD INTERNATIONAL People are not kind about **Ashford**. If Kent were ever to need an enema, they suggest, then Ashford is where you'd insert the tube. But, as it happens, the town is the site for the Eurostar high speed rail-link (scheduled for 2006), which is attracting huge investment and a surge in house prices. In the Seventies it was designated as a growth area. Thousands of new houses were built, the population swelled to nearly 100,000 and a lot more housing is planned. Ashford is zoned for growth. Next to the domestic station used by South Eastern Trains trains, there is now the International Passenger Station used by Eurostar, with combined traffic of more than 8.5m passengers each year. Lydd Airport is just a few miles away; Sainsbury's, Asda, Tesco and the UCL multiplex cinema have set up shop alongside junction 9 of the M20.

Among the swathes of modern housing, a three-bedroom semi with a garage will cost £140,000 to £170,000; a modern four-bedroom detached house £200,000 to £250,000. A two- to three-bedroom period cottage will be over £250,000. Ashford has two good grammar schools, Highworth School for Girls and Norton Knatchbull for boys, and three mixed high schools. Ashford Girls' School is private and takes both boarders and day-pupils.

All the villages within reach of Ashford are feeling the hope factor created by the new rail link. On the slopes of the North Downs are several tiny hamlets amounting to little more than clusters of houses. **Boughton Aluph** (pronounced Borton Aluf) is rather more substantial. It is centred around a village green on which cricket has been played since 1752. This is flanked on one side by neo-Georgian houses and on the other by the green-painted, corrugated iron village hall, known as the Iron Room. The village has one or two distinguished Elizabethan houses, but there is no shop, and the church (a mile away since the village was displaced by the Black Death) is used only in summer. In winter it is too expensive to heat. The Stour Music Festival is an annual thrill for lovers of early music. The big house, Eastwell Manor, has become a hotel with a spa and restaurant. A two-bedroom cottage in Boughton Aluph will start at £175,000; a family-size period house over £300,000.

Challock (pronounced Chollock), also in the north, is similarly priced. The name Challock means "enclosure of calves". The village has a considerable number of new houses squeezed in between the old, and there are a couple of modern closes. A four-bedroom modern detached house will cost £250,000 or more. Challock is high up on the Downs, 630ft above sea level, and there are some spectacular footpaths and bridleways. The price you pay is that it can be very cold, windy and foggy in winter. The village has a post office-cum-general store, a pub and a farm shop. Each September it hosts a Goose Fair to support village projects.

'Challock is high up on the Downs, 630ft above sea level, and there are some spectacular footpaths and bridleways'

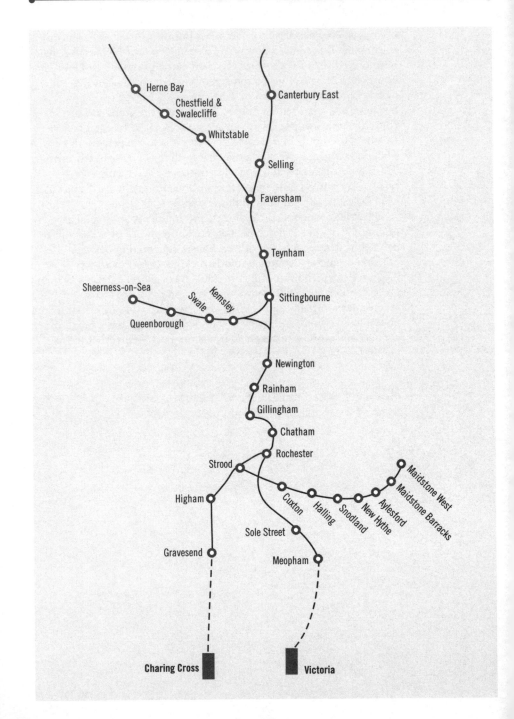

Herne Bay

Chestfield & Swalecliffe

Whitstable

Canterbury East

Selling

Faversham

Teynham

Sheerness-on-Sea

Swale

Kemsley

Sittingbourne

Queenborough

Newington

Rainham

Gillingham

Chatham

Rochester

Strood

Maidstone West

Maidstone Barracks

Aylesford

New Hythe

Higham

Cuxton

Halling

Snodland

Sole Street

Gravesend

Meopham

Charing Cross

Victoria

Charing Cross/Victoria
> Herne Bay and Canterbury (via Rochester)

> Line from Victoria to Meopham and Sole Street

Journey: 47 min
Season: £2020
Peak: 3 per hr
Off-peak: 2 per hr

MEOPHAM The cricket green at Meopham really grabs all the attention, being overlooked by a marvellous wooden mill. The village is long and straggly with a main street dotted with 16th- and 17th-century houses mixed with new. There are four pubs, a post office, fish-and-chip shop and hardware store. You would pay £170,000 to £200,000 for a two-bedroom cottage; £240,000 for a three-bedroom semi built in the Sixties or Seventies.

Journey: 49 min
Season: £2020
Peak: 3 per hr
Off-peak: 2 per hr

SOLE STREET is deceptively small and, because it really is very rural, it can be rather expensive. It has a general store, a pub, a little shop and a post office. The Tudor Yeoman's House is owned by the National Trust, though you have to make a written request to see it. Houses rarely come on the market. Older, two-bedroom Victorian terraced houses sell for around £140,000; four-bedroom modern detached houses for £350,000 to £500,000.

Cobham is a very pretty north Kent village in an Area of Outstanding Natural Beauty on the crest of a hill. The big house, Cobham Hall, is now a girls' boarding school, but the grounds – landscaped by Repton – and the deer park are open to the public in summer. The Street has a good range of 18th-century houses, some Victorian and some weatherboarded, plus the village hall and three pubs, including the Leather Bottle which Dickens used as a setting in *Pickwick Papers*. There is also a Victorian flint primary school and a general store. It is an expensive village in which a one-bedroom 18th-century cottage will cost upwards of £130,000. A modern detached house will be at least £300,000.

> Main line from Charing Cross

Journey: 52 min

Season: £1588

Peak: 4 per hr

(plus 3 per hr to Cannon Street)

Off-peak: 4 per hr

GRAVESEND For centuries the local economy of Gravesend, London's trade and defensive gateway, has been bound to the River Thames. Many of the traditional riverside industries have closed down, but the paper mills and cement works are still going. The riverside part of town is heavily atmospheric, with narrow streets and alleyways peppered with old churches, inns and historic fortifications. The best place to watch river traffic ploughing the Thames is from the Gordon Promenade gardens, where you can look across the water into Essex. The potential of the river is now being realised with redevelopment, parks and new housing coming on apace.

Efforts to work the London Docklands miracle by replacing old industrial sores with mix-and-match housing are well under way. The district council and Kent County Council together have allocated funds for a town rejuvenation scheme which they have called Towncentric, but its thrust is mainly commercial. The headquarters of the Port of London Authority and Customs and Excise have moved here, and by 2005 there should be a new international station with a fast track to London.

There are swathes of Edwardian and Victorian houses, and some handsome Georgian houses. It is a good hunting ground for first-time buyers. A small two-bedroom Victorian house would cost around £120,000 to £130,000. On the river there are some new developments in which two-bedroom flats with balconies sell from around £170,000. Large Georgian terraced houses with four or five bedrooms can be bought for up to £450,000 depending on condition.

Property prices are higher to the south of the town, especially in the Thirties-built roads around the golf course. A detached house will cost from upwards of £200,000 to around £650,000, for which you would also get a very large garden. Another more expensive part of Gravesend is the Windmill Hill conservation area, a mile from the town centre, where some of the houses have giddy river views. A two-bedroom Victorian house would cost at least £150,000. Some of the larger houses have been converted into flats. If you were looking for a house on a decent modern estate, then the answer could be Rivermount, built in the Eighties, where a four-bedroom detached house costs £250,000 to £300,000, a three-bedroom semi £200,000, and you might get a good view thrown in.

The village of **Shorne**, two miles east, is pretty and old (though with its fair share of new), and very much sought after since this part of north Kent can seem rather bleak. It is also close to the A2. Snob value adds to the prices of the 15th- and 16th-century timber-framed cottages. You would have to pay £150,000 for one-and-a-half bedrooms, £250,000 for a modest three-bedroom house in a terrace. There are a few five-bedroom detached Thirties' houses, valued at around £800,000.

Journey: 58 min
Season: £2024
Peak: 2 per hr
(plus 2 per hr to
Cannon Street)
Off-peak: 2 per hr

HIGHAM is mostly a soup of houses built in the Sixties and Seventies with a few older properties thrown in for flavour. A Victorian two-up-two-down will cost around £135,000; a modern three-bedroom semi around £200,000. There is a butcher, a hairdresser, greengrocer, pub and takeaway. Gad's Hill Place was Charles Dickens's home from 1856 until the end of his life, and is now an independent girls' school. He left *Edwin Drood* unfinished when he died in 1870.

Journey: 68 min
Season: £2160
Peak: 3 per hr
(plus 2 per hr to
Cannon Street)
Off-peak: 2 per hr

STROOD is linked to Rochester by a bridge over the River Medway. Its small High Street has a broader choice of shops than Rochester's, and B&Q, Homebase and Matalan draw people from over the water. The houses in the centre are flat-fronted, late-Victorian terraces, which cost around £150,000 for three bedrooms and are attractive to first-time buyers. Close to the station is a surge of Fifties' housing where a three-bedroom home would cost around £150,000. In the more sedate Thirties' developments near the fringes of the town, a three-bedroom house would cost around £165,000.

It is a popular area for boating. Further out along the Medway estuary, the marina at **Upnor** throngs with hundreds of small craft. Developers have begun to cater for the sailors' needs by providing small town houses and semis along the riverbank. Prices are similar to those in Strood. The main street is rather pretty, with old weatherboarded houses. Upnor Castle, now a museum, was built in the mid-16th century to defend Chatham dockyard. The Isle of Grain, which thrusts out like a hammerhead over the mouth of the estuary bristles with oil terminals and refineries. It is one of the fastest growing container ports in the country. British Gas has 900 acres of land earmarked for future industrial development.

'Developers have begun to cater for the sailors' needs by providing small town houses and semis along the riverbank'

> Branch line to Maidstone West via Cuxton, Halling, Snodland, New Hythe, Aylesford and Maidstone Barracks

Journey: 83 min
(from Aylesford)
Season: £2380
(£2420 via
Maidstone)
Peak: 3 per hr*
Off-peak: 2 per hr*

*Change at Strood.
There are no
through trains. It is
also possible to
travel in the
opposite direction
and change at
Maidstone West
(footpath to
Maidstone East)

CUXTON is one of the Medway villages that boomed with the cement industry during the 19th century. It has an attractive mock-Tudor station with a hand-operated level crossing and an old-fashioned signal box, however the Stategic Rail Authority is thinking of curtailing the service in the future. Some of the houses are Victorian terraces suitable for first-time buyers, selling for around £120,000 for two bedrooms.

On the borders of Cuxton, **Halling** is dominated by the large riverside cement works. This part of north Kent is not very popular, but it does offer the prospect of affordable housing and property here is selling fairly fast. A detached family house can be bought for £240,000. **Snodland**, too, has been stigmatised by association with the cement industry. Blue Circle and the area around the cement works is plagued by dust and lorries. Snodland has a plain Victorian centre where terraced houses sell for about £115,000. Or you could pay around £140,000 for a three-bedroom semi.

New Hythe is very close to the old Aylesford paper mills, which have now been converted to light industrial use. Victorian and Thirties' semis start at about £160,000. **Aylesford** is marginally more appealing and is thought to offer good value for money. Nearby is a retail park with a Sainsbury's, Comet, Homebase and so on. It has a 14th-century ragstone bridge and some very old houses overlooking the River Medway. These might sell in the region of £150,000 and upwards for two bedrooms. For **Maidstone West** see **Victoria to Ashford International line via Maidstone**, page 314.

Converted oast house

> Continuation of main line

To Victoria
Journey: 42 min
Season: £2260
Peak: 3 per hr
Off-peak: 4 per hr

To Charing Cross
Journey: 74 min
Season: £2260
Peak: 2 per hr
(plus 2 per hr to
Cannon Street)
Off-peak: 2 per hr

'Rochester is
stiff with
locations used
by Dickens in
his novels,

ROCHESTER Most of this apparently seamless string of north Kent towns looks as if it might have detached itself from the north of England and slipped southwards during the night. Rochester, however, is something of an exception, having managed to sustain a policy of architectural conservation on the back of the Charles Dickens industry, just as in the past it was able to create fine buildings on the back of its maritime trade. The pedestrianised High Street has an intimate villagey atmosphere with tourist shops, gift shops, antiques shops and small businesses packing the narrow streets around it. It is pleasant to stroll and enjoy some of the older Elizabethan buildings and excellent Georgian houses. The town is stiff with locations used by Dickens in his novels. The Royal Victoria Hotel is The Bull in *Pickwick Papers*; The Bull is The Blue Boar in *Great Expectations*; Miss Haversham's home was loosely based on Restoration House; *Edwin Drood* was set in Rochester. The Charles Dickens Centre at Eastgate House has the reconstructed Swiss chalet workshop in which the author worked while he lived at Gad's Hill. Every year the town dresses itself in 19th-century costume for the summer Dickens Festival and Christmas Dickensian festivities.

One of the most prestigious areas is close to the castle. This was built during the reign of Henry I, and has a well-preserved square keep that overlooks the river. Nearby are the Cathedral, largely 12th-century, and King's School Rochester, the co-educational public school. One of the best places for period properties is St Margaret's Street, where a four-bedroom early Georgian house with garage will fetch £300,000 to £600,000. In the streets just off it, and lying within the same conservation area, are large, five-bedroom Victorian houses which fetch up to £600,000 depending on size and position. For less expensive homes you need to travel five or 10 minutes out from the centre. Here you will find row upon row of Victorian terraces. They front straight on to the pavement and sell at around £125,000 for two bedrooms. New building has been kept at bay, but there are a few small estates where you could buy a four-bedroom, detached house for about £280,000. To the south is a large area of Thirties' housing with some bay-fronted terraces and semis, and a few bungalows. The average price for a three-bedroom semi in good condition is about £165,000.

You have to suffer a little to commute from Rochester. The one-way system makes driving to the station difficult, and parking is not easy. The area is earmarked for growth by the Government and development sites are being prepared for new houses.

To Victoria
Journey: 44 min
Season: £2260
Peak: 3 per hr
Off-peak: 4 per hr

To Charing Cross
Journey: 76 min
Season: £2260
Peak: 1 per hr
(plus 3 per hr to
Cannon Street)
Off-peak: 2 per hr

CHATHAM
Little flat-fronted Victorian terraced houses, ideal for first-time buyers at around £100,000, cram the steep hillsides around Chatham dockyard, once the industrial heart of the town. Its first ship was launched in 1586 to join the fleet against the Spanish Armada. Four centuries and 400 Royal Navy ships later, the docks were closed in 1984 and handed over to a trust. The 80-acre site, which contains 47 scheduled monuments, is the most complete Georgian and early Victorian dockyard in the world. Now it is almost as much of an attraction to house-hunters as it is to tourists. Part of it has been turned into a living museum where you can see rope- and sail-making. Other parts have been converted to residential use with a choice of both restored and new properties. The new developments include one- and two-bedroom flats starting at about £150,000, and town houses modelled on the Georgian officers' terraces, priced up to £550,000. Restored properties include 12 houses in a terrace built on five floors between 1722 and 1732. These are the cream of the bunch. Old naval stable blocks have been converted into three-bedroom mews houses selling at about £220,000. For cheaper

Schools in Kent

Kent still has some of its old grammar schools, though parents should remember that entry is highly selective. At Tonbridge there are two grammars for girls and The Judd for boys, as well as the Tonbridge independent boarding and day school for boys.

Tunbridge Wells is full of good schools, including the Tunbridge Wells Girls' Grammar, Tunbridge Wells Grammar for boys and The Skinners' School for boys. Also, there is Kent College Pembury independent girls boarding and day school.

Sevenoaks is rightly proud of Sevenoaks School, an independent co-educational day and boarding school beside Knole Park, and Walthamstow Hall independent day school for girls.

At Cranbrook, close to Staplehurst station, is the Cranbrook co-educational day and boarding grammar school. It is so popular that houses within a five-mile catchment area may carry a premium price. Nearby is the girls' public school Benenden.

Maidstone has its Girls' Grammar and Maidstone Grammar for boys (girls in the sixth), plus Oakwood Park Grammar for boys. Nearby is Sutton Valence, an independent co-educational day and boarding school.

Girls can also look to Ashford where there is Highworth Grammar for girls, Invicta Grammar

and Ashford independent day and boarding school. Boys in Ashford can go to Norton Knatchbull, which does well in the school league tables.

Canterbury offers a wide choice. King's Canterbury, the independent co-educational day and boarding school, is set in the cathedral precinct and has a strong musical tradition. Its rival is Kent College, the independent co-educational day and boarding school with its own 90-acre farm. There are also two grammars – Simon Langton Boys' and Simon Langton Girls'.

Gravesend has Gravesend Boys' Grammar and Gravesend Girls' Grammar. Chatham has Chatham Girls' Grammar, which accepts boys into the sixth form. Chatham House boys' grammar also performs well in the school league tables, as does Ford Pitt Grammar. Other good grammar schools can be found in Gillingham, Broadstairs, Sittingbourne and Faversham.

Rochester also has a cathedral school, mostly for day pupils. King's is co-educational, independent and fiercely no-nonsense. The alternative is Rochester Independent College, which is non-selective and co-educational. Rochester Girls' Grammar was founded in the 1880s to produce girls "fit to adorn the homes of England".

modern housing you could look at the Walderslade area, a huge estate with two-bedroom terraced houses at £115,000 and four-bedroom family houses at £220,000 to £250,000. The Walderslade Woods area is more sought after and prices can rise to £400,000 for a five-bedroom house.

To Victoria
Journey: 48 min
Season: £2264
Peak: 3 per hr
Off-peak: 4 per hr

To Charing Cross
Journey: 80 min
Season: £2264
Peak: 1 per hr
(plus 3 per hr to
Cannon Street)
Off-peak: 2 per hr

GILLINGHAM is the largest of the Medway towns and commercial

big brother to Chatham, with which it shares the former naval dockyards and depot. The large shopping centre has a pedestrianised High Street with the usual chain stores. There are very good leisure facilities – an ice rink, leisure centre, leisure pool, indoor bowls and cricket, and Gillingham Football Club, currently playing in the first division of the Football League. The dockyard here is ringed by an old Georgian fortification system known as the Brompton Lines, one-and-a-half-miles of moats and ramparts overlooked by the Napoleonic Fort Amherst.

Near the town centre, in the tightly-packed Victorian streets, first-time buyers can still pick up small terraced houses for around £110,000 to £120,000. One of the better areas is Darland, a Thirties' estate where four-bedroom detached houses sell for upwards of £220,000.

To Victoria
Journey: 53 min
Season: £2340
Peak: 3 per hr
(plus 3 per hr to
Cannon Street)
Off-peak: 4 per hr

RAINHAM is much more suburban in character than either

Gillingham or Chatham and has the atmosphere of a dormitory town. It was once popular with hop-pickers coming down from London. The station is large and the London trains are fast. Housing is a mixed bag, from turn-of-the-20th-century farmworkers' terraced houses at £110,000 to £115,000 to Thirties' houses in the Wigmore area, where three-bedroom detached homes now sell for £180,000 upwards. Hempstead is another attractive area with an old villagey heart and an outgrowth of new estates: you can pay from £110,000 for a starter home, up to £400,000 for a large detached house. The Riverside Country Park, which extends along the southern shore of the Medway Estuary between Gillingham and Rainham, offers escape from the relentless housing. The park was created from reclaimed salt marshes and is linked from west to east by the Saxon Shore Way, a coastal footpath which runs 140 miles between Gravesend and Rye.

'The Saxon Shore Way runs 140 miles between Gravesend and Rye'

To Victoria

Journey: 76 min

Season: £2380

Peak: 2 per hr

(plus 2 per hr to

Cannon Street)

Off-peak: 2 per hr

NEWINGTON

The countryside does try to breathe here, but it is soon submerged again by Sittingbourne. Newington is thought to be more rural, but in fact it's bisected by the busy A2 and is beginning to blend at one end with Sittingbourne and at the other end with Hartlip. A two-up-two-down terraced house will cost about £140,000; a modern three-bedroom semi close to £160,000. Calloways Lane is particularly smart. A large four-bedroom detached house on up to an acre of ground here would sell for over £300,000.

Hartlip, a mile or so to the south-west, is more sought after. It has a villagey feel and is close to the Medway Towns. This is one of the first conveniently-placed, attractive villages that you reach on your way out of London through this part of Kent. The conservation area in the village centre encompasses a handful of listed buildings, 15th-century thatched cottages and a fine half-timbered pink-and-white house. The rest is brick and weatherboarding, plus some modern houses built in the Eighties. It is a good address. You will have to pay £435,000 or more for a four- or five-bedroom property with a garden. There is a primary school with about 85 pupils, a church, a Methodist chapel and a village hall. The local parish pump is The Rose And Crown – symbolic of Kent's reputation as the Garden of England and its allegiance to the sovereign. The village is friendly to newcomers and used to commuters. The main worry is that Gillingham might burst at the seams and engulf it.

To Victoria

Journey: 60 min

Season: £2460

Peak: 3 per hr

(plus 3 per hr to

Cannon Street)

Off-peak: 4 per hr

SITTINGBOURNE

Like the Medway Towns, Sittingbourne is more affordable for first-time buyers and is likely to grow hugely in the next few years. Much of the town centre looks more like Coronation Street than Kent, with terraces fronting straight on to the pavement. A two- or three-bedroom house here could be bought for between £80,000 and £115,000. Yet it is still only an hour by train from London. The north side of town is the old industrial area, now joined by smart new developments where prices for a four-bedroom house are between £180,000 and £300,000. On the south side of town Thirties' detached houses and semis – some of them with good long gardens – sell for £200,000 or more. There are new estates here, too, with three-bedroom terraced houses at just over £140,000.

The mile-long High Street still displays something of its history as a market town (there is a Friday market) and coaching stop. Pilgrims used to rest here on their way to Canterbury. The Red Lion, The George Inn and Ypres Tavern are still there, and there is evidence of Georgian buildings behind the High Street's modern facades. Sittingbourne was also once a busy harbour town. The muddy Milton Creek that runs into town from The Swale is lined with warehouses, factories and reedy inlets, some of which might be given over to new housing. The Dolphin Yard Sailing Barge Museum repairs and

Restored timber-
framed house
north Kent

restores barges. The town's prosperity used to depend on the hugely
expanding demand for bricks, paper and cement in the late 19th
century. Of these traditional local industries only paper-making now
remains: the rest have been replaced by modern light manufacturing.
For recreation there is The Swallows, a huge, multi-million-pound
leisure centre.

House prices rise a little as you move out to the villages. To the
west is **Stockbury**, which has a pub, green and farm shop. It would be
difficult to find a property here at less than £200,000, for which you
might be lucky enough to get a two-bedroom bungalow. A four-
bedroom house would be closer to the £425,000 mark. Closer to
Sittingbourne is **Borden**. It is quite smart and attracts executives.
Some parts of it are very old indeed: a 13th-century church is set in
the conservation area which contains some quaint, white-painted
weatherboarded cottages. You would pay £150,000 for a semi-
detached house. Four-bedroom bungalows start at around £300,000.
Much of the building is in brick, with some timber-frame and some
modern infilling. At the heart of the village is the Playstool, a Kentish
name for a playing field on two levels. From the top level you have
wonderful views across the countryside. The main street is called The
Street and has a pub. The village has a high proportion of elderly
people as well as a thriving primary school.

Less than a mile away is **Tunstall**. Prices here are similar to those in
Borden, though the village itself is very tiny, with a good primary
school, but no shops. Due south of here is **Milstead**. Opinions and
signposts vary about the correct spelling (several maps and guides,
though not the Ordnance Survey, omit the a) though there's no
doubt about its status as the most sought-after village in the area. It
has a truly Kentish feel to it, with leafy lanes on the slopes of the
North Downs giving on to a church, pub, thatched cricket pavilion,

primary school and old thatched cottages which tend to be occupied by well-paid professionals. A three-bedroom detached cottage will come with a price tag of over £300,000. The village itself is a conservation area. The surrounding countryside is a designated Area of Outstanding Natural Beauty. At the centre is a tiny green with an old cedar tree growing on it, framed by a row of tile-hung cottages, the church and Milstead Manor. It is a busy place, but residents are worried about it becoming a dormitory village, though there are truly local families who have lived here for years. The cricket attracts people from neighbouring villages. A car is essential for those who don't want to have to use the post bus.

> Branch line to Sheerness-on-Sea via Kemsley, Swale and Queenborough

Journey: 81 min
(from Sheerness)
Season: £2460
Peak: 3 per hr*
Off-peak: 2 per hr*
*Change at
Sittingbourne.
There are no
through trains

KEMSLEY was built to house workers from the nearby papermills and is rather formally laid out with a central square containing a modern social centre built in Queen Anne style. The area is not greatly sought after. Three-bedroom terraced houses cost about £115,000. There is also a large new estate on the outskirts where prices are low: three-bedroom semis sell for £135,000 and four-bedroom detached houses for £180,000 or more.

Swale station is in a bleak and remote spot where the only housing to speak of is the occasional farmhouse on the flattest of horizons. It was named after the channel that separates the Isle of Sheppey from the mainland, now spanned by the Kingsferry Bridge (the central section of which opens up for coasters). The Royal Society for the Protection of Birds' Elmley Marshes Nature Reserve begins here and stretches across the southern part of the island. At **Queenborough** once again you find the typically north Kentish combination of relentless turn-of-the-20th-century housing in a harbour setting. The High Street, which provides for local shopping, ends in an esplanade where you can watch the boats using all-tide landing gear. New housing is going up, but locals are worried that the infrastructure may not keep pace with it. Construction of a second crossing over the River Swale to link the Isle of Sheppey with the mainland has just started. At least the area has been spared the blight of hosting a new airport on the marshes at Cliff. Two- and three-bedroom Victorian terraced houses sell for about £105,000.

Sheerness-on-Sea, at the north-west tip of the Isle of Sheppey, is protected by a massive sea wall above the clean shingle beach, from which there are good views over the Thames estuary. The design of the old dockyards was supervised by Samuel Pepys in his capacity as

Secretary to the Navy Board in 1665. This is where Nelson's body was brought in *HMS Victory* after the Battle of Trafalgar in 1805. Today Sheerness has a flourishing cargo port. Most of the town consists of Victorian terraced housing, built for dockyard workers and now selling at around £95,000 for two bedrooms. Ex-council semis sometimes fetch £120,000. **Minster**, two miles to the east, is more popular. Semis and bungalows here tend to sell in the range of £120,000 to £160,000. Established between World War I and II by speculative developers who sold plots to Londoners who wanted seaside homes, Minster is still growing. There is a community hospital and local shopping. The coast from Minster to Leysdown is a more or less continuous run of caravan sites and chalets.

'Sheerness-on-Sea is where Nelson's body was brought in *HMS Victory* after the Battle of Trafalgar in 1805'

> Continuation of main line

To Victoria
Journey: 86 min
Season: £2460
Peak: 2 per hr
(plus 2 per hr to
Cannon Street)
Off-peak: 2 per hr

TEYNHAM is a sprawling village unromantically sandwiched between the A2 and the railway. It was once 10 hamlets, hence its name. Though only a few trains stop here in peak hours, Teynham is very much a commuter village. Most of the houses were built during the Sixties and Seventies. A three-bedroom semi of that vintage will sell for around £160,000. A run of older, turn-of-the-last-century housing flanking the A2 provides two- or three-bedrooms for around £130,000. Outside the road-rail sandwich lie the hop fields which supply the Faversham breweries.

To Victoria
Journey: 69 min
Season: £2600
Peak: 3 per hr
(plus 3 per hr to
Cannon Street)
Off-peak: 4 per hr

FAVERSHAM is a hugely popular old market town. The historic Market Place lies within a mainly pedestrianised conservation shopping area, and still has markets on Tuesdays, Fridays and Saturdays. Tudor and Georgian houses exude period charm, and Faversham Creek brings the sights and smells of the river. It was this navigable tidal inlet that earned Faversham its status as one of the Cinque Ports. The warships built here won it the further title of King's Port. There are still some medieval warehouses left on the banks, though today it is the brewing industry that dominates. Shepherd Neame was founded here in 1692 and there are great pubs in the town, including The Chimney Boy, The Bull and The Phoenix. There are barge races in summer and a hop festival in September.

Small, plain terraced houses sell for between £100,000 and £150,000. For more expensive property, the most sought-after streets are West Street and Abbey Street, which contain some of the oldest half-timbered buildings in Kent. They very rarely come on the market, but their current value is probably about £350,000 or more. People looking for new houses and flats should consider Wheeler Court, with prices up to £200,000. The villages around Faversham benefit from their proximity to such an attractive and popular town. Stretched along a valley bottom to the south-west is **Newnham**, which has a conservation area and a gastro-pub, The George, and where everyone knows everyone. A three-bedroom weatherboarded cottage might fetch £210,000; a four-bedroom detached £295,000 to £330,000. Newnham's big house is an interesting Tudor pile with two chalk fireplaces and decorative plasterwork in the form of tumbling leaves. It is privately owned.

Eastling, a mile from Newnham, has 14th- and 15th-century timbered hall houses and ancient weatherboarded homes scattered along country lanes. The cheapest two-bedroom weatherboarded house costs around £150,000; a four- or five-bedroom house with paddocks £500,000 or more. The village has a pub and a church (with a yew tree reputedly more than 900 years old), and a primary school with a toddlers' group, but there are no shops. The village has a number of vigorous societies, but the character of the place has changed over the years as commuters have replaced agricultural workers. Two or three miles away is Belmont House, an 18th-century mansion set in fine parkland which is open to the public.

Boughton village, a couple of miles east, has a charming main street lined with period houses, laced with a few shops and two good pubs. It has a complete cross-section of residents, including quite a few commuters. A modern three-bedroom terraced house would sell for £160,000. A larger four- or five-bedroom early Victorian house would be expected to fetch around £350,000.

> Fork from Faversham to Herne Bay

To Victoria
Journey: 81 min
Season: £2680
Peak: 2 per hr
(plus 3 per hr to
Cannon Street)
Off-peak: 2 per hr

WHITSTABLE The sea can be a force to be reckoned with in Whitstable. New sea defences now keep it snug and dry, but in the terrible storm of 1953, waves breached the sea wall and the tide surged miles inland. The oyster industry was severely disrupted then, too, though it has been built up again so successfully that the harbour area now contains the largest oyster hatchery in Europe. There is an annual summer oyster festival, and the beginning of the oyster season is marked by the blessing of the sea.

The housing market has been frisky recently, boosted by commuters and second-home hunters. The town centre is full of little Victorian terraces of two-up-two-downs. These now sell for about £135,000. There are also some well-established newer developments. In Bay View Road, for example, a four-bedroom modern detached house overlooking the sea would cost £250,000 upwards. On the seafront there are some 200-year-old smugglers' and fishermen's cottages with added cutesey value, but they very rarely come onto the market and buyers must move quickly to catch them. As a resort Whitstable is fairly restrained, though there are the usual seaside amusements and it is popular for yachting and watersports. The rows of weatherboarded fishermen's cottages and old boat-sheds along the shingle beach (there is sand to the east and west) are the subject of a Turner sketch.

'The harbour in Whitstable now contains the largest oyster hatchery in Europe'

Tankerton, on the east side of Whitstable old town, is sedate, slightly more expensive and a popular retirement haven. There is a charming promenade, cliff walks and beach huts. Houses on the seafront sell for between £200,000 and £395,000, and overlook the Tankerton Slopes, a wide grassy verge that runs down to the beach. Extending from the beach is a long shingle spit known as The Street. This is where two tides meet, and at low water you can walk out along it into the sea. **Seasalter**, to the west, is another retirement area with its own parade of shops and ration of bungalows. In Joy Lane you will find some of the most expensive houses in the area. This is where Somerset Maugham, whose uncle was vicar of Whitstable, learned to ride his bicycle. If you fancy one of the large detached houses he must have wobbled past, you'll need to spend anything from £320,000 upwards. A three-bedroom ex-local authority house will cost around £110,000.

CHESTFIELD & SWALECLIFFE

To Victoria
Journey: 85 min
Season: £2680
Peak: 2 per hr
(plus 1 train to Cannon Street)
Off-peak: 1 per hr

There is a bit of snob value attached to Chestfield. It is a cut above the seaside tat, thinks of itself as a village and has a private golf club. The new dual carriageway on the A299 has affected it, though. There are some very large period houses that sell for over £550,000. Between these are new developments or individually-built modern houses on small plots. On the Churchwood Park estate, family houses sell from just under £300,000 to £350,000. The village does also have some properties for first-time buyers. Expect to pay around £105,000 for one-bedroom starter homes. Chestfield now spills over into Swalecliffe, which has lots of ex-council houses in the £120,000 to £140,000 range. It also has a primary school.

HERNE BAY

To Victoria
Journey: 86 min
Season: £2680
Peak: 2 per hr
(plus 3 per hr to Cannon Street)
Off-peak: 2 per hr

The Victorian seaside resort has spread its tentacles over quite a large area, but the retirement town atmosphere of Herne Bay is being rejuvenated as young buyers arrive from Canterbury. Spacious Victorian and Edwardian houses line the seafront and a flat in one of them will cost around £100,000 or more. Numerous roads lead down to the sea, fitted snugly with two- to three-bedroom terraced houses which sell at around £130,000; and modern detached houses which rise to £250,000 depending on the views. Herne Bay's long exposed foreshore can be sealed off when there are severe storms; otherwise it is extremely popular with day-trippers, and with sailing and fishing enthusiasts. The seafront has had a £3.5m makeover and the pier (the second longest after Southend), which was damaged by storms in 1953 and 1978, is due to get one, too. The 1920's Art Deco bandstand also gleams with fresh paint.

One mile inland is the parent village of **Herne**, a collection of pretty white weatherboarded cottages on a hillside with a restored working 18th-century smock mill. A mid-terraced cottage here would cost just over £140,000.

Large family house, Herne Bay

> Main line from Faversham to Canterbury East

To Victoria	
Journey: 79 min	
Season: £2600	
Peak: 1 per hr	
(plus 1 per hr	
changing at	
Faversham)	
Off-peak: 1 per hr	

SELLING This is a nice position to be in. You are close to the pretty market town of Faversham, near enough to Canterbury for special shopping, and also handy for the sea. The countryside starts to roll south-east of Faversham, and at Perry Wood is a huge area of unspoilt accessible woodland. From the Pulpit, a wooden structure built on a mound at the highest point, you have panoramic views over Kent. There are some very fine half-timbered houses and oasts scattered in the deep lanes around here. A three-bedroom cottage might cost £275,000; a five-bedroom oast conversion £725,000.

To Victoria
Journey: 86 min
Season: £2760
(also valid at
Canterbury West)
Peak: 1 per hr
(plus 1 per hr
changing at
Faversham)
Off-peak: 2 per hr

See also
Canterbury West
on the Charing
Cross to
Canterbury line,
page 311

CANTERBURY EAST Canterbury charmingly combines

modernity and tourism with its medieval heritage. Parts of the
centre were bombed in World War II and nasty Sixties' infills are
now being replaced. Beneath the modern shopping precinct that
lies here now are Roman mosaics which are open to the public.
Large parts of the centre are pedestrianised, which makes it a
pleasant place to shop, and it is also very beautiful. The new
Whitefriars shopping centre will boost choice. Much of the old
medieval city remains in the narrow streets of timber-framed
houses around the Cathedral, where Thomas Becket was
murdered. The most sought-after area is within the city walls,
close to the Cathedral and King's co-educational public school.
The latter occupies many of the buildings that were formerly part
of the monastery attached to the Cathedral. Grade II listed houses
here are snapped up very quickly. Anything with a garage sells at a
premium as parking in Canterbury is a nightmare. At the cheaper
end of the market, a tiny turn-of-the-20th-century terraced cottage
within the city walls would be likely to fetch £150,000. Smart
high-spec flats in the city centre are now coming on stream at
£200,000 to £250,000.

The city margin is ringed with roomy Victorian detached and
semi-detached houses. In Ethelbert Road, to the south, haunt of
doctors and academics, the houses have as many as 10 bedrooms
and sell for around £600,000. There are also plenty of modern
developments from the Fifties, Sixties and Eighties. A 10-year-old
town house with three bedrooms within the city walls in the south
of the town would cost around £300,000.

The University of Kent, built in the Sixties high on a windy hill
just outside the city, attracts a lot of students to the St Stephen's
area. Many of the bay-windowed Thirties' semis here are rented –
some are bought by the parents of wealthier students. A three-
bedroom house could be bought for around £170,000. Investors
and professionals also buy in the area around St Peter's Grove,
where a flat-fronted late Victorian house may be picked up for
£150,000.

In the countryside around people prefer to look to the south
where the landscape is prettier. Two-and-a-half miles south-east is
the village of **Bridge**, which is extremely pretty and
commensurately expensive. It has a butcher, bakery, post office,
primary school and offers a mix of thatched cottages, turn-of-the-
last-century and modern houses, but remains very compact. A
five-bedroom family house on the outskirts would cost £500,000.
Further east is **Patrixbourne**, which is very tiny, but also very pretty
and so popular that half-timbered houses and thatched cottages
often sell by word of mouth. Period houses around here cost

335

£400,000 to £600,000. The Nail Bourne river runs through it, though it fills only after heavy downpours. For most of the year it is dry.

Looking north-east you find **Wickhambreaux**, a typical Kentish village with a green and an old church on one side, the Little Stour running through it with a watermill now converted into flats, and a manor house. It once formed part of the Kentish estates of Joan Plantagenet, the Fair Maid of Kent, wife of the Black Prince. There are no shops and a minimal bus service, but the village does have a pub and a Church of England primary school. Two summer fêtes on the green bring the villagers together. There has been little new development for 40 years. A large village house would cost £700,000. One way of telling old villagers from new is by the name they give to the main street. Incomers rather grandly call it The Street. To old villagers it is Gutter Street.

At **Stodmarsh**, slightly to the north, the landscape becomes very rural, with good views across the Stour valley. Stodmarsh itself is a small village with an excellent pub. Properties rarely come on the market and when they do prices are much the same as in Wickhambreaux and Bridge. The old coal-mining area has been turned into a nature reserve with man-made lakes to attract birds and wildlife.

'Wickhambreaux once formed part of the Kentish estates of Joan Plantagenet, the Fair Maid of Kent'

Index

Stations are in
bold type

A

Abbotts Ann 215
Abinger Hammer 277
Adstock 118
Aldbourne 160
Aldbury 115
Aldeburgh 28
Aldermaston 182
Aldershot 210
Almondsbury 163
Alresford, Essex 23
Althorne 36
Alton 210, 211
Amberley 261
Amersham 132
Amesbury 221
Ampney Crucis 163
Ampney St Mary 163
Ampney St Peter 163
Ampthill 103
Anchorage Park 249
Andover 215
Ansford 191
Appledore 309
Appleford 163
Apsley 113
Apsley Heath 120
Architecture *see House Style*
Ardingly 263
Arkesden 59
Arlesey 79
Arundel 251, 256, 262, 281

Ascot 200
Ascott-under-Wychwood 175, 177
Ash Vale 201, 202, 209
Ashby St Ledgers 129
Ashford 310, 318
Ashford International 309, 313, 318
Ashingdon 38
Ashridge 115
Ashton Keynes 162
Ashurst 289
Ashurst New Forest 231
Ashwell 73
Ashwell and Morden 73
Aspely Guise 119, 120
Aston 70
Atch Lench 179
Audley End 59
Avington 223
Avoncliff 167
Awkley 163
Aylesbury 131, 135, 141
Aylesford 324
Aynho 144
Ayot St Lawrence 68
Ayot St Peter 68

B

Badby 126
Bagnor 186
Bagshot 201

Balcombe 262
Baldock 73
Banbury 145, 175
Bancroft Park 123
Barby 129
Barcombe 269
Barcombe Cross 291
Barkham 206
Barkway 74
Barley 74
Barling 45
Barming 313
Barmpton 83
Barnack 86
Barrington 75
Barrowby 88
Basildon 41
Basingstoke 213, 221
Bassett 229
Bassingbourn 74
Bath 167, 168
Bath Spa 168
Batheaston 170
Bathford 170
Bathwick Hill 169
Battle 300
Battlesbridge 36
Bayford 91
Bayfordbury 92
Beaconsfield 139
Beare Green 279
Bearsted 316
Beaulieu 232
Bedford 97, 104, 119
Bedford St Johns 119, 121
Bedhampton 247
Bedwyn 188
Beeston 80
Belton 88
Beltring 305
Bendish 101
Benenden 307
Benfleet 42
Bengeo 93
Benington 70

Bentley 211
Berkhamsted 114
Berwick 270
Betchworth 279
Bethersden 309
Bicester 143
Bicester North 143
Biddenden 308
Biddenham 105
Biddestone 165
Biggleswade 79
Bildeston 29
Billericay 35
Billingshurst 260
Bilton 128
Binfield 203
Birdingbury 129
Bishop's Itchington 146
Bishop's Stortford 56
Bishop's Tachbrook 146
Bishopstoke 224
Bishopstone, Bucks 135
Bishopstone, Wilts 160
Bitterne 227
Bladon 176
Bledlow 140
Bletchely 118
Blewbury 159
Bloxham 146
Boars Hill 174
Bodenham 191
Bolney 265
Borden 329
Botley 225
Boughton 332
Boughton Aluph 319
Bourne End 153, 154
Bournemouth 233
Bourton-on-the Water 177
Bovingdon 113
Bow Brickhill 119
Bowerchalke 219
Box 165
Box Hill 277
Box Hill & West Humble 277

Boxford 23
Boxley 316
Boxmoor 113
Bracknell 203
Bradford-on-Avon 167
Bradley Stoke 164
Bradwell 123
Bradwell-on-Sea 37
Braintree 19
Bramley, Hants 181
Bramley, Surrey 237
Bratton 190
Braughing 54
Bray 152
Breachwood Green 101
Breamore 219
Bremhill 165
Brentwood 35
Brickendon 92
Bridge 335
Brighton 251, 262, 267
Brinkworth 161
Bristol 149
Bristol Parkway 163
Bristol Temple Meads 170
Britford 219
Broad Chalke 220
Broadbridge Heath 259
Broadway 178
Brockenhurst 232
Brockham 278
Bromham 105
Brookmans Park 65
Brookwood 210
Broome Manor 160
Broughton Gifford 168
Brownsover 128
Broxbourne 51
Buckingham 125
Bucklebury 183
Bures 20
Burgess Hill 265
Burnham 151
Burnham-on-Crouch 36
Burpham 236, 262

Burton Latimer 108
Burwash 299
Bury 261
Bury St Edmunds 30, 63
Busbridge 239
Buscot 160
Buxted 290

C

Calne 166
Camberley 201, 202
Cambourne 61
Cambridge 51, 61, 72, 76
Cannon Street 293, 305
Canterbury 305, 310, 321
Canterbury East 334, 335
Canterbury West 311
Canvey Island 42
Carterhouse 239
Castle Cary 181, 191
Castle Combe 165
Castlethorpe 124
Catsfield 301
Cavendish 22
Caversham Heights 157
Caversham Park 157
Chalcombe 170
Chalfont & Latimer 132
Chalkwell 43
Challock Lees 319
Chandlers Ford 225
Chappel 20
Chappel & Wakes Colnes 20
Charing 318
Charing Cross 293, 305, 321
Charlbury 175, 176
Charlcutt 166
Charlton, Herts 71
Charlton, Northants 144
Charlton, Worcs 178
Charlwood 254
Chartham 311
Chatham 326
Cheapside 199
Chearsley 142

Cheddington 116
Chelmsford 15
Chenies 132
Cherhill 166
Chertsey 198
Chesham 133
Chesham Bois 133
Chestfield 333
Chestfield & Swalecliffe 333
Chiddingfold 240
Chiddingstone 253
Chignall Smealy 17
Chignall St James 17
Chilham 311
Chilton Foliat 187
Chilworth, Hants 229
Chilworth, Surrey 238
Chippenham 165
Chipperfield 114
Chipping Campden 178
Chipping Hill 18
Chipping Norton 177
Chipping Sodbury 164
Chiswell Green 98
Chobham 209
Cholsey 158
Chorleywood 131
Christ's Hospital 259
Church Langton 109
Church Lench 179
Cippenham 151
Clacton-on-Sea 23, 24
Clandon 237, 280
Clavering 58
Clifton 79
Clifton, Brighton 267
Clifton, Bristol 171
Clifton upon Dunsmore 129
Clifton Village, Bristol 171
Coalpit Heath 164
Cobham 321
Cockfield 30
Codford St Mary 220
Codford St Peter 220
Coggeshall 20

Colchester 22
Colchester Town 23
Cold Ash 183
Coleshill 160
Colnbrook 150
Colne Engaine 23
Combe 175, 176
Comberton 62
Compton Basset 166
Cookham 153
Cooksbridge 268
Copthorne 255
Corringham 49
Corsham 165
Coryton 49
Cottenham 76
Cowden 288
Cowfold 259
Cowplain 247
Cranbrook 307
Cranleigh 237
Cranleigh 280
Crawley, Hants 223
Crawley, Surrey 256
Cressing 19
Cropthorne 178
Crowborough 289
Crowhurst 301
Cuckfield 264
Cuddington 142
Cuffley 91
Culford 30
Culham 173
Cumnor 174
Cuxton 324

D

Damerham 219
Damerham 191
Danbury 16
Datchet 194, 195
Datchworth 68
Daventry 126
Debden 59
Deddington 145

Dedham 26
Deeping Gate 85
Deeping St James 85
Denham 137
Denham Golf Club 137
Denmead 247
Denton 88
Denvilles 247
Desborough 108
Devizes 188
Dickleburgh 31
Didcot Parkway 159
Digswell 67
Dinton 135
Diss 31
Ditcheat 191
Ditchling 266
Donnington 184
Dorking 277
Dorking Deepdene 279
Dorking West 279
Dormans 286
Dormans Park 286
Dovercourt 26
Down Ampney 163
Downham Market 78
Downswood 316
Downton 219
Dullingham 63
Dummer 213
Dunbridge 230
Dunchurch 128
Duns Tews 175
Dunsfold 239
Dunstable 101
Duxford 60

E

Earley 206
Earls Barton 127
Earlswood 253
East Bergholt 25
East Chiltlington 268
East Farleigh 305, 306
East Garston 185

East Grafton 189
East Grinstead 285, 286
East Hagbourne 159
East Hendred 159
East Ilsley 185
East Langton 110
East Malling 313
East Meon 246
East Tilbury 48
East Tytherton 165
Eastbourne 251, 268, 271
Eastbury 185
Eastleigh 224
Eaton Central 150
Eaton Ford 81
Eaton Socon 82
Ecchinswell1 86
Edenbridge 251, 252
Edenbridge Town 287
Edlington 190
Education *see Schools*
Egham 197
Eight Ash Green 23
Elmswell 30
Elsenham 58
Elstead 239
Eltisley 82
Elton 86
Ely 77
Emberton 124
Emmer Green 157
Englefield Green 197
Epping Green 92
Eridge 289
Etchingham 299
Euston 113
Eversholt 120
Evesham 173, 175, 178
Eye 32
Eynesbury 82

F

Fair Oak 224
Fairford 161
Falksworth 85

Fambridge 36
Fareham 225
Faringdon 160
Farnborough 212
Farncombe 238
Farnham 210
Farnham Common 151
Farnham Royal 151
Faversham 331, 332, 334
Faygate 257
Feering 20
Fenchurch Street 41, 47
Fenny Stratford 119
Fenny Stratford 119
Finstock 175, 176
Fittleworth 261
Fladbury 178
Flamlingham 29
Flamstead 100
Flatford Mill 25
Fleet 212
Fletching 264
Fletching 291
Flitwick 103
Fordham 23
Fordingbridge 218
Fornham St Martin 30
Foxton, Cambs 75
Foxton. Leics 110
Frampton Cotterell 164
Frant 298
Fratton 248
Freshford 167
Frimley 201, 202
Frinton 23, 24
Frome 190
Fulbourn 63

Fulmer 138
Furze Platt 153
Fyfield 55

G

Gatwick Airport 255
Geddington 108
Gerrards Cross 137
Gillingham 327
Girton 62
Glynde 270
Godalming 238
Godmanchester 83
Godstone 252
Gomshall 279
Good Easter 17
Goring 157, 158
Gosmore 71
Goudhurst 306
Grand Pont 174
Grantchester 61
Grantham 87
Grateley 217
Gravesend 322
Grays 47
Grayshott 242
Grayswood 242
Great Addington 107
Great Amwell 53
Great Bedwyn 188
Great Bentley 23, 24
Great Braxted 18
Great Chesterford 60
Great Comberton 179
Great Durnford 221
Great Gransden 82
Great Missenden 133
Great Shelford 60
Great Somerford 161
Great Stukeley 84
Great Tew 175
Great Tey 20
Great Totham 18
Great Wakerling 45
Great Wymondley 71

Grendon 107
Groombridge 289
Grundisburgh 28
Guildford 235
Gumley 110
Gunthorpe 84

H

**Haddenham and Thame
Parkway, Bucks** 142
Haddenham, Cambs 77
Haddon 85
Hadstock 60
Halling 324
Hamble 227
Hambledon, Bucks 156
Hambledon, Surrey 240
Hambrook 163
Hampden Park 270
Hampton 84
Hamstreet 309
Handborough 175, 176
Harbourside 171
Harbury 146
Harlaxton 88
Harlington 102
Harlow Mill 55
Harlow Old Town 55
Harlow Town 55
Harpenden 98
Harpole 127
Harrietsham 317
Hartley Wintney 212
Hartlip 328
Harwell 159
Harwich International 26
Harwich Town 26
Haslemere 241
Hassocks 266
Hastings 293, 302
Hatfield 65
Hatfield Broad Oak 57
Hatfield Peverel 17
Haughley 29
Havant 247

Hawkhurst 299
Hawkwell 38
Haxted 252
Haywards Heath 263
Headcorn 308
Headington 174
Heddington 166
Hedge End 225
Hedgerley 138
Helpston 86
Hemel Hempstead 113
Hemingford Abbots 83
Hemingford Grey 83
Hempstead 60
Henley 156
Henley-on-Thames 156
Henlow 79
Herne 334
Herne Bay 321, 332, 333
Hertford East 52, 54
Hertford North 92
Hertingfordbury 94
Hever 287
Heyford 175
High Brooms 295
High Easter 17
High Wycombe 139
Higham 323
Higham Ferrers 106
Highclere 186
Highfields 111
Hildenbrough 294
Hilsea 248
Hindhead 242
Hinksey 174
Hinton Charterhouse 169
Histon 62
Hitcham 29
Hitchin 71
Hoby 111
Hockely 38
Hocombe 225
Hoddesdon 51
Hollingburne 317
Holmbury St Mary 278

Holmwood 279
Hook 213
Hopcroft's Halt 175
Horley 254
Horringer 30
Horsell 209
Horsham 258, 277, 281
Horsted Keynes 264
Horton 194
Houghton Regis 102
Houghton, Cambridgeshire 84
Houghton, West Sussex 261
House style
   East Anglia 17
   Hertfordshire 70
   Kent 315
   South Midlands 120
   Surrey and Hampshire 223
   Sussex 258
   West 161
Hove 272
Hoxne 32
Hullbridge 38
Hungerford 160
Hungerford 187
Hunsdon 54
Huntingdon 82
Hurley 153
Hurst 206
Hurst Green 285, 287
Hurstbourne Tarrant 184, 215
Hurstpierpoint 266
Hythe 23

I

Ickwell Green 80
Ifield 257
Ingatestone 15
Inkpen 186
Ipswich 26
Iron Acton 164
Itchen Abbas 222
Itchingfield 259
Iver 149
Ivinghoe 116

J

Jericho 173
Jordans 138

K

Keevil 168
Kelshall 73
Kelvedon 20
Kemble 162
Kemleey 330
Kempston Hardwick 119, 121
Kennett 63
Kensworth 101
Kersey 27
Kettering 108
Keymer 266
Kilsby 129
Kimpton 100
King's Lynn 61, 65, 72, 78
King's Sutton 144
Kingham 175, 176
Kings Cross 61, 65, 95
Kings Cross Thameslink /
   St Pancras 97
Kingston 269
Kintbury 186
Kippington 294
Kirby Cross 23
Kirby-le-Soken 25
Kirtlington 143
Kislingbury 127
Knebworth 68

L

Lacey Green 140
Lacock 167
Laddingford 305
Laindon 41
Lamberhurst 298
Lambourn 184
Lancing 274
Lane End 139
Langley, Berks 149
Langley, Kent 317
Langton Green 289, 297

Launton 143
Lavenham 22
Laverstock 221
Leagrave 101
Leamington Hastings 129
Leamington Spa 129, 137, 146, 175
Lechlade 160
Leckford 215
Leckhampstead 186
Lee Common 134
Leeds 317
Leicester 97, 110
Leigh Old Town 43
Leigh, Kent 295
Leigh, Surrey 278
Leigh-on-Sea 42
Leighton Buzzard 116
Lenham 317
Letworth 72
Leverstock Green 114
Lewes 251, 268
Ley Hill 132
Liddington 160
Lidlington 119, 121
Limpsfield 284
Limpsfield Chart 284
Lindfield 263
Lingfield 285
Liphook 243
Liss 243
Little Addington 107
Little Badstow 16

Little Bealings 28
Little Bedwyn 187
Little Berkhamsted 92
Little Chalfont 132
Little Chesterford 60
Little Comberton 179
Little Gaddesden 115
Little Gransden 82
Little Hadham 56
Little Horkesley 23
Little Horstead 291
Little Kimble 141
Little Shelford 60
Little Somerford 161
Little Stukeley 84
Little Tew 175
Little Tey 20
Little Wymondley 71
Littlebury 59
Littlehaven 257
Littleport 77
Littlewick Green 153
Liverpool Street 15, 35, 51, 63
London Bridge 251, 283
London Colney 98
London Road (Guildford) 237
Long Buckby 128
Long Crendon 142
Long Melford 21
Longcross 198
Longparish 215
Longthorpe 85
Lower Beeding 259
Lower Caversham 157
Lower Earley 157
Lower Slaughter 177
Lower Stondon 79
Lower Woodford 220
Ludgershall 216
Lullington 191
Luton 100
Luton Airport Parkway 100
Lydiard Millicent 162
Lymington 232
Lyne 198

M

Madingley 62
Maidenhead 152
Maidstone 313
Maidstone Barracks 324
Maidstone East 314
Maidstone West 305, 324
Malmesbury 161
Manningford Bruce 188
Manningtree 25
Manthorpe 88
Manuden 57
Mapledurwell 214
Marden 306
Market Deeping 85
Market Harborough 109
Marks Tey 20
Marlborough 162
Marlborough 189
Marlow 153, 154
Marsh Gibbon 143
Marsh Green 252
Marshfield 166
Martin 219
Martin 191
Martin's Heron 203
Marylebone 131, 137, 175
Mashbury 17
Maxey 86
Melbourn 75
Meldreth 75
Mellis 32
Melton 28
Mentmore 117

Meopham 321
Meppershall 79
Merrow 236
Micheldever 221
Michelmersh 230
Middle Barton 143
Middle Wallop 217
Middle Woodford 220
Middleton 28
Midgham 183
Midhurst 242
Milford 239
Millbrook, Beds 119, 121
Millbrook, Hants 229
Milstead 329
Milton 76
Miton Bryan 102
Milton Keynes Central 122
Milton-under-Ashwood 177
Minster 331
Mistley 26
Mollington 145
Monks Risborough 141
Monxton 216
Moorgate 91
Morden 73
Moreton 55
Moreton-in-Marsh 175, 178
Mortimer 181
Mottisfont 230
Much Hadham 56

N

Needham Market 29
Nether Wallop 217
Netherton 85
Netley 227
New Alresford 223
New Hythe 324
Newark Northgate 89, 95
Newbury 184
Newdigate 278
Newington 328
Newmarket 63
Newnham 332

Newport 58
Newport Pagnell 124
Ninfield 301
North Cadbury 191
North End 249
North Fambridge 36
North Grays 47
North Holmwood 279
North Laines 267
North Stifford 47
North Tidworth 216
North Wraxhall 170
Northampton 113, 125
Northbourne 159
Northend 170
Northill 80
Norton St Philip 169
Norton, Herts 72
Norton, Worcs 179
Norwich 15, 33, 63
Nunton 219
Nutborne 260
Nutfield 251
Nuthurst 259
Nutley 291

O

Oadby 111
Oakley 104
Ocean Village 228
Ockley 280
Odstock 219
Old Alresford 223
Old Basing 213
Old Headington 174
Old Marston 174
Old Portsmouth 249
Old Town 160
Old Town 303
Old Warden 80
Old Welwyn 67
Old Windsor 196
Old Wives Lees 311
Olney 124
Orton Goldhay 84

Orton Malborne 84
Orton Wislow 84
Osney 173
Otham 316
Over Wallop 217
Overton 214
Oxford 173, 175
Oxted 283

P

Padbury 118
Paddington 149, 173, 181
Paddock Wood 305
Palgrave 31
Pangbourne 157, 158
Parkstone 303
Patrixbourne 335
Paxhill Park 264
Peasedown St John 169
Peaselake 277
Peasenhall 29
Pembury 297
Penn 138
Penshurst 295
Penton Mewsey 216
Perry 82
Peter's Green 101
Peterborough 84
Petersfield 244
Petham 311
Petworth 261
Pewsey 188
Pilley Bailey 232
Pinkneys Green 153
Pirton 71
Pitsea 41, 42, 47, 49
Pleshey 17
Pluckley 308
Plumpton 268
Plumpton Green 268
Podington 107
Polegate 270
Poole Keynes 162
Port Solent 249
Portslade 273

Portsmouth 235
Portsmouth & Southsea 248
Portsmouth Harbour 248
Potten End 114
Potters Bar 65
Potton 80
Pound Hill 255
Preston Park 267, 272
Princes Risborough 140
Prittlewell 39
Puckeridge 54
Pulborough 260
Purbrook 248
Purton 162
Purton Stoke 162

Q

Quainton 135
Queenborough 330
Quendon 58
Quorn 111

R

Radley 173
Rainham 327
Raunds 107
Ravenstone 124
Rayleigh 38
Reading 149, 157, 193, 207
Reading West 181
Redbourn 99
Redbridge 229
Redgrave 31
Redhill 251
Redland 171
Reigate 251
Reigate 253
Rickling Green 58
Ridgmont 119, 121
Ringmer 270
Roade 127
Robertsbridge 300
Rochester 321, 325
Rochford 38
Rockbourne 219

Rockbourne 191
Rodmell 269
Roedean 267
Romsey 230
Rothwell 108
Rowland's Castle 246
Roydon 55
Royston 74
Rugby 113, 128
Ruscombe 155
Rushden 106
Rusper 259
Rye 309, 310
Rye House 52

S

Saffron Walden 59
St Albans 97
St Catherine 170
St Denys 226
St Helen's 303
St Ippollits 71
St Ives 83
St Leonards Warrior Square
302
St Margaret's 52
St Mary Bourne 215
St Neots 81
Salfords 253
Salisbury 209, 214, 217
Sandhurst 300
Sandon 16
Sandy 80
Sandy Lane 167
Saunderton 140
Sawbridgeworth 56
Sawston 60
Saxmundham 28
Scanyne's Hill 264
Schools
   Bedfordshire 104
   Berkshire 154
   Bristol, Bath and Somerset
      166
   Cambridgeshire 62

East and West Sussex 269
Essex 45
Gloucestershire 162
Hampshire 228
Hertfordshire 98
Kent 326
Leicestershire and Rutland
   108
Norfolk 32
Oxfordshire 174
Suffolk 27
Surrey 239
Warwickshire,
   Northamptonshire,
   Lincolnshire and
   Peterborough 127
Wiltshire 218
Seasalter 333
Sedlescombe 301
Seer Green and Jordans 138
Selborne 243
Selling 334
Sevenoaks 293
Shalford 238
Shawford 224
Sheerness-on-Sea 330
Sheet 245
Shelford 60
Shenfield 15
Shenington 146
Shenley 98
Shepreth 75
Shere 277
Shillingford 159
Shillington 79
Shiplake 156

Shipton 175
Shipton Bellinger 216
Shipton-under-Ashwood 177
Shirley 229
Shoeburyness 41, 45
Sholing 227
Sholing 227
Shoreham-by-Sea 273
Shotley Gate 27
Shotteswell 145
Shurlock Row 155
Sibford Ferris 146
Sindlesham 206
Sion Hill 168
Sissinghurst 307
Sittingbourne 328
Slindon 262
Slinfold 258
Slough 149
Smallfield 254
Smarden 308
Snape 28
Snodland 324
Sole Street 321
Somerford Keynes 162
Sonning Common 157
Soulbury 117
Souldern 144
South Cadbury 191
South Cerney 162
South Harting 246
South Heath 134
South Holmwood 279
South Nutfield 251
South Tidworth 216
South Woodham Ferrers 36
Southampton 209, 221, 228
**Southampton Airport
   Parkway** 226
Southampton Central 228
Southend 35
Southend Central 43
Southend East 44
Southend Victoria 39
Southminister 36, 37

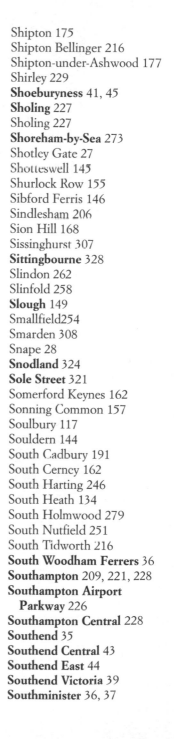

Southsea 249
Southville 171
Southwater 259
Sparsholt 223
Staines 193
Standon 54
Stanford Dingley 185
Stanford-le-Hope 49
Stanstead Abbots 52
Stanstead St Margaret's 52
Stansted Airport 57
Stansted Mountfitchet 57
Stanton St Bernard 188
Stapleford 60
Staplehurst 307
Steep 245
Steeple Ashton 168
Steeple Aston 175
Steeple Barton 143
Steppingley 103
Stevenage 69, 91, 95
Stewartby 119, 121
Stewkley 117
Stilton 85
Stock 16
Stockbridge 216
Stockbury 329
Stocking Pelham 56
Stodmarsh 336
Stoke Gifford 163
Stoke Golding 124
Stoke Lyne 143
Stoke Mandeville 135
Stoke Poges 150
Stoke-by-Nayland 23
Stokenchurch 139
Stonegate 299
Stoneygate 111
Stony Stratford 124
Storrington 261
Stotfold 79
Stowmarket 29
Stratton Audley 143
Streatley 157, 158
Stretham 77

Strood 323
Stutton 27
Sudbury 20, 21
Summertown 174
Sunningdale 199
Sunninghill 199
Sunnymeads 194
Sutton, Cambs 77
Sutton, W. Sussex 260
Sutton Green 235
Sutton Valence 315
Swaffham Bulbeck 62
Swaffham Prior 62
Swale 330
Swalecliffe 333
Swaunswick 170
Swaythling 226
Swindon 160

T

Tackley 175
Tandridge 284
Tankerton 333
Taplow 151
Tempsford 81
Teynham 331
Thame 142
Thatcham 182
Thaxted 58
The Lawns 160
The Lee 133
Theale 182
Therfield 74
Thornborough 118
Thornbury 164
Thorney 85
Thorpe 197
Thorpe Bay 43, 44
Thorpe Langton 110
Thorpe-le-Soken 23
Thorpeness 28
Three Bridges 255, 256, 262
Thurston 30
Ticehurst 299
Tilbury Riverside 48

Tilbury Town 48, 49
Tilehurst 157, 158
Tillingham 37
Tingrith 102
Toddington 102
Tollesbury 18
Tonbridge 294, 305
Totton 231
Tring 115
Tring Station 115
Trowbidgre 167
Tunbridge Wells 296
Tunstall 329
Tur Langton 109
Twein 67
Twyford 155

U

Uckfield 287, 291
Uffington 160
Ufford, Cambs 28
Ufford, Suffolk 86
Ugley 58
Upnor 323
Upper Heyford 175
Upper Lambourne 184
Upper Slaughter 177
Upper Weald 125
Upper Woodford 220
Upper Wraxhall 170
Upton Grey 214
Urchfont 188

V

Victoria 251, 277, 283, 313, 321
Virginia Water 197

W

Wadhurst 298
Wakes Colnes 20
Walkern 70
Wallingford 159
Waltham St Lawrence 155
Walton on the Naze 23, 25
Wanborough 160
Wansford 86
Warborough 159
Ware 52, 53
Waresley 82
Wargrave 156
Warmington 145
Warnham 281
Warninglid 265
Waterbeach 76
Wateringbury 305, 306
Waterloo 193, 209, 235, 237, 277
Waterlooville 248
Watlington 78
Watton-at-Stone 94
Wedon's Ambo 59
Weedon 126
Weekley 109
Weeley 23
Welham Green 65
Wellingborough 106
Wellow 170
Welwyn Garden City 66
Welwyn North 67
Wendover 134
Wepham 262
Werrington 84
West Burton 260
West Byfleet 209
West Chiltington 260
West Hagbourne 159
West Horndon 41
West Humble 277
West Ilsley 185
West Langton 110
West Malling 313
West Meon 246

West St Leonards 302
Westbury 190
Westcliff-on-Sea 43
Westerfield 28
Westhill 267
Westleton 28
Westmeston 266
Weston Turville 134
Weston Underwood 123
Westown 84
Wetherden 29
Wheathampstead 66, 100
Whelford 161
Whitchurch 214
White Notley 19
White Waltham 153
Whiteknights Road 157
Whiteleaf 141
Whitley 240
Whitstable 332
Whittlesey 85
Whittlesford 60
Wicken 125
Wicken Bonhunt 59
Wickford 35
Wickham Bishops 18
Wickham Market 28
Wickhambreaux 336
Widdington 59
Willen 123
Willian 72
Wilton 220
Wimbish 59
Winchester 221
Winchfield 212
Windlesham 199
Windsor 150
Windsor & Eton Riverside 194, 195
Wineham 263
Wing 117
Winkfield 200
Winnersh 206
Winnersh Triangle 206
Winterbourne 164

Wisborough Green 260
Witchford 77
Witham 18
Witney 176
Wivelsfield 265
Wivenhoe 23
Woburn 120
Woburn Sands 119, 120
Woking 209
Wokingham 204
Wollaston 107
Wolvercote 174
Wolverton 124
Wood Street 237
Woodbridge 28
Woodbridge Hill 236
Woodhurst 84
Woodley 155
Woodstock 176
Woolhampton 183
Woolley 170
Woolston 227
Wootton Bassett 161
Wootton Rivers 189
Wormley 240
Worplesdon 235
Worthing 251, 272, 275
Woughton-on-the-Green 123
Wrabness 26
Wraysbury 194
Writtle 16
Wroxton 145
Wye 310
Wymington 107
Wyton 84

Y

Yalding 305, 306
Yarlington 191
Yattendon 186
Yaxley, Cambs 85
Yaxley, Suffolk 32
Yoxford 29